THE DIVINE ORDER

ACTA THEOLOGICA DANICA

EDENDA CURAVERUNT:
TORBEN CHRISTENSEN . EDUARD NIELSEN
REGIN PRENTER . HEJNE SIMONSEN

VOL. XI

THE DIVINE ORDER
A STUDY IN
F. D. MAURICE'S THEOLOGY

by

TORBEN CHRISTENSEN

LEIDEN
E. J. BRILL
1973

THE DIVINE ORDER

A STUDY IN
F. D. MAURICE'S THEOLOGY

by

TORBEN CHRISTENSEN, D.D.

Professor of Ecclesiastical History
at the University of Copenhagen

LEIDEN
E. J. BRILL
1973

Index

III. THE MANIFESTATION OF THE DIVINE ORDER

FOREWORD

A scholarship, generously granted by the then Church of England Council on Foreign Relations, made it possible for me to spend the academic year 1946/47 in Oxford. During that time I happened to read some of Maurice's books. I became fascinated. Maurice seemed to me in a remarkable degree to have anticipated what was to be the concern of the Lutheran as well as the Barthian reaction against Liberal theology. At the same time many terms and ideas in his thinking puzzled me. Alongside lucid statements there were obscure passages. In many cases, if one took his words at face value, Maurice appeared to contradict himself in the exposition of his ideas. Nevertheless I was convinced that he was a great thinker; his incoherence I attributed to my failure to grasp the significance of certain aspects of his thought and to interpret his words and ideas correctly.

Naturally I consulted works on Maurice for help in trying to understand the essentials of his teaching, but discovered that no extensive and fully documented treatment of his thinking had been produced. Those who had written on Maurice did not appear to feel the same difficulties in understanding him as acutely as I did. At any rate, they could not offer any substantial help in elucidating the problems I had discovered. I could fully agree with Maurice B. Reckitt when he wrote in 1947: "The greatness of Maurice is perhaps more widely recognized to-day than at any time since his death, though that we still have no adequate study of his teaching and its significance is surely the most curious and the most deplorable *lacuna* in English theology."[1]

The following year A. R. Vidler issued *The Theology of F. D. Maurice*. A more appropriate title would have been "Gleanings from Maurice's Writings" as the book consists mainly of a wealth of excellent quotations. However, as a contribution to an understanding of Maurice's theology it was of limited value, unlike A. M. Ramsey's brilliant book: *F. D. Maurice and the Conflicts of Modern Theology. The Maurice Lectures 1948*, published in 1951. This book was a sympathetic and discerning study of Maurice's teaching, particularly on the Atonement and the interpretation of Scripture. Despite certain critical reservations I regretted that the author of this slim volume had not produced a work, dealing with Maurice's theological thinking in its entirety. Reckitt's *desideratum* was still unfulfilled.

In 1954 I published my doctorate thesis: *Logos og Inkarnation. En Studie i F. D. Maurice's Teologi*. Whatever its defects, it had attempted to treat all aspects of Maurice's theological thinking. Furthermore, in it I argued that Maurice's teaching was basically coherent and consistent, though undeniably different from what recent Maurice studies had indicated.

---

1 *Maurice to Temple. A Century of the Social Movement in the Church of England. Scott Holland Memorial Lectures 1946* (London 1947), 14.

Considering the great interest in Maurice I thought that the book might interest an English-speaking public. Consequently I wrote to various publishing houses in England, presenting them with an English translation of about two thirds of the book and asking whether they were willing to publish it. I was unsuccessful; the Maurice market was already fully stocked according to those who courteously replied. As my time and attention were engaged by many other things, the idea of having the book published in English virtually disappeared.

However, students of Maurice repeatedly wrote to me, asking whether the book would be available in English, and it is in response to their requests that I have decided to prepare an English edition. I was well aware that it was a risky matter to publish a work that had been completed 20 years previously and had originally been written in Danish. I have disregarded these objections because, to my knowledge, there is still no book available in English which gives an exhaustive examination of Maurice's theological thinking. It may be somewhat presumptuous to think that my book can supply this want. Nevertheless I am still convinced that my interpretation of Maurice's teaching holds good, and I would welcome criticism of it by other Maurice students. If they should arrive at a better and truer understanding of Maurice than I have achieved I should be the first to rejoice.

The English version follows the Danish book in both substance and argument. It has, however, been rewritten; some passages have been left out because they seemed superfluous, or too dogmatic or irrelevant to the theme. Thus I have cut out a section which gives a detailed discussion of the most important Maurician studies prior to the publication of my book.[2] Similarly I have considerably reduced my criticisms of other works on Maurice.

My analysis of Maurice's theological thinking is based upon Maurice's entire literary production. The first time a work is referred to I give the full title with the year of publication and indicate the abbreviation which is used for further references. In quotations I follow the spelling and punctuation of the work in question.

I have quoted Maurice extensively instead of merely referring the readers to the particular books and articles. I have done this so that readers may check the correctness of my interpretation of Maurice's statements. Also I hope that these quotations will help to give an otherwise dull book a spark of life.

For invaluable help in preparing this English edition I wish to thank most heartily John Kendal, M. A., Copenhagen, and Rev. Peter S. Grierson, Aston, Sheffield, England.

Finally, I wish to thank Rask Ørsted-Fondet for a financial contribution to the work of translation and Statens Humanistiske Forskningsråd for a grant to cover the printing costs.

Hørsholm, February 4th, 1972.

Torben Christensen.

2 See p. 26–35.

INTRODUCTION

On January 26th, 1834 John Frederick Denison Maurice was ordained deacon by the Bishop of Lichfield. This event, which indicated his burning desire to spend his life as a clergyman in the service of the Church of England, was the outcome of a unique spiritual development.

Maurice had grown up in the home of a highly cultured Unitarian minister with a keen interest in the spiritual, social, and political questions of the day. During his childhood he received such a strong impression of Unitarianism that he embraced his father's beliefs. Later, however, his home was divided by violent religious differences when his sisters and his mother came under the influence of the Revivalist movement and joined various Church bodies. In this way the religious and theological differences and controversies of the age were reflected in the daily life of the family and even broke up its harmony. The young Maurice was forced to make up his mind as to his own future course but felt unable to see his way clearly. He found it impossible to accept his father's Unitarianism any longer. Nor could he endorse the various beliefs of his mother and sisters. In fact he felt a growing disgust at the various manifestations of religion which he had come across at home.

Undoubtedly in the hope of finding a world of wider horizons Maurice decided to go to Cambridge in 1823. Apart from Julius Hare's lectures on some of the Dialogues of Plato – which kindled an undying admiration for the greatness and intrinsic value of Platonic thought –, he did not find anything of value for him in its educational system. He derived the greatest benefit, however, from the friends he made amongst some of the best and most gifted Cambridge undergraduates. Contact with them, together with his own voracious reading, opened up new vistas of thought for him. He became deeply influenced by Samuel Taylor Coleridge. At the same time, true to his Unitarian background, he was keenly interested in the political and social problems of the time – and held opinions similar to those of the Philosophic Radicals, the adherents of Jeremy Bentham and James Mill.

The Cambridge years had made Maurice a man of *belles-lettres,* equally conversant with the problems of literature, history, philosophy, and politics. Intercourse with the most alert of his fellow-students had given him an opportunity of sharpening the powers of his intellect and of having his convictions tested in the fire of criticism. Under the influence of Plato and Coleridge he was well on his way to developing a clear, consistent and comprehensive view of the problems of human existence – supplemented with progressive Radical views on political and social questions.

In 1826 Maurice moved to London where he threw himself into journalism. He contributed a series of articles to the *Athenæum* and other periodicals, in which he expounded his views brilliantly. It appeared that Maurice's spiritual development had been brought to a close. He had broken with the philosophy of the Enlightenment and had, in the train of Coleridge, but independently and far more consistently, become a convinced expounder of the romantic-idealistic school of thought. He was readily recognized as an outstanding figure by those young intellectuals who, because of their sharp criticism of the existing society and of current modes of thought and because of their courage in treading new paths, seemed destined to wield a great influence on the shaping of the future of their country. But suddenly, to their amazement and even bewilderment, Maurice turned his back on them and denounced the ideas that he had been propagating. Even worse, he joined the very Church which they had regarded as the main hindrance to the progress and freedom of humanity.

This unexpected step followed a spiritual crisis which Maurice experienced during 1828. Through the influence of one of his sisters, who had become an Evangelical, the question of a living personal faith in God became a vital concern for him. He was led to a critical self-examination of his previous life and thought. He saw that his view of life was unable to lead him to fellowship with God. He came to realize that the abyss, separating God as perfect love from man as a sinner, could only be bridged when God had revealed Himself and cleansed him from all evil.[1]

This insight gave a new direction to his thinking. He now became wholly absorbed in religious and theological problems. He came under the influence of two outstanding Scottish theologians, Thomas Erskine and Edward Irving, who opened his eyes to the essentials in the Reformed tradition. At the same time he was drawn to the Church of England in whose ordinances, liturgy and doctrinal standards he came to see the true embodiment of God's revelation to mankind.

As a result of his new spiritual experiences Maurice decided to be baptized into the Church of England on March 29th, 1831. When in 1834 he took the step of receiving ordination in this Church, it was the outward expression of the fact that his quest for truth had come to an end: he had found the truth about God and man for himself. Now it became his duty to proclaim this truth as a minister in the service of the Church of England.

Maurice had joined this Church at an extremely critical moment. In the heated debates, preceding the passing of the Reform Bill, it had become notorious as the stronghold of political reaction – a staunch advocate of an Engand built upon the rights and privileges of the aristocracy as the ruling class. The ecclesiastical machinery was cumbrous, brimming with abuses, and completely inadequate to cope with the new problems of a rapidly changing society. It was with good reason that the Church of England was regarded as a tottering building, a remnant of the past, doomed to downfall unless it was radically reformed and reshaped for the new pattern of society which was emerging.

The demand for Church reform was in the air. Some even expressed dissatisfaction within the Church itself. The Evangelicals felt that the main problem was to awaken the Church from its spiritual lethargy, the result of the baneful influence of the Latitudinarian Christianity of the Enlightenment. For decades and with increasing success they had worked for a spiritual regeneration of the Church and the nation.

1 Cf. *The Life of Frederick Denison Maurice Chiefly Told in His Own Letters. Edited by His Son Frederick Maurice* (3rd edition. London 1884. Cit. *Life)* I, 94–6 (letter to Maurice's father from February 1829).

Now in the 1830's they were joined by the Tractarians under John Henry Newman's inspiring and powerful leadership. Although they had the same starting-point as the Evangelicals, the Tractarians reacted against Evangelical subjectivism and adherence to the Reformed tradition and stood up for the piety and Catholic tradition found in the great Caroline divines. By 1840, although few in number, they wielded a considerable influence. Not the least important result of the Tractarian movement was that their attacks constrained the previous liberal breadth of the Evangelicals and welded them together into a clearly-defined party which stood for Protestant and Biblical Christianity in sharp contrast to all "Romanizing" deviations.

However, besides these two dominating parties, there was also a small group of talented clergymen and scholars who were equally dissatisfied with the Evangelicals and the Tractarians. They desired a reform in which the Church would cast off the irksome strait-jacket of the orthodoxy of a bygone age and reformulate the message of the Bible in accordance with current scientific and philosophical insights. Although these men did not act as a group and were not as articulate as the Evangelicals and the Tractarians, we see here the characteristics of what was later to be known as the "Broad Church" movement.

Thus the 1830's was a time of great upheaval in the Church of England. The traditional groupings were giving way to be replaced by the three emergent parties which, in conflict and interaction, were to shape the Church and, with shifting emphasis, to set the pattern of its religious and theological debate for the rest of the century. Broadly speaking this was the situation of the Church when Maurice decided to devote his life to its service.

The unique religious and intellectual development which had brought Maurice to the Church of England explains his peculiar, even lonely, position in it. He felt unable to join any of the parties which were being formed with clear religious and ecclesiastical policies. For him all of them distorted, and even subverted, the message with which, according to his vision, God had entrusted His Church.[2] Nor did the various proposals which had been put forward, inside and outside the Church, for Church reform find much favour with him since they stemmed from a complete misunderstanding of the nature of the Church and its task.

Maurice readily admitted that the Church of England, in its actual life, was denying its own foundation. It had to be called to order to fulfil its true vocation of proclaiming Christ as the Lord and Redeemer of the human race. The severe self-searching and humiliation that would ensue were necessary if God's purposes for His Church were to be realized. "I tremble to think," Maurice wrote to the young Daniel Macmillan, "what a crushing of all systems, religious and political, there must be, before we do really feel our gathering together in Christ to be the hope of the Universe; before we acknowledge that the manifestation of the actual centre of so-

2 Cf. *Life* I, 349: "But neither in our modern church notions [High Church] which leave us so generally to the dream of a new scheme or system into which we are artificially put for the purpose of being fitted and ripened for what is called our salvation; nor in the Protestantism which sets up individual salvation as the end, only not admitting the Church as the necessary means to it; nor in Rationalism which equally glorifies self, only deifying it under the name of Intellect or Insight instead of soul, do I find that which we and all men have need of."

ciety, not the creation of some circle for ourselves or the indefinite enlargement of the circumference of our thoughts and notions, is what we should be looking for."[3]

Maurice was well aware that a renewal of the Church could not be achieved through the endeavours and efforts of man. God Himself must perform the work.[4] At the same time he knew that God calls forth men as His prophets and messengers to achieve His ends. Maurice himself felt convinced that God had called him forth to be a prophet of God's truth and love to a Church and a nation which had exalted man instead of the living God. He knew perfectly well the cost of being a prophetic witness – it meant to be a sign of contradiction, to be delivered up to mockery and persecution, to raise up contention among men where one only desired to be a peacemaker. But the man whom God had chosen as the means of purifying and renovating His Church could not choose his own way. He was under constraint and had to follow the course appointed by God.[5] Even though he felt his own incompetence and unworthiness, was afraid of wounding others and recoiled from opposition, he had to proclaim the message the Lord had put into his mouth. "I often feel," Maurice wrote,[6] "as if I ought to have a deeper sense than I have of being called to work in some way for the reformation of the Church. Sometimes I do feel it very strongly and begin to gird myself to the work; and then comes a shame over me as if I had no business to think that I was born to set things right. But the fact is that one can only speak when the fire is in one's heart, and that when it is, one *must* speak, in spite of the diffidence, despair, and all the devils outside and within one."

To discharge his task as a prophetic witness within the Church of England, Maurice issued pamphlet after pamphlet, book after book, took part in debate after debate, proclaiming his vision. To this end he repeatedly turned down any idea of ecclesiastical promotion so that he could be free to proclaim his message.[7]

His prophetic office was to point out to men that God is the sole reality and that in His love He has created the universe and continues to sustain it and the whole life

3 *Life* I, 349. Cf. also II, 354: "we have much to learn, perhaps a tremendous crisis to pass through before we learn, respecting our own position as baptized with the Spirit and so made children of God. I foresee a terrible breaking down of notions, opinions, even of the most precious beliefs, an overthrow of what we call our religion – a convulsion far greater than that of the sixteenth century – in our way to reformation and unity."

4 Cf. *The Prophets and Kings of the Old Testament* (5th edition. London 1894. Cit. *The Prophets),* 438: "No one [as Jeremiah] had entered so deeply into the truth that God Himself is the reformer, – that all real renovation must come from Him."

5 Cf. *Life* II, 253: "a higher voice said in me, 'That is not the way, walk not in it! Never mind being called Jesuitical, bigoted, half-hearted, eclectical, any name that you hate most, never mind who bestows it upon you, that does not signify a jot. You are not sent into the world to get credit for freedom of mind, liberality, manliness, sincerity, but, so far as you are shown how, to bear witness of that which you know, to testify that which you have seen'."

6 *Life* I, 499–500. See also p. 350.

7 When Julius Hare strongly encouraged Maurice to apply for the Preachership at Lincoln's Inn, which was considered a stepping-stone to episcopacy, and, later, to apply to be Principal at King's College, Maurice bluntly refused: "If I am ever to do anything for the Church, it must be in some subordinate position. The moment I am tried in another I shall have the bitter mortification of hearing principles which I hold most sacred derided, from the feebleness of the person who should be the practical expounder and manifester of them" *(Life* I, 356. See also p. 415).

of mankind. Accordingly Maurice could say: "if ever I do any good work, and earn any of the hatred, which the godly in Christ Jesus receive, and have a right to, it must be – – by proclaiming society and humanity to be divine realities, *as they stand,* not as they may become, and by calling upon the priests, kings, prophets of the world to answer for their sin in having made them unreal by separating them from the living and eternal God who has established them in Christ for His glory."[8] In bearing this witness Maurice was only expounding the full counsels of God as they had been revealed to man: "I have affirmed continually – – that I have discovered nothing; that what I am saying is to be found in every creed of the Catholic Church; in the Prayers and Articles of the Church to which I belong; most emphatically in the Bible, from which they derive their authority, and to which they refer as their ultimate standard."[9]

Maurice looked on himself simply as the unworthy instrument which God had been pleased to use to proclaim His Divine Order. Therefore men were not to heed him but God, who in Christ had revealed the perfect truth. They were bound to reject his teaching if he said anything contrary to the Divine revelation.[10] Likewise he declined to be a leader of a group or a party in order to bring his views to victory in the Church. On the contrary, knowing his own incapacities, he hoped that God would send a more qualified person to carry out the task.[11]

Maurice's strong conviction of a prophetic calling was directly displayed in his letters to his friends, especially when they attempted to involve him in tasks which he considered would distract him from his appointed course. This conviction also permeated his mammoth literary output and made itself felt to anyone who read his books.

8 *Life* II, 137–38. Cf. p. 137: "my business, because I am a theologian, and have no vocation except for theology, is not to build, but to dig, to show that economy and politics – – must have a ground beneath themselves, that society is not to be made anew by arrangements of ours, but is to be regenerated by finding the law and ground of its order and harmony, the only secret of its existence, in God."

9 *The Doctrine of Sacrifice Deduced from the Scriptures* (Cambridge 1854. Cit. *Sacrifice*), XI.

10 Cf. *Life* II, 231: "I do hope and trust that I should be glad to see every notion of mine exposed and annihilated if it blocks up the way to truth. To exhibit that truth, not in notions but in a Person, has been, and is the object of my life", and *The Unity of the New Testament: A Synopsis of the First Three Gospels, and of the Epistles of St. James, St. Jude, St. Peter, and St. Paul* (London 1854), 197, where Maurice warns his readers in the following way: "I hope every one will reject any interpretations of mine which seem to them strained and artificial. I hope I shall not cling to any of them merely because they are mine and have seemed plausible to me. The more I read the Bible and believe it, the deeper is my sense of the fearful sin of sacrificing truth in the slightest degree, for the sake of making out a case in favour of it. God has confounded many such tricks which have been resorted to in support of His cause. May He confound mine if I have committed what I know must be a more grievous offence in His eyes than many open professions of doubt or unbelief."

11 Cf. *Life,* II, 44: "For that distinction [God's order as the antagonist of man's systems] I exist only to testify. The sooner God pleases that I shall finish my testimony for it, and that some other and more faithful and wise protestant shall appear, the less will be my sorrow. For having considered and tried to count the cost, I see this only before me, ever increasing misunderstanding, ever increasing incapacity of being a fellow-worker even while I desire to be that and nothing else."

But how did Maurice's contemporaries receive his message?[12] From the publication of his first great work, *The Kingdom of Christ; or, Hints on the Principles, Ordinances and Constitution of the Catholic Church,* in 1838, and right through the 1840's he was regarded as an original thinker and able theologian. He was held in great esteem and admiration. It was admitted that he had his special way of presenting and pleading for what he considered the truth. It was recognized that many of his statements were obscure and, taken at their face-value, might appear unsound. But what appeared strange was either overlooked or ascribed to his idiosyncracies. No one within the Church of England challenged the basic soundness of his theological thought. In fact, he was considered a valuable advocate for the Church. It was an obvious choice when, in 1846, he was appointed Professor of Divinity at King's College in London.

By the end of the 1840's Maurice was becoming a figure in the Church of England. His strong personality, his great charm, his unselfishness and humility, and the earnestness of his convictions, attracted an ever-widening circle of adherents, especially among young people who were growing tired of the prevailing orthodoxy. His combination of a deep and sincere spirituality with breadth of intellect led them to regard him as the man who could help them to solve their religious and intellectual problems. The nucleus of a Maurician party was in fact being formed. Through the emergence of Christian Socialism they hoped to bring their views to bear upon the problems of the day. The same years saw a prolific literary activity on Maurice's part. In book after book he proclaimed his message to the Church and the nation at large, always making it quite clear that he was expounding the whole truth of God's revelation to mankind in contrast to the sects and Church parties which had misunderstood or even distorted it.

As Maurice's influence grew, people naturally began seriously to consider his thought and the merits of his approach. The weeklies and quarterlies of the various Church bodies and parties began to deal more extensively with Maurice and his views.

The first serious attack against Maurice was by William Parker, the staunch well-known advocate of High Church orthodoxy. He saw Maurice as a powerful representative of "a Coleridgean school", tainted by German rationalism and idealism, forces subversive of true faith. The powerful Evangelical weekly, *The Record,* followed this up by a continuous and generally unfair campaign against the Coleridgians. Maurice was now marked out as a dangerous man, expounding "Coleridge's Platonic Christianity". Furthermore, he was the founder of Christian Socialism, and on this account he could be attacked for propagating dangerous political and social doctrines under the cover of Christianity.

However, these attacks were unrepresentative of the general attitude towards Maurice in the Church of England and the Nonconformist bodies as well. The great majority of the reviewers of his books were keen on giving him both a fair hearing and fair treatment. They were anxious to point out his personal qualities and intellectual ability. They did complain of the obscurity of his thought and its apparent inconsistencies, and even passed strictures on many of his statements, but still con-

12 For a further treatment, see my: *F. D. Maurice and the Contemporary Religious World* in *Studies in Church History* II (Leiden 1966), 69–90.

sidered Maurice to be an original, powerful, and inspiring theological thinker, a man of good will and good intentions. For this reason it was right to give him more rope than was usual and to interpret his more doubtful ideas and views favourably.

This was the situation up to 1853, the year in which Maurice published his *Theological Essays*. This publication, which led to his eventual dismissal from his professorship at King's College, became a turning-point in his relations with his religious contemporaries. At one blow he became the centre of a furious religious and theological debate.

Maurice had intended his book to be a challenge to the orthodoxy of his day. This challenge could not pass unheeded. Up till then not all religious papers and reviews had dealt with Maurice, but now not one neglected to discuss *Theological Essays*. Immediately it was felt that the book laid bare the core of Maurice's theological thinking, and that it needed detailed discussion in the religious press.

It is generally agreed that *Theological Essays* is a difficult book to master. The violent attacks on contemporary orthodoxy for being a betrayal and distortion of the revelation of God were expressed unambiguously. But Maurice's own contribution to the problems dealt with in the book often appeared to be most elusive. No wonder many of the reviewers misunderstood many aspects of his thought! On the whole, however, they displayed great intellectual energy in grasping his ideas and revealing his intentions. Admittedly the treatment of *Theological Essays* varied in quality, approach and standards of judgment. Different portions of the book attracted the attention of the various reviewers. Yet, in spite of all difference, the critics were unanimous in their final verdict of *Non placet*.

Of course it was impossible to give an exhaustive treatment of *Theological Essays* within the scope of an article, but this deficiency was rectified by R. S. Candlish, a Scottish minister in the Free Kirk. In his *Examination of Mr. Maurice's Theological Essays,* a large book of nearly 450 pages, published in 1854, he gave a detailed and painstaking analysis of Maurice's book. In spite of misunderstandings his exposition must on the whole be described as correct. His critical remarks were often justified. Candlish had given the contemporary orthodoxy competent help in unravelling Maurice's ideas.

In January 1855 the Methodist divine, James H. Rigg, published an article on Maurice, which was later reprinted in his *Modern Anglican Theology,* 1857.[13] Rigg set himself the task "to find out Mr. Maurice's principles, – to discover the root of all his heresies, – the πρῶτον ψεῦδος of all his errors."[14] This was to be found in his Platonic realism: "A sort of Platonism is his fundamental creed; and his Christianity is adjusted accordingly."[15] As soon as it was realised that his theological thinking was based upon Platonism, everything became clear and consistent.[16] Because Maurice's

13 The following quotations are taken from the second and revised edition, 1859.
14 p. X.
15 p. 133. Cf. p. 200–01: "The vital and characteristic doctrines of Christianity are metamorphosed and dislocated. They are bleached into the pale complexion of Platonism or Neo-Platonism; and their relations to each other, as well as to man, and God, and the Bible, are essentially altered."
16 Cf. p. IV: "Having once obtained the clue, I found myself comparatively at home in the Labyrinth of Mr. Maurice's speculations. The master-key fitted all the locks."

contemporaries had failed to grasp this, they were unable to understand what he was driving at and consequently incapable of refuting him efficiently – they simply did not expect to find in him "Platonism – – in a gown and cassock, expounding Christian theology."[17] But Rigg maintained that Maurice had done his best to veil his true aims. When his ideas were obscure and misty, this was because he had clothed his Neo-Platonic rationalism and mysticism in the dress of orthodox terminology. Rigg's treatment of Maurice is not without its blemishes – often he misunderstood Maurice and did not always take sufficient pains to ascertain what he was saying. Nevertheless he had shown erudition and ingenuity in substantiating his charge that Maurice's thinking was contrary to Biblical Christianity.

Candlish's and Rigg's books further developed and supported the criticism already made of Maurice's theology. They were received as a ratification of the judgment previously passed upon him. Those who wanted to vindicate the orthodox faith, whether Evangelicals, Tractarians or Nonconformists, agreed that Maurice's theology meant an evasion and a denial of the authority of the Bible and the fundamentals of the Christian faith. Thus the challenge of *Theological Essays* had forced contemporary orthodoxy to examine Maurice's credentials as a prophet and had found them wanting. Maurice's message was rejected as heretical.

Apart from the small group of ardent and devoted Mauricians there were some who greatly sympathized with Maurice. They approved of his deep religious feelings and agreed to his criticism of orthodoxy. Nevertheless they found his teaching inadequate because he had tried to reconcile it with the institutional life and dogmatism of his Church. This attitude is represented by the great James Martineau. In 1856 he published an article in *The National Review: Personal Influences on Present Theology*,[18] in which, with rare understanding and insight, he discussed the significance of the thought of John Henry Newman, Thomas Carlyle and Maurice. Martineau presented a masterly sketch of Maurice's theological thinking. He pointed out that Platonic Realism "is the inner essence of the system [of Coleridge's] itself, and the living seed of its development in the school of Mr. Maurice. It is chiefly from inapprehension of this character, and from the inveterate training of the English mind in the opposite habit of thought, that so many readers complain of obscurity in the writings of the Chaplain of Lincoln's Inn."[19] Likewise Martineau pointed to what he considered the fundamental weakness in Maurice's thought: "So long as it advances on the ground of religious philosophy, it appears to us to make its footing good: and the first questionable step is, perhaps, at the point where it enters *history* and hands itself over from Plato to St. John. – – we do not see that the links of relation have hitherto been adequately supplied."[20]

The criticisms of *Theological Essays* made no impression on Maurice. He was fully convinced that he had expounded the whole truth contained in the Scriptures and in the doctrinal standards of his Church. He looked on this opposition as motivated by the desire to suppress his teaching. He had only received the lot that always

17 p. 159.
18 Reprinted in *Essays, Reviews and Addresses* I (London 1890), 219–81.
19 p. 258.
20 p. 264.

befell the prophets of God when they attacked the self-centeredness and self-sufficiency of the religious world! He felt himself bound to go on proclaiming the truth by issuing new books. Now and again they were noticed in the religious press. Although they were discussed with due respect for him personally, it was obvious that they no longer held any attraction. Maurice had receded into the background of the religious and theological debate of his day. His thinking had been weighed and found wanting.

This is well illustrated by the treatment accorded to Maurice's reaction against H. L. Mansel's Bampton Lectures on *The Limits of Religious Thought Examined*, delivered in 1858.[21] Mansel was prompted by a desire to stem the growing scepticism and rationalistic criticism of Christianity which had made a special impact on the younger generation. His work was hailed as a great help in the maintenance of orthodox faith. Maurice, who rightly saw Mansel's whole argument as a virtual refutation of the fundamentals of his own thinking, reacted violently in *What is Revelation?*, 1859, and in *A Sequel to the Inquiry, What is Revelation?*, 1860. The passionate vehemence with which Maurice attacked Mansel did not pass unheeded. Once more the attention of the religious press was focused on Maurice and his theology. But it was evident that the champions of the orthodox faith had grown impatient with him. They did not care to listen to him and examine his arguments on their own merits. Maurice was treated in a superficial, and often unfair and sarcastic, manner. The orthodox world had become prejudiced against him – he was categorized as a well-meaning but erring theologian.

However, the great interest which Mansel's Bampton Lectures had aroused was eclipsed by the publication of *Essays and Reviews* in 1860. It struck the adherents of orthodoxy with alarm. The book demonstrated, to their minds, that the Broad Church school stood for the surrender of Christianity to rationalism and Biblical criticism. The Evangelicals and the Tractarians, suspending their internal controversies, rallied their forces to the defence of the citadel of orthodoxy.

Maurice was in an awkward position in the battle around *Essays and Reviews*. On one hand, he approved of the Essayists in their attacks on contemporary orthodoxy. They even appeared to be carrying out the principles which he always had advocated: a fearless regard for truth, wherever and by whomever it was uncovered, a protest against isolating the Christian faith from science and philosophy, and the necessity of meeting and dealing with all doubts and questioning in a frank and honest way. On the other hand, he was convinced that the Essayists were robbing men of God's revelation, which proclaimed the truth about man and the history of mankind. Maurice felt it incumbent upon him to show that both orthodox and liberals had distorted the truth, but that in God's revelation a true reconciliation of that which was a genuine concern for each of the conflicting parties was to be found. With this aim he and some of his friends published *Tracts for Priests and People* in 1861-2.

The *Tracts* attracted a certain amount of attention but were considered to offer little help. The orthodox camp quickly disposed of the Tracts as part and parcel of the dangerous Broad Church movement. All the accusations previously launched against the Essayists were now flung indiscriminately at Maurice and his friends. This

21 Cf. below p. 66-7.

was further evidence that the orthodox reviewers did not find it worth while dealing with Maurice's thinking.

The Essayists and their adherents were dissatisfied with Maurice because he did not appear to understand the essence of their problems and thoughts; he had stopped half-way between his convictions and the consequences to be drawn from them.

From now on Maurice was a lonely figure in the religious and theological life of England. He still published books but small interest was paid to them. In contrast to the situation in the 1840's and in the early 1850's Maurice no longer had the attention of the rising generation, now haunted by doubt. He had nothing to offer them in their crisis of faith. Even more significantly, many who had been ardent Mauricians now drifted away from him, finding his thinking inadequate to cope with the new problems presented by scientific research and Biblical criticism.

In 1872 Maurice died. His death was noticed in many obituaries in the press – also in the weeklies and quarterlies of the religious world. Nobody doubted that he had been a man of more than common ability and had displayed great sincerity and earnestness of purpose. But for all that the obituaries only ratified the previous rejection of his message as being either erroneous or insufficient for solving the burning questions of a new age. In 1874 Leslie Stephen, a former admirer of Maurice, summed up the situation harshly but aptly in the following words: "Mr. Maurice's characteristic doctrines have ceased to have much interest for the world at large. Most men who claim to be, and all who claim not to be, orthodox, see in them a painful waste of intellectual ingenuity; and even the [Broad Church] party which would appropriate Mr. Maurice's reputation has drifted widely from his principles."[22] The following years only confirmed the correctness of Leslie Stephen's estimate. Maurice was considered a figure of the past; the message he had proclaimed in his numerous books was almost forgotten.[23]

However, Maurice was not allowed to sink into oblivion. Suddenly he was rediscovered, his books were re-read and new editions were sought. The primary cause of this unexpected change was the publication of Maurice's *Life and Letters* in 1884.

---

22 *The Fortnightly Review* XV (1874), 595 ("Frederick Denison Maurice"). The correctness of this statement is confirmed by Stopford A. Brooke who on the occasion of Maurice's death wrote: "the real religious leader of liberal theology, the true author of our movement, has but little fame, and has had no worldly success. – – – It is nearly forty years ago since he stood by its springs, and many who are now borne upon the surface of its river have forgotten or never knew its origin. Moreover, it has entered on a new reach of its career in which Maurice would be likely to find himself a stranger, and the tide of which has left behind many of the forms in which he cast his thought" *(The Late F. D. Maurice. A Sermon Preached by the Rev. Stopford A. Brooke, M. A., Honorary Chaplain to the Queen, at York Street, St. James's, on Sunday, April 7, 1872, 3–4).*

23 Thus in 1884 the judicious J. Llewelyn Davies, one of the faithful disciples of Maurice, made the following observation: "during the twelve years that have passed since his death, only the few who have been drawn to him by an inward sympathy have studied with any appreciative interest the volumes which he has left behind him. It is probable that his writings become less easy to understand as the circumstances which called them forth, and of which they are full, pass out of memory" *(The Contemporary Review* XLV (March 1884), 304–05 ("Frederick Denison Maurice")).

In his own lifetime Maurice had charmed and spellbound those who got to know him intimately. Now through his published letters he continued to fascinate. His letters revealed the innermost thoughts of a man who was convinced that he had a prophetic calling to proclaim the good tidings of Christ as the Lord and Saviour of mankind to his Church and nation; a man who unswervingly followed his appointed course, in spite of resistance and misunderstandings of his true motives.

Instead of the rather vague idea of Maurice as a well-meaning, but erring, theologian, the readers of *Life and Letters* saw a man of unique personal grandeur and saintly character. They were ready to believe that, from the time of the publication of *The Kingdom of Christ* in 1838, Maurice had been shamefully misunderstood, misrepresented, and persecuted by the religious world of his day. The reviewers of Maurice's *Life and Letters* accepted this estimate, which Maurice's son had taken over from his father and made the basis of his account of the relationship between his father and his religious contemporaries.

In spite of their great admiration for Maurice's personal character some reviewers still had reservations, not least about the soundness of various aspects of his theological thinking. But he was treated with the respect which was due to a saintly person and was no longer branded as a heretic and a false prophet. Far more prominent, however, was the desire of other reviewers to point out that Maurice was a great theologian and prophet, who had a message for those who took the pains to make themselves acquainted with his work. Thus, while the publication of *Theological Essays* caused the eclipse of Maurice's theological repute among his contemporaries, the publication of his biography marked the beginning of his posthumous fame.

At the time of Maurice's dismissal from King's College Daniel Macmillan wrote to his brother: "He is a grand man and must endure like other prophets. The good people of the next age will build his tomb."[24] This prophecy proved to be true. The criticism which appeared against Maurice in several reviews of his *Life and Letters* soon faded away – and what critics remained kept silent. Those who were enthusiastic about Maurice had the field to themselves – and they were not sparing in their praise. A few quotations will illustrate how successive decades added to his fame.

At the turn of the century W. E. Collins wrote: "But however our estimates may be falsified by the judgment of posterity, there is one of whom it is safe to say that he must always stand out preeminently: Maurice the seer. During the great part of his lifetime, although greatly trusted and revered by an ever-widening circle of friends, he was about the most generally hated of all men in the religious world at large. To-day there are few names that are more generally honoured amongst us than his."[25] Maurice was, according to Collins, the greatest thinker of the nineteenth century, and his greatness consisted in having brought men back to reality and in having proclaimed in its fullness "the Faith which was once for all delivered to the Saints."[26] Charles E. Raven reiterated the same thought twenty years later: "Among all the Churchmen of the nineteenth century it seems certain that we shall reckon him

---

24 *Memoir of Daniel Macmillan* (Cambridge 1882), 251.
25 *Typical English Churchmen from Parker to Maurice* (London 1902), 328.
26 p. 360.

as incomparably the greatest, alike in life, in vision and in achievement."[27] Time, he maintained, had vindicated Maurice. His opponents disappear, but "Maurice lives and grows."[28]

Indeed this was true. The liberal theologians were not allowed to monopolise Maurice. The new theological trends that turned in protest against Liberal theology found in Maurice a spiritual giant who had been struggling for precisely their own aims. Thus A. G. Herbert maintained that Maurice was a "seer and prophet of the future whose importance has never yet been fully recognized. The whole centre of his teaching was his faith in the reality of God and his constant endeavour to distinguish between the Divine and the human. – – there never was a theologian more radically opposed to the spirit of Liberal theology, or a more thorough dogmatist."[29] H. Hodkin found that Maurice had anticipated the teachings of Barth and Brunner on the Continent, and that a deeper understanding of Maurice would give rise to a similar theological renewal in England.[30] Only now, he continued, was it possible truly to understand the depth of his thought and to realize how closely he adhered to the Bible: "Although he was underestimated, disparaged or misunderstood by the great majority of his contemporaries – – in our day he is coming into his own."[31] Maurice was not only recognized by some as the greatest Anglican theologian of the nineteenth century, he was also ranked with the most outstanding theological thinkers of the Church such as Augustine and Thomas Aquinas.[32] Posterity had truly built Maurice a fitting tomb. He was considered a prophet firmly anchored in the fundamental truths of Christian faith, with a message so profound and so much in advance of his time that later generations would benefit from studying and appropriating its principles.

It must be said, however, that these eulogies are the outcome of personal impressions and not the result of an intensive study of Maurice's theological thinking and its significance. They are strikingly unsubstantiated. That is not to say that no studies on Maurice have appeared since the publication of *Life and Letters* in 1884. On the contrary, many books and articles have been devoted to his work, and there are a

27 *Christan Socialism 1848–1854* (London 1920), 75. Cf. *ibid.*: "In these days when the idols of our grandfathers are being thrown irreverently from their pedestals, he almost alone holds his place secure and attracts to him wider circles of disciples, and not the least proof of his quality is this, that he stands as a test of his contemporaries; by their attitude to him we can with remarkable accuracy determine their true and abiding worth."

28 p. 81.

29 *Liturgy and Society* (London 1935), 108.

30 *Theology* XL (1937), 108 (*"The Theological Teaching of F. D. Maurice"*).

31 p. 97. Cf. also p. 101: "The centre of his mind and teaching, 'the master light of all his seeing', was the Incarnation," "the cardinal event in the history of mankind."

32 Cf. V. Landmead Casserley: *The Retreat from Christianity in the Modern World. The Maurice Lectures for 1951* (London 1952), 164–65: "Wherever true dialectical Christian thinking is going on, it is contemporary thinking, redeeming the prevailing intellectualism of the place and the time by setting it in a wider and more comprehensive context, so that our particular position in space and time is no longer an intellectual prison whose walls enclose our vision and stunt our minds, but a genuine point of view from which a man may look out freely upon all space and time. This, as I believe, is the ideal of Christian thought and theology as we find it in the writings of its great masters, in Augustine, and Aquinas, Butler and Maurice, for example."

large number of references to Maurice in books not otherwise concerned with him and his thought.

It is not our purpose here to supply an annotated Maurice bibliography. But it must be pointed out that although the studies on Maurice vary in quality, their common deficiency is that they deal only with certain problems and aspects of his thinking. On the whole too little energy has been spent on ascertaining what exactly Maurice meant by the terms and ideas he employed, and too little attention has been directed to tackling the apparent inconsistencies in his writings. More often than not the studies on Maurice must simply be qualified as "Lesefrüchte", since their authors have only picked out what was of interest and value to them personally and even interpreted it in the light of their own theological presuppositions. No wonder, then, that the various publications present a rather confused picture of the essential character of Maurice's theological thinking and of its significance. One's bewilderment is of course only increased when one takes into account the verdicts which competent contemporary critics had pronounced upon Maurice!

Once the deficiencies in Maurician studies have been admitted, it must be considered whether it is not Maurice himself who is in the last analysis to be held responsible for this state of affairs. He did not produce a systematic account of his teaching. We find his message expounded in numerous collections of sermons and in books and pamphlets which dealt with what he considered to be the burning questions of his day. They seem to defy any attempt to discover a coherent pattern of thought in them. Small wonder so many have complained about the tormenting obscurity of his writings. Maurice's style leaves a confusing impression. Frequently he is content to do no more than to throw out hints as to the right solution to the problems he has raised. Similarly, the meaning of his words is difficult to grasp; he seldom tried to define or explain them, as if his audience knew what they signified. His statements appear most elusive, even inconsistent and contradictory.

It can be argued that these conflicting interpretations of Maurice's thought are due to the fact that it was moulded by various influences. So Maurice appropriated truths from divergent philosophical, religious and theological movements whilst at the same time reacting vehemently against much in these various movements which he considered false and misleading. Maurice appears a confused thinker, lacking the ability to weld various ideas into a coherent whole.[33] Since he was an uncritical eclectic, his

33 This was the view of the astute J. B. Mozley. In the article: *Professor Maurice's Theological Essays* in *The Christian Remembrancer* for January 1854 (reprinted in *Essays Historical and Critical* II (London 1892), 254–309) he maintained that Maurice is "a writer whose strength is that of vehemence rather than accuracy, and who thinks less like a reasoner than a rhetorician; who employs, to prove his conclusions, rather a determination of the will than the ordinary instrument of argument, and is too generally almost as obscure as he is emphatic" (p. 256). Mozley generously places Maurice in "the order of prophets", of whom "strength of conviction rather than of argument" (p. 257) is characteristic. A few years later, however, on the occasion of Maurice's controversy with Mansel he spoke his mind: "we may be permitted to say that we have never seen anything in him which indicates any other characteristic than that of an earnest, illogical mind, endeavouring to find its way out of a labyrinth of error in which it has been educated, and torn asunder by the contradictory influences to which it has been subjected, catching at truth wherever a glimmer of it could be seen" (*The Christian Remembrancer* XXXIX (June 1860), 297).

teaching represents a *complexio oppositorum*. So all the highly divergent estimates of what constitutes the inner core of Maurice's thought can be said to be equally true. A case can be made for his having been basically a Platonic realist, an expounder of Biblical realism, a Liberal theologian, an Anglo-Catholic of the *Lux Mundi* type, a dialectical theologian or even a genuine Lutheran theologian. It is all a question of which aspect of this theological *complexio oppositorum* one chooses to emphasize at the expense of the other aspects, which can be ignored as basically irrelevant.

Although it is tempting to regard Maurice as an uncritical ecletic, there is, however, much which makes it difficult, *a priori*, to accept this solution. If Maurice often appears to be obscure and even inconsistent in exposition, it is worth noting that prior to his spiritual crisis in 1828 he expounded his romantic-idealistic philosophy in a lucid and consistent manner. Furthermore, Maurice repeatedly indicated the main ideas in the message which he felt himself called to proclaim to his age with almost epigrammatic clarity and concision, especially in his letters.

Maurice's writings confirm that he knew his own mind. From the publication of *The Kingdom of Christ* in 1838 to his death his teaching was dominated by the same ideas, not to say peculiarities, which led to inevitable repetition and monotony. Neither the criticism of his contemporaries nor the shifts in the spiritual and religious climate during his life induced him to revise his ideas or polemics. However strange it may sound in consideration of the repeated accusations against him of indistinctness and obscurity, Maurice himself was firmly convinced that his teaching was clear and could easily be grasped by anybody.[34] Finally, Maurice demanded of any book worth anything – and we are probably justified in adding any body of thought – that it be dominated by a leading idea or principle, which binds its parts together into a coherent and consistent whole.[35] This must imply that Maurice was confident that he had satisfied this demand in his writings.

These observations cannot be reconciled with the idea of Maurice as an uncritical eclectic whose thinking was a hotchpotch of the most diverse elements. On the contrary, they lead to the conclusion that we are entitled to look for coherence and consistency in Maurice's teaching. The aim of the present study is to examine if these qualities are to be found. It requires, however, that all aspects of his theological thinking are drawn into account. I shall pursue this end by adopting the method

34 Cf. *The Church a Family: 12 Sermons on the Occasional Services of the Prayer Book Preached in the Chapel of Lincoln's Inn* (London 1850), 40–41: "It is looseness and vagueness against which I protested – –, the habit of using words as if they might stretch or contract according to our convenience; of uttering a great proposition concerning the acts of God to man, and then annulling it by some exception, or some ambiguous phrase a moment after. This is a perilous course for our sincerity and faith; perilous in proportion to the largeness and reality and awfulness of the question about which we are occupied."

35 Cf. *The Unity of the New Testament*, 167: "Is any book worth anything to any human being, unless there is some idea or principle in it which binds the different parts in it together? Can a person sit down to write a book which shall last for any time, and convey a living impression to a number of minds, unless there is such an idea or purpose within it? Supposing it to be within it, will not every part of this record be penetrated by it? Will he not see every fact in the light of it? And, so far as he imparts an impression to us, will he not do so by making us see every fact in the same light?"

which Maurice wished to use in analysing the New Testament: "I desire to inquire whether there is a leading truth which goes through these documents, which binds them together, which explains the differences of their form and their apparent incongruities. Such a truth, if it exists, ought to present itself on their very surface. It should bear to be tested by minute criticism, but yet it should reveal itself in the general course of the narrative, in the enunciation of the discourse. No ingenuity should be needed for the detection of it; the only business of the lecturer should be to shew that this principle compels the reader to acknowledge a coherency in these writings, even though his theories incline him to deny it."[36]

36 *The Unity of the New Testament,* 2.

I

THE TRIUNE GOD AND THE DIVINE ORDER

Chapter I

THE TRIUNE GOD AND THE CREATION OF THE DIVINE ORDER

1. God as the Triune God

Nothing is more striking about Maurice than the fact that his thinking dealt with every aspect of human life. Yet this was implied in his calling as a theologian: "I have felt as a theologian, thought as a theologian, written as a theologian; – – all other subjects in my mind are connected with theology and subordinate to it."[1] In theology he had "a much broader as well as firmer meeting-ground with men as men, with men of all kinds and professions, of all modes and habits of thought, with men who attack my convictions, with men who are indifferent about their own convictions, than any maxims of trade, of convenience, of modern civilization, of modern tolerance, can supply me with."[2]

But this holds good only if theology is defined strictly as "that which concerns the Being and Nature of God."[3] In contrast to contemporary theology which was based, according to Maurice, on the religious man's experiences and notions about God he stated the principles for true theology in the following way: "My desire is to ground all theology upon the Name of God the Father, the Son and the Holy Ghost; not to begin from ourselves and our sins; not to measure the straight line by the crooked one. This is the method which I have learnt from the Bible. There everything proceeds from God; He is revealing Himself, He is acting, speaking, ruling."[4]

For Maurice it was self-evident that nothing can claim to be scientific unless it dealt with *that which is,* "the substantial and real", or, as this is in itself unchangeable and perfect, "the permanent" and "the eternal".[5] According to this definition theology must be described as a divine and human science since its subject-matter is God, the Perfect and Eternal Being, and those immutable principles which direct His dealings with mankind.[6]

1 *Moral and Metaphysical Philosophy* II (London 1873), IX.
2 *The Conflict of Good and Evil in Our Day. Twelve Letters to a Missionary* (London 1865. Cit. *The Conflict*), 182.
3 *Moral and Metaphysical Philosophy* II, IX.
4 *Sacrifice,* XLV.
5 Cf. *Macmillan's Magazine* IX ("Christmas Thoughts on Renan's *Vie de Jésus*", January 1864), 195: "science means – – a reverence for that which is; for the permanent; for laws which live on through a multitude of changes, and direct these changes."
6 Cf. *Theological Essays* (London 1904), 90–91: "If Science concerns that which is fixed and absolute, *that which is,* then to believe that God has declared Himself, that He has withdrawn the veil which hides Him from His creatures, that He has in a wonderful and orderly history enabled us to see what He is, and what He is to us, what those eternal laws and principles are which dwell in Himself and which determine His dealings with us, is to believe that there is a divine and human *Science."*

Maurice followed in the steps of all Christian Platonists when he described the nature of God by reference to Ex. 3,14, where Jehovah reveals His nature as "I AM THAT I AM", the One who can be described as "I AM".[7] God is the totality of all being, the perfect and almighty life, whereas all other beings must always be dependent upon Him for their existence. By calling Himself "I AM" God has revealed Himself as the One who is immutably the same – He is what He is. God cannot change nor be subject to the changing conditions of time and space.

Maurice repeatedly spoke of God as "He who was, and is, and is to come" and described Him as "He who is the same yesterday, today and for ever", in order to drive home the truth that the categories of time and space, which belong to the visible world, do not apply to God. God's being and work can only be described in the present tense, the eternal *now* which knows neither beginning nor end.[8]

It is precisely the same concern which made Maurice insist that theology must begin with God and not with man. The starting point is the eternal world, whose centre is God as the perfect Being and not the finite world of time and space. This enables the theologian to rise above the appearances of the visible world to the real and substantial, that is, to know God as He is.

God's revelation of Himself as "I AM THAT I AM" means at the same time that God is a personal will. His will is dependent only upon His own nature and being. Since He is immutable, it follows that His will is unchangeable and irresistible.

Maurice was at pains to point out that "He who rules all is not a destiny, but a loving will, not an abstraction, but a Person; not a mere sovereign, but a Father."[9]

---

7 Cf. *The Kingdom of Christ* (2nd revised and altered edition 1842, reprinted in *Everyman's Library*. Cit. *The Kingdom of Christ*) II, 312–13: "Do we not mean when we use the awful name of God, 'THE BEING, HE who IS'? If there be no certainty, how dare we take that name into our lips? Are not the very words, 'I believe in God the Father Almighty', an assertion that there is something fixed and eternal upon which the pillars of the universe rest? Do not the next words mean, 'He who Is has revealed Himself to us? We are not to live upon probabilities and plausibilities. He who is Truth does wish that we should know the truth, and that the truth should make us free?'"

8 Cf. *The Religions of the World and their Relations to Christianity, Considered in Eight Lectures Founded by the Right Hon. Robert Boyle* (6th edition. London 1886. Cit. *Religions*), 134–35: "Nothing [in the O. T.], you see, is set forth in the Hindoo manner, as a dream, or thought, or reflection *about* God; all is set forth as coming *from* Him; He *is*, and He is doing. – – It [the O. T.] is a record – – but not merely a record – it tells us of Him who was, and is, and is to come; of One by whose command the world was made, and by whose command it subsists; who rules and directs in the affairs of men, not less now than of old. I conceive that there is nothing in Christianity so primary and fundamental as this belief; nothing which it is so necessary for us to assert, in the simple practical language of the Old Testament, and not to dilute by any modern phrases or unreal substitutes." The last words are aimed at those of Maurice's religious contemporaries who maintained that we only know God through His revealing acts in history and that for this reason we must use the common grammatical tenses: the past, present, and the future (see also *The Prayer-Book, Considered Especially in Reference to the Romish System, and the Lord's Prayer* (London 1893. Cit. *The Prayer-Book*), 289).

9 *The Prayer-Book*, 380.

Love as the essence of God's nature dominates His will and His mind.[10] Thus God is not a despotic tyrant who lives for Himself and whose acts merely serve His own gratification and selfishness. He is that perfect fatherly love which must create fellowship.

Maurice was fully aware that his insistence on the idea of God's unchangeable love towards men coincided with Unitarian doctrine,[11] and indeed he praised the Unitarians because they had always upheld the idea of the unity of God.[12] But this did not lead him to reject the orthodox doctrine of the Trinity. On the contrary, he considered the belief in the Trinity to be the only safeguard of the true insights underlying Unitarianism.

When the Unitarians interpreted the unity of God to mean that God is numerically one,[13] they in fact conceived of Him as a sovereign power, who in His innermost nature lives for Himself and only finds pleasure in Himself and in His own perfection. On this presupposition the fatherhood of God and His love for man must always be but a chance attribute having no necessary relation to His essential nature. It merely expresses the arbitrariness and capriciousness of a ruler whom man can never rely upon as an unchangeable reality.[14] Basically, then, Unitarianism represents "that ghastly solitary *singleness* of the Godhead which ends in the acknowledgement of a mere imperial Power removed from all sympathy with his creatures."[15]

So the true principles of Unitarianism are preserved in the doctrine of the Trinity to which the Creeds of the Church bear witness.[16] A personal will which originates in and is determined by love can never be self-sufficient: "We cannot think of a Being of perfect love as wrapt up in Himself, as dwelling in the contemplation of His own

10 Cf. *The Patriarchs and Lawgivers of the Old Testament. A Series of Sermons Preached in the Chapel of Lincoln's Inn* (London 1890. Cit. *The Patriarchs*), 183: "this Love as the essence of the divine Mind, – as the spring of all its purposes, as directed towards it [the spirit of man] and the whole universe."

11 See *Theological Essays*, 4.

12 *ibid*.

13 Cf. *The Kingdom of Christ* I, 138–39: "With deep awe they [the Unitarians] had acknowledged the Unity of God as the unfathomable foundation of thought, and faith, and being. Now they heard that unity asserted, not as mysterious and unfathomable, but as the escape from mystery. It was a purely material notion; all the arguments in its favour were deduced from the impossibility and contradiction which a Trinity presents when it is contemplated materially."

14 Cf. *Theological Essays*, 110: "We have sometimes fancied we could dwell simply on the thought of a Father; all others should be discarded as unnecessary. But soon it has not been a Father we have contemplated: it has been a mere substratum of the things we saw, a name under which we collected them."

15 *The Contemporary Review* XV ("A Few More Words on the Athanasian Creed," October 1870. Cit. *The Athanasian Creed*), 487.

16 Cf. *The Kingdom of Christ* I, 139: "Such thoughts brooded in their minds, and led them by very slow processes and through bitter conflicts to the conviction: 'If the Unity of God is to be asserted it *must* be asserted on quite different grounds from those which the so-called Unitarians have chosen, and the true assertion of it *may* possibly be contained in those creeds which we have rejected!' "

excellence and perfection."[17] Such a Being must communicate: "It must speak, it must utter itself. A Will cannot be without a *Word*. A Will that is, and lives, must utter itself by a living Word. That is what St. John, in his divine theology, declares to us. But if he speaks in one sentence of a Word, he speaks in the next of a Son."[18] The Father's eternal life with the Son makes it clear that the idea of fatherhood is implied in His very nature. God's fellowship with His Son teaches us that He is eternally sacrificing Himself as the Father. He keeps nothing for Himself but freely gives everything to the Son. But the Son for His part has as little desire as the Father to live for Himself, self-sufficient and independent. His life is willingly sacrificed in faith and obedience for the realization of the Father's loving will.[19] Christ freely passes on what He has received from the Father. The unity between Father and Son is thus based upon the love in and through which they both sacrifice themselves for each other.[20] Following St. Augustine, Maurice interpreted this love as the Holy Ghost, who is the bond that unites Father and Son.[21] Therefore "the Divine Unity is not a narrow selfish individuality but the unity of a Father with a Son in one Spirit."[22]

Inasmuch as God eternally exists as the Triune God, we know that love and fellowship belong to God's own immutable essence. This fact furthermore reveals that the sacrifice of love, and not independence and selfishness, is the fundamental law of the universe, rooted in the Divine Being. Sacrifice never presupposes sin. It is the expression of the highest and most perfect life imaginable – the inner life of the Trini-

---

17 *Theological Essays,* 109.

18 p. 108.

19 Cf. *The Prayer-Book,* 254–55, where Maurice made Christ say: "I am under no stern law of Necessity, binding me to a certain act which it is physically impossible for me to leave undone. I am under a law of obedience; I cannot break that law without self-destruction. And why? Because I am under the law of a Son to a Father, under a law of eternal Love. Here is the secret of my freedom, of my inherent power; here is the secret of my perfect, entire subjection. I could not be free except I were bound by this fetter; there is no freedom without it. I could not be obedient except I had the power of not being obedient. I should not be submitting to the control of love, but of something else over which I am entirely master. My Father loves me, because I lay down my life. That perfect internal delight which He has in me expresses itself in this act, binds me to this act. It would be suspended, there would be a clashing and contradiction in the eternal Unity of our Being, if I did not lay down my life. The perfect fulfilment and unfolding of that Unity is in my giving up of myself. The love of the Father sees itself, realises itself in this act and is satisfied. Here is the manifestation of that love; here it shines forth full upon you; here you must see it, confess it, submit to it." For Maurice the Son's relation to the Father during His earthly life, as it is described in the Gospel of St. John, is a perfect reflection of the eternal fellowship between the Son and the Father.

20 Cf. *The Gospel of St. John. A Series of Discourses* (London 1894), 154: "And this union of Wills, this inward substantial Unity, [Christ] declares to have its basis in love, the underground of Deity."

21 Cf. *Theological Essays,* 109: "To think of the Father resting in the Son, in the deepest sense knowing the Son, and of the Son knowing the Father, we must think of a uniting Spirit."

22 *The Prophets and Kings of the Old Testament. A Series of Sermons Preached in the Chapel of Lincoln's Inn* (London 1894. Cit. *The Prophets*), 491.

30

ty.[23] So, as His life with the Father had been eternally one of unceasing sacrifice,[24] Christ is truly "the Lamb slain before the foundation of the world."[25]

Because the doctrine of the Trinity leads man to a true knowledge of God and His mind and will,[26] it never becomes obsolete or superfluous. Indeed, time will only demonstrate the necessity of retaining it since it proclaims the fact that the Triune God constitutes the very reality upon which the universe and humanity rest.[27] Therefore Maurice can say: "No change of place or circumstance, no progress in the world's history, no development of the Divine purpose, must interfere with the calm belief of a unity of the Father and the Son in the Spirit which was in the beginning, is now, and ever shall be, world without end."[28]

2. The Creation

Being perfect self-sacrificing love, God's sole delight is to impart His own being to that which is nothing. God is by inner necessity a Creator who eternally has decreed the creation of the universe and mankind.[29] As He is the totality of being, all created things not only owe their origin to God but are also dependent on Him at all times. So the creation is founded on God's love and bears witness to that love's continual presence.

Although for Maurice God is the Creator, he more often spoke of Christ as "the Author and Upholder of the true order of the world", "the actual foundation of the universe".[30] Of course this is not contradictory because the creation originates

23 Cf. *Sacrifice*, 182: "I have maintained that sacrifice is entirely independent of sin – that the most pure and perfect state we can conceive, is the state of which sacrifice is the law", and *Dialogues between a Clergyman and a Layman on Family Worship* (London 1862. Cit. *Family Worship*), 108–9: "Sacrifice is evidently the opposite of the sin of the world. For that sin is, as we all feel it to be, the self-seeking, the self-willing, which sets us at war with each other."

24 Cf. *Sacrifice*, 119: "sacrifice is implied in the very Original of the universe – – it is involved in the very nature and being of God – – it was expressed in the divine obedience of the Son before the worlds were."

25 See *Sacrifice*, 255–6. Cf. p. 110–1: "the apostles – – lead us back to a ground of sacrifice in the divine nature; in that submission of the Son to the Father, that perfect unity of Purpose, Will, Substance, between them, whence the obedience and fellowship of all unfallen beings, the obedience and fellowship of all restored beings, must be derived, and by which they are sustained."

26 Cf. *The Prayer-Book*, 255: "We must be taught what lies at the foundation of things, whether it is a hard power, a hopeless compulsion; whether it is nothingness; whether it is something which we can have projected out of our own minds; or whether it is this truth of a Father united with a Son in an eternal Spirit of Love; which Love is the ground of his Nature, which Love has been ever coming forth to us in acts of Creation and Redemption."

27 Cf. *The Kingdom of Christ* (1838) I, 61: "When we assert the doctrine of the Trinity, we do so, because we believe it to be the grand foundation of all society, the only ground of universal fellowship, the only idea of a God of love."

28 *The Gospel of St. John*, 238.

29 Cf. *Christmas Day and Other Sermons* (London 1843. Cit. *Christmas Day*), 161: "But he created nothing for his own glory in the sense that dark and selfish men give to the word; for love delights to shed itself abroad to everything. It is satisfied in itself already, and it would bring all things to its own satisfaction."

30 See, e. g., *Life* II, 138.

in the Triune God. So the Father keeps nothing for Himself but in love gives up everything to the Son. For His part, the Son receives that which His Father has given in order to realise the Father's will and purpose.[31] In this sense Christ is the Creator and "the Head of all Creation"[32]: "The *name of Jesus* is the name to which all the intelligences of the universe refer themselves, and all the energies and impulses of the unconscious creation. They bow *to* it, as denoting the only source of their strength; they bow *in* it, as containing the only secret of their humiliation."[33]

Because God, in and through Christ, is the ever active and ever present Creator, it is an indisputable fact that it is in God that everything lives, moves, and has its being.[34] As the created universe originates in God's eternal decree and is the expression of His love, man can rest assured that God will always uphold it and preserve it from all destructive forces. Man can remain confident that the creation is imbued with order and harmony. This is an unchangeable truth because the Triune God "underlies and bears up the universe".[35]

This message is good tidings to common people.[36] Yet they are being deprived of it by contemporary theology with its notion of a universe, once called into existence by God but then left to run its own course independent of God.[37] The reason is that the Mosaic account of the creation has been interpreted as "the history of the for-

31 Cf. *The Prayer-Book,* 249: " 'God so loved the world, that He gave His only-begotten Son, that whosoever believeth in Him should not perish, but have everlasting life.' That love is the original ground of all things, of ourselves, of our acts, of our creation, of our redemption," and *Family Worship,* 107–8: "I have learned that if the Father did *not* give up the Son, if the Son did *not* give up Himself, the one commanding, the other obeying – the mutual sacrifice, not destroying the idea of authority, but sustaining it, – there is nothing to hold the universe together."

32 *Family Worship,* 197.

33 *Sacrifice,* 226. Cf. *The Kingdom of Christ* (1838) I, 254, where Christ is spoken of as "a person, actually living and reigning, upholding the earth and the pillars thereof, when all things but for him would have been out of their course."

34 Cf. *The Conflict,* 179: "We tell all men, those who are most incredulous of our message, most hostile to it, that this Name is about them, that they are living, moving, having their being in it." Maurice never tired of quoting Acts 17,23.

35 *Sermons Preached in Lincoln's Inn Chapel* IV (London 1892. Cit. *Sermons* IV), 38.

36 Cf. *The Patriarchs,* XIX: "Toiling and suffering men want to know, not how the world was governed thousands of years ago, but how it is governed now; whether there is any order in it, whether there is any one who can and will rectify its disorders. They must have plain straightforward answers to these questions," and *Life* II, 253: "Doctrines about heaven and earth which are separated from trust in the Creator of heaven and earth, and in Christ in whom heaven and earth are reconciled, had better perish – the sooner we can get rid of them the better. But these are negative doctrines – opinions which we hold by dint of tradition or argument, not a faith which upholds us when we are most feeble and tottering. Of that faith no man or devil can deprive us."

37 Cf. *Moral and Metaphysical Philosophy* I, XXVI: "But the oldest [teaching] is that the Word of God put life into all creatures, bidding them grow and multiply. According to the Scriptures, this creative power is never wearied or exhausted but is new every morning. These are, or ought to be, our nursery lessons. If we divines have grafted upon them any conception of a dead universe which was called into existence, and has had no renewing life-giving power in it, the more completely such conceptions are exposed the better, for they have arisen from an implicit Atheism, and are likely to produce an explicit one."

32

mation of the material world"[38] according to "notions of a material manufacture".[39] However, a close and strictly literal reading proves this interpretation to be false, Maurice maintained.

The first of the two accounts of the creation of man in Genesis must refer to the creation of the ideal man, or the idea of man, while the second describes the creation of an individual, the first member of the human race.[40] As this observation is bound to apply to the interpretation of the creation of the universe as described in the first chapter of Genesis, "we are forced to the conclusion, that in the one case, as in the other, it is not the visible material thing of which the historian [Moses] is speaking, but of that which lies below the visible material thing, and constitutes the substance which it shows forth."[41] Moses' concern is to show that "the going forth of God's Word, the expression of His mind and will," means the creation of "living powers".[42] Visible things, on the other hand, are called into being "through the communication of that inward power and substance, without which matter is but a dream".[43] The living or productive powers were admittedly imparted once but only in order to be "in continual exercise and manifestation".[44] Thus Moses did not describe the creation as an event in the past. On the contrary, by giving an account of the creation of "the living powers" and their unceasing activity in and through matter he revealed what always holds good of the created universe.

Although Maurice's understanding of the creation is obscure in places,[45] the main argument stands out quite clearly. God created "the living powers" which imparted life and being, order and harmony to matter and so the visible world came into being. It was no accident that Maurice did not speak of the creation of matter, as he always described it as something shapeless and changeable, gravitating towards nothingness. All emphasis lies on "the living powers" or, as Maurice says, on the substantial, eternal world, which is the pattern according to which the material world

---

38 *The Patriarchs*, 43.
39 *The Claims of the Bible and of Science. Correspondence between a Layman and the Rev. F. D. Maurice on Some Questions arising out of the Controversy respecting the Pentateuch* (London 1863. Cit. *The Claims*), 42.
40 In *The Patriarchs*, 35 Maurice argued that "Moses has contemplated the creation of man not from our point of view, but from God's. He has told us what man was in His mind; and how He brought forth the purpose and intent of His mind into act. — — we are told afterwards that He did [invest him with something visible]; but this cannot have been the special, essential, act of Creation."
41 *The Patriarchs*, 37.
42 See p. 37–39.
43 p. 37.
44 p. 39.
45 Thus, apart from the problem of the creation of matter, it is not clear whether "the living powers" proceeded directly from God, representing an independent spiritual world of archetypal ideas. Generally, however, Maurice argued that the "Eternal Word — — in St. John's Gospel — — is affirmed to be that form or type after whom the Divine Artist fashioned the whole universe" (*The Epistles of St. John. A Series of Lectures on Christian Ethics* (London 1867), 131), and asserted that Christ is "*the* image of God, the ground and pattern of the visible and invisible creation, the Head of all powers and governments in the unseen world" (*The Unity of the New Testament*, 565).

is fashioned.[46] Because of this fact all visible things are worthy of respect and honour[47] – they must never be considered as "actual separate phenomenal existences, such as they present themselves to the senses of man."[48] Only by taking our starting-point in eternity, in the mind and will of God, can we "regard the whole universe as very good, even as it was when it came forth at the call of the divine word."[49]

3. Christ as the Head of the Human Race

Within God's created universe man occupies a unique position. Being a voluntary creature,[50] endowed with reason and will, "God's higher and more glorious creation",[51] man stands highest in the hierarchy of creation.[52] The involuntary creatures are subordinated to him and only "find their meaning and interpretation in man, as

---

46 Cf. *Sequel to the Inquiry, What is Revelation? in a Series of Letters to a Friend* (Cambridge 1860. Cit. *Sequel),* 14–5: "the Bible – – spoke of a substantial, eternal world, in which men were intended to find a home. If what it said was true, the words which described that substantial, eternal world must be most strictly metaphysical words. And yet they must be also most strictly popular words; words for the people, for human beings as such. I found temporal things in the Bible opposed to eternal, but not in the way of contempt or disparagement. The greatest justice was done to both. The world which we see with our eyes was never treated as popular preachers treat it. It had its own honour. It derived honour and grandeur from its associations with the other. – – I looked upon the permanent as the standard for the changeable and fleeting, and did not attempt to deduce the nature of the higher from that of the lower." – J. H. Rigg maintained that Maurice borrowed the idea of the creation of the transcendental spiritual world from Philo (see op. cit., 140). Although it is possible to demonstrate certain points of similarity with Philo's *De Opificio Mundi,* everything points to St. Augustine as his source of inspiration. Thus it is significant that Maurice, in the sermon on Genesis 1–2 *(The Patriarchs,* 33–49), where he gave his most elaborate exposition of the creation of the spiritual world, quoted, with approval, a passage from *De Genesi ad Litteram* lib. I § 39. Elsewhere Maurice agreed with St. Augustine's account of the creation in his *Confessiones:* "throughout the Confessions, the unchangeableness of God is not a negation of the changeable, but the very ground of all changeable things; the thought and belief of it alone make them endurable. Augustine can find his rest nowhere but in the Infinite and the Eternal" *(Sequel,* 72). Also Maurice's conception of the ideas as living powers is similar to St. Augustine's *rationes seminales.* So, in many ways, St. Augustine appears to have influenced Maurice's idea of the creation. So much is at least clear that Maurice reproduces the ideas of the Christian Platonists of the Early Church on this subject.
47 Cf. *Sequel,* 17: "they could never deal bravely and manfully with changeable and transitory things, or pay them the reverence to which they have a right, while they raised them into gods; – – they could see the earth and all its beauty clearly, and love it heartily, while they walked in the heavenly sun which is looking down upon it."
48 *The Patriarchs,* 37.
49 *The Gospel of St. John,* 253.
50 Cf. *The Unity of the New Testament,* 392: "a beautiful order [extends] from the highest to the lowest, through every rank of creatures, man being the one who has the power of disobedience, the privilege of cheerful, voluntary obedience."
51 *The Kingdom of Christ* (1838) II, 211.
52 Cf. *The Patriarchs,* 46: "– – the fact of which the human conscience testifies so strongly that a creature endued with a will and a reason must be higher than all the things which his senses contemplate, which his mind can conceive of, that have *not* a will and a reason."

man finds his meaning and interpretation in God".[53] Yet man's position as ruler over the rest of creation is due to the fact that he alone is created in the image of God.[54] This means that man is created in Christ, who by His self-sacrificing love and obedience to God reflects God's mind and will and thus is the perfect Image of God. Furthermore, man's creation in Christ means that he is created to have fellowship with Him and to be fashioned in His likeness.

It is important for Maurice to insist that Christ did not initiate His relation with mankind through His incarnation. The relationship between Christ and man is of no accidental character since God from eternity decided to create the human race in Christ.[55] Maurice can, therefore, maintain: "The sense of our substantial union as men with Christ, and of His union with the Father, sometimes comes to me with overpowering conviction – – of its stern, hard, scientific, reality".[56]

As Creator of man Christ is "a Fountain of Life – a divine life from which human life is derived, by which its springs may be renewed, in which it can find its full repose and satisfaction."[57] But men have never received life from Christ in such a way that they become independent and able to live without Him. As the ever present life-giver Christ always upholds man.[58] To exist as a man means to live with Christ and always receive life from Him. Conversely, to be without Christ is to be cut off from the only source of life and be in the grip of death.

To be created in Christ, then, means that man is to have nothing in himself; everything comes from Christ as man's only Lord and Creator.[59] All men are to live by

---

53 *The Patriarchs*, 34.
54 Cf. *Religions*, 191: "We turn to the earliest of the Jewish records, and we find it declared that God made man in His own image, and gave him dominion over all the other creatures He had formed. Before a word has been said about the difference of one people from another, here is a broad fundamental assertion respecting man as man," and p. 194: "Man, the race of Man, is treated as formed in the image of God, as intended for rule over the creatures."
55 Cf. *The Unity of the New Testament* 518, where Maurice commented on Eph. 1, 3–4: "Here as the Predestinarian school rightly assures us, is the assertion of a divine purpose which was to be executed in time, but which was not formed in time, which cannot be contemplated in reference to it and under its conditions. And they cannot be wrong in saying that the rest of the Epistle is unintelligible if the divine purpose, the Eternal Order, of which the Apostle speaks almost in the first words of it, is forgotten, or merged in any of the acts or events by which it was realised."
56 *Life* II, 326.
57 *The Epistles of St. John*, 170.
58 Cf. *Sermons Preached in Lincoln's Inn Chapel* I (London 1891. Cit. *Sermons* I), 7: "from Him they receive the life of their bodies and the life of their spirits, the power to see and hear, the power to think, believe, hope, love; – – in Him they are constituted by God's eternal law, – – apart from Him they have no life at all," and *Sermons* IV, 130: "To suppose the grace of our Lord Jesus Christ absent from any age or any set of circumstances becomes difficult, all but impossible, to those who ascribe every good thing to that grace, who cannot conceive how men could exist a day or a moment, if they were left to themselves and the wayward impulses of their own nature."
59 Cf. *Sacrifice*, 15: "the Creator is goodness and truth, and – – all creatures have goodness and truth, so far as they disclaim them in themselves and seek them in Him," and *Religions*, 201: "The Scripture starts from the divine ground; assumes that man according to his constitution is nothing but an image; denies that he can originate anything."

His creative acts. Maurice meant it quite literally when he said that "Christ is the Centre of the universe, the source and spring of life to all men".[60] Because Christ's fellowship with man originates in God's eternal will and love, His work amongst men does not depend upon their acknowledgement and confession of Him as their Lord and Creator or on any qualities or merits of their own. If faith was to be the condition of Christ's continued presence and work in men, there would be something in them entitling them to be the object of His love. Apart from the fact that man cannot offer God anything, this would be a denial of God who creates and gives without regard to human worthiness and merit. Inasmuch as Christ sacrifices Himself to carry out God's will, man can determine with certainty that Christ is always present and gives life to everybody. Men may deny that this is the case, but this denial does not destroy the relationship between Christ and man: "It is awful to think that if we take the wings of the morning, or ascend into Heaven, or dive into Hell, we cannot escape from the Divine Presence."[61]

Christ, as the Creator and Upholder of all human life, is the Head of the human race and the actual Head of every man. In expressing this idea Maurice only claims to have expounded the Bible.[62] However, this cardinal truth had been completely forgotten by contemporary theology, robbing men of the true knowledge of their own existence. Maurice considered it his appointed task to bring this truth to light and show its bearing upon the lives of ordinary people.[63]

Christ is, however, not only the Creator of mankind and the Giver of life to every man, but also "the ground and archetype" of man.[64] As "the true man after God's

60 *The Epistles of St. John*, 331.
61 *Sermons Preached in Lincoln's Inn Chapel* VI (London 1891. Cit. *Sermons* VI), 125. Cf. also p. 44: "He is with us in our walks, and with us when we sit down to eat; by the very constitution of our being we cannot be alone; – – He is there when we perceive it least," and *The Prophets*, 253: "there is – – some One beneath ourselves – the ground of all that we desire and believe and are, the spring of our hopes and the consummation of them, the fountain of all love in every creature and the satisfaction of its love – –. There is a presence near us and within us that cannot be put by."
62 Cf. *Theological Essays*, 25: "In Him, and for Him, we were created, this is our doctrine or rather the doctrine of St. Paul; for *we* have said little enough about it"; *Sermons Preached in Lincoln's Inn Chapel* III (London 1891. Cit. *Sermons* III), 107–8: "The theology of St. Paul declares Christ to be the foundation that is laid for every man, not one that men by their faith and feelings can lay for themselves; the theology of St. John declares Christ to be the Light that lighteth every man, whether the Light is acknowledged or denied", and *The Epistles of St. John*, 335–6: "We do not honour Christ by disparaging that which took place before He dwelt on earth. If we believe St. John, He was before all worlds. He was in the world and was the Light of men." Maurice based his arguments upon I Cor. 8,6, Col. 1,14, Eph. 1,4–5, and last, but not least, upon St. John, 1,1–4, to which he repeatedly referred. Maurice's favourite expression "Christ as the Head of every man" represents his rendering of I. Cor. 11,3.
63 Cf. *Life* II, 161: "I hope also by God's grace that no fear of offending my best and dearest friends will keep me from proclaiming that truth of Christ as the actual Head of Man, which I was sent into the world to proclaim – –."
64 *What is Revelation? A Series of Sermons on the Epiphany; to which are Added Letters to a Student of Theology on the Bampton Lectures of Mr. Mansel* (Cambridge 1859. Cit. *What is Revelation?*), 220. Cf. *Introduction to Archdeacon Hare's Charges* in *The Victory of Faith* (London 1874), XXV: "Thanks be to God who has forced me to acknowledge that

own heart"[65] Christ is the pattern according to which every man is created and which reveals the purpose of their creation. Consequently Maurice rejected the idea that Christ became the true man, or the pattern of humanity, by His incarnation. From eternity He is *the* man, the archetype of which every man is meant to be the image, the only one from whom man receives his own humanity.[66] It is in this sense that Maurice spoke of "the divine humanity of Christ".[67] This perfect humanity is, however, nothing but Christ's eternal Sonship; to see Christ's eternal life as the life of the Son with the Father is to see the true humanity in the image of which mankind is created.[68] Thus to attain to a true anthropology, we must begin with christology.[69]

Maurice understood man's creation in the image of Christ to mean that man is created to share Christ's Sonship and to live the life that Christ eternally lives with the Father. In Christ men "were originally created to be the sons of God".[70] Because "the Sonship of Christ is the type and ground of the relation in which the human stands to the divine,"[71] God may be said to have predestined Christ to be the first-born of all creation,[72] "the elder Brother", an expression frequently used by Maurice.

---

there is an ideal, in which and after which man is created; an ideal which explains and justifies all the ideals men have perceived and followed, and found themselves unable to reach; an ideal which tells us what our sin is; an ideal which can lift us out of it."

65 *The Prophets*, 55. Cf. also *The Epistles of St. John*, 61: "He is the Man. It is in Him that we know what we are, and why we were created."

66 Cf. *Sermons* II, 215: "[Christ is] the deep root of all the humanity which is or ever has been in the earth."

67 p. 333.

68 *Life* II, 408.

69 Cf. *What is Revelation?*, 399: "admitting the union of the two Natures in Christ – – as a fundamental article of faith, – – we ought more distinctly to allow, first, that there is a divine standard for human morality; secondly, that this standard is in such direct affinity with humanity in its highest form, that the one is the exact reflex of the other." It is important to emphasize that to Maurice the relation between the divine and the human does not apply to the incarnate Christ, because Christ eternally, as perfect God and perfect Man, represents "the union of the infinite and finite, the divine and human" (cf. p. 392). However, in reality the divine and the human are fused, as the Son of God Christ is eternally the true Man, *the* Man. Maurice accepted the orthodox christological beliefs, but where they spoke of the divine and human natures of Christ in reference to the Incarnation, Maurice applied these doctrines to the eternal being of Christ without reservation. As we shall see later, this interpretation, that true humanity is expressed in Christ's eternal life with the Father, had important consequences for his conception of the Incarnation. Here it is sufficient to point out that it served the practical purpose of showing that in Christ, who is above time and space, man finds the purpose and foundation of human life – eternal truths, not historical events, are the object of theology. There is, however, this difference between Christ and man, that He is eternally God's Son, whereas all men are God's sons only because they have been created to receive Christ's divine humanity. His divinity thus consists in the fact that He is eternally with the Father, and that the Father has entrusted Him with creative power in order to create the human race and to endow it with His own life. He alone is the creative archetype whereas mankind is merely its reflection.

70 *The Epistles of St. John*, 314.

71 *The Kingdom of Christ* II, 271.

72 Cf. *Sacrifice*, 221: "He was the original man, the type of all creation, as it is expressed in the Epistle to the Colossians, *'the first-born of every creature'*."

As the relationship between Christ and the Father is a personal relationship, a fellowship between personal wills, so man is created as a voluntary being, a personal will – which is another way of saying that he is created in the image of God.[73] When Maurice spoke of man as will it was his vital concern to maintain that man's relationship to God is to be understood as a personal fellowship between an "I" and a "Thou". God does not coerce man to live in fellowship with Him. The relationship between God and man is not a mechanical cause and effect relationship in which a sovereign power forces man into submission. On the contrary, God deals with man as a responsible being and freely calls man to receive the life of love in Christ. God's purpose is perfected only when man submits freely and gladly to His will and desires with his whole being to live in trust and obedience.[74]

Maurice carefully avoided the term "free will" and spoke only of "will". This is characteristic. Man is created with a will but that does not mean that he is free and independent of God. Such a view would involve a diminution of God's power and glory. It is to His glory, as almighty God, that He has elected mankind to sonship, to live in a personal fellowship with Him according to the pattern established by His Son. Man is called to accept life freely and willingly from God but this high position, for which God created man as "His chief and highest creature",[75] entails, on the other hand, the terrible possibility that he might choose to resist His love and disobey His will.[76]

Maurice's idea of man as created with a personal will is elucidated further by his view of Calvinism. Maurice welcomed the Calvinist assertion that it is God alone who has the initiative and acts, with man as the receiver.[77] There is nothing whatever in man

---

73 Cf. *The Epistles of St. John,* 289: "The Will of man was made in the image of God", and *The Prophets,* 10: "He, the Perfect and Absolute Will, has created beings with wills, beings made in His own image."

74 Cf. *The Patriarchs,* 179: "the Bible – – throughout exhibits God's operation upon the will of the creature whom He has made in His image, as something quite distinct from that operation by which He compels the obedience of involuntary creatures. He treats the first always as creatures capable of resisting Him; yes, and as creatures whom no *mere* power can ever bring into submission to Him", and *The Prophets,* 413: "everywhere [in the Scriptures] men are assumed to have wills, upon which no mere blind mechanical power can operate, but upon which God, a living Person, is operating by gracious, mysterious, orderly processes that He may make them in His own likeness."

75 *The Patriarchs,* 175.

76 Cf. *Christmas Day,* 186–7: "But none of them [the other creatures] is able to say, 'I will do this or I will not.' They follow their instincts; they do just what is marked out for them. We can choose for ourselves. A command is given us; but let the power that gives it be as great as it may, we can still refuse to obey it."

77 Cf. *Life* II, 317–18: "The strength of Calvinism lay of old in the proclamation of *God* as the originator of all faith and righteousness in man. The reformation of Calvinism must come from the steadfast grasp of that truth. Resolve not to let it go or dilute it with any philosophical explanations or theories, and you must come to a gospel that God is seeking after man to bring them back to His fold, that He has redeemed the race, that there is no good of any kind in any creature which must not be referred to Him, which it is not a sin to claim for the creature, under any miserable subterfuges, such as that 'this only means the natural conscience' or 'only means some beautiful relic of the fall' – as if these phrases meant anything at all!"

that can dispose him to do any good works or incur any merit from God. It is to the credit of the advocates of predestination that they asserted this principle against the Pelagians and Arminians.[78] By the law of his creation man is dependent entirely upon God. Man's will signifies that he can subordinate himself freely to God and willingly receive his life in Christ as his Head. So there is no question of the human will limiting God's power and activity. The fellowship between God and man is based solely upon the will of God and is a free act of love on His part. The difference between man and the rest of creation is that God's dominion and dealing with him alone unfold themselves in a personal fellowship in which man is meant to live as a responsible person.

Created in the image of God, man is made to know God just as Christ, his archetype, knows the Father and His innermost nature and will and finds His life and joy in trusting and obeying Him.[79] In correlation to this God always reveals Himself, as He truly is, to man.[80] However, to see and know God is not an egocentric *fruitio Dei*. Just as Christ's sole pleasure is in carrying out God's will of love, so man is created to be God's fellow-worker and the instrument in furthering His purposes.[81] As all human life is created to be the reflection of God's love in and through Christ, no human morality can exist independent of theology. The life of Christ with the Father in eternity is the pattern of human activity.[82] Man is not to work and strive in order to win merit in God's eyes. It is an act of divine mercy that God has given

78 Cf. *Theological Essays*, 32: "Every redeemed person must, according to me, as much as according to the Calvinist, refer every good that is in him, that he does, that befalls him, to the Father of Lights, – must consider his will as freed by Him from a bondage, and as freed, that it may become truly a servant." Frequently Maurice expressed a desire to preserve the idea of predestination as represented in orthodox Calvinism (see *The Conflict*, 59–60; *Family Worship*, 32 and 43; *The Prophets*, V–VI; *Sacrifice*, XIV–XVI and *Life* II, 588–9). However he regarded Calvinism as false when it made naked sovereign power and not love and righteousness the essential attribute of God (see *Life* I, 376), and when it limited the predestination to a group of individuals, thus failing to understand that God had predestinated the whole human race to receive life from Christ and to live in Him.

79 Cf. *Sermons* III, 24: "the knowledge of God, which is eternal life, was that for which He formed, not sages or saints, but men, in His Son," and VI, 219: "God who never acts from caprice or self-will, who governs all things in heaven and earth according to the order which He has imposed upon them, who seeks to bring all voluntary beings into an understanding of His order and into cheerful consent with it – –."

80 Cf. *The Patriarchs*, II: "My chief object in preaching and writing upon the Old Testament, has been to show that God has created man in His image; that being so created he is capable of receiving a revelation of God, – of knowing what God is; that without such a revelation he cannot be truly a man; that without such knowledge he cannot become what he is always feeling that he ought to become."

81 Cf. *The Patriarchs*, 264: "We affirm that He [God] calls out men to be His agents and fellow-workers; to understand the purposes which He has at heart", and *The Prophets*, 95: "A personal God dealing with men, will employ man as the agents and executors of His purpose." See also *The Patriarchs*, 197 and 213.

82 Cf. *The Prophets*, 451: "the theology of the prophets was the ground of all their human morality. Every perception of what man is and what he ought to do must rest upon some perception of what God is and of what He does. To affirm what image it behoves a man to show forth without reference to the archetype: to lay down rules how a man should govern himself and others without declaring how God governs, was in their minds a vanity, nay, an impossibility." See also p. 345–6.

man the privilege and responsibility of being His fellow-servant.[83] Therefore man must pass on to his fellow-men that love which he himself has received from God.[84] So, by regarding Christ as his true archetype, man learns what he is and what his life is.

The creation can never exist independently of God. To exist means nothing else than to be surrounded and supported by God and His creative acts. Even man is created to live in complete dependence upon God.[85] Therefore man cannot attain to the knowledge of God by himself and has in himself no power to perform the will of God. If man is to live the true human life, it must always be given to him.[86] God imparts it to man when he turns from himself and clings to Him who alone enables him to fulfil the purpose of his creation.[87]

To be created to dependence upon God means that faith or trust constitutes the law of human existence.[88] Faith is not limited to religious men, and its necessity is not

83 Cf. *The Epistles of St. John, 160:* "We often speak as if people were to be paid for being good; not as if the being good were itself God's highest gift and blessing. Such an opinion comes from our not thinking of God Himself as the good and the true Being, or else from our not thinking that He has made us capable of entering into His goodness and knowing His truth. The Bible from first to last is proclaiming that it is possible to know Him and be like Him, that this is the end which men are to desire and expect, and that they cannot be content with any lower end."

. 84 Cf. *The Gospel of St. John, 388–9:* "The love of the Father is at the root of all. The Son can do nothing but in obedience to that. He believes it, obeys it, and so lives in it. The law of the disciples' being is the same. They are to believe in the love which is the manifestation and reflection of this love, to obey it, to live in it," and *Lectures on the Apocalypse or Book of the Revelation of St. John the Divine* (London 1885. Cit. *The Apocalypse*), 61: "The glory of Him who sits upon it [the throne] is to be imaged in His creatures; what He is absolutely and entirely, they are to set forth in their different measures and relations."

85 Cf. *The Patriarchs, 51–2:* "God did not look upon the order He made – and lo! it was very good – because each creature was standing in its own separate excellence – because the highest creature of all held that excellence in its fullest measure. He pronounced it very good because *no* creature was standing in itself; because each was formed according to its kind in relation to every other; because the highest creature, that to which all others looked up, and in which they saw their own perfection, himself looked up to his Maker, and saw his perfection in Him."

86 Cf. *The Epistles of St. John, 43:* "If we are made in the image of God, it is a false and unnatural state for a man, not to be looking up to God but only to be looking down upon himself", and *The Patriarchs, 47:* "he [man] only realizes his own glory when he beholds it in God; – – he was not an independent being, but made in the image of another."

87 Cf. *Sermons* II, 198: "What then was the Law [for man]? A law of simple dependence on One Who does not pay, but Who gives; from Whom we take, not as bargainers so much price for so much work done, but the power of working, the privilege of working; Who does not remit so much punishment in consideration of so many petitions offered, but Who gives the privilege and ability to pray; Who does not return so much praise rendered to Him, but confers the wonderful gift and energy to praise, the joy and freedom of being grateful, the still higher power of giving Him thanks, not only for what He *does*, but for what He *is*, for His own great glory."

88 Cf. *Family Worship*, 208: "Every word in the New Testament presumes that a man is created to depend and to trust; that in dependence and trust is his life; that in self-satisfaction and distrust is his death", and *The Ground and Object of Hope for Mankind. Four Sermons Preached before the University of Cambridge in November 1867* (Cambridge 1868. Cit.

derived from the fact that man is a sinner who can only be saved by faith. It is the gift which God imparts to every man and can never be the exclusive privilege of any group of men. Faith is simply the expression of true humanity because Christ, as man's archetype, eternally lives by trust in God. Nor is faith an effort, or an act, on the part of man. This is a cruel distortion of its nature. Faith represents the attitude in which man renounces every claim to be anything, or to possess anything, in himself and instead trusts God for everything: "faith is the giving up of your own will to God's will; resting in Him, because you cannot rest in yourselves; living in Him, because you have no life of your own."[89] Faith can only exist when it forgets itself and turns to God as the object of faith.[90]

Maurice regarded faith and love as inseparable. It was a fatal error to consider love of God and of one's fellow-men as originating in man himself.[91] He maintained emphatically that "without Faith and Trust in God's Love it is impossible, by the laws of the Universe, by the relation in which the creature stands to the Creator, that there should be any love in us."[92] The confession that there is no good in man in himself is therefore not due to the fact of his being a sinner, Christ's eternal sonship revealing that this is the truth of perfect humanity. Christ possesses no love in Himself, since His love for mankind originates in God and is received by submission to God. In the same way man can only love when God through Christ imparts His love, received in submissive trust.

Hope for Mankind), 85: "He [St. Paul] said – – that all boasting of a man in himself on any ground whatever, personal or national, was excluded by that law of faith which he had been setting forth as the true law of all human creatures."

89 *Christmas Day*, 184. Cf. also p. 348: "– – by this act of trust we put ourselves under his guardianship. We acknowledge that we cannot do without him, we give up that effort and violence of will which is striving against him."

90 Cf. *Sermons* I, 71: "How often are we told of our faith, to consider whether we have a right to claim Jesus Christ as our Saviour! The Epistle [of the Hebrews] bids us to look from our faith to a Living Person Who is the only root of it, the only end of it. Our faith is not in itself, but in Him; if we think of it instead of Him, it perishes", and *The Epistles of St. John*, 256: "The man can boast of nothing; least of all can he boast of his faith. That is not something which belongs to him, a gift which he can carry about with him, and say 'Now I am a believer'. It is exactly the reverse of this. It saves him, by emptying him. It delivers him from himself; it attaches him to another. – – That is more essentially, more characteristically human, than seeing, hearing, smelling, speaking. To be wholly without it, is to be a beast or a devil. To be endued with it in the highest measure, is only to be a true man."

91 Cf. *Sermons* VI, 107–8: "What is the original falsehood of all who speak of their love to God and to man? This: they take credit to themselves for a love which is moving them to noble thought and good deeds but which has another source than their hearts; which is divine, not earthly; universal, not partial. – – the horrible vanity and conceit of their supposition, that they loved men better than their Father in Heaven loved them; that their love was anything but the result and reaction of His; that they can be anything but His agents and ministers to declare by words or deeds a little of what He is."

92 *Sermons* I, 203. Cf. also *The Gospel of St. John*, 290: "He [Christ] boasts of no love to man as dwelling in Himself, – it is all derived from His Father. He merely submits to His will, merely fulfils it. And because that will is a will of absolute love, the mere submission to it, – the mere consenting that it should be accomplished upon Him and in Him, – involved the most perfect love to men, – the most entire communion with them, – the dying for them."

Maurice placed the greatest emphasis upon the idea of Christ as the Lamb slaughtered before the foundation of the world. Because Christ eternally sacrifices Himself to carry out the will of His Father the whole creation rests upon His sacrifice. Inasmuch as Christ is the archetype of man, it furthermore follows that men are created to live a self-sacrificing life for God and their fellow-men. Self-sacrifice cannot denote an extraordinary quality exhibited by believers for which they can be even given credit.[93] Every man is created in Christ and called to reflect Christ's self-sacrifice as the only law of human existence.[94]

To live a life of sacrifice is nothing else than to live in faith and love.[95] However, it is of no little importance to Maurice to establish the fact that man is created to sacrifice himself. Again and again the true understanding of faith and love has been distorted and turned into a travesty by religious selfishness. Faith and love have been considered means to the performing of meritorious acts to be rewarded by God's favour and love, which man can then enjoy for his own benefit. The awareness that sacrifice is synonymous with faith and love means that they can be released from the grasp of man's self-assertion and their true nature be established.

Consequently, man sacrifices himself in faith for God, renouncing every claim to live in and for himself. In this act he subordinates himself to God and His love. As the Divine love never seeks its own but always sacrifices itself, man must give himself up for his fellow-men in order to bring them as a sacrifice that which he himself has received from God. He who in faith sacrifices himself for God is bound to sacrifice himself for his neighbour too.

In regard to Maurice's anxiety to establish the fact that self-sacrifice is the law of human life, it is necessary to bear in mind that for him there is no question of an idea to be realized in the future. Every man is able to live in faith and love because Christ is his Head and imparts these gifts to him always.[96] Christ and man can never be

93 Cf. *The Epistles of St. John*, 209: "The law of sacrifice is not a law for moments or crises of our existence; it is the law for the whole of it", and *Sacrifice*, 65: "self-sacrifice can never be an ambitious thing – a fine way to get the reputation of saints or the rewards of another world. It will be regarded as the true ground of all action; that on which all the blessed relations of life stand; that upon which all the charities and sympathies of life depend; that which is at the same time the only impulse to and security for the hard and rough work of the world – –."

94 Cf. *Sacrifice*, 43–4: "he [Abraham] had begun to understand the principle upon which God rules it [the universe], and the law of man's position in it. He had found sacrifice to be no one solitary act, no sudden expression of joy, no violent effort to make a return for blessings which we can only return by accepting; but that it lies at the very root of our being; that our lives stand upon it; that society is held together by it; that all power to be right, and to do right, begins with the offering up of ourselves, because it is thus that the righteous Lord makes us like Himself."

95 Cf. *Sacrifice*, 112: "So it is proved that obedience and sacrifice are the very conditions of truth and righteousness, that they belong to man who is made in God's likeness, because they are involved in the very character and being of God Himself."

96 Cf. *The Gospel of St. John*, 363–4: "If God demands that we should bring this offering [of love] to Him or perish, we must perish. But if He says, 'My name and nature is love; my Son has manifested my name and nature to you; you are created in Him; you are created to obey Him; you need not resist Him; His Spirit shall be with you that you may do His will as He has done mine', – then the precept is not cruel, but blessed and divine."

separated, with Christ living in heaven, and man living upon earth and left to himself to realize the law of his being. Christ is always near to man, offering, in self-sacrificial love, His divine humanity.[97]

4. Christ as the Eternal Mediator

Maurice's understanding of the significance of man's creation in Christ also dominates his idea of justification, a theme which played a prominent part in the theological debate of his day.

The Evangelicals together with the other revivalists regarded justification by faith alone as the cornerstone of Christianity. They believed that, owing to the fallen condition of mankind, man was corrupt and unable to do the deeds of righteousness which God, as a righteous and holy Being, demanded from His creatures. Man had forfeited fellowship with God and was punished with death and eternal damnation. However, Christ, the Son of God, through His vicarious death on the Cross, offered a satisfaction to God's holiness and wrath for the sins of mankind. Through faith man receives Christ's righteousness and holiness as his own. Only in this way could it be maintained that salvation was dependent wholly upon the grace of God and not upon the works of man.

This idea of justification was attacked by the Tractarians who regarded an imputed righteousness and holiness as contrary to the idea of God as truth and justice. God can only declare those righteous and holy who are truly righteous and holy. Furthermore, only by maintaining an actual justification and sanctification can the necessity of a righteous and holy life be upheld. If notoriously sinful men are declared righteous and holy and made equal to pious saints by virtue of Christ's imputed righteousness and holiness, then the motivation for every struggle to mortify and sanctify man's sinful nature disappears. The Evangelicals reacted to this criticism by accusing the Tractarians of teaching justification by works.

In Maurice's eyes the argument between the Evangelicals and the Tractarians on this question had reached an impasse. Maurice agreed with the criticisms which the conflicting parties had launched against each other, but he could not accept either alternative because they argued from the same false premises.

Thus, when the Evangelicals presumed that Adam was created perfect in possession of all goodness and righteousness, they presupposed that *justitia propria* belonged to the sinless state of man. The imputed righteousness was, on the other hand, necessitated by the fact that because of his sin man had lost the capacity of being righteous in himself. To say that, by virtue of Christ's expiatory death, God has declared men righteous therefore implies that He has dispensed with the principle that only the truly

---

97 Cf. *Theological Essays*, 75: "it is impossible, without violating the law of my being, the eternal order and constitution of things, that I should separate myself from Christ. He is the Lord of my own self, of my spirit; whether I confess Him or not, I must continually hear His voice, be open to His reproofs. Wherever I am, whatever I am doing, He must be there; He must be the standard of my acts; the right in them must be that which has originated in Him, – the wrong must be the revolt from Him. No present or possible condition of our being can change this order."

righteous are righteous in His eyes. The Evangelical concept of justification debases God by making Him deviate arbitrarily from truth as well as undermining man's moral integrity.[98] As Maurice insisted that God's decrees and judgments must always accord with unchangeable truth, he could only describe the current idea of imputed righteousness as a fiction.

Although the Evangelicals, and with them even the Reformers,[99] proclaimed a real truth – that God regarded man as righteous because of Christ and not because of his own qualities and deeds, they were led to these blasphemous conclusions because they had a false understanding of the Biblical account of Adam's life in Paradise and his subsequent fall. According to Maurice this account clearly demonstrates that Adam, and thereby the whole human race,[100] was created to live in complete dependence upon God: "So far from saying that God endowed man with an independent righteousness, with an innocency of his own, it tells us that God said, "Let us make man in *our* image, after *our* likeness." Such words absolutely exclude the idea that man according to his original constitution possessed *any thing* of his own. They affirm him to be good only in so far as he reflects that which exists perfectly in another, so far only as he confesses Him to be *the* Good. Personal, self-existing righteousness is not only not imparted to him by the law of his creation; it is denied to him."[101] Adam's sin was that he denied that he was created to be nothing in himself and to receive everything from God: "He would be a God; he was not content to be in the image of God. His offence consisted in giving up that position of dependence, which some would tell us only became his when he fell. His wrong consisted in setting up that claim to be something in himself; – which they would tell us that he was, so long as he continued right."[102] It was sin for Adam, and for all men, to imagine that man could or must exist before God by virtue of his own righteousness, whether that

98 Cf. *The Gospel of St. John*, 499–500: "Personal holiness is weakened, nay, is destroyed, by everything that could lead a man to think that it was fictitious in him, or that God was sanctioning a fiction. And therefore it is greatly imperilled by any notions which speak of the individual man having a righteousness imputed to him, in consequence of his faith, which is not truly and actually his."

99 Cf. *Sacrifice*, 149: "Still I do not doubt they [the Reformers in their translation of the Bible] put a force upon the phrase '*justified*', which would not have been expressed by the phrase *made righteous*. They were afraid to use that form of expression, lest it should seem to intimate that men became righteous in *themselves*, and are not, as our Article expressed it, 'accounted righteous only for the sake of Christ'. I believe that fear had a most reasonable ground; though there may have been another fear as reasonable, to which they were not equally alive. They dreaded lest men should fancy they had a righteousness of their own; and that dread no one could entertain so strongly as St. Paul. But they did not tremble as much as the Apostle did, lest men should suppose that the judgment of God was not *according to truth;* lest they should ever charge Him with acting upon a legal fiction."

100 Cf. *The Patriarchs*, 55: "The principle that man was made in the image of God, is not a principle which was true for Adam and false for us. It is the principle upon which the race was constituted and can never cease to be constituted."

101 *The Patriarchs*, 51–2. Cf. p. 53: "We may add what we please out of our fancies about their [the first man's and woman's] transcendent knowledge or their seraphic virtues. Nothing of it is to be found in the Bible. No hint of any vast endowments, or wide-reaching thoughts, or great projects."

102 *The Patriarchs*, 55.

righteousness was achieved through works or received as a divine virtue to be disposed of as his own possession. Both views treat man as a self-existent being who can claim something for himself before God. This attitude represents "the greatest pride and self-righteousness."[103]

Only the doctrine of imputed righteousness can demonstrate that man is meant to be dependent upon, and live by, a righteousness which is given him.[104] That this is the eternal truth is demonstrated by Christ's eternal sonship. Christ Himself is justified by faith: "God justifies the Man who perfectly trusted in Him; declares Him to have the only righteousness which He had ever claimed, – the only one which it would not have been a sin and a fall for Him to claim, the righteousness of His Father, – the righteousness which was His so long as He would have none of His own, so long as He was content to give up Himself."[105] As Christ, the archetype of man, lives by God's righteousness, so man must always live by a righteousness not his own but given to him in Christ: "It is by claiming to be united with Christ that a man becomes righteous. Whilst he tries to be righteous in himself, whilst he wishes to be separate from his true Lord, he cannot be righteous."[106]

So justification by faith is not God's special provision because of man's sin and fall. Instead it is an emphatic expression of the fact that man is created to be wholly dependent upon God in and through Christ. As God in His eternal will elected Christ to be the Head of the human race, His body, so it is forever true that God can never consider man apart from Christ: "God can only look upon us in Christ; that for Him to account us righteous in Christ is not a fiction (which it would be blasphemy to attribute to Him) but that judgment according to truth which alone is possible for Him."[107]

---

103 *The Epistles of St. John*, 176.
104 Cf. *Life* II, 166: "[St. Augustine] distinctly lays down the proposition that man is not in his normal condition unless he is looking out of himself, walking *secundum Deum*. Suppose that to be true, and that the prelapsarian state was a normal state, which all assume, it cannot have been a state in which the man had some goodness of his own (as our doctors teach). It must have been a state in which he neither had nor pretended to have any. And his fall must have been when he began to set up some, and not to walk *secundum Deum*. Justification by faith (to use the speech of these doctors) – – must be the only law for men in paradise or anywhere else."
105 *Theological Essays*, 51.
106 *Sermons Preached in Country Churches* (London 1903. Cit. *Country Churches*), 68. Cf. *Sermons* II, 154–5: "It was a bold thing to talk of clothing himself with the Righteousness of Christ, of putting on His qualities. Very bold; but if this is our proper humanity, – if no other is intended for us –, if all that we have substituted for it has been assumed in spite of God's Will, – He Himself will clothe us with our right mind, He Himself is clothing us day by day."
107 *The Faith of the Liturgy and the Doctrine of the Thirty-Nine Articles* (Cambridge 1860. Cit. *The Faith of the Liturgy*), 41. Cf. *The Gospel of St. John*, 500: "If by the very law and constitution of His universe God contemplates us as members of a body in His Son, we are bound to contemplate ourselves in the same way. We have a righteousness and holiness in Christ. We have no right to deny it; our unrighteousness is the very effect of denying it. Imputation of righteousness *then* becomes no fiction. It means only that God beholds us as we are, as we have not learnt or do not choose to behold ourselves. The fiction has arisen because the truth has been denied."

Thus Maurice rallied in defence of the doctrine of justification by faith. He bluntly rejected the doctrines of justification by works and of man's inherent righteousness. He was, however, anxious to point out that it is possible to understand justification by faith in such a way that it turns out to be a more subtle form of man's own self-justification. This happens when man is told to produce a faith by which he can appropriate Christ's justification. Such an approach leads, inevitably, to the same pitfalls as justification by works. In both cases man, in the final analysis, must achieve his own salvation. The believer imagines that, by virtue of his faith, he stands in a unique relation to God and this leads to pride and self-glorification. This, in turn, leads to the setting up of barriers, with the few believers saved, and the rest of mankind damned. In contrast to this counterfeit Maurice strongly asserted that every man is created to be wholly dependent upon Christ and receive everything from Him, even his faith.

Justification by works must be rejected in any form whatsoever. It presupposes that God and man are separated from each other, throwing man back on himself and making him believe that he himself must establish fellowship with God. But for man to rest upon his own achievements means that he can never be sure whether he can count himself a child of God or not; his whole life becomes a hectic search for God's favour and for assurance that he really possesses it. If, on the other hand, man accepts the fact that he has been created in Christ, he is assured of his status as a child of God, clothed with righteousness. Self-righteousness deprives man of the right to depend on God in all the walks and works of his life, whereas justification by faith enables him to give God the glory and honour of being the Creator at work in him.[108]

The Tractarians accused the Evangelicals of disregarding in their preaching of justification by faith the need to live a sanctified and holy life. Maurice agreed with them that justification and sanctification essentially belong together. Yet he opposed the Tractarians, because they made purity and holiness inherent virtues in man to be acquired through his own efforts. He saw this as another way of denying that man is created in the image of God: "God has constituted men holy in His Son; – – all unholiness is the result of the selfish desire of men to have something of their own, and not to abide in God's order."[109] To believe that Christ is man's holiness means to

---

108 Cf. *The Acts of the Apostles. A Course of Sermons* (London 1894), 212: "I conceive the Jews did think too meanly of themselves. That they thought too meanly of themselves was the main cause of their self-righteousness. And, again, their self-righteousness kept down their thoughts to the low level which they had attained; yes, and depressed them continually to a lower. If they had estimated what their capacities were, what they might ask for and expect, as creatures made in the image of God, they could not have been content with their own righteousness; they could not have made that the measure for other men."

109 *The Gospel of St. John*, 499. Cf. *Sermons* I, 81: "– – the purity or innocence of any human creature is not and cannot be his own; – – we are only innocent so far as we claim nothing of our own, so far as we look out of ourselves, so far as we forget ourselves in another." See also *The Acts of the Apostles*, 159 and *Religions*, 227.

have an open, receptive attitude which allows Him to perform His own works in man.[110] So, to live by Christ's holiness rules out any idea of moral passivity.

To all appearances Maurice was reproducing traditional theology when he maintained that Christ is the Mediator between God and man. However, he stressed that Christ did not become the Mediator by virtue of His incarnation and His death upon the Cross when He made atonement for man's sin. This would make Christ's work dependent upon man's fall and sin instead of upon God's unchangeable will. For Maurice Christ is "the High Priest, the perfect Mediator between God and man, not in virtue of an arbitrary decree, but of an eternal constitution."[111] Christ is eternally the Mediator who unites God and man.

This idea underlay Maurice's favourite description of Christ as "the Son of God and the Son of Man", the latter term meaning "the Man", "the perfect Man". As previously mentioned, this expression does not refer to the incarnate Christ, but to the eternal Christ. Christ eternally knows the Father, reveals Him and carries out His will, and at the same time He is the Head of created humanity, man's creative life-giving idea. Thus Christ represents God before man and man before God. As this is due to God's eternal decree, Christ is for ever the Mediator between God and man.

Christ, however, only fulfils God's will and purpose by His sacrificial life. By sacrificing Himself in trust and obedience to His Father He performs the work of creation and sustains the universe and the life of mankind. Therefore Maurice could declare: "Only a living sacrifice – – could be the bond of a living covenant between man and his Creator, of a covenant which should declare that their union stood on an eternal, unchangeable ground, that it was upheld in a Divine Person, the High-priest of the universe."[112]

Because Christ's eternal sacrifice to the Father originated in self-denying love, the Father was well-pleased with it.[113] Since the whole universe, together with mankind, has come into being, and is upheld, through Christ's sacrificial life, the Father can only look upon the creation as pure, righteous and holy. So God never looks upon man in himself, but always regards him in Christ and considers His life to be the only source of his righteousness and holiness.[114]

Man can never cease to be a child of God. He may choose to resist God and try to live an independent life, yet nothing can destroy the fact that he is a child of God,

110 Cf. *The Epistles of St. John*, 213: "To keep God's commandments is to remember what that law is which He has established for the universe; what the law of His own mind, of His own life, is. When we submit to that law, His life acts upon our life. As St. John says, 'He dwells in us, and so we are able to do the things that He would have us to do – –.' Nay, he says, 'If you ask me what God's first commandment is, I should say, *that we should believe in the name of His Son Jesus Christ'*."

111 *The Conflict*, 161–2.

112 *Sacrifice*, 174–5.

113 Cf. *The Acts of the Apostles*, 221: "His sacrifice was one which perfectly satisfied and delighted His Father, because it is the image of His own perfect goodness."

114 Cf. *Sermons* I, 214: "It is His Will that we should believe constantly and daily that He does regard us, not as poor separated creatures such as we have taken ourselves to be, but as a body united in Christ, justified in Him, presented by Him as a pure and holy sacrifice," and *The Acts of the Apostles*, 158: "He was the Lord of all before He came in the flesh; therefore God must have looked upon mankind in Him – –."

elected, created, and existing in Christ.[115] Christ is truly "the Son of God in whom all things had stood from the first, in whom God had looked upon His creature Man from the first."[116] Man must never rely upon his faith, his works, or his own mood in order to assure himself of being a child of God and a brother of Christ despite his own sin, disbelief, and lack of religious feeling; by God's eternal decree he is created to sonship and is always considered pure and holy by God on account of Christ's eternal sacrifice.[117]

115 Cf. *Life* II, 271-2: "You know, I think, how much it has been the effort of my life to assert a ground for men's sonship to God, which is – – grounded on the eternal relation of God to man in the Living Word," and *The Gospel of St. John,* 416: "The only true God knows the creature in all its wanderings and ignorance and falsehood, knows him in that Son in whom He has created him."

116 Cf. *The Unity of the New Testament,* 367.

117 Cf. *Sermons* I, 97-8: "I said that men found continually that the further they went down into themselves, the more there was of corruption, and darkness, and evil, till at last they supposed the very root of their being was nothing else. St. Paul had gone down into these depths; he had found this rottenness; in himself he says he found only that. But he discovered that there was a root below himself, a true divine root, for himself and every man. He found that each men, when he tries to contemplate himself apart from Christ, is that evil creature in which no good thing dwells. But no man, so he teaches, has a right to contemplate himself apart from Christ; God does not so contemplate him. He was formed at first in the Divine Word; in Him he lives and has his being still."

Chapter II

MAN IN THE DIVINE ORDER

1. Man as Spirit and Flesh

Besides saying that God has created man in His own image, Maurice can, without any change of meaning, maintain that God has created man as a spirit.[1] It is the spirit that represents "the true man, the man after God's heart".[2] The spirit is that in man with which God establishes fellowship and towards which He directs His love and care.[3] Actual, existing man came into being, however, when the spirit was clothed in the flesh, the earthly, that which was taken from the dust. Hence Maurice spoke of men as "spirits having bodies"[4] or as "spirits with an animal nature".[5]

It was quite clear to Maurice that the spirit, as originating in the eternal world, is of greater dignity than the flesh, which belongs to the changeable visible world. On the other hand, he was ambiguous when defining the relation between the spirit and the flesh. Maurice could declare that, just as man is created to rule over all the involuntary creatures, he, as a spirit, is meant to rule over his own body, control and use it as his servant.[6] The body, as well as the visible things with their material nature, are means placed at man's disposal for the carrying out of God's will. Therefore they are by themselves morally neutral.[7] If man lives in trusting dependence upon God, the body with the whole visible world is subservient to him and is good. If he turns away

1 Cf. *Theological Essays*, 69: "the spirit is the substantial part of man; –– he *is*, because he is made in the image of God, who is a Spirit;" *The Prophets*, 316: "Were not the covenant and the law and the promises, all so many declarations that God who is a Spirit claims the spiritual creature whom He had formed in His own image, as His servant and child?," and *Country Churches*, 152: "In all these ways he [David] was taught that it is the spirit that is in a creature – not its size or its fierceness – which makes it victorious, and that this spirit is what God put into man when He made him after His own image."

2 *Sermons* V, 78.

3 Cf. *The Prophets*, 60: "God himself –– is working with and for the spirits whom He has formed."

4 *Theological Essays*, 68.

5 *Life* II, 272.

6 Cf. *The Unity of the New Testament*, 40: "God has given us the earth to enjoy. He has given us the appetites and senses wherewith to enjoy it. But He has not given us the earth to be our master. He has not given us our appetites and senses to be our masters," and *The Patriarchs*, 225: "there is a spirit in man which is created to govern the sensible world, not to be governed by it."

7 Cf. *Sermons* I, 279–80: "The flesh, as such, is not an enemy: if it means the body, we believe in the redemption of the flesh, in the resurrection of the flesh. But the lusts of the flesh, the desire of the flesh to be supreme – to make the man its subject, – this involves *sin*, or separation from God; this involves the degradation of both spirit and body. The world in itself is not our enemy: it is loved by God; it has been redeemed by Christ. –– And because these distinctions were necessary respecting the flesh and the world, because it is a dangerous

from God, whom he is created to trust and obey, the body and the sensible things will get the upper hand and take the spirit into bondage – so they become evil. Thus Maurice's concern was to show that the fundamental contrast does not run between the visible world and the immaterial, spiritual world as such, but between trust and distrust, obedience and disobedience in man as spirit, and this alone decides whether visible things turn out to be good or evil.

But Maurice also maintained that there is a "radical and everlasting distinction between the flesh and the spirit in the *man*."[8] By virtue of the spirit man belongs to the eternal world and aspires towards it as his true home, whereas the flesh with its senses chains him to the earth.[9] The spirit and the flesh clash, there being "a twofold life in man, – – a struggle upwards and a tendency downwards."[10] As the animal, fleshly nature has its origin in the changeable world of time and space, and is always gravitating away from *that which is,* it represents "the gravitation downwards".[11] This "grovelling tendency",[12] which is difficult to bridle, impedes the spirit, the truly human, in its desire for God and His eternal world.

Man, as spirit, has to struggle against the flesh, which is always striving to make him "a brute", "a beast" or "an animal creature". In every existing man spirit and flesh are at war with each other, one trying to draw him upwards, so that he may live in fellowship with Christ as the true Lord of the spirit, the other trying to draw him down and chain him to the sensual world.[13] When Christ told His disciples that they must not throw pearls before swine nor give that which is holy unto the dogs, he was teaching that "there is in every one of us a holy thing, – there is in every one of us a bestial nature."[14] The Gospel is directed not to man's bestial, fleshly nature, but to the spirit, lying hidden in man like a pearl, representing that which is holy.

and inhuman and ungodly thing to count either as evil itself, as having anything but a derivative evil, we were obliged to speak of an evil spirit or evil will." Maurice does not wish corporality to be understood as something evil in itself, but nevertheless he attributes to it a desire to rule over the spirit and draw it down into sensuality. Thus an evil principle adheres to it.

8 *Use of the Word Revelation in Scripture* (in *Present-Day Papers, On Prominent Questions in Theology. Edited by the Right Rev. Alexander Ewing, D. C. L., Bishop of Argyll and the Isles.* 2nd Series, 1867. Cit. *The Word Revelation),* 20.

9 Cf. *Sequel,* 23: "I found that I had in myself that which aspired to rise above its own level and that which was content to stay upon its own level. The one I learnt from St. Paul to call the spirit, the other the flesh. I learnt also from him that it was possible to live after the flesh and so to die, or to live after the spirit, and so to enter into fellowship with those eternal things which eye hath not seen, nor ear heard, nor hath it entered into the heart of man to conceive."

10 *The Kingdom of Christ* (1838) I, 17. Cf. *Religions,* 172: "The Christian Church – – claims to be a witness of that mighty privilege which men have of conversing with the Unseen and Infinite, as well as a witness of the tendency which there is in man to be merely animal and sensual."

11 *The Prophets,* 188. Cf. also p. 156: "the gravitation of our nature to the earth."

12 *The Prayer-Book,* 53.

13 Cf. *The Kingdom of Christ* (1838) I, 93: "God had been – – teaching man respecting his own condition. For he had been teaching him to know that he was a spiritual creature, and that he had a fleshly nature; he had been teaching that his spirit was united to the Divine Word, that his flesh was chained to earth."

14 *Sermons* I, 223.

This spirit aspires towards heaven, towards fellowship with its invisible Lord, seeking to be free of its prison and its jailers, the sensual nature and its fleshly desires.[15] Often the spirit seems to have been smothered by the fleshly, animal nature, but this is only so on a superficial view. In spite of all that debases and enslaves man to the things of the earth, the spirit with its aspirations and longings for God,[16] will never be "at ease in a world of shows and outsides".[17]

So the Gospel about God's union with every man and man's deliverance from everything hindering the satisfaction of his yearnings for that which really and truly is, must be addressed to man's spirit. That spirit will recognize the voice of the Father, drawing it upwards to its true everlasting home. The spirit will open itself to God when it is told that God has chosen and loved it as His child and protects it from the flesh and the visible world.[18] On the other hand, the Law, with its threats and judgments, must be directed at the flesh, which seeks to escape from God and the eternal world and is in revolt against the desires of the spirit. The spirit can never be subjected to the Law as it is always seeking God. But the flesh, since it is earthly, must always be under its discipline. Thus the Gospel and the Law address themselves to the higher and the lower parts in man, that is, to the spirit and the flesh respectively.[19]

Though Maurice's description of the relation between the spirit and the flesh is ambiguous, the implications of the fact that man is a spirit are clear. Man is created

15 Cf. *Sermons* I, 226: "the more the fleshly tendencies which make us akin to the dogs and the swine, tremble and are confounded, the more the Spirit, the holy thing which they have imprisoned, the pearl which they have trampled upon, lifts itself up and gives thanks to God, because in these curses upon its tyrants it hears the voice of the Deliverer, the assurance of its redemption."

16 Cf. *Sermons* I, 222: "For there *is* a holy thing in that creature whom, for his snapping, biting temper, I have reckoned among dogs. There is a man beneath all that which is so disagreeable, even so morally offensive."

17 *Sermons* I, 286.

18 Cf. *Sermons Preached in Lincoln's Inn Chapel* V (London 1892. Cit. *Sermons* V), 70: "There are tendencies in you which are earthly, sensual, idolatrous. He has not chosen *these*, He has chosen *you*, that He may separate you from these; that He may overcome them in you; that He may give you your true and proper rights as men; that He may save you from sinking into animals yourselves; that He may save you from worshipping animals or anything – even the most vast and glorious things – which you see with your eyes," and *Family Worship*, 58: "I am certain that you are as conscious of the struggle of a lower nature in you against higher impulses and instincts as I am. – – It belongs to man as man. Some may be more conscious of it than others. Those who have been most conscious of it have been the best and wisest men. But still it is in all. – – Supposing then there were a revelation of a God who had taken part with these higher instincts and impulses in men, who had Himself inspired them, who had *justified* them, saying, 'This higher thing in the man is the true man. This is my child.' – – Suppose again that He who had given this revelation, had given a sign and pledge that He recognizes this in the man as the true man, that whatever is fighting against this He regards as the man's enemy and as His enemy."

19 Maurice asserted that "the distinction between the flesh and the spirit has been so forgotten and misinterpreted", because "an actual union of the spirit of man with Christ has been lost sight of." This has had the harmful consequence that "the blessings and curses of God, the Gospel, and the Law, are not directed against different parts of the same man, – the blessings to himself, the curses against the evil nature to which he has no right to be in bondage, – but against two sets of persons, whom the minister assumes the divine prerogative of defining" (*The Kingdom of Christ* (1838) I, 35).

to live in fellowship with God in the eternal unchangeable world. It might appear that he finds his whole satisfaction in the visible world of time and space, living a bestial animal existence in ignorance of God, and yet this is not the whole truth. Man always remains a spirit, and this betrays itself in a feeling of restlessness, a sense of discontent with the outward and visible. This yearning can be stirred by the beauty of the visible world, by its order and harmony, but man aspires beyond this in a search for the perfect beauty, order and harmony that are not subject to change and vicissitude.[20] The visible world mirrors the eternal world, but man can never be satisfied with the image – he must know and see the archetype.

The restlessness of the spirit and its unsatisfied yearnings may take widely different forms. But all such longings, however they appear, are prompted by man's longing for God and fellowship with Him.[21] Nothing but God can satisfy man. If, in his blindness, he cannot find the God in whose image he was created, then he raises up gods in his own image. He knows that he is not meant to live for himself, but for another, whom he is bound to serve and to worship, and from whom he must receive life.[22] Man can never be content with his own achievements. He always pursues happiness, but being created by God he will only find his true happiness and satisfaction in God.[23] In the last analysis the whole history of mankind is determined by this longing for union with God. This quest for God is also at the bottom of all religious, philosophical, political and social systems.[24]

20 Cf. *Sermons* VI, 96: "That desire [for God] is kindled by a number of objects in nature; the sunrise and sunset, the still lake, the faces of children, the music of the human voice. In all these things there is a witness of something calmer, brighter, truer than himself. There is a witness to man that he is to cry after this; that only this will satisfy him. But there is a witness, also as strong, in them and in him, that they do not contain that treasure," and *Sermons* I, 247: "These visible things are not your masters; all their beauty cannot satisfy the cravings for beauty in you; all their order cannot satisfy the craving for order in you; all the knowledge you can have of their secrets cannot satisfy the craving for knowledge in you."

21 Cf. *Sermons* I, 257: "The heart and flesh of all human beings, whether they know it or not, are crying out for the living God. And they do give a thousand indications everywhere, that they cannot be contented with dead gods, or with any religious notions and forms which try to put themselves in the place of a living God," and *Life* I, 384: "You cannot go north or south, east or west, without finding men full of restless desires after a knowledge of God and of union with Him."

22 Cf. *Sermons* III, 122: "There is a thirst of the soul to create something in its own likeness; but the first and deepest thirst is to find in what likeness it is itself created; whence all its living powers are derived; who has fixed their ends; who can direct them to their ends."

23 Cf. *Sermons* III, 121: "the thirst for God is the thirst of man. The thirst for happiness means this, ends in this. The thirst for those particular finite things which try to sum themselves up in the thirst for happiness have here their true centre, their final explanation," and *The Epistles of St. John*, 339: "Man cannot be satisfied with anything short of what is Perfect. He must have perpetual 'unrest' till he finds what is Perfect."

24 Cf. *The Kingdom of Christ* (1838) I, 259: "Communion with God in the largest and fullest sense of that word, is not an instrument of attaining some higher end, but is itself the end to which he is leading his creatures, and after which his creatures in all kingdoms, and nations, and languages, – by all their schemes of religion, by all their studies of philosophy, by art, by science, by politics – – are secretly longing and crying, and without which they cannot be satisfied."

52

The life of man is a confused mixture of truth and falsehood; of truth, because it originates in his search for God, the root from which he has sprung; of falsehood, because it has been shaped by his animal nature and by his selfishness. This is why every man feels his own life to be a dark riddle demanding a solution. Man yearns to unravel the tangled threads of human life.[25] His rootlessness and restlessness only spur him to thirst even more strongly for a God who can satisfy him and in whom he can find truth.[26] Thus the search for God and the perfect life in the eternal world is the fundamental problem that haunts mankind. All other questions stem from this, and the answer to it contains the solution to all the other problems of mankind. The riddle of human existence can only be solved in God, man's Lord and Creator.

Maurice's description of the spirit's yearning and longing for God and the unchangeable, eternal world often directly echoed Plato's idea of the soul's flight to heaven.[27] In many passages Maurice even appeared to conceive of the spirit, man's true being, as that which has its origin in the eternal world but is chained to the body and now desires to return to its true divine home.[28] Furthermore, Maurice always refers to Plato's view of man as fundamentally true. However, he did not accept this Platonic idea uncritically. Without giving a detailed examination of Platonic anthropology, Maurice interpreted it in such a way that he maintained that man, as a spirit, is a creature dependent upon his Creator at every moment. Man is not a perfect and divine being in himself, nor is he capable of ascending to the eternal world by himself. Man is unable to achieve anything himself but must live in and by Christ always, if the spirit is to achieve its goal. It can only rise towards God when it forgets itself and waits, in trust, for God Himself to come and lead it to its true home: "to walk in the spirit is to be dependent, self-distrustful, seeking help and satisfaction in One Who has all that you want. A spirit must be ascending above itself; it becomes devilish when it sinks into itself. Therefore is the spirit rightly described as desiring or lusting; therefore is communion with a higher Spirit the only way of appeasing its lusts."[29]

25 Cf. *Has the Church, or the State, the Power to Educate the Nation? A Course of Lectures* (London 1839), 35: "in all ages and nations men have been wanting to be informed concerning the mysteries of their own being, wanting to have the riddle of this world solved to them, wanting to know what they are, and whence they came, and whither they are going."

26 Cf. *Sermons* V, 93: "For they would perceive that they want – that mankind wants – the actual knowledge of God; that for this men have sighed and cried in every country and age of the world; that if this knowledge is not to be had, what is called self-knowledge is either a miserable delusion or a curse and a horror."

27 Thus when Maurice states that "there is in Man a spirit which gives him wings, which carries him into the highest and most distant worlds" *(The Prophets, 453)*, the allusion to *Phaedrus* 246A–E is obvious.

28 Cf., e. g., *The Gospel of St. John*, 202: "The spirit in man is – – impatient of those fetters which bind it to the earth."

29 *Sermons* V, 242. Cf. *Christmas Day*, 332: "When man has been conscious that there is a spirit within him, he has always cried for something higher than himself to help him; when he thinks only of himself, his wings soon drop, he falls back into the very charnel-house which he had found so degrading and so loathsome. Whenever he has been conscious that he had spiritual powers, he has lifted up his voice to a higher spirit to raise him to himself, he has felt all his misery came from the separation between him and some being whom he ought to trust in and obey; he has felt, at the same time, that he could not destroy the

To blur or destroy the qualitative difference between God and man is to deify man and to deprive God of His exclusive right and glory of being the Creator. On closer inspection, however, such deification does not exalt man at all; instead it disparages and defrauds him – he is left to himself and must trust to his own powers and achievements, being a solitary atom wandering aimlessly in the universe and an easy prey to earthly things and his own sin.

Man, in himself, cannot draw near to heaven. Even the yearning of the spirit for eternity, and its discontent with earthly things, come from God.[30] He does not want man to rest satisfied with the fragile earthly happiness with which sin and his animal nature try to beguile him. Christ is near to man, inspiring him with the longings and aspirations that make him restless and impatient of falsehood and all counterfeits of true reality.

Man is ever restless until he finds his true rest in God. He must question, criticize, investigate and explore that which has been handed down to him from previous generations, and everything around him, to find out whether it is permanent and substantial or merely changeable and transient. The entire history of mankind is a great Socratic dialogue of question and answer, the purpose of which is to find *that which is*. Philosophers, theologians and politicians, indeed all men take part in this dialogue, for it is simply a necessity for man to seek the firm foundation of his existence.[31]

Even here it is God Himself who, through Christ, carries on the Socratic dialogue

separation, that the being whom he had invoked must descend to him, or he could never rise." – In the same way Maurice strongly protested against any attempt to identify the spirit in man with the Holy Spirit. It was necessary to "to distinguish with great accuracy between the faculties which a man is enabled to exert through the power of the Spirit, and that Spirit itself. The difference is a radical one; it lies in the nature of things" *(The Church a Family,* 83). Cf. also *Queen's College, London. A Letter to the Right Hon. and Rev. the Lord Bishop of London, in Reply to the Article CLXXII of the Quarterly Review, entitled 'Queen's College, London'* (London 1850. Cit. *Queen's College*), 31: "I need not remind your lordship what fearful fanaticism has arisen from the identification of the acts and operations of the divine, indwelling Spirit, with those of the human. Again, what fearful coldness, what terrible denial of all communion between earth and heaven, has resulted from the reaction against that fanaticism."

30 Cf. *Sermons* I, 239: "He [St. Paul] said he knew whence these lusts of the spirit in man came; that they came from the Spirit of God; that they were awakened in each human being by Him; that He watched over them to give them strength and victory over their enemies."

31 Cf. *Sacrifice*, XI–II: "there is a sense in which I earnestly desire to be original myself; and in which I desire that you, and all the young men of England, should be so likewise. An original man is not one who invents – not one who refuses to learn from others. I say, boldly, no original man ever did that. But he is one who does not take words and phrases at second hand; who asks what they signify; who does not feel that they are his, or that he he has a right to use them till he knows what they signify. The original man is fighting for his life; he must know whether he has any ground to stand upon; he must ask God to tell him, because man cannot. – – All men are capable of this originality; it is not a special talent; it comes from that earnestness of purpose, that longing to find what is not dependent on ourselves or on human caprice which, I believe, is awakened in us by the Spirit of Truth, and by Him only. If I have not this originality, may that Spirit impart it to me, for to be without it is death."

to lead mankind to truth.[32] That is why all doubts and questionings, in whatever form they appear, must be treated seriously and not be rejected bluntly as foolish or even frivolous and impious. Because Christ is the Inspirer of this quest for reality and truth, the history of philosophy and of religion is a living book in which the lessons of God's dialogue with man through the ages have been preserved in such a way that later generations might profit from them and be helped to true knowledge. Everything that stirs man is meaningful and must be taken in earnest. As God Himself has awakened this quest for truth man can rest assured that he will receive an answer. Man will find the perfect satisfaction for all his longings and questions when God, by revealing Himself, imparts knowledge of Himself and of the true foundation of human life.[33]

2. Man's Knowledge of the Universe and of God

a. Reason and Understanding

Maurice was insistent that there is in man "a Divine faculty, meant for fellowship with that which is Divine, not realising its own properties but in that fellowship."[34] This faculty signifies that man is created for "the internal and spiritual apprehension, the recognition of the Eternal Being."[35] As long as the fact of its existence was maintained the question of nomenclature was of minor importance for Maurice. Indis-

---

32 Cf. *Sermons* V, 91: "I believe that Christ has been asking questions from that day to this; that He is asking questions of us all, divines and laymen, now; that the questions come to us in multitudes of shapes, through a multitude of lips; – through children tormenting their parents and teachers about the wonderful meaning of *words* which have become to *them* mere familiar sounds, of *things* which they have gazed at till they have forgotten that there is any life or mystery in them at all; through men who have been exercised with the puzzles of Philosophy, and want to find some ground upon which they may stand, a ground of reality, not of convention; – through the cravings of men who know nothing of Philosophy, but who have found enough in their own thoughts and in the world to amaze and confound them; – through the frivolous, even, who appear to be engaged in no search at all, who only wish to throw down some system or build up one for their own fame, but who nevertheless, because they are men, cannot be merely busy in that poor occupation, and will be sure to start some inquiry which we may pursue to its issue if they will not. I am greatly afraid that when we try to silence any of those questions we are trying to silence the voice of Christ, in others and in ourselves," and *Moral and Methaphysical Philosophy* I, XVII–III: "When I find men occupied with a number of strange thoughts and questionings about the universe and themselves, and their relations to each other, – about their origin and their final destiny, – when I observe how easily they lose all care for such investigations – –, can it seem wonderful to me that the Father of their spirits – – should have awakened them to ask, and seek, and knock for answers, which without this asking, seeking, and knocking, could not, by their very nature, be granted to them?"

33 Cf. *Sermons* I, 241–2: "Live in the habitual recollection that these lusts of the spirit which you have often sought to stifle, which you have often supposed to be strange aspirations after the distant, the fantastical, the impossible, are gifts from the Father of your spirit, – monitions from Him of your own glorious origin and high destiny, – pledges that He wishes you to inherit the substantial treasures of His own Truth and Goodness."

34 *The Kingdom of Christ* II, 106.

35 *What is Revelation?*, 136.

criminately he could call it "the spirit" or "the inward eye", but just as frequently he used the term "reason".[36]

Whatever the term, the faculty which enables man to grasp true being, *that which is*, must be contrasted with "the understanding" or "the intellect".[37] A clear distinction must be drawn between them and their specific ways of functioning. Only then will it be possible to solve the fundamental problem of human knowledge: "Have we anything in us which can apprehend that which *is*? Are we merely circumscribed by that which we think? – – Can we come into contact with the meaning, the substance, the reality of anything in earth or Heaven? Have we nothing in place of that knowledge but a semblance or appearance which is presented to us?"[38]

By calling the faculty which apprehends true being "the reason" and by contrasting it with "the understanding" Maurice deliberately followed Coleridge, whom he considered to be the greatest philosopher of his age. Coleridge was a new Socrates, whose importance lay less in his actual solutions to philosophical and theological problems and more in posing the right questions and helping others to seek the truth for themselves. Coleridge's greatness was not impaired if the seeker, faithfully following his method of inquiry, was led to different conclusions.[39] When Maurice pointed to Coleridge as having shown the right method in the search for truth and reality, he was specifically thinking of his attempts at working out the distinction between the understanding and the reason and their respective ways of functioning.

Although Coleridge never gave a systematic account of the problems of the understanding and the reason, he dealt with them so extensively in connection with his discussion of theological, philosophical, and political questions that his fundamental position is clear.[40] In elaborating his views Coleridge made use of Kant's distinction

36 Cf. *The Kingdom of Christ* (1838) II, 87–8: "the reason – – is the organ wherewith we apprehend spiritual matters."
37 Cf. *The Kingdom of Christ* I, 178: "There is an organ in man which speaks of that which is absolute and eternal. You believe that this organ, call it reason or what you will, is distinct from the one that merely forms notions and affirms propositions," and *The Contemporary Review* XIX (January 1871. *"On the Mode of Dealing with Words which Occur Most Frequently in Treatises on Mental Philosophy"*. Cit. *Mental Philosophy*), 272: "still men have felt that, besides this [the calculating faculty] – which they have been in no wise inclined to disparage – there was something which delighted in Order for its own sake, which abhorred disorder; something not contented with phantoms and shadows, which desired to lay hold of that which is. It may not be Reason. Call it by any other name which you like better. But it deserves to have a name, seeing that it points to a reality – seeing that it must be connected somehow with Knowledge or Science."
38 *What is Revelation?*, 136.
39 What Maurice found valuable in *The Friend* (1818) aptly sums up his evaluation of Coleridge's philosophical thinking: "Its merit is, that it is an inquiry, that it shows us what we have to seek for, and that it puts us into the way of seeking" *(The Kingdom of Christ* I, 4). *The Kingdom of Christ* I, 1–15 gives the most complete statement of what Maurice considered to be his indebtedness to Coleridge. Here as elsewhere Maurice's declaration of his debt to other men must, however, be critically sifted before they can be made use of.
40 For a more detailed treatment see my: *S. T. Coleridge's religiøse Udvikling (Teologiske Studier Nr. 10*, København 1949), 51–9. See also René Wellek: *Immanuel Kant in England 1793–1838* (Princeton 1931), 65–135, and Elisabeth Winkelmann: *Coleridge und die Kantische Philosophie (Palaestra* 184, Leipzig 1933), 48–104.

between *Verstand* and *Vernunft,* which he translated as "the understanding" and "the reason". Although the problem of the relation between discursive and intuitive thought has always been a burning question in the history of philosophy, Coleridge considered Kant the first to have demonstrated, by a stringently logical analysis of the structure of the human mind, that man possesses both "understanding" and "reason" and that there is a qualitative difference between these two kinds of apprehension. Coleridge agreed with Kant that the understanding receives, through the senses, the material, which it classifies and arranges by virtue of its inherent forms of perception and categories of thought, thus making the cognition of the phenomenal world possible. Whereas Coleridge carefully followed Kant with regard to the functioning of the understanding, the influence of Platonic and Neo-Platonic thought made him go his own way with regard to the reason.[41] The reason is the faculty through which man intuitively apprehends true being and, with self-evident clearness, becomes aware of God, with whom his true self is related.

Thus Coleridge's idea of the understanding and the reason represented a fusion of Kantian and Platonic elements respectively. In Kant he had found a solidly argued analysis whereby the understanding was deprived of its false sovereignty. Kant had provided him with the weapons that enabled him to settle accounts with the prevalent empirico-materialistic philosophy and make room for a Platonically conceived reason. The assertion of the validity of the reason was his real concern, enabling him to lay a critically sound foundation for his own philosophy of life, made up by influences from Platonism and orthodox Christianity.

Maurice readily acknowledged his debt to Coleridge – he had especially, he pointed out, learnt from him the importance of the distinction between understanding and reason for theology.[42] Maurice himself clearly wanted to be faithful to Coleridge's concern, and therefore he never launched any direct criticism against Coleridge. It is nevertheless evident that on many points he found fault with Coleridge's philosophical and theological exposition. A consistent application of the Coleridgean

41 Like Kant Coleridge could distinguish between "spekulative Vernunft" and "praktische Vernunft", but in fact this distinction was of no importance to him. At bottom "practical reason" is the reason proper, which has absorbed "theoretical reason".

42 Maurice found special help in the search for truth in Coleridge's *Aids to Reflection* (1825), which built upon this distinction between reason and understanding: "I can testify that it was most helpful in delivering me from a number of philosophical phrases and generalisations, which I believe attach themselves to the truths of the Creed, even in the minds of many who think that they receive Christianity with a most childlike spirit – most helpful in enabling me to perceive that the deepest principles of all are those which the Peasant is as capable of apprehending and entering into as the Schoolman. I value and love his philosophy mainly because it has led me to this discovery, and to the practical conclusion, that those who are called to the work of teaching must cultivate and exercise their understandings, in order that they may discriminate between that which is factitious and accidental, or belongs to our artificial habits of thought, and that which is fixed and eternal, which belongs to man as man, and which God will open the eyes of every humble man to perceive" *(The Kingdom of Christ* I, 7). Cf. equally p. 12: "though it was your father's [Coleridge's] honour that he asserted them [the essential principles of the Reason] to an age and a nation which had not yet discovered the need of them, he certainly did not pretend, and no one should pretend, that he was the first reviver or expositor of them. But the application of these principles to *Theology,* I believe, we owe mainly to him."

method would often lead to conclusions that differed from Coleridge's. This was in actual fact the case with respect to man's way of arriving at knowledge both of the created universe and of God.

b. The Understanding and Human Science

Maurice followed Coleridge in representing the understanding as "the conditions under which the intellect combines, distinguishes, classifies; the forms through which it conceives the matter that is external to it; the machinery of propositions, argumentation, inference."[43] With its "terms and forms of logic"[44] it is "a faculty which forms notions, judges of opinions, criticizes documents."[45] The understanding, or intellect, forms conceptions or notions, indicating through its logical laws and rules the conditions of sense and coherence in words and sentences. If the understanding confines itself to its proper task, it is useful and good.[46] But if it transgresses its limits and considers itself capable of delivering judgment on reality itself, it must be sharply opposed as harmful and pernicious.[47]

Maurice agreed with Coleridge that, with its forms of perception and categories of thought, the understanding moulds our sense-impressions and thereby creates an image of reality.[48] But even if the understanding is unable to arrive at "das Ding an sich", Coleridge, with Kant, considered its cognition valid with respect to the phenomenal world. Here Maurice, however, parts company with him. Inasmuch as the understanding, because of its structure, only deals with "abstractions from the Finite and the Temporal", it is disqualified as a means of arriving at true knowledge of the essential nature of the created universe. By classifying the sense-impressions according to its inherent patterns of thought it even distorts reality. Hence Maurice ranges the understanding or the intellect among the forces of the flesh which have to be fought.[49]

43 *The Contemporary Review* XIV (May 1870. "Dr. Newman's Grammar of Assent". Cit. *Grammar of Assent*), 168.
44 *What is Revelation?*, 267–8.
45 p. 255.
46 Cf. *Sequel*, 196: "What I feel and have always felt is, that there is a Logic of the Understanding, which deserves all honour whilst it confines itself within its own limits, and contents itself with telling us under what laws and in what forms we must discourse."
47 Cf. *Sequel*, 198: "It is this imposition of the Logic of the Understanding upon the Conscience and the Reason, arising from a disbelief in their distinct objects and obligations, which I think we are bound to resist to the utmost."
48 Cf. *What is Revelation?*, 324: "the restless eagerness of our intellect to conceive and create objects for itself out of the things we see."
49 Cf. *The Epistle to the Hebrews, Being the Substance of Three Lectures Delivered in the Chapel of the Honourable Society of Lincoln's Inn, on the Foundation of Bishop Warburton. With a Preface Containing a Review of Mr. Newman's Theory of Development* (Cit. *The Epistle to the Hebrews*), LXXIII: "to cast away all conceptions of the carnal understanding, all creations of the mere systematizing faculty"; p. XCII: "They had a flesh in them as well as a spirit, and therefore, no doubt, they were disposed to exalt the notions and opinions of their own minds," and *The Gospel of St. John*, 202: "The spirit in man is as impatient of those fetters that bind it to the earth, as the carnal understanding is of all that is not of the earth, earthly."

Maurice allowed that the understanding, with its logical principles indicating the rules for coherent and meaningful discourse, was valuable but he never worked this idea out; nor is it of any importance to his thinking. The explanation is not difficult to find. Maurice was merely echoing Coleridge in his description of the function of the understanding. For Coleridge, however, this was relevant since he considered the understanding constitutive for knowledge of the visible world. But Maurice denied this, and his statements on the understanding and its validity are consequently left hanging in the air. Maurice used Coleridge's terms, and some of his arguments, in order to reduce the understanding and demonstrate its subordinate role in cognition. Indeed, a closer inspection reveals that he attributed to the understanding no significance and importance whatsoever. On the contrary, by virtue of its structure it prevents man from arriving at true knowledge, either of the created universe, or of God.

True knowledge, even of the visible world, can never be achieved through the understanding or the intellect. As it moulds the sensual impressions according to its own forms of thought, the knowledge it gives is nothing but "a feat of ventriloquism" – man only hears "echoes in Nature of his own voice".[50] By making the understanding the only instrument of knowledge man not only falsifies reality, but also makes himself the centre of all things. To exalt the understanding means that man has asserted himself as an independent and self-sufficient being free to shape reality at his will and pleasure – therefore the understanding stands for a pernicious and godless principle.

True knowledge of the visible universe can only be obtained if man rejects the understanding and its falsifying patterns of thought. He must be a learner, ready to be taught by reality itself. In accordance with this principle Maurice insisted that man must found his knowledge upon facts. Man must not build on the theories and speculations produced by the understanding, but, by the observation of facts, renounce himself and reach out towards that which comes to him from the world around him.[51] Induction from facts, and not deduction from the logical principles of the intellect,

50 *The Claims,* 61.
51 Cf. *What is Revelation?,* 477–8: "It [the Bible] tells us what we are when we are shut up in ourselves, in our own conceptions; how we abstract and form notions from names; how they are to be distinguished from the things which they set forth; how impossible it is for them to exhibit a single living process. For every process of bodily life – seeing, smelling, tasting, handling, walking, breathing – is an act of rising out of ourselves. Not to do that is to die. The Bible consistently and harmoniously shows us that every process of life in the man himself, – every movement of thought, feeling, affection – is, in like manner, a rising above ourselves, an ascent into another region," and *The Contemporary Review* XIX *(Mental Philosophy),* 270: "every act of sense [is] a paradox. No sense has an existence in itself; it is not a sense till it goes out of its organ – till it has communion with something that is distinct from it. That is no law devised by transcendentalists; it is a law which goes through our lives."

is the method which leads to true knowledge.[52] Scientists have demonstrated this when they have rejected all preconceived theories and speculations in order to stick to facts: "Physical Science – – presumes a world which exists, and which we did not create. Science was impossible while men glorified their own thoughts and speculations more than that which nature presented to them. It has become firm and safe since they have humbled themselves into the condition of learners. This has been the security for progress."[53]

Maurice's requirement that all knowledge be founded upon the observation of facts does not mean, however, that man must rest satisfied with the impressions which the senses convey of the facts of the visible world. In that case man would have taken notice of the external appearance of things only. As this represents the changeable and transient, such a cognition would be shadowy and indistinct. It has nothing whatsoever to do with science, which refers to the unchangeable and permanent alone, to *that which is*.[54]

The essential characteristic of "a fact" is, for Maurice, not its visible appearance, but the inner principle, the power, the idea or "meaning", that alone constitutes its essence. The facts in the universe consist of permanent principles, or of unchangeable being, clothed in external, sensible and changeable shapes – hence they can be the object of genuine knowledge. Consequently science cannot rest content with externals but must penetrate the visible disguise or veil and discover *that which is*, "the truth of things", their substance and reality, instead of "the semblance or appearance" with which our senses bring us into contact.[55] The true scientist apprehends the facts by means of sense-impressions, but he must penetrate beyond their visible, outward shape and find the hidden principle manifesting itself through it. Therefore Maurice can say that "physical science begins in the trampling down of sense, and in penetrating into the secret heart of things."[56]

52 Cf. *The Word "Eternal" and the Punishment of the Wicked. A Letter to the Rev. Dr. Jelf, Canon of Christ Church and Principal of King's College, with a New Preface* (Cambridge 1854. Cit. *The Word "Eternal"*), 10: "In Physics, induction is the means of escaping from arbitrary definitions and classifications, and of bringing nature to tell her own secrets in her own way."

53 *Theological Essays*, 90.

54 Cf. *Macmillan's Magazine* IX (*Christmas Thoughts on Renan's Vie de Jésus*), 195: "science means what I take it to mean, reverence for that which is; for the permanent; for laws which live on through a multitude of changes, and direct these changes."

55 Cf. *The Prophets*, 247: "all outward appearances [are] but signs of some power or principle which is working unseen. What is the function of the physical student or philosopher but to discover the power or principle of which any appearances or facts in nature are the indexes?"; p. 82: "He [the man of science] is always seeking for that which is. He seeks, believing that he may find. That faith rests upon the conviction that he is not investigating a world which he created for himself, nor a world which is lawless and ungoverned, but one of which the meanings and harmonies lie deep; to be reached only by him who feels that he is a little child and bewails his ignorance, and desires clearer light that he may wonder more"; *What is Revelation?*, 467: "The realities which are behind the veil express themselves through the forms of sense, because that is the order and principle of God's universe," and *Theological Essays*, 111: "The philosopher must ask to what reality the perception or intuition corresponds; of what substance that which he sees is the shadow."

56 *The Kingdom of Christ* (1838) II, 272. Cf. also *The Prophets*, 82: "the man of science – – is

The true man of science who forgets himself and the preconceived notions of the understanding and humbly submits to facts will discover their inmost meaning and significance. Maurice can equally say that the facts themselves reveal *that which is* to the student who, in rejection of all dogmatism, is intent on pursuing truth alone. Whatever the approach Maurice's contention is, however, that the attainment of knowledge is never an act of man. It is God who imparts knowledge of the universe whether man acknowledges it or not: "Science makes [nothing] be which was not. It rejoices to disclaim any such faculty. It boasts of *finding* fixed, permanent, universal laws. I do not ask the scientific man to say that GOD discovers to him any law or principle. To many that might not be real or honest language, – or they might not feel it to be so, – therefore they should not adopt it. To many, I doubt not, it is the most simple, genuine expression of their inmost thoughts. But at all events, *I* am bound so to speak. Believing the Bible to be true, I cannot suppose that any discovery can be made to a man except by God. I must suppose that when at last it bursts upon him it is a gift from God."[57]

Science, which implies forsaking and forgetting oneself to stretch out towards the truth in the confident expectation that it will be revealed, pursues the same method as theology. Both can learn from each other. In the past science has helped theology in rediscovering its true method. This was the case when Sir Francis Bacon pointed out the baneful effects of preconceived speculations and theories for anyone who wanted to find the truth.[58] Even now every scientist who follows the right scientific method teaches the divines this needful lesson.[59] The time has, however, come for

fearful of being imposed upon by the idols of sense, by the conclusions and anticipations of his own mind," and *The Kingdom of Christ* I, 129–30 "the experimental philosophy in physics held out to students the hope of attaining an actual knowledge of things by delivering them from the impressions of the senses, and from the notions which the understanding generalises out of those impressions." We should now be able to explain the apparent ambiguity in Maurice's conception of the sense-perceptions. He welcomed them because they established man's connection with facts, the inner principle of which is denoted and manifested by the sensible appearance of things. At the same time he spoke of the tyranny of the sense-impressions because, taken by themselves, they forced man to rest content with the changeable appearance and prevented him from penetrating to the inward invisible principle. Thus Maurice's conception of what is implied in the observation of facts reveals the inherent conflict in his thought between the temporal and the eternal. This is the reason why he sometimes described the knowledge of the senses as the true point of departure for genuine science, and sometimes opposed it as an enemy.

57 *The Claims*, 22–3.
58 See *What is Revelation?*, 155.
59 Cf. *Sermons* II, 143: "The pursuit of natural science has had this blessed effect, that men demand something which is not hypothetical, which their own thoughts and conceptions do not supply, as a ground for their thoughts and conceptions to stand upon. The Spirit of God, I am sure, urges them to make this demand, in the spiritual world as much as in the natural," and *The Conscience, Lectures on Casuistry, Delivered in the University of Cambridge* (London 1868. Cit. *The Conscience*), 137: "The scientific man bids us seek the thing as it is. He tells us that we are always in danger of putting our thoughts or conceptions of the thing between us and that which is. He gives us a discipline for our thoughts that they may not pervert the facts which we are examining."

theology to repay its debts and, profiting from its own bitter experiences, to point out to science the dangers which are threatening it from the acceptance of the understanding as the means of arriving at knowledge.[60]

Theology is able "to make us understand the ground upon which science stands, what science itself is."[61] This must not be taken to mean that theology is the guardian of science and must dictate the results to be attained. Maurice believed that the contemporary religious world was acting in this way and, by so doing, falsifying both Biblical truth and the findings of science.[62] Theology is not to dominate science but to serve it and help it to perform better its divinely appointed task. It renders this service when it warns science of the pernicious consequences of making the understanding the supreme and only source of knowledge. Because of its inherent thought-forms, which produce only their own image of reality, it deprives science of any possibility of attaining a universally valid knowledge of reality. It shuts man up in himself and fetters him to his own prejudices and notions and condemns him to rest satisfied with appearances. Furthermore, it presupposes the universe to be a chaos, void of order, harmony and purpose. Inevitably such a view fosters scepticism or dogmatism. Despairing of arriving at knowledge, man must either declare every opinion to be equally true or false or, in order to avoid such scepticism, erect a human authority to prescribe what is to be maintained and what to be denied, what is to be sought for and what is to be rejected as conflicting with the authorized idea of meaningful reality. If truth be nothing but the opinions of the individual or of a group of individuals, then the foundation of science is undermined and the search for true knowledge becomes impossible.[63]

Against this false conception of the universe and man, which lies behind the attempt to make the understanding the basis of science, theology proclaims the universe to be created as an ordered, harmonious whole, constituted by unchangeable laws and principles which can be sought and found. Behind the changeable, sensible appearances lies *that which is,* and so the visible universe can be made the object of knowledge. Furthermore theology bears witness to the fact that man, created in

60 Cf. *The Claims,* 60–1: "The writer of the 'Novum Organum' did so much for us divines in throwing down the idols which the logicians had set up, that we are bound, as far as we can, to return the service in kind. The idols are rising up again under new names; we have the most intense interest in breaking them into pieces, and grinding them small. If we can do that, we may protect the physical student from assaults which may ultimately render all his investigations abortive, though, in his devotion to those investigations, he may be indifferent and secure."

61 *Has the Church, or the State, the Power to Educate the Nation?,* 146.

62 Cf. *Theological Essays,* 71: "There are those among us who think that the facts of science, unless they are well sifted and sorted by religious men, and mixed with religious maxims, are likely to disturb the faith of the people – –. Our education in the Bible ought to have taught us to believe in a God of Truth; to reverence facts, because they must be His facts; to long that laws should be discovered, because they are His; to fear nothing but what is false – that being certainly of the Devil."

63 Cf. *Has the Church, or the State, the Power to Educate the Nation?,* 143–4: "Do you think the results of science are safe, or that there is the least security for scientific progress, if the scientific principle be lost? Do you think that this scientific principle can be retained, when the notion is afloat, that knowledge and opinion are the same, that that is, which seems to each man; that truth is what every man troweth?"

the image of God, is not only created to know God Himself but also to know the laws and principles implanted by God in the created world and constituting its existence, order and harmony. So theology can safeguard the true foundation of scientific knowledge, since, believing in God as the Supreme Being and Reason, it teaches that true being exists and can be found, and that God is the ever acting God working to bring man to the knowledge of *that which is*.[64] For this reason theology declares that it is a work well-pleasing to God to investigate the created universe in order to discover its principles and well-ordered harmony.[65]

Theology not only teaches that knowledge is possible, but it also provides the attitude which alone enables man to receive knowledge. We have seen how necessary it is for the man of science to have a mind which is self-denying, open and receptive. Only he who, like Socrates, acknowledges that he knows nothing can attain knowledge. The scientist must forsake his own prejudices, opinions and systems and be dependent entirely upon that which is given to him. The same applies to the theologian. Self-assertion and self-sufficiency are as dangerous for theology as for science. The Bible uproots this false state of mind when it teaches man to understand himself as created to depend on God and receive everything from Him.[66] There is but

64 Cf. *Has the Church, or the State, the Power to Educate the Nation?*, 145–6: "We are able to prevent you from losing the idea of science, from losing the feeling that it is possible to know at all. We are able to tell you the spiritual and moral dignity which belongs to you, and so to teach you that you are not part of these physical things – that you are meant to overlook them, and investigate them, and rule them – –. We are able at the same time to give an impression of the dignity and majesty of the world with which you are thus freely and, as its lords, able to converse, by showing you that the creator of it has himself explained how every portion of it is pregnant with symbols of that which is higher and more divine," and *Queen's College*, 15: "But how is truth to be sought, how is God to be honoured, in them [the visible things]? Not, surely, by some artificial and irreverent introduction of religious phrases and topics into them, but by inculcating the uniform habitual belief that this universe is God's; that all our powers and faculties of every kind are God's; that He will have us to know the laws of His universe; that the knowledge of them is to be sought in the same humble, self-suspecting, patient temper, which is required for attaining the knowledge of Himself, and of His own inmost mind; that He makes known the secrets of His creation to those who in this spirit inquire after them; that we hold every energy and capacity as a trust from Him; that it is a violation of His commands to engage in any study, as if it were not a godly study."

65 Cf. *The Kingdom of Christ* II, 258–9: "the study of the laws according to which God has framed this universe is – – a solemn and religious work, to be carried on reverently, in connexion with the study of the laws upon which He has constructed the moral universe. – – A national Church must believe in the highest sense that what *is* is right. This is the pillar of her own existence; this is what she opposes to the maxim of the world, that things are right which we make so by our rules and conventions; therefore she must teach her children to ask bravely and boldly, 'What is?', encouraging them by all means to expect an answer; teaching them in what frame of mind to wait for it, to receive it, to give thanks for it."

66 Cf. *Social Morality. Twenty-One Lectures Delivered in the University of Cambridge* (London 1893), 359–60: "What I maintain is that the hindrances to experimental philosophy were also the great hindrances to theological belief. As long as men are counted infallible the investigation into the meaning of facts will be checked, precisely because the belief in a God of Truth, in a God who stirs men to pursue truth and leads them on in the pursuit of it, is checked. The practical denial of God, not faith in Him, makes us afraid that if we seek we shall not find, if we knock it will not be opened to us."

one method leading to the true knowledge of reality: man must renounce himself, spurn the understanding and acknowledge his ignorance in order to be instructed by God Himself.

Our analysis has demonstrated that although Maurice apparently assented to Coleridge's conception of the understanding and its functioning, he in fact completely rejected it as a means of arriving at knowledge of the visible world. This rejection is not really based on a deep study of the epistemological problems. But when Coleridge, following Kant, claimed that the understanding and its categories are constitutive of empirical knowledge, which on that account can only be phenomenal, Maurice reacted instantly. The understanding must be rejected partly because it assumes man to be independent of God in his search for knowledge, partly because it cannot penetrate and grasp "the truth of things".

At the same time our analysis has demonstrated that Maurice's criticism and his own idea of knowledge were inspired by a Platonic conception of reality. Sense perception and the synthesizing classification of the sense-impressions by the intellect are characterized as δόξαι, notions, opinions. They reflect the changeable and fluctuating which can never be the object of true knowledge. But knowledge is possible because the visible world is constituted by *that which is,* and because man is created to grasp *that which is,* the reality hidden behind the sensible and external.

Maurice never felt bound to give a critical analysis of epistemological problems and to substantiate his own views. Apparently the Platonic theory of knowledge was so obviously true that it was unnecessary to argue further about it.[67] For him truth needed no substantiation or argument; it was enough to proclaim it and let it assert itself as self-authenticating. Epistemology is no exception to this rule. Yet there was another reason why Maurice refrained from giving a detailed explanation of his epistemological views. He was convinced that man is nothing in himself, but that everything is given to him by God if only he is willing to receive it. No more need be said. It is not important, it is even harmful to analyse the actual processes by which the individual attains knowledge. By so doing the temptation arises to attribute to man a creative power of his own instead of pointing to God as the only source of knowledge.

Invariably Maurice eloquently proclaimed his deepest convictions and presented his own conclusions, but left only hints and fragments of a detailed argumentation. This also applies to his epistemology. He clearly assumed the truth of the Platonic idea of reality and did not feel the need to argue about it. However, Maurice did not adhere rigidly to Plato, but attempted to absorb new elements taken from quite different systems of thought. This is apparent in his admiration of Francis Bacon and his scientific method – it even makes him attempt to place Plato and Bacon side by side by insisting that Plato, like Bacon, was wholly intent on exploring facts by means of an experimental, inductive method.[68] Because of this influence Maurice

---

67 That Maurice was convinced of the essential truth of Plato's epistemology is apparent in *Moral and Metaphysical Philosophy* I, 147–51.

68 See *Moral and Metaphysical Philosophy* I, 157 and 175–6. Maurice admitted that Plato had not carried out his method in the sphere of natural science, as *Timæus* bears witness. In contrast Bacon rightly maintained that induction from facts is the means by which true knowledge of the physical world is to be obtained. But this did not entitle Bacon to criticize

wanted to build upon the observation of facts and emphasized induction from facts as the true method for arriving at knowledge. The idea of man as created to receive knowledge demands that the facts which meet man from outside must be the starting-point of knowledge. But this was not a refutation of Platonic thought, since Maurice interpreted the facts in such a way that the Platonic conception of reality was preserved. Therefore he was not interested in concrete existing things but in their principle and constitutive being. Maurice was not concerned to explain how man is able to penetrate appearances and apprehend *that which is*; he was simply content to state that this is so.

Maurice's view of human knowledge lacks completeness and stringency in exposition. His attitude towards the various philosophical schools of thought was never based on any profound knowledge of them. His reactions depended on whether a system was compatible with his own Platonic idea of reality and whether, at the same time, it was capable of expressing the idea of man as created to receive everything from God. He made generous use of any idea which fulfilled these conditions. If he wished to refute a false point of view, he did not hesitate to collect ammunition from other quarters in order to demolish an opponent. Thus, he did not scruple to use Coleridge's idea of the understanding in order to undermine an empirical philosophy. But, torn out of its context and interpreted according to Maurice's basic intentions, it becomes void of all meaning. Maurice had no use for it as a means of arriving at a knowledge of the created universe.[69]

c. The Reason and the Knowledge of God

Man is related through the senses to the visible world of time and space. As spirit, or reason, he is at the same time related to the invisible eternal world. Maurice was convinced that there is "a faculty in man which can take cognizance of the Eternal and Absolute".[70] In this respect he agreed completely with Coleridge and drew upon the Coleridgean exposition of the unique character of the reason in its contrast to the understanding. Thus Maurice was echoing Coleridge when he declared that the reason is that which is truly human, common to all men, and possessed by all equally. The understanding, on the other hand, has not only been given to men in various degrees of strength, but is also largely dependent in its use upon an intensive and pro-

---

Plato's thought as a whole: "Would that our countryman, for the honour of his own character, for the sake of the ages which were to follow him, had been as willing to recognise the truth of Plato, as he was acute in detecting his falsehood; as honest in acknowledging him for a guide, as he was right in pointing him out for a beacon. He would then have seen that the *Timæus* was in contradiction to the principle of induction, because it was inconsistent with the principle of Plato" (p. 175. Cf. also *Sequel*, 31: "that method [of Plato] of rising by questionings of common facts into the perception of eternal realities").

69 In his published writings Maurice never directly criticized Coleridge for attributing a positive importance to the understanding as constitutive of our knowledge of the empirical world. The reason is that Maurice never explicitly attacked those from whom he thought he had learnt something. He always acknowledged his debt, but this was not always followed by a direct criticism of what he considered false in his teachers' views. At best he hinted at what he thought had been stated inadequately.

70 *Sequel*, 237.

tracted intellectual training which is possible only for the few. The understanding is exclusive, varying greatly from individual to individual, whereas the reason is common to all men – it alone is entitled to be called "the human faculty" or "the universal faculty".[71] Every man is created to know God, and as it is precisely through the reason that man attains to direct knowledge of God, it qualifies man as man and constitutes his true humanity. Being created by God every man has "a faculty of knowing the Being in whom we live and move, as a child knows its father."[72]

Maurice considered the reason such an integral part of the Christian view of the relation between God and man that to part with it would be to destroy Christianity itself.[73] This is evident in Maurice's attack on Mansel's Bampton Lectures for 1858: *The Limits of Religious Thought Examined*.

Mansel was a disciple of Sir William Hamilton, who maintained that all metaphysics must be rejected as illegitimate, since because of the very structure of the human mind knowledge can only refer to that which belongs to the finite world of time and space. Hamilton was influenced by Kant but kept exclusively to the latter's conception of phenomenal cognition, whilst rejecting Kant's idea of the practical reason as being false. Mansel constructed his Bampton Lectures on the same epistemological foundation. He wished to show that the criticism directed by a rationalistic philosophy against the Christian faith was philosophically untenable, since human knowledge cannot reach beyond the world of time and space without involving itself in insoluble 'antinomies'. By means of a stringently philosophical analysis of human thought Mansel wished to cut away the ground under all rationalist criticism of the Bible and orthodox Christianity. God has adapted Himself to the structure of man's apprehension and has imparted, by revelation, all that is necessary for Him to live a pious, holy life. Man must submit to this revelation since the reason has no means of criticizing it. Because his knowledge is conditioned by time and space, it follows that man can never conceive God as He truly is.

Maurice considered Mansel's Bampton Lectures a "critical event in the history of the English Church".[74] In the name of Christianity Mansel had attempted to enslave man to the world of time and space and had thereby denied that man is created

---

71 Cf. *The Kingdom of Christ* (1838) II, 69: "that universal faculty by which we converse with God, and which the learnedest and the poorest possess equally, is superior to every other faculty, and the real characteristic of our humanity"; *Life* I, 299: "the truth which is highest, as well as the highest faculty which apprehends it, is the most universal. I certainly do find very few who see this as clearly as I wish them to see it: some form of intellectual worship, some exclusiveness or other mars the fulness of this conviction", and p. 334: "I was desirous, therefore, to act upon the principle which I have always acknowledged: that the faculty which deals with the spiritual truths and mysteries is the universal faculty; that it is the intellect, which meddles with propositions, that is wanting or only exists very feebly in the poor – –."

72 *What is Revelation?*, 47.

73 Cf. *What is Revelation?*, 256: "It is because the Bible addresses that human faculty and not some special faculty, that it can bear to be translated into every tongue of the earth, that it can speak to all tribes and nations. For *us* to deny the existence of such a faculty, is simply to deny our work [as ministers of the Gospel]. Any one who tells us that it does not exist is bound also to tell us that if we are honest men we must relinquish that work."

74 *What is Revelation?*, 141.

to know God and true reality.[75] The grave issue which Mansel had raised was "the question whether the Infinite and Eternal God has or has not unveiled Himself to human beings, and whether, though all distinctions and the very names Finite and Infinite should be utterly dark to them, they may not dwell in His light, and have fellowship with it, and gradually come to see all things by it. This I believe is the question of questions for our generation."[76]

This being the case, it was no wonder that Maurice felt compelled to remonstrate. Immediately he produced the lengthy *What is Revelation?* (1859), in which he embarked upon a passionate polemic against Mansel, upbraiding him for the un-Christian consequences of his argument. Mansel's reply was calm and dignified, pointing out that Maurice had not only often grossly misunderstood and misrepresented him but had even missed his point. Maurice was not at all convinced. Although in a more dispassionate temper he restated his position and with only slight variations reproduced his arguments in a new book: *Sequel to the Inquiry, What is Revelation?* (1860).

These two works are of the utmost importance to an understanding of Maurice's theological thought. Mansel's Bampton Lectures displayed great philosophical insight and the power of stringent philosophical reasoning. To make his counter-attack effective and establish the truth of his own position, Maurice was forced to enter into a more detailed discussion and argumentation than was his wont, thus affording us precious glimpses into the working of his mind.

The crux of Maurice's disagreement with Mansel was on the reason. To demonstrate its existence he was bound to discuss the validity of Kant's philosophy. Without displaying any profound knowledge of Kant's philosophical thought[77] Maurice recognized that Kant's lasting achievement had been that his astute and penetrating analysis of the conditions of human thought had forced him, besides the understanding, to admit the existence of the reason.[78]

---

75 Cf. *What is Revelation?*, 163: "This is the ground of my conflict with Mr. Mansel. He seems to me to crush the search after Truth, all that is expressed in the word *Philosophy*, by crushing at the same time the discovery of Truth, all that is expressed in the word *Revelation*."

76 *Sequel*, 141.

77 Maurice's exposition of Kant was not based upon any study of his writings nor upon any serious preoccupation with the problems which are raised by his thought. He inherited his respect for Kant from Coleridge, and what he learnt at second-hand he interpreted in the light of his own Platonically inspired epistemology.

78 Cf. *Sequel*, 189: "I was likely to be somewhat jealous in claiming the distinction between things as they are, and phenomena, as *not* a specially German distinction. – – I am as little inclined as any one can be to underrate the merits of Kant in giving fixedness to that distinction as one of the most important in Philosophy," and *What is Revelation?*, 254: "You will see there that the tendency of Kant's mind was destructive, – that he applied the severest logic to the overthrow of the metaphysical or ontological notions of his predecessors, – that he did effectually sweep away, so Sir W. Hamilton thinks, all mere notions and conceptions about the Infinite. It was this man who, *because* he was a logician, could not bring himself to deny that there is something in us which takes hold of fact, something which will not be circumscribed by notions and conceptions, which confesses that which is. He felt that if there is no such faculty in man as this, there is not and cannot be any morality for man, there is not and cannot be any truth for man."

Kant had distinguished between "spekulative Vernunft" and "praktische Vernunft". "Spekulative Vernunft" denoted that faculty in man which, on the basis of knowledge obtained through the forms of perception and the categories of thought of the understanding, strives after an embracing view of the ultimate principles of reality. Its regulative ideas – the world, God, and the soul – manifest our aspiration towards absolute perfect knowledge, but they can never become the object of clear unequivocal knowledge. If we seek to give an account of them we are led into 'antinomies'. Mansel, following Sir William Hamilton, concluded from this that we can only attain knowledge of finite things within time and space. The very structure of our thought does not permit any knowledge of the infinite. Therefore all ontology and rational metaphysics are impossible. As proof Mansel refers to Kant's "spekulative Vernunft" with its 'antinomies'. As it does not produce valid knowledge, it must be rejected as "a faculty of lies". We have no organ of knowledge capable of apprehending ultimate reality. All such attempts are due to human knowledge trying to transgress the limits appointed for it.

Maurice challenged Mansel's assertion that the reason was "a faculty of lies". He did not deny that the reason could function as a faculty of lies, but from this fact it would be rash to deny it any validity whatsoever. Maurice conceded to Mansel that, on the basis of Kant's analysis of "the Dialectic of the Reason", the reason must be considered "a faculty of lies". This was, however, due to the incomplete and unsatisfactory nature of the Kantian analysis. But to Maurice it was worth consideration that Kant did not on that account dismiss the reason as Mansel did. Although Kant was unable to solve the problems of the reason, the facts were too strong for him and forced him, despite all logical inconsistencies, to assert the existence of a faculty dealing with ultimate reality.[79]

Maurice regarded Kant's account of "the Dialectic of the Reason" as erroneous because it confined itself to an analysis of the inner structure of the reason. His inquiry was based on the presupposition that it could be examined as a self-existing entity, the source of man's knowledge of the ultimate foundation of his existence. This approach implies, however, that the reason possesses the power of reaching towards that which transgresses time and space. On these premises it was small wonder that Kant was able to describe only "the *disorderly* operation of the Reason" and because of its 'antinomies' was compelled to characterize it as "a faculty of lies".[80]

79 Cf. *Sequel*, 174: "Kant had only to say that there is no distinction between the Reason and the Understanding, and to call the illusions of the Reason the impotence of the Understanding; then the illusion would cease. The German, I suspect, had considered that way of cutting the knot as seriously as Mr. Mansel. It was the natural and obvious one which his inclination would have led to him to embrace. It was the pressure of evidence, the sternness of his actual observation, which compelled him to refuse it. At all hazards, in spite of all apparent contradictions, he must confess that there is that in us which grasps at the Infinite and Eternal, – which will not be content with phenomena, or with any arguments and deductions from phenomena."

80 Cf. *Sequel*, 192: "I have shown you that I do confess these difficulties, and confess them to be inseparable from the independent exercise of the Reason. The questions at issue between us are, whether these difficulties and contradictions are proofs that there is nothing in man which really demands a knowledge of the Infinite and Eternal, and that what seems to demand it is an impotency of the understanding, attempting unlawful and impossible

In contrast Maurice maintained that it is only possible to arrive at a true analysis of the reason and its function when it is realised that the reason is created to depend upon God for its knowledge.[81] The reason is bound to display 'antinomies' when it trusts to itself for true knowledge – thereby acting contrary to the law of its creation.[82] Instead of being an argument for the rejection of the reason, its 'antinomies', on the contrary, point to the fact that the function of the reason is that of receiving.[83] Only when it is understood that the reason is created to receive the revelation of God in His true nature and of the ultimate foundation of the universe does everything fall into place. Depriving the reason of its independence delivers it from its 'antinomies' and allows it to recover its true position as the faculty which is created to receive knowledge of *that which is*.[84]

Thus the idea of God as the Creator, imparting everything to man as His dependent creature, also applies to the reason. To give expression to this fact Maurice often called it "the spiritual eye".[85] Just as the bodily eye does not create its object, so the reason does not possess the light of truth, but is created to receive it. Without a revelation, an enlightenment from without, it remains in darkness. The reason has knowledge only in so far as it renounces its autonomy and self-sufficiency and loses

> flights; or whether these difficulties and contradictions only show that the faculty which God has given us for the apprehension can only put forth its full powers when He meets it and illuminates it," and *What is Revelation?*, 251: "there is a *disorderly* operation of the Reason in us to which we are all prone, that which is busy in creating the object which it beholds, or else argues about it instead of contemplating it."

81 Cf. *Sequel*, 196–7: "Believing that Kant deprived the Reason of its proper complement, so far as he did not accept a Revelation, I must suppose that his Dialectic of the Reason may be very instructive, and must be imperfect."

82 Cf. *Sequel*, 177: "And most devout Englishmen will, I think, be disposed to admit that there must be paralogisms and antinomies in any faculty which is created to seek after that which is above all sense and experience, and which does not perceive that that which it seeks is coming to meet it, is seeking for it."

83 Cf. *Sequel*, 175–6: "The visible world meets the senses and gives them their objects. What meets the faculty which rises above sense and experience, and gives it its object? Is not that "appearance of objective principles" in the Reason, which Kant speaks of, precisely the indication of this want? Could there be a more faithful exposition than that phrase contains of the need in the highest region of our being, of something to commune with it and save it from the endless and frightful contradiction into which it falls from making its own thoughts its objects?"

84 Cf. *Sequel*, 75: "while we set up Revelation against Reason instead of regarding the first as God's discovery of Himself to the other, we shall be in the double peril of degrading the Reason, and of giving it an unfair and dangerous exaltation."

85 Cf. *Sequel*, 177–8: "You may easily persuade Englishmen to regard the faculty which they are told is spoken of in Kant's Critique on the Pure Reason as a faculty of lies; but you will not persuade them, if they are serious, godly men, that what they speak of under the name of their inward eye is a faculty of lies; though they know too well, and will confess with profound sorrow, how quickly, how of necessity, it falls into lying, when it is not in communion with its true Enlightener," and *What is Revelation?*, 252: "Now he begins to perceive that what he has to thank God for with his whole heart, was not for giving him something which He has refused to the race generally, but for opening in him that eye which belongs to us as men, and which, through our desire to magnify our own individual souls and to separate them from other men's, we put out."

itself in God as its sole enlightener.[86] The reason is "a Divine faculty, meant for fellowship with that which is Divine, not realising its own properties but in that fellowship."[87] Only when it lives in trust in God, does it live a true life in accordance with the law of its creation.[88]

Through this corrective to Kant's analysis of "the Dialectic of the Reason" Maurice found that he had demonstrated that man possesses the reason, which – in contradiction to the understanding – receives knowledge of God as the Supreme Being. That man is created with the reason implies, on the other hand, that he is not confined to the visible world of time and space. He is meant for a direct contemplation and vision of the eternal God as ultimate reality. Through the reason man transcends the limits of time and space and lives in direct communion with God and His eternal world.[89]

With this conception of the reason Maurice found himself in opposition to orthodox contemporary theology. When he upbraided it for proclaiming "conceptions", "notions", "opinions", "propositions", "theories", "dogmas" about God and His revelation, instead of proclaiming the living God Himself,[90] he was expressing a protest against the intrusion of the understanding and its categories into the domain of theology. Maurice's polemic had a far wider scope than a mere protest against the idea that man can know God and describe Him by virtue of the human mind and

86 Cf. *The Kingdom of Christ* II, 22: "This [the reason] only knows itself when it forgets itself; this only sees while the sense of sight is lost in the object of it. Accordingly the Reason also finds its deepest meaning and expression in worship," and *Life* II, 147: "Our highest human reason asks for the knowledge of God as the ground of itself – as that which is to deliver us from notions, conceits and imperfect apprehensions which belong to us as individuals."

87 *The Kingdom of Christ* II, 106.

88 Cf. *The Contemporary Review* XIX ("Mental Philosophy"), 272: "If it [the reason] owns itself not to have knowledge, not to possess in itself that which it always seeks after, then it will, I apprehend, acknowledge a Perfect Reason. And the Trust in that as a Power which is unfolding our Reason and drawing it to itself will be what we have been used to call *Faith*."

89 Cf. *The Kingdom of Christ* I, 179: "this Being of whom the reason speaks is one who transcends the conditions of space and time; – – this one faculty in man has the power of beholding that which is not under these conditions."

90 Cf. *The Conflict*, 187: "We have accused each other of being heretics, and we have all been heretics. We have all set up notions and dogmas of our understandings against Him who has given us understandings, against Him who is guiding us to seek for that Truth which passes all our understandings. We have said that there is such a Truth, that in it we have eternal life. And then we reduce this too down to the level of our conceptions. What *we* hold about the Name which we declare in the most solemn language to be incomprehensible and eternal, is substituted for the Name; we believe in ourselves – in what we think – not in God. – But such a belief as this cannot last; our notions will not uphold us when we are sinking in deep waters. We may call in evidences, arguments, authority, what we will; but if they are not GOD, they will not help creatures who are made in the likeness of God, who demand Him as the object of their trust," and *Sermons* I, 262: "Do not let us complain that the age is weaker or worse than others, because men are no longer satisfied with their opinions, because they cannot find any opinions upon which they may cast anchor. Thanks be to God if they are making that discovery! For as long as there is any resting upon opinions, so long will the Apostle's words, 'Other foundation can no man lay than is laid' (or, is lying), 'which *is* Jesus Christ', be but dead letters to us. We shall think that it is our notions about Christ, not He Himself, who is upholding the pillars of Heaven and earth."

its concepts, so that self-appointed human opinions and theories take the place of God's revealed truth. Maurice aimed at nothing less than a refutation of all assertions that God's revelation of Himself to man takes place in a specific history in the world of time and space. The contrast between the understanding and the reason is between time and eternity. Hence, to proclaim the living God in rejection of the understanding and its categories means to assert that God reveals Himself directly to the reason, which is capable of apprehending true being.

Because man, by virtue of the reason, is created to enter into direct relation with the ultimate Being, God, he can never be satisfied with that which belongs to the visible, ever fluctuating world of time and space. He must always aspire towards the living God, towards the direct knowledge and contemplation of that which remains unshaken through eternity, *that which is*.[91] But this also implies that the reason is capable of distinguishing that which belongs to the eternal world from that which belongs to the visible world: "there is a true and normal operation of the Reason, which we all recognize in reference to common things, an operation by means of which we discern that which is from that which merely seems or appears."[92] Where St. Paul speaks of the spiritual man judging everything (1. Cor. 2,15) Maurice interpreted the passage to mean that it is the reason which is able to distinguish clearly between truth and the appearance of truth, between that which truly is and that which is shadowy and unreal.[93] The reason is capable of unmasking everything that pretends to be true and real but is in fact merely "abstractions", "opinions", "propositions", "systems" and "theories", deduced by the understanding from its sense perceptions.

This power of discernment is not the privilege of a few. It belongs to every man, inasmuch as all are created with the reason as "the universal and human faculty". This is why Maurice was not concerned to argue or substantiate that which he proclaimed. It would commend itself directly to men's reason, which can intuitively discern whether it is true or not. Maurice, then, was consistent in eschewing argument and appealing to "the reason and conscience of mankind" as that which possesses the only criterion for judging the truth of his teaching.[94] It is understandable that Julia Wedgwood felt annoyed when Maurice, instead of giving real arguments for his views, always introduced "the bedridden woman – – as the infallible arbiter of spiritual problems perplexing to the minds of scholars, generally in order to rebuke the

---

91 Cf. *What is Revelation?*, 261: "Our preaching is continually encountered by the argument, 'We are fallen creatures; what can we know of God? How can we ever rise to the perception of the Eternal Truth and Goodness?' Must we not answer that argument by appealing to every witness of the heart, the Conscience, the Reason, – if you will, to every contradiction of Philosophy, – that the spirit of man within us demands the knowledge of God, demands the perception of Eternal Truth and Goodness."

92 *What is Revelation?*, 251.

93 Cf. *What is Revelation?*, 252–3: "Is not the spiritual man, as we are told in that very Epistle, the man who – – will not make his own notions or opinions the standards for men, or the measures of God's acts, – who will receive the things that are freely given him of God – who *therefore* has a faculty of discrimination, which does not suffer him to be deluded by imposters, or to confound the Devil with the true God?"

94 No special references are needed since this appeal to the conscience and reason of mankind occurs repeatedly in Maurice's writings.

pride of our intellect, but nearly as often that she might reflect upon our spiritual exclusiveness".[95] This ironical comment is not wide of the mark. It must, however, be added that this method of appeal stems from Maurice's basic assumptions. Argument and substantiation in support of a certain idea imply the use of the understanding. Its categories of thought would then become the final criterion of truth; the many would be at the mercy of those few who had mastered the use of the understanding and would have to depend upon their "opinions" and "systems" and not upon reality itself.[96] But there can exist no arbiters who, by virtue of the understanding, can decree what should be maintained and what should be rejected regarding true reality. On the contrary, every man possesses in his reason the measure that can intuitively discern what is true and false, real and unreal. To the reason alone all appeals must be made.

When Maurice referred to "the bedridden woman", to ordinary people contending with poverty and disease, want and vice, it was because he thought that, under the pressure of the stern hardships of life, they had gained a knowledge of man's deepest needs and longings, just as they had been taught how powerless the understanding, with its "propositions" and "opinions", is to satisfy them.[97] But the more it is demonstrated that the understanding only gives false solutions because it never penetrates to that which truly is, the more clear-sighted the reason becomes: "One sees it in the liveliest exercise among those who are utterly incapable of drawing conclusions, who are not logicians, who can neither form dogmas nor understand them when they are formed. Among pure, true-hearted women, among honest mechanics, among those upon whose powers of sense and even of reflection death has laid his hand, this power of discerning the truth from the lie, the thing that is from that that is not, dwells often with enviable clearness."[98] Because the discriminatory power of the reason is made more acute in simple people by want and suffering it is sufficient to proclaim the truth to them. It can safely be left to them to decide whether it is true or not.

95 *Nineteenth Century Teachers and Other Essays* (London 1909), 40.
96 See *What is Revelation?*, 161–2.
97 Cf. *Sermons* III, 172: "This process of proving or testing the phenomena of the moral and spiritual world is not exercised as much in schools by learned men – though they have great need of it, and should use all the aids they have for conducting it – as on sick-beds, by men and women who are fighting with sore temptations, and are asking God's help against them"; *Religions*, 233–4: "Experience of sorrow, a sense of weariness and dissatisfaction with all that was visible, the feeling of a good almost within reach and yet never quite attained; above all, the bitter consciousness of something wrong within, which needed to be purged away, of a hollow which needed to be filled up; these were intimations to men of an unseen treasure which they were intended to possess, which only One mightier than they could enable them to possess. Such thoughts and longings would especially haunt the hearts of poor and suffering people; they would be rarer in men who had outward ease and comfort," and *The Conscience*, 96: "All such propositions look very plausible upon paper; bring them to the test of living experience and they melt away."
98 *What is Revelation?*, 251. Cf. also *Sacrifice*, 103: "It was not in the schools, from any illuminated or initiated teachers, it was in their closets when they had to confess that all their illuminations and high conceits had failed, when they felt as if they had no standing-ground at all, when they were on the brink of despair, that these truths appeared to them as solid and eternal resting-places for themselves and for all."

Thus, we have seen that Maurice, like Coleridge, maintained that man possesses a faculty, the reason, by which he can attain a clear and direct knowledge of God and the ultimate principles of existence, *that which is*. This concept is based upon a Platonic idea of reality. However, there is a fundamental difference between Maurice and Plato. Plato understood νοῦς as that which is divine in man, his necessary affinity with true being. Maurice rejected this view as implying a fusion of God and man. He had to interpret the reason and its functioning in accordance with his basic conviction that man is created to depend upon God for everything. Therefore the reason, though created to contemplate reality, is not in itself capable of achieving this goal. It is always completely dependent upon God's revealing self-communication. The reason only truly exists and lives when it forgets itself in the vision of "the absolute Reason", a term Maurice uses for God as the ultimate source of its knowledge.[99] The reason in itself is death, darkness, and complete ignorance, not because it is enslaved by sin and finite things, but because this is its true state in accordance with God's eternal will. It lives a true life when it reaches out towards God and lets Him grant it true knowledge.[100] Despite this important modification of the Platonic conception of νοῦς the fact nevertheless remains that Maurice retained its fundamental structure. He assumed it to be self-evident that man is not a finite being, bounded by time and space, but that he is destined to know and contemplate the eternal world, *that which is* – to know the living God.

3. The Conscience

For Maurice every man also possesses "the conscience", a term used alongside "the will", "the heart", "the reason"[101] and even "the spirit".[102] The conscience is inextricably connected with the "I"[103] and describes that which is truly human, "the

---

99 Cf. *The Kingdom of Christ* I, 179: "Does it [the reason] not – – demand that which is homogeneous to itself? Does it not demand an absolute Reason? And if there be such an absolute Reason to which the reason in man looks up, a real Being, is it more consistent to believe that the reason found him out, or that he revealed himself to the reason?" Another title Maurice used to describe God was "the Being, the essential Reason" (*ibid.*).

100 It might seem that Maurice ascribed to the reason the power to distinguish between truth and its appearance, but even here it is in fact God Himself who, through the reason, conducts the Socratic dialogue. As Maurice put it: "God teaches me to question, that I may separate the one from the other, that I may not accept Opinions for Realities" (*What is Revelation?*, 200).

101 Cf., e. g., *The Gospel of St. John*, 9: "They [the words of God] addressed themselves to the wills, hearts, consciences of man; into these only could they enter"; *What is Revelation?*, 107: "Is it, as the word [revelation] seems to intimate, the actual unveiling of a Person to the conscience, heart, reason of human beings?", and *The Prophets*, 263–4: "I know that there is a conscience and reason within me which say, 'Such a One there *must* be'."

102 See *Sacrifice*, 194.

103 Cf. *The Kingdom of Christ* (1838) I, 226: "the conscience is essentially that which causes each men to feel that he is a distinct person."

73

man".[104] Hence it is common to all men. Just as appeal can be made to the reason, so it can be made to the conscience. [105]

It is because of the reason and the conscience that men are men and not brutes. Maurice can use the terms indiscriminately as synonyms of humanity. Yet they are quite distinct: "if there is a faculty which speaks of what *is* right or wrong, there must be one which speaks of that which *is* true and false. The faculties are clearly not identical; one has relation to me, to what *I* do and think; the other belongs to the region – – of the absolute."[106] In other words, the reason deals with the knowledge of that which truly is, whereas the conscience is occupied with the question of what is right for man to do. Although each of the two faculties has its own function, they are related so intimately that the denial of one faculty necessarily leads to the denial of the other. They stand and fall together.[107]

Through the conscience man meets the demand to do right, a demand which is inseparably bound up with his "I" as a personal will, responsible for his acts.[108] Hence the conscience and man's "I" constitute two different aspects of the same thing.[109] When the conscience is alive, man is called forth as a distinct "I" who must take the sole responsibility for his actions.[110] Man's conscience always confronts him with the demand to do what is right, accusing and convicting him of sin when

---

104 Cf. *The Conscience*, 196: "he must be reminded that the Conscience in him is the man in him; he cannot divide himself from it."

105 Cf. *The Conscience*, 90: "There is a Conscience in each of them, whether he owns it or not. Give him credit for it; appeal to it; let him keep his theory along with it, if he likes, and if he can."

106 *Sequel*, 180.

107 Cf. *Sequel*, 180–1: "But there is so close an affinity between their processes, they blend so curiously and intricately, that it is scarcely possible for a man of logical and coherent mind, who is convinced of the non-existence of the general judge, to recognize, for actual use, the existence of a personal judge. – – All I mean is, that the non-recognition of a Reason which takes account of what is, as distinct from what appears, involves the non-recognition of a Conscience which affirms this to be right for me and that to be wrong."

108 Cf. *The Conscience*, 31: "we should find [no] more exact account of a conscientious man than this, He is one who is always considering what he ought or ought not to do; – – there is [no] more exact description of the Conscience than this, It is that in me which says, I ought or I ought not."

109 Cf. *Life* II, 578: "The conscience is not a part of my soul, but is I myself. Parting with it, I lose not like Chamisso's hero my shadow, but the substance from which my shadow is cast"; *The Conscience*, 19: "['Consciousness' and 'Conscience'] involve that duplicity [I and myself], they associate it with all my acts and thoughts, they remind me that I am stooping to the condition of a brute, not asserting my rights as a man, if I disavow it," and p. 30: "it is this conscience which binds the different parts of my existence together, which assures me that the past still belongs to me. It seems very terrible. But banish it, and there is no drama, no biography, no history: human existence becomes the dreariest blank; men only brutal."

110 Cf. *The Conscience*, 96–7: "There is that in me which asks for the Right, for that which ought to have dominion over me; there is that in me which says emphatically, 'This is not that Right, this ought not to have dominion over me.' – – But always there will be a witness in me that what I have made or any one has made, is not what I ought to serve; that is not the Right, not what I am seeking for, not what is seeking me."

he performs unrighteous deeds.[111] It is "the adversary who is within us,"[112] because there is "that in me which passes judgment on my own acts and states of mind, and pronounces some to be right and some to be wrong."[113]

Maurice thought that these observations expressed the common experience of mankind. However, he was bound to enter into a closer analysis of the workings of the conscience because of the great importance and influence of Joseph Butler's investigations in this field.

Maurice held Joseph Butler in great esteem as a thinker. Butler pursued the right method since he wished to stick entirely to facts. All human systems and theories were to be rejected, so that the facts themselves could be studied and disclose the truth.[114] Applying the inductive method to the study of human life Butler came to the conclusion that man has a conscience and that it functions as "the lordly faculty". This faculty recognizes what is right and bids man follow it – therefore Butler felt obliged to speak of "the Supremacy of the Conscience". Despite his grateful respect for Butler[115] Maurice could, however, not fully approve of Butler's analysis of the conscience. It was incomplete, and so his conclusions were insufficient and even misleading.

It was Butler's fundamental error that he treated the conscience as an independent self-sufficient entity.[116] Hence he was bound to describe the conscience as a faculty able to issue laws by itself. The fatal consequence of this view is that man is regarded

111 Cf. *The Prayer-Book*, 351–2: "For each man says within himself, Are not these debts *mine* in the strictest sense? Are they not obligations which *I* have contracted, and which *I* have violated? Upon me lies a burden which I cannot shift upon any other creature – the burden of duties unfulfilled, words unspoken, or spoken violently and untruly; of holy relationships neglected; of days wasted for ever; of evil thoughts once cherished, which are ever appearing now as fresh as when they were first admitted into the heart; of talents cast away; of affections in myself, or in others, trifled with; of light within turned to darkness. So speaks the conscience; so speaks or has spoken the conscience of each man."

112 *The Epistles of St. John*, 213.

113 *Sequel*, 180.

114 Cf. *Theological Essays*, 61: "he [Butler] is pursuing precisely the same end as the physical inquirer, by an inductive process as nearly as possible the counterpart of his. He is as unwilling to accept hasty generalisations as every disciple of Bacon must be; he is as ready to look at facts and test them; he seeks to be delivered from vague hypotheses, that he may feel the ground upon which he is actually standing," and *What is Revelation?*, 171: "Our frivolity, our delight in our conceptions rather than in the observation of facts and the reflection upon them, *this* kind of danger was constantly present to his mind."

115 Cf. *Theological Essays*, 56: "I should find it difficult to say how much I honour Butler or how much I owe to his discourses on Human Nature," and *Sequel*, 144: "And because I am convinced that all our deepest experiences, – all our experiences of the struggle between right and wrong, between the apparent good and the real good, – are common experiences which the peasant and the scholar share together, – it is therefore that I do not think Butler was uttering vain and idle words when he put forth his idea of Human Nature as inseparable from the idea of a Conscience."

116 Cf. *Sequel*, 182: "in Butler it [the idea of the Conscience] was inevitably incomplete, not from a fault in him, but because he was criticizing the mind of man from its own ground, not contemplating it from a higher ground." See also p. 183 and *The Conscience*, 73.

as his own master and law-giver.[117] In fact, when Butler spoke of "the Supremacy of the Conscience" and defined it as "the lordly faculty" belonging to the nature of man, he deified man. Furthermore, if the conscience is described as "the lordly faculty", endowed with absolute authority, it will be necessary to uphold its integrity and inviolability. But this runs contrary to experience: the conscience is not invulnerable and constant in its activity.[118] It can be subjected to sin and enslaved to the visible world. Since Butler had not taken these facts into account, his exposition of the conscience was untenable. Either we must deny that there exists any authority that can rule over man,[119] or, in order to assert its existence, we must both deify man and close our eyes to the antinomies that characterize its workings.

However, this dilemma can be avoided, and a true description of the nature of the conscience be reached on the basis of the observation that conscience and consciousness are related.[120] The conscience is not autonomous but must be described as a 'consciousness' of something else. In other words, the conscience is intended to exist in fellowship with another being. We arrive at a true understanding of the conscience only when we view it in the light of the object of which it is a 'consciousness'.[121] Thus, instead of speaking in Butlerian terms of "the Supremacy of the Conscience", the appropriate description must be "the Conscience of Supremacy", which indicates that the conscience is not self-existing and divine but has consciousness of a power which alone has authority to rule over it.[122] It does not possess any power in itself; it only bears witness to One above it who has sovereign power to

117 Cf. *The Conscience*, 161: "If the Conscience is a *property* of mine, and if it implies judgment, superintendence, direction, I must be my own judge, superintendent, director. Then *jura nego mihi nata*. They are created by me, not for me," and *Theological Essays*, 57: "Is not every practical student of Butler obliged to put the question to himself, 'This faculty belongs to my nature, then – What to *me?* Is the conscience *mine?* Do I govern it, or does it govern *me?*'."

118 Cf. *Sequel*, 182: "there are paralogisms and antinomies of the Conscience as there are of the Reason."

119 Cf. *What is Revelation?*, 443–4: "What has been said and felt and suffered by those who have found that in themselves, that is, in their flesh, dwelleth no good thing, has worked more than all the logic and ridicule of Mr. Rogers and Mr. Mansel – though these may contribute their quota – to make men distrust that testimony to which Butler attached so much worth."

120 Cf. *The Conscience*, 148: "Above all, I wished to give the word *Conscience* its original import, to restore that link between it and Consciousness, which is almost inevitably severed when it is treated as a faculty of Human Nature." See also p. 124–5.

121 Cf. *Theological Essays*, 57: "The great facts [of the Conscience] to which Butler bore so brave a witness cannot, I think, be explained while we regard them *merely* as facts in man's nature. The more we look into them, the more they imply an ascent out of that nature, – a necessity in man to acknowledge that which is above it, that which is above himself. When we take in this necessity, as implied in our constitution, the difficulties which beset the most full and masterly explanation that can be given of these facts gradually disappear."

122 Cf. *The Conscience*, 149: "'The Conscience of Supremacy' may seem to be no substitute for the 'Supremacy of Conscience', but the very opposite of it. Nevertheless it may show us *what* 'judgment, direction, superintendency is involved in the very idea of the Conscience', in *what* sense 'it may have a right to govern the world'."

command.[123] Likewise it is misleading to speak of "the laws of the Conscience" as though the conscience was able to create laws. But as "the Conscience of Laws", that is, as the consciousness of laws, it bears testimony to the fixed, unchangeable moral laws which only the Lord of the conscience can promulgate. The conscience does not chain man to himself and make him self-sufficient and independent. Instead it is the organ through which God speaks, commands, and judges.[124] It avows and testifies to the One whom man must obey as his true Lord.[125]

Only when it is understood that that which the conscience proclaims does not proceed from it but comes to it from without, is it possible to give proper emphasis to its greatness. If it is treated as autonomous it falls victim to finite things, human authorities, and man's own delusions. When it is seen to be the organ in man through which God reveals the eternal laws of His kingdom and claims man's responsible obedience,[126] then we see the celestial and divine origin of the conscience.[127] Once it was established that God, as the Lord of man, speaks through the conscience, Maurice had no scruples about describing it as "the lordly faculty", as Butler had done, nor about calling it the noblest organ in man.[128] Yet this dignity is its due only insofar as it has fellowship with God and subjects itself to Him.[129]

The idea of the greatness of the conscience is, however, in no way incompatible with the assertion that man has "a corrupt or evil Conscience", since this statement

123 Cf. *The Conscience*, 160: "the Conscience in itself has no authority; its authority begins when it goes out of itself, its supremacy consists in its abdication of supremacy."

124 Cf. *The Epistles of St. John*, 12: "the conscience is not a power of its own, but is a witness to us of some One speaking to us, commanding us, judging us," and *What is Revelation?*, 444: "Does not what was said of Consciousness apply with deepest emphasis to Conscience? Is not that the witness – not of some part of the man, but of the man himself – to a Word nigh him, even at his heart; to a divine Teacher from whose sentence he cannot fly; who judges him, whose judgment he owns, even when he is resisting it most, to be according to truth?"

125 Cf. *Theological Essays*, 59: "The name Conscience would seem to import, not a power which rules in us, but rather our perception and recognition of some power very near to us, which has a claim on our obedience. – – But if I am entitled to say, 'There is a Lord over my inner man to whom I am bound, apart from whom I cannot exercise the functions which belong to me as a man, according to the law of my being,' conscience can be restored to its simple and natural signification; it does not demand sovereignty, but pays homage."

126 Cf. *The Prophets*, VII: "the conscience in man which God has created to bear witness of what He is and of what Man, His image, is intended to be," and *Sermons* IV, 170: "when we speak of the conscience in a man, we mean that which God has created to hear His voice, and to answer it."

127 Cf. *The Conscience*, 161: "if there is that in me which is higher than anything I call my own; if there is that in me which carries me beyond myself – if the Conscience is this, – then I may indeed speak loftily of it; for it testifies of every man in whom it dwells, that *Igneus est illi vigor et coelestis origo*. He may have a clothing of earth, he may have wrapped himself closely in it. But there is in him a fire which the earth did not kindle, there are the signs of a parentage which must be divine."

128 See *Theological Essays*, 59.

129 Cf. *Theological Essays*, 60: "Till the true Lord of the conscience has made Himself known to it, of necessity it must go about seeking rest and finding none. Every false king will assume dominion over it; as it bows to the impostor, it will become beclouded in its judgments."

simply means that man has a consciousness of the fact that he is corrupt and evil. In reality it presupposes "the Conscience of Supremacy". Man can refuse to follow his conscience and deny its sovereignty, but this does not destroy it since its force rests not upon its inherent perfection but upon its being the consciousness of the supreme will of God, who speaks through it. Man can only be judged sinful and disobedient because the conscience in him is "a Conscience of Supremacy". The more the conscience, as the consciousness of a sovereign power outside man, asserts itself, the stronger is his conscieneess of his own depravity.[130]

So Maurice believed that he had brought Butler's analysis of the nature of the conscience to a satisfactory conclusion. He never denied that man possesses a conscience which confronts him with an absolutely binding authority, but this conscience is in itself neither perfect nor autonomous. Its very structure demands that God reveal Himself and proclaim His will to it. It works properly only when, in trusting dependence, it lives by God's revelations. When this has been said, its existence cannot be too strongly stressed. The conscience witnesses that man is not chained to the world of time and space but is created to hear God's will directly, as a responsible "I".

4. Christ as the Light of Man and the Word of God

Maurice described Christ as the Head of every man in order to emphasize that every man always stands in Christ and owes his entire existence and being to Him. Alongside the idea of Christ as the Head of man, he also spoke repeatedly of Christ as the true Light, "which lighteth every man that cometh into the world" (St. John 1,4, 9).

There is a close analogy between the visible sun and Christ as Light, just as there exists a necessary analogy between the visible and the invisible world.[131] As the sun gives life to the visible creation, so Christ quickens and calls forth true humanity in

---

130 Cf. *The Conscience*, 161–2: "Once admit that the Conscience is that in a man which points to what is above him, which declares the supremacy of a right that he did not mould and cannot alter, and the meaning of these expressions [a corrupt or evil conscience] becomes frightfully evident. – – The more there is of Conscience in me – the more I confess a higher law – the greater will be my degradation and the sense of it. – – the depth of this degradation is measured by the elevation of which I have the Conscience." In the same way Maurice dealt with the question of the free and the enslaved conscience. He cannot accept the term "the Liberty of Conscience", as it may suggest that "the Conscience left to itself is always grand and glorious, incapable of debasement or degradation" (p. 126). On the other hand, it is right to speak of "the Conscience of Liberty", since the conscience is then understood as that which bears witness to the freedom and deliverance bestowed upon it by its Lord. This can exist perfectly well alongside "the Conscience of Slavery", for its witness will awaken the feeling of slavery: "there *always* will be a Conscience of Slavery where there is a Conscience of Liberty" (*ibid.*).

131 Cf. *What is Revelation?*, 94: "May not all sensible things, by a necessity of their nature, be testifying to us of that which is nearest to us, of that which it most concerns us to know, of the mysteries of our own life, and of God's relation to us?" The visible world, as an image of the eternal heavenly order and harmony, can be a sign and a symbol of true reality.

man.[132] And just as the sun gives light to dispel the darkness and to allow man to see clearly, so Christ dispels the darkness of man's ignorance and gives the clear light of knowledge by which he can perceive the true nature of things and distinguish truth from its counterfeit.[133] Again, the sun shines upon all men and gives life, light, and clearness to all; so Christ, as "the Universal Light",[134] is always near to every man, and so every man can be exhorted to turn to the light and open himself to Christ, shining in him.[135] Thus the idea of Christ as "the light that lighteth every man" is simply another way of expressing what is implied in Christ as the Head of every man.

But Christ, as the Head of man and the universal Light, at the same time is "the living Word", who is with God and is God eternally.[136] One cannot study Maurice long before realizing how greatly he valued St. John's Gospel. For him it provided the key to the true understanding of the entire history of the Bible and of mankind. This Gospel points to the living Christ as the Divine Word, who created the universe and is near to man, always imparting life, goodness, and righteousness.[137] As God's eternal Word, Christ speaks to every man and calls all men to live in con-

132 Cf. *Sermons* IV, 61: "Christ proclaimed Himself to be as much in contact with the hearts and understandings of men as the sun is with their bodily senses, – to be as mighty in unfolding the true human life as that is in awakening the vitality of the vegetable and animal creation."

133 Cf. *The Gospel of St. John*, 136: "The Light entered into the separate hearts, and showed them their dark passages. And yet it was a common Light; it gave them a sense of being men, which they had never had before. And, moreover, it was a light which scattered confusions, ignorance, falsehoods, that had been dwelling undisturbed within them, or that had only been disturbed by what they felt must have been a ray of this same Light."

134 *What is Revelation?*, 94.

135 Cf. *Christmas Day*, 7: "This light is with us, above us, at every hour and moment," and *Theological Essays*, 30: "There is a light within you, close to you. Do you know it? Are you coming to it? Are you desiring that it should penetrate you through and through? Oh, turn to it! Turn from these idols that are surrounding you, – from the confused, dark world of thoughts within you! It will reveal yourself to you! It will reveal the world to you!" It is not surprising that Maurice approved of the idea of the inward Light of the Quakers. His criticism of the Quakers is limited to a protest that they never consistently carried out their fundamental conception of Christ as the inward Light. (For Maurice's attitude to the Quaker doctrine of the inward Light, see *The Kingdom of Christ* I, 45–74).

136 Cf. *The Kingdom of Christ* I, 50: "Christ, the Living Word, the Universal Light", and *Christmas Day*, 5–6: "This unseen Teacher of men, this source of our light and our life, was perfectly one with Him whom no man hath seen or can see; the brightness of his glory, the express image of his person."

137 Cf. *The Gospel of St. John*, 121: "For that Gospel begins from the principle that Christ, the living Word of God, is the life and light of men, the life and light of all men. If that is true, it must have been the work of the Son of Man, of the Word made flesh, to let all manner of people know that He was the source and spring of their life, – that apart from Him they had none", and *Life* I, 253: "St. John's [Gospel] is emphatically the Christian Gospel, exhibiting the relation of Christ as the Head of humanity to Christ as the Son of God." See also *The Gospel of St. John*, 36, 470 and *The Epistles of St. John*, 131.

formity with the truth He proclaims.[138] That is why Maurice pointed repeatedly to the ever present voice in man which speaks to him even when he believes himself to be forsaken and in the power of evil.[139] Because man is created to live in fellowship with Christ, he knows intuitively that it is the voice of his true Lord which is calling him to life and truth.[140]

However, this revelation is imparted to the reason and the conscience of man, which is why Maurice so strongly maintained that they do not possess the truth but are created to live in dependence upon Christ and to receive the truth from Him. But just as it must be vigorously asserted that Christ brings the knowledge of truth to man, so it is necessary to emphasize that man has been created with the reason and the conscience to enable him to know and receive the light that Christ gives, and to hear and understand when Christ speaks. Man must be as his archetype, Christ, who knows the Father and His mind and will. This is more than a theoretical possibility. The existence of the reason and the conscience demonstrates that man transcends the world of time and space and is enabled to perceive God directly as the ultimate reality and, thereby, the truth of his own existence. However, the reason and the conscience can function properly only when it is realized that Christ, as the universal Light and the eternal Word, is the necessary foundation of their existence.

Maurice distinguished between the reason and the conscience as the two faculties in man which deal with the knowledge of absolute reality and of absolute moral obligation respectively. But, since Christ is the only One in whose fellowship man is created to live, there can be no dualism between knowledge and morality. To know that which truly is, reality itself, is to know God. But the absolute Being, "He who Is", is the personal God of absolute love and righteousness. As He is the Creator and Lord of man, to know God as He is, inevitably leads to the demand that man be obedient to God's love and righteousness. Conversely, insight into man's absolute obligation leads to the knowledge of God, in whom the foundation and purpose of all things are to be seen. When knowledge of *that which is* and of that which is right

138 Cf. *Sermons* VI, 73–4: "You are to think that every man who, amidst whatever confusion, is striving to be faithful and righteous, is obeying a word speaking in his heart – and because that is God's word and not man's, will be led by Him into all truth", and *The Gospel of St. John*, 18: "this Word must be a Friend, a Person; One who could work with with him, reprove him, illuminate him."

139 Cf. *The Gospel of St. John*, 288–9: "Truly, the voice of him who was a liar and murderer from the beginning is speaking to us and in us all, – is tempting us all down into death. But the voice of the true Shepherd is also speaking to us, inviting us, claiming us as His sheep. And there is not one who has not at times heard that voice, – who has not been sure that he had a right to follow it, and that no man or devil had a right to say, 'Thou art not His; thou hast not a claim on Him; and He does not desire thee to follow Him'," and *The Patriarchs*, 59: "Each of us, I think, must, at some time or other, have felt the reality of the first words of this narrative [Gen. 3,8–9]. He must have said within himself, 'Such a voice of an unseen being have I heard speaking down in the depths of my heart, awakening me to a consciousness of His reality and His personality, and of my own'."

140 Cf. *The Prophets*, 270: "The voice which spoke to them was mighty because the heart and conscience confessed that it was a divine voice," and *The Kingdom of Christ* (1838) II, 2: "His [Fox's] doctrine of the essential connection between man, as man, and the Divine Word, I have all along contended to be involved in the very idea of Christianity and of a Christian Church."

80

is considered in relation to the reason and the conscience, they appear to fall apart, but in Christ, the image of God and the archetype of man, they are by inner necessity united.[141] Because being, love and righteousness constitute an indivisible unity in God, the distinction between the reason and the conscience disappears and we can understand why Maurice used them as synonyms. All is based on the knowledge of God, which Christ imparts to man.[142]

As truth is always directly revealed by Christ Himself to be received by the reason, revelation is universal and encompasses the whole history of mankind.[143] That is why Maurice protested against the traditional distinction between Natural and Revealed Theology. He was well aware that the distinction had been established to ensure reverence for the Bible and to safeguard the uniqueness of its message.[144] Nevertheless, it actually caused the Biblical testimony to be distorted so that revelation came to be identified with the Scriptures themselves, with something susceptible to sense perception.[145] Furthermore, the concept of Natural Theology is unscriptural because it implies that man, by himself, can attain a certain amount of knowledge of God through deduction from nature or from his own life. This is a

---

141 Cf. *Sequel*, 201: "In this way those two faculties or perceptions, which are necessarily diverse, and appear sometimes as if they could not well be brought into harmony when they are looked at as faculties of ours, become united and harmonize by that light which falls upon them from above. Each finds that which meets its own need. The man in whom they dwell is no longer a dislocated being, no longer a mere philosophical compound; he is a living unity." See also p. 200–1.

142 Cf. *What is Revelation?*, 117: "the knowledge of God [is] assumed to be the ground of all good to man. Grace and peace proceed from that knowledge. Whatever belongs to life and godliness, whatever leads to glory and virtue, comes through that knowledge. -- Knowledge of God is that which enables us to become *'partakers of the divine Nature'* [2. Pet. 1,4]."

143 Cf. *What is Revelation?*, 91: "What is eternal is mysterious, inconceivable. Our Lord admits that it is. He speaks of *mysteries*. But He speaks of knowing mysteries. He means apparently what St. Paul meant when he says, 'Eye hath not seen, ear hath not heard, neither hath it entered into the heart of man to conceive the things which God hath prepared for them that love Him' [I. Cor. 2,9]. But He affirms that the Disciples – taken from the commonest order of men, sharing in their ignorance – have a capacity for *knowing* these mysteries, these eternal things which cannot be conceived." The gist of Maurice's exegesis is that the mysteries are always revealed to the reason but remain hidden to the understanding.

144 Cf. *The Word Revelation*, 5: "Modern usage has determined that the name [of revelation] shall denote the lessons which we receive from the Bible, as contrasted with those which we receive from the natural world, or from our own conscience and reason. To depart from that usage is, it is said, to show that we do not care for the testimony of the Bible; that we wish to substitute for it some theories or conclusions of our own."

145 Cf. *The Word Revelation*, 14, where it is stated that revelation is not "a communication from without in letters and propositions such as the eye and ear could take in. But a Revelation of Christ, the Son of God, by the Father in Heaven, a discovery to the man himself of his Lord and King. Surely on that rock Christ would build His Church; not on a man, not on the teaching of a book, but on the Son of God discovered to men as the ground of their thoughts, their life, their fellowship."

direct denial of the fact that no man knows God's nature and will unless it is revealed to him. The false distinction between Natural Theology and Revealed Theology need, however, never arise if man acknowledges Christ as the ever acting Divine Word, giving him true knowledge of God regardless of his own efforts or merit.[146] Nature, the life of man and the history of mankind remain a closed book until Christ unveils their true character and imparts a kowledge of *that which is*.[147]

Since Christ always reveals the truth about God and the creation, the entire history of the human race, even the life of every man, belongs to the history of revelation and is a witness to that which Christ makes known to men. Thus the history of philosophy testifies how Christ has imparted truth to philosophers, and how this truth has struggled with darkness and sought to penetrate it.[148] The belief that every man through Christ is under "an actual Divine guidance"[149] involves not only the duty of being attentive to all that is narrated in the annals of history, but also the duty of having a genuine respect for the convictions of one's fellow-men in order to learn from them. Even if they are often mixed with falsehoods which may even threaten to distort and eclipse the revealed truth which has prompted them, man must take his fellow-men seriously, discover what they really have at heart and be willing to learn from them.[150]

146 Cf. *The Contemporary Review* XIV ("Grammar of Assent"), 170: "I fully admit, then, that the nations had, as Dr. Newman says they had, perceptions of God and of His purposes; but I submit to St. Paul's decision that their perceptions came from a *revelation* of Him – a continued, daily, hourly revelation – not from the nature of things or from the nature of men acting independently of a revelation," and *Introductory Lectures Delivered at Queen's College, London, by F. D. Maurice, C. Kingsley, and Others* (London 1849), ("On Theology), 248: "I do not feel able to speak of Natural and Revealed Religion, or Theology, meaning by the former that Religion or Theology which is contained in the world around us; and by the latter, that which is contained in the Scriptures. This distinction, it seems to me, is set at nought by history, by our own consciences, and by the Bible itself. Nothing is more clear than this fact: that the heathens received Nature or the outward world as a revelation. They believed that invisible powers were manifesting themselves, or that *the* Invisible Power was manifesting Himself in the forms of nature. They did not and could not separate Nature from Revelation. They could not suppose that they were merely finding out evidences of a Divinity in the world; they felt that, in some way or other, He must be speaking to them in it." See also p. 249.

147 Cf. *What is Revelation?*, 95–6: "these secret processes of Nature, – – the transactions of human beings, had been, from the foundation of the world, the lesson-books out of which God was instructing men, and revealing Himself to them."

148 Cf. *Moral and Metaphysical Philosophy* I, XVI: "And as I think these philosophers were not always in error, but had glimpses of precious truths, I believe they were not without revelation", and p. XXXI: "To one who accepts the teaching of the old Hebrew, – *'In the beginning was the Word, and the Word was with God, and the Word was God. In Him was life, and His life was the light of men'* – every conception that men have formed of a Divine Wisdom who was illuminating them, whatever shape it may have taken, with whatever local or material accidents it may have been clothed, must be profoundly interesting, not for its falsehoods, but for its truth. The study of the divided forms under which the light has broken in upon the human heart and intellect – of the efforts of the senses to draw it down into themselves – of the corruptions which have darkened it – will be pursued by one who takes this clue with him, reverently, in sympathy and in fear."

149 *Moral and Metaphysical Philosophy* I, XV.

150 See *Sequel*, 189, 197–8, and *Sermons* I, 169.

Thus Maurice took the view, simply and practically, that Christ, as the Head of every man, is the Universal Light and the Divine Word, always enlightening man and revealing God to him, conducting the Socratic dialogue, which tests and sifts all that surrounds him, distinguishing truth and its counterfeit and thereby leading him to a true knowledge of his own life and the whole creation. Because Christ is present to every man, nobody lives without knowledge of God,[151] and since man possesses the reason and the conscience, he is able, as a responsible "I", to hear, to perceive, and to live in the truth which Christ reveals to him.

151 Cf. *Life* I, 266–7: "We know that the Word of Wisdom does dwell in all; in those who kick against that very doctrine as in those who receive it; the reception of the doctrine being, indeed, in *their* account everything, not in ours. To make them aware of its presence, to bring them to submit to it, and for this end to sympathise with whatever light there is in them, however hidden under dark notions of life, however stifled by unkind and uncharitable surmises, must be our aim."

Chapter III

THE HUMAN ORDER AND ITS FELLOWSHIPS

The analysis of Maurice's conception of man as a spirit might lead to the conclusion that man's true lot is to yearn for release from the changeable and transient world in order to live in the vision and contemplation of God in the eternal world. However, the idea of the heaven-aspiring flight of the spirit is sharply repudiated by Maurice.[1] God, being self-sacrificing love, finds no pleasure in solitude and self-sufficiency. His sole delight is in creating, in communing with and imparting love to His creatures. Therefore it is inconceivable that man be intended to enjoy God individually and selfishly. To see God is to participate in perfect love which never seeks its own.

Man is created in the image and likeness of Christ, who submitted to God's love and sacrificed Himself in His service in order to become the brother and servant of every man. As Christ is the archetype of man, His presence in every man implies that He makes him the brother and servant of his fellow-men, to whom he must give what he himself has received from Christ. He who lives with Christ is led to his fellow-men and, conversely, man is only capable of living a life of fellowship when he receives Christ's self-sacrificing love.[2]

1. The Kingdom of God and the Fellowships of the Human Order

Man is created to live in fellowship not only with Christ but also with his fellow-men. However, he need not seek them out and establish relations with them, since God

1 See, for instance, *The Prayer-Book*, 54, where Maurice stated that the recognition of "the spiritual condition of man" implies "his deliverance from the fetters of time and place", and then goes on to say: "Worship there as much as you please; the more the better. But take care that you do not fly thither to be out of the way of those who live in close alleys, damp cellars, dark garrets. Take care that you are not running from your kind to be easy and comfortable in your own grand thoughts. If you do so, you may worship a spirit of the air, but you will not worship GOD who is a Spirit. You may exalt yourself, but you will not feel that you are a spirit; for a spirit seeks for a real fellowship with all other spirits."

2 Maurice realized that the conception of human life as a life of fellowship was alien to Greek philosophy (see *The Kingdom of Christ* (1838) III, 291: "But perhaps you think that Pagan *philosophy* helps to make this subject [of human relationships] intelligible. Now it happens, that this is just the one point of which ancient philosophy takes scarcely any cognisance. Of the powers of man, his inclinations, destinies, ultimate objects, it may say much that is most interesting and important for us to hear. It may speak even of the struggles of conscience, of the sense of evil, of the desire after good, of the divine element in humanity. It may speak of the necessity to man of something above man, of his unceasing endeavours to apprehend it. On all these points I have never concealed my opinion, that the ancient philosophers were led by the Spirit of God into many deep and precious discoveries, which Christianity interprets and makes practicable, but never for a moment seeks to set aside." But the Greek philosophers have not "perceived the deep meaning of their own human relationships" (p. 292)).

has ordered human life in such a way that the only existence open to man is an existence with his fellow-men. He constituted fellowships in which all individuals are placed and bound together under the law of love.[3]

An analysis of human life clearly demonstrates that man can never be considered in isolation but only in relation to other men. Every person is a son or a daughter, a brother or a sister, a father and a husband, or a mother and a wife. Furthermore every person is a subject in a country whose inhabitants speak the same language and have a common law and government. So nobody can deny that his life is part and parcel of that of a family and a nation and that these fellowships are founded upon human relationships.[4] Thus the sheer facts of ordinary human existence show that man belongs to a Human Order.[5] Similarly, they make it clear that man lives and acts in these fellowships as a distinct person, a responsible "I". He is bound to his fellow-men through human relationships and must follow a different law to that which applies to his relation to the Natural Order.[6]

This Human Order owes nothing to man's efforts and achievements for either its existence or its continuance. God alone created and upholds it with its fellowships of family and nation. Since it embraces all men as spirits, or voluntary beings, it can, in contrast to the Natural Order, be called "a spiritual constitution".[7] Maurice also frequently described the Human Order as belonging to the Kingdom of God. Thus he asserted strongly that God had set up His Kingdom upon earth with the creation

---

3 Cf. *The Prayer-Book*, 380: "All creation is ordered upon this law of mutual dependence and charity."

4 Cf. *The Conscience*, 54–5: "I recur to my old question, 'What am I?' There are a few simple answers to that question which show me that there is an Order in which I am placed, a real order, not an imaginary one – not an order which might be desirable but which exists. I *am* certainly a son, I *am* a brother. I *am* a citizen. Perhaps I *am* a husband, perhaps I *am* a father."

5 Cf. *Social Morality*, 21: "In what region do you find a man who is not born a son, who is not related to a father and mother? It is a fact for me surely, but it is a fact for you and for every man. And if you determine not to take notice of this fact, not to give it precedence of every other, the effect is, that instead of contemplating the world at large you will only contemplate yourself. *You* will be the unit about which all events and persons will revolve. Each man will regard himself as the centre of the universe," and p. 59: "I would not have you think of relations as if they were – what some seem to consider them – the ornaments and embellishments of our existence; additions on the whole, though with many drawbacks, to the sum of its happiness. It is of relations as the core of human society that I speak, as implied not only in its well-being but in its very being."

6 Cf. *The Kingdom of Christ* I, 230: "we are obliged to speak of every man as being in two conditions. He is in a world of objects which offer themselves to his senses, and which his senses may be fitted to entertain. He is a son, perhaps he is a brother. These two states are equally inevitable; they are also perfectly distinct. You cannot by any artifice reduce them under the same law or name. To describe the one you must speak of what we see, or hear, or handle or smell; to describe the other, you must speak of what we are: "I *am* a son", "I *am* a brother". It is impossible therefore to use the word *"circumstances"* in reference to the one state with the same strictness with which you apply it to the other. All the things which I have to do with I naturally and rightly call my circumstances – *they stand round me;* but that which is necessary in an account of myself, seems to be entitled to another name. We commonly call it a *relationship*."

7 *The Kingdom of Christ* I, 231.

of man and that it encompasses family and nation.[8] Men may deny the existence of the Kingdom of God, and seek to escape from its Order, but it endures and is always the sole foundation of all human life without any qualification.[9]

As God accomplished His creative acts in and through Christ, it can also be said that Christ set up His reign at the time of the creation. Christ had created a great human fellowship, which embraces all mankind and in which each individual has his ordered place and function.[10] Christ is not only the Head of every man, but "the Head of the universal Family".[11] Because the Human Order receives its existence from Christ and finds its harmony and unity in Christ, it is rightly called the Body of Christ.[12]

The conviction that every man is placed in a well-ordered, harmonious Human Order was at the bottom of Maurice's "system-phobia".[13] He feared all attempts to reshape existing society. He consistently waged bitter war against all organisations which put up a political, social, or ecclesiastical programme to be realised.[14] All such

8 Cf. *The Prayer-Book*, 310–1: "Our Lord speaks of His Kingdom, or His Father's Kingdom, not as if it were to set aside that constitution of the universe, of which men had seen the tokens in family and national institutions, of which they had dreamed when they thought of a higher and more general fellowship; but as if it were that very constitution in the fulness of its meaning and power. He who is the ground of the world's order, He in whom all things consist, reveals Himself that we may know what its order and consistency are, how all disorder and inconsistency have arisen from the discontent and rebellion of our wills."

9 Cf. *The Acts of the Apostles*, 225: "The Kingdom of God was never, for them, merely a Kingdom in the future, or in the present, or in the past. It was the Kingdom of Him who is, and who was, and who is to come, the Eternal Kingdom. They could speak of it as surrounding men, and as acting upon them when they were most unaware of its presence, when they were most trying to live independent of it."

10 Cf. *Christmas Day*, 190–1: "He [Christ] had made them feel that they could not live apart from each other; He had formed them into families; He had established the bonds of fatherhood and brotherhood, of wife and husband; He had taught them to feel the need of laws, and had given them laws, and had brought them into neighbourhoods and cities, and had set kings over them – –."

11 *The Prayer-Book*, 55.

12 Cf. *The Unity of the New Testament*, 536: "So the truth dawned upon him [St. Paul], that all men, of whatever race or tongue, do constitute one body in Him – – they are one, by the law of their creation, and become actually one, when they believe that law and submit to it," and *Sermons* I, 212–3: "But His [Christ's] blessed order stands firm, however little we abide in it. The affinities in the world of human beings, like the affinities in the natural world, have all been constituted by Him, are all maintained by Him. The unity between the different parts of the frame in each man is not so mysterious as the unity between the different members of the body politic. The latter is certainly indestructible, whatever may happen to the former. And this, because our polity is in the Heavens. We are made one in Christ. Therefore it is that the dream which each man dreams, that he is the centre of the world, and that he can refer all its movements to himself, is so monstrous and ridiculous."

13 *Life* II, 43.

14 Cf. *Life* II, 44: "God's order seems to me more than ever the antagonist of man's systems; Christian Socialism is in my mind the assertion of God's order. – – Every attempt to hide it under a great machinery, call it Organisation of Labour, Central Board, or what you like, I must protest against as hindering the gradual development of what I regard as a divine purpose, as an attempt to create a new constitution of society, when what we want is that the old constitution should exhibit its true functions and energies. For that distinction I exist only to testify."

attempts are evil, without exception, because they presuppose that the world as being without God, as a meaningless chaos, receives structure and shape only when men provide it on the basis of their own schemes and principles. This is practical atheism, a denial of the fact that God has already structured human life through His acts of creation. God's Order does not need to be improved by man. Man's function is to recognize its existence and let it assert itself as true and good.

Man is sadly mistaken if he believes that he can take better care of his fellow-men through his own systems and policies than God does through His created Order. All new attempts to create fellowship among men only mean, in reality, that man does not care for his actually existing fellow-men but selects his own fellowship. The criterion for this choice will, in the last instance, always be whether men approve of the systems and policies in question.[15] Thus all system-builders who do not acknowledge the existence of the Divine Order deny God and forsake their fellow-men. They make themselves, and their own groupings, the centre of the world. But when they believe themselves to have the power and the ability to create human society, they are deluded. As man does not possess any creative power all their attempts are doomed at the outset to failure and ruin. The only true reformer of society is he who sweeps all human systems and constructions aside in order to unveil the Divine Order which is established in Christ.

As God has established here on earth His Kingdom as a living fellowship which encompasses all men, Maurice naturally opposed any view which made men believe that the earth is without God and left to follow its own maxims. He protested strongly against those who made selfishness the constitutive element of human fellowship.[16] Above all he directed his polemics against the contemporary religious world, which, in his opinion, was chiefly responsible for the promotion of a secularized view of the world and human society.

15 Cf. *Social Morality*, 59–60: "If we do not take account of those societies in which we must exist, we shall attach a very disproportionate value to those in which we *may* exist. The Class and the Club will be superlatively precious and dear as the Family is lost out of sight. Men will recognize themselves more and more by their badges and colours when they cease to care about the ties of blood. So with all our talk about the greatest happiness of the greatest number, the number to which we attach any real importance will be after all a very small one. The greatest number for which we shall care will be that which uses our shibboleths, which favours our sect. If we can persuade the greatest number to identify their greatest happiness with those shibboleths and that sect we shall pay it honour; if the greatest number should have some other conception of happiness we shall regard it with as much contempt as the most exclusive haters of the common herd."

16 Here Maurice was thinking primarily of those who share Thomas Hobbes' view of society, according to which man is fundamentally an isolated individual who, egoistically, considers the formation of states to be the only way of not falling a prey to the *bellum omnium contra omnes* (see *Social Morality*, 329–30). He was thinking also of the Manchester School, which maintained that the stability of society depended upon the free play of individual forces, and that the man who seeks his own ends will at the same time serve the well-being of society. Maurice could not agree that man should be regarded as an independent creature, whose only maxim is selfishness, and that this should also be regarded as the fundamental principle of the rise and continued existence of society (see *Sermons* III, 220). This fallacious view involved a striking denial of God, who created the Divine Order with love as the fundamental law of human life.

This happens when it is maintained that the Gospel only deals with the individual and his personal salvation. Then Christ is reduced to being the Saviour of individual persons with the result that His Lordship over mankind, and over the entire universe, is denied. The dire effect of this preaching is that ordinary human life is regarded as being outside Christ's dominion, as a sphere in which man can act as he pleases. Against such an anti-social distortion of the Gospel Maurice raised an emphatic protest: "the Bible does not accept that position which men have courteously assigned it. It does not profess to provide rules or comforts for men as individuals, and to leave their condition as portions of a Community out of its calculations. It speaks from first to last of a Kingdom. It promulgates a social Law. It tells all men that this is the law which makes communion among men possible; that there is positively no other."[17]

Since the Kingdom of God embraces all mankind and all human fellowships, to maintain that any part of human life falls outside the reign of God is to deny God as the Creator and Lifegiver of the universe and to despise Him and His love.[18] Nonetheless, Protestants, and not least the Church of Rome, have been guilty of this blasphemy by separating God's Kingdom from earthly life.

A fatal consequence of this secularized view is that the world is considered the place where sin and selfishness reign and have free scope.[19] The false impression is created that the followers of Christ are called to live a life which has nothing to do with ordinary human life. Christ's demand of love is virtually restricted to self-elected religious cliques, or sects, which are regarded as the only true fellowships. This is nothing less than to use the Gospel as a pretext for excusing oneself from the obligation of love towards one's fellow-men in the fellowships of family and nation. Yet Christ did not come to create a religious sect that was to live an isolated life cut off from the life of the rest of mankind. He came to reveal that God had created and established His Kingdom upon earth and that every man had his place in His Divine Order. Further, Christ did not intend to establish a new humanity that was to live according

17 *Sermons* III, 223–4.
18 Cf. *Sermons* III, 212: "[God] was the Ruler of all the nations, had created the earth and all its treasures for His service," and *Sermons Preached in Lincoln's Inn Chapel* V (London 1892. Cit. *Sermons* V), 35: "he [St. Paul] would bid them give thanks for a present King and Deliverer, for One who makes this earth, with all its confusions, a blessed place, in which they may be well content that their lines are cast, because it is full of tokens of His love and of occasions for serving Him."
19 Cf. *The Prayer-Book*, 102: "Romanism had secularised and degraded common life. – – It had treated that life as most heavenly which was most separated from earth; so far as the system prevailed – in spite of the ten thousand counteractions which there were in the constitution of the Church itself, in its Creeds, in its noblest teachers – the feeling grew up that what is inhuman, not what is human, is the image of the Divine. Here, out of the book which was felt to be of transcendent authority, the opposite lesson was inculcated day by day. The sanctity and dignity of all social relations; the direct connection of all earthly acts with God himself. Men were divinely taught *not* to touch the things of earth with scrupulous superstitious hands, as if they were unholy; they were told that is was a sin against God to do so," and p. 105: "Divines and religious people have been too fine to meddle with such [earthly] things; they have supposed that religion had nothing to do with them. And since religion could not touch them, something else must. Selfishness undertakes this charge; the external world is surrendered to its dominion, provided the internal is saved for God."

to specific laws having no connection with the laws applying to ordinary human life. He proclaimed that the earth was surrounded and ordered by God's will of love, and that love was the only law of human existence. To follow Christ and to fulfil His law does not mean to withdraw from the world of men in order to live in an isolated and exclusive religious sphere; it does mean man's being freed from his selfish inhumanity and becoming a true man by sacrificing himself in the service of love in the human fellowships of family and nation.[20]

It is an illusion to think that isolation and exclusiveness from ordinary human life promote fellowship with God. However much religious people may pour contempt upon earthly life as lying outside God's rule, they have to take part in it. But they then think themselves at liberty to deal with it at their pleasure, and this in reality means that they themselves conform to the supposedly selfish maxims of this world. This is proved overwhelmingly by the behaviour of the religious world. Maurice unsparingly described how, in disregard of Christ's law of love, and even of all human decency, it performed the most revolting and inhuman acts in its dealings with ordinary people.[21] Such an attitude by inner necessity corrupts man's fellowship with God. For no matter how much it is maintained that heaven and earth have nothing to do with each other, man cannot dissolve that unity which exists in the very order of things. He who deals with his fellow-men according to the law of selfishness, and not according to the law of love, makes selfishness the basis of all his thoughts and deeds.[22]

20 Cf. *Sermons* III, 226: "Assuredly there is this great and eternal distinction between the new and old man, the regenerate and unregenerate. But the new man is he who consents to follow the true law of humanity which is in Christ Jesus, and so to be at one with his fellow-men; the old man is he who obeys the inclinations of his nature, and so is at war with his fellows. The law of Christ is *not* the law of a select few, but the law for man," and p. 225: "To bear one another's burdens – – is not to act upon some sublime, heroical maxim, wholly apart from the common daily business and routine of life; it is simply to fulfil a law, simply not to break loose from the order and government under which our hearts and lives are actually constituted, simply to yield ourselves to the real Lord and Master of our spirits, Who has power to mould them according to His will, instead of choosing another service – the service of the Spirit of Division and Selfishness."

21 Cf. *Sermons* VI, 268–9: "We speak scornfully and disparagingly of this earth, as if it were a fit place for poor, fallen, wicked creatures to inhabit; as if those whom the Spirit makes meet for the Kingdom of Heaven are to look down upon it; at best to regard it only as a place in which they are compelled for threescore and ten years to dwell. Those words stand out often in the strongest contrast to the acts of those who use them; sometimes one would think they were determined to establish the truth of their sayings and prove how wretched the things of the earth are by the preference which they exhibit for the very meanest and most frivolous of them; especially by their devotion to the earth's money, the love of which is said to be the root of all evil. And so I believe it must be more and more, if we are not taught reverence for the earth as an article of faith; if it is not declared to us more and more, that the Bible commands this reverence, gives us the strongest and most sacred reasons for it; warns us against the sins into which we must fall when we esteem it lightly."

22 Cf. *Sermons* III, 227: "A Christian man must believe that the law of Christ is applicable to all persons and all cases, or he will very soon apply it really and practically to no persons and in no cases. He must acknowledge it as the human law, or it certainly will not be the law of his church, or circle, or caste; he must believe that it lies at the root of all politics and of all daily business, or he will not make it the guide of his individual conduct, not even of his most sacred and solemn transactions."

He abuses not only his fellow-men but also God for his own selfish ends. It is necessary to reject the contrast between holy and profane, between the Kingdom of God and the earth, as false and being a denial of the Divine Order if man is to attain true love of God and of his fellow-men as well.

Maurice knew perfectly well that both politicians and ecclesiastics had maintained that Christianity had important functions to perform in and for society. As a religious and moral force it was needed for the establishment of a harmonious body politic. However, Maurice did not approve of this utilitarian idea, since it implied that society was ultimately regarded as a human creation, prompted by selfish considerations, which therefore needed help from outside to secure its stability.[23] But a society which considers itself built upon the selfishness of men, and acts accordingly, is based upon a lie and ought to perish rather than be endorsed and strengthened by Christianity.[24] There can be no alliance between Christianity and a society that denies God as the Creator and acts as if selfishness was the law of human life.[25] When the Church is content to be a stabilizing factor in a society that regards itself as man's own achievement, it will merely serve to confirm that society in its practical atheism and promote its secularization. Instead the Church must proclaim that human society belongs to the Kingdom of God, with love as its only foundation.[26]

Similarly, Maurice repudiated the idea that human life becomes good and holy when it is lived under the rule of the Church and its sanctifying influence as presupposing that the Church is a spiritual entity in contrast to common human life which, being isolated from God, is regarded as profane. This false idea paves the way for all hierarchical demands for power and a setting up of a priestly despotic rule over human life.[27] In Maurice's mind the sacerdotal lust for power and a secularized view of man and society always go hand in hand and support each other.

23 Cf. *Sermons* III, 222–3: "You may fancy that – – I am trying to convince you that Religion, or, as it is sometimes called still more vaguely, *the Religious Principle,* has been necessary for the conservation of society, and is necessary for it still. But there is much confusion and mischief, I fear, lurking in the use of such language. It may mean that Religion prevents a society from perishing, which has selfishness for its root, and which would naturally fall to pieces if it had not some supernatural power, or the dream of some supernatural power, to keep it together. Such a religion statesmen have unquestionably been desirous of, and priests have been found ready to supply them with it."
24 Cf. *Sermons* III, 223: "A society which has reached the point of confessing no principle but that of rivalry, no maxim but that of "Every man for himself", may in its dying agonies ask help of the Gospel – but assuredly too late. – – Religion, or the Religious Principle, if it is worth anything, – if it is not another name for the worship of the God of this world, of the Evil Spirit, – cannot be the instrument of preventing or even delaying that destruction which the Righteous and True God has pronounced against all unrighteousness and untruth."
25 Cf. *ibid.*: "But if by Religion be meant the Gospel of Christ in a living, practical sense, it declines such an honour altogether. It does not exist to keep men comfortable in their contradictions, or to avert the consequences of them. It exists as a perpetual witness against those contradictions, and a perpetual prophecy of the result which must come from them."
26 Cf. *ibid.*: "Either the Gospel declares what Society is, and what it is not; what binds men together, what separates them, or it has no significance at all."
27 Cf. *The Patriarchs,* 134–5: "May it not then be that, instead of the theocratic element having been too strong, at any time, in the politics of the world, it has always been far too weak; and that to this weakness we owe very much of the vagueness and imbecility of politicians, as

So, with great vigour, Maurice asserted that the Kingdom of God was established on earth with the creation and that it encompasses all human life. Any separation between heavenly and earthly, holy and profane, must be rejected as false. The Church must in no way endorse or promote the practical atheism to which man, in his blindness and ignorance, is more than prone. The Church is called to testify that human life, with its common fellowships of family and nation, is created by God and is good and holy because it has Christ as its creative and life-giving Head and Centre.[28]

2. Vocations and Human Relationships

Every man is a citizen of the Kingdom of God, a member of the Body of Christ. For Maurice this meant that all men are called by God to an office in which they can serve their fellow-men.[29] Man's earthly vocation, of whatever kind, whether high or low, is a ministry in the Kingdom of God to be performed in responsibility to God alone.[30] God has placed man in a specific relation to his fellow-men, with specific tasks to be discharged in trust and obedience to Him.[31] To attempt to serve God other than through the vocations is to follow the way of self-elected works and to

well as very much of the unfair dealings and dangerous pretensions of priests? Yes, brethren, of *priests;* for the priest, who is sent into the world to testify that God is the King of the earth, may set up himself to be the king of it; he may secularize the Universe, that he may be the one spiritual person in it. If he does so, he will assuredly become, in the most radical and dreadful sense, secular himself. And if you acknowledge his falsehood, if you submit to be secularized by him, – if you say that your civil transactions have nothing to do with God, – he will establish his power over you; not a divine, godly power, but a very earthly, sensual, devilish power."

28 Cf. *The Unity of the New Testament*, 547: "In the God-Man in whom all things were created, in whom men were chosen, in Him who was born of the Virgin, and was subject to her, who had brothers and friends, who loved Martha and her sister and Lazarus, St. Paul found the eternal centre round which all the different portions of human society are moving in their different orbits, who keeps them from ever becoming discordant or from disturbing the unity of the system."

29 Cf. *The Prayer-Book*, 341: "every man, in every position, has an office and ministry which it is his privilege to exercise for those over whom he is set."

30 Cf. *Sermons* I, 70–1: "they [the offices] are stewardships from God, to which men must appoint, and which they must hold every hour under a sense of God's presence and judgment; for the abuse of which they must therefore seek His forgiveness, for the right performance of which they must cast themselves upon His grace; otherwise their acts will be done either in cowardly deference to other men's judgments, or in self-willed dependence upon their own, in each case equally to the injury of those whom they are sent into the world to serve."

31 Cf. *Sermons* I, 176: "every common calling upon earth, to do the most humble work, may be taken as a summons from the great Husbandman to bear our part in cultivating His vineyard, to serve Him with His own free Spirit, to enter into His own joy," and *The Prophets*, 69–70: "He [David] showed that he could trust God to put him in the position that was best for him; that he knew God did not send him into the world to provide either for his body or his soul, but to glorify His name and to bless His creatures. He was most devoted to God when he was most devoted to His work. He prayed fervently because he lived fervently. He found out the necessity of seeking God continually, of meditating upon His law, of blessing His name, – because he learnt how weak and how little he could be a king over men when the image of the divine kingdom was not present to him."

shirk obeying God's will as it confronts the individual in the tasks of his vocation. Obedience to God implies that man sacrifices himself in the fulfilment of the duties of his vocation.[32] This is the true imitation of Christ.[33] So every vocation is "a divine office" and every man in his vocation is "a minister of God", "a servant of God".[34]

Maurice was well aware that this idea ran counter to the generally held view according to which only priests hold a divine office by virtue of their Ordination, which imparts to them the gift of the Holy Spirit for its proper functioning. This concept must, however, be rejected as false. Any distinction between divine and profane offices introduces a secularized view of the common vocations of men as self-established tasks which they can consequently perform by themselves and discharge at pleasure. Furthermore, the exclusive privilege of the clergy gives them a pretext for acting as a sacerdotal caste with the right to assume dominion over other men.

These grave consequences will, however, not be removed merely by abolishing Ordination.[35] On the contrary, both the secularized view of ordinary vocations as well as the emergence of a sacerdotal rule are due to the fact that its significance has neither been understood nor taken seriously. The truth about the Ordination is that it proclaims that priests are not appointed to act on their own behalf, but are called and sent by God to serve their fellow-men. They can perform their ministry only if they forswear their own interests and place their sole trust in the Holy Ghost and His help. All lust for power is removed immediately when it is realized that priests are not installed as rulers, in place of God, but are entrusted with the task of being God's self-effacing servants. That they have been appointed to a certain service does not mean that they alone are called to work under the guidance of the Holy Spirit.[36] The

32 Cf. *The Gospel of the Kingdom of Heaven. A Course of Lectures on the Gospel of St. Luke* (London 1899. Cit. *The Kingdom of Heaven)*, 46: "They were not to forsake their work that they might serve God more punctually and faithfully, – that would be a distrust and denial of Him. They were to serve Him *in* their work; they were to avoid those things which they knew were inconsistent with fidelity to it; they were to do the acts of simple kindliness and good neighbourhood which belonged to their position, and which came in their way." See further *Christmas Day*, 182–3.

33 Cf. *Sermons* VI, 219: "no office can be looked upon as anything less than a calling; in the highest and in the lowest Christ's own voice is saying 'Follow me'."

34 Cf. *Country Churches*, 188–9: "remember, that whatever your place in the world, you are called by God, your Almighty Father, to that place. He calls you to be farmers, labourers, school-masters, magistrates, physicians, clergymen. They are all His servants", and *Sermons* I, 46: "Must it not be that all offices among man were now, as heretofore, divine offices? Did not the revelation of this King show under Whom they were held, by Whom each person was called to the one for which he was intended, to Whom each person was responsible for the duties which were entrusted to Him? Did it not behove any one, who would do his work faithfully, to confess whence his trust was derived, and to seek strength from Him Who had laid it upon him, that it might not be abused?"

35 Cf. *Life* II, 417: "The clergy you know are obliged to say that they believe themselves to be called by the Holy Ghost to the office of the ministry. Many object to that language. They think it marks out the clergyman as different from other men. They wish it blotted out of our service. They think it leads him to falsehood."

36 Cf. *ibid.*: "He [the clergyman] is different from other men inasmuch as he has tasks to perform which other men have not to perform. He is like other men inasmuch as they have all a general calling as men, and have all their specific callings as physicians, soldiers, tradesmen."

uniqueness of the priest's office is to be found in the very fact of his being elected to tell all men that they are called by God to a specific service, and that they must receive the Holy Spirit in order to be able to act as God's servants in their respective vocations.[37] Thus the priest's ordination reveals the truth of every man's vocation: "every one of us is a servant or minister in this [Christ's] kingdom. Some of us have the name of Ministers. That is not that we may be separate from our fellows, but that we may give them a sign what Christ would have them be. *All* of us are ministers. Every father is a minister of Christ to his children. Every mother is a minister of Christ to her children. Every brother and sister is a minister of Christ to his brothers and sisters. Wherever we are going, whatever we are doing, in a house or in a field, we are ministers of Christ. That is our calling. We may be faithful or unfaithful ministers; but He is our Master, and He has sent us to wait upon some or other, upon more or fewer."[38]

Because the office of the priest is a visible sign which proclaims how each man is to understand his own calling, he who combats the divine calling of priests, denying it all significance and purpose, only undermines the true foundation of his own calling. It is even more serious if the priest, in the actual performance of his office, betrays the truth about his own ministry.[39] For Maurice the proper fulfilment of the vocations, within the fellowships of family and nation, depends quite simply upon how the priests understand and discharge the office to which God has called them.[40]

37 Cf. *ibid.*: "If he [the clergyman] supposes his specific calling to be higher than theirs, it can only be on this plea; that he is appointed to tell all men *what* they are, *who* calls them to their works, what strength they have for fulfilling their works. He is only entitled to the epithet of a divine so far as he believes in his heart, and can declare with his lips to all his fellows, that their position is fixed for them by God, and that they will have His help day by day in understanding it and maintaining it," and *The Patriarchs*, 135: "Believe priests to be perpetual witnesses in their words, lives, sacraments, that you all of you stand in a direct relation to God; that you all of you are in covenant with Him; that every work of yours is a vocation from Him; that no part of your civil transactions is indifferent to Him, or can be excluded from His cognisance."

38 *Country Churches*, 204.

39 Cf. *Life* II, 53: "I would have all laymen feel that they are called by GOD to their different offices, but I do not think they will feel it if we [the clergy] do not feel our call more distinctly, and assert it against all doubts in our minds and apparent contradictions from without. We are called, and we may believe that we are; anything that the devil says to the contrary in any wise notwithstanding"; and *The Patriarchs*, 216: "We [the priests] are sent into the world in this day, as the tribe of Levi was sent into the world under the old dispensation, to bear witness for the consecration and holiness of God's entire family. We become guilty, as they did, when by our words or our acts we lead you to think that you have not received this consecration, that you are not set apart to God; that you and your children and your occupations are not holy in His sight. Our sin in all times has been not that we have proclaimed too loudly and too practically our calling by God; it has been – that with these words on our lips, we have acted as if we had some power of our own, some inherent sanctity, some right to put ourselves in His place," and *The Church a Family*, 146-7: "In denying that we are called to our ministry by anything more than an earthly summons, that we hold it by anything more than an earthly tenure, you are undermining the sacredness, and with the sacredness the dignity of the lawyer's, the physician's, the statesman's character."

40 See *The Prayer-Book*, XIV–XV.

As Christ in obedience to the will of God brings His love to men, even so is every man called to bring God's love to his fellows. This is the purpose for which God has established the various offices, or ministries, in the Human Order and appointed men to be His fellow-workers and servants within their respective vocations.[41] That God entrusts man to perform and mediate His love through the vocations testifies to the great honour God conferred upon him when He created him in His image.[42]

So the sole purpose of all vocations is to serve one's fellow-men. For this end God provides each office-holder with the necessary personal abilities and the material means. These are a trust from God to be used according to the law of love.[43] Consequently, they can never be considered as a personal possession nor be used to exalt or glorify the office-holder. Conversely, all the spiritual and material blessings which men receive through the vocations of other people must be regarded as gifts from God, who works through men, His fellow-servants.[44]

Every office is holy because God has established it and appointed men to perform acts of love towards their fellow-men. But, as noted earlier, man is incapable of loving his neighbours unless God Himself imparts the love. The tasks of even the meanest, and apparently least spiritual, vocation cannot be fulfilled unless man relies upon God for his help and support. Dependence on God and fellowship with Him are conditions necessary to the realization of the meaning and purpose of his vocation.[45]

Maurice made the same point by asserting that man can perform nothing

---

41 Cf. *The Prayer-Book,* 34: "As the Old Testament is throughout a history of God's deliverances of men, so it is throughout a history of His deliverances of them by men. Every Jewish lawgiver, patriarch, chieftain, judge, prophet, and king, is said to be called out for the purpose of filling some part in the scheme of God's deliverance – –. God was the Deliverer, man was the instrument and agent of His deliverance." Se also *The Patriarchs,* 134.

42 Cf. *The Epistle of St. John,* 259–60: "He is intending the creatures whom He has made in His image to share His own nature, to show it forth in their intercourse with each other and with the world in which He has placed them." See also *The Apocalypse,* 121.

43 Cf. *Christmas Day,* 272: "By the order and design of God, we are placed in certain vocations for the good of mankind and for His glory. To the fulfilment of this vocation, certain outward and material blessings are attached. If we faithfully depend upon Him, these will come to us at such times and in such measures as are best for us; if we keep them constantly before us as an object, we shall be restless and dissatisfied, incapable of pursuing one of those duties rightly, of which they are meant to be not so much the rewards as the needful supports and appliances."

44 Cf. *Country Churches,* 15: "Whatever any physician does for you, is done by His [Christ's] power: it is His work. Be sure that you confess that it is; and then you will love all that act as His servants to your bodies or your spirits, for His sake."

45 Cf. *Sermons* I, 13: "I know no ground for the relationships among men but their common relation to God. I know no security for the permanence of fellowship among men but that fellowship which depends upon no chances, which the Unchangeable God Himself has established." Man's inability to fulfil his office without God was to Maurice the true principle in the Corporation and Test Acts of 1661 and 1673, according to which "the State looked upon this Communion of the Lord's Supper as a qualification for its offices." Rightly understood, this principle contained "the secret of all moral and social reformation" *(Sermons* I, 70).

without Divine inspiration.[46] By proclaiming that the priest cannot discharge his ministry without the inspiration of the Holy Spirit, the Ordination Service is merely stating the truth about every vocation. The Spirit is always near every man.[47] The work of the Holy Spirit in men has the sole purpose of making them obedient servants of God so that they can carry out His will where He has placed them.[48] Therefore the Holy Spirit inspires man with the love which he shall show forth to his fellow-men in his vocation.[49] Far from imparting spiritual gifts which raise men above their fellow-men, the Spirit unites them in the bond of love.

In order to prevail with the idea of the Holy Spirit as the Guide and Inspirer of every man Maurice felt bound to settle accounts with the various theories of inspiration rampant in his day. Thus, according to Maurice, contemporary orthodoxy restricted the work of the Spirit by maintaining that by virtue of the possession of an exclusive inspiration the Biblical authors occupied a unique position in the history of mankind. In this way their lives became isolated from those of other men and could have no significance for them. Maurice agreed with the criticism made by the poets and philosophers of Romantic Idealism that no distinction should be made between the inspired prophets and apostles and every true poet and philosopher. All who were seeking ultimate reality, beyond the world of the senses, were inspired.[50] However, Maurice could not agree with their interpretation of the gift of the Holy Spirit to man as a beautiful, but antiquated, mode of expression, as if man were capable

46 Cf. *Family Worship*, 185: "It is not vanity to think that God will inspire me when I am praying, when I am working, when I am studying. It is the root of all vanity to suppose that I can be anything or do anything if He leaves me to myself," and *Sermons* VI, 104: "His Spirit is the author of whatever love men are able to exhibit in acts or to feel within."

47 Cf. *Christmas Day*, 258–9: "the Spirit of the Father and the Son, the Spirit of love, and peace, and order, is intended to dwell with men, to bring their hearts into conformity with this divine scheme and order; to teach them what is their own position in regard to it."

48 Cf. *Religions*, 243: "There is a Power which can bring us not into some imaginary condition of excellence, but precisely into our true condition: which can remove the individual interests, selfish feelings, national antipathies, narrow apprehensions, that all our efforts to produce unity have only evoked and strengthened; which can bring down our high notions and conceits of what we are and what we do; which can enable us to be God's servants and to do His work in the world He has redeemed."

49 Cf. *The Gospel of St. John*, 94: "are we not to learn that, at every moment of the day, the Spirit of the eternal God is moving around us, speaking to us, acting upon us; but that His mightiest operation, that which alone fulfils His purpose towards us, is when He enables us to become the willing servants and children of our Father in heaven?", and *Family Worship*, 56: "whenever you see a person who shows you gentleness and loving-kindness, who calls forth gentleness and loving-kindness in you, who resists the work of the devil in you, I tell you, the Bible tells you, that you are to say, that that person is acting under the inspiration of God's Holy Spirit, and cannot be acting by any other inspiration than His." See also *Life* I, 246, 274–5 and *The Conflict*, 147.

50 Cf. *The Kingdom of Christ* II, 128: "The man of letters and the man of science, I believe, are called of God to the work in which they are engaged; they are His ministers – I would earnestly wish that they might feel themselves to be so. I will go further; I will admit that their function, especially that of anyone who has a real poetical gift, does answer in several important respects to that of the ancient prophet; that they may, without any impropriety, be said to perform a similar office, and to be endowed with powers which correspond to the circumstances of their different periods."

of grasping and contemplating true reality through his own spiritual powers.[51] Apart from the fact that this Romantic-Idealistic theory of inspiration makes man a creative being and thereby glorifies and deifies him, it only leads to a new form of exclusiveness. Its adherents regard only the exceptional few as spiritually gifted, destined to be the masters of the rest of mankind, whom they despise as being devoid of spiritual capacities.[52] So, for Maurice, both the orthodox and the Romantic-Idealistic view of inspiration lead to a dead end.

Maurice agreed with the orthodox in asserting a clear distinction between the Holy Spirit and man. As a creature, man can perform nothing without the guidance and inspiration of the Spirit.[53] They were, however, mistaken in limiting the work of the

51 Cf. *Theological Essays*, 93: "in our own day, a number of persons fancy they have discovered a sufficient equivalent of the doctrine of Scripture respecting a divine Spirit imparted to man, in the belief that man himself has a spiritual nature, – that all his powers, energies, affections, show him to be more than a creature of flesh and blood. The doctrine of the Creed, they say, is only an old theocratic mode of enunciating a truth which belongs to the consciousness of all men, and of which some races have had a much keener intuition than the Jews."

52 Cf. *Theological Essays*, 97: "But oh, how melancholy if we must resolve this Spirit into the spiritual movements, affections, powers of the creatures whom He came to guide and animate! Thanks be to God for the witness which is borne in our own day for the spirituality, not of a few men, but of man as man. It is His teaching, His way of declaring His Son to us, the battle of His Spirit with our pettishness and vanity. But if we substitute the lesson for the Teacher; if man falls down and worships his own faculties of worship; if he determines to be a God because he has the capacity of knowing God, what a tyranny of particular spiritual men is he preparing for himself, what a slavery to mere gifts, what a rivalry of impostors, each pretending to be *the* spiritual and divine man who can guide the rest; ultimately, what an abyss of Materialism!", and *The Kingdom of Christ* II, 129: "By all means, then, let those who feel their gifts strong in them, train themselves to an awful and humble acknowledgment of them, and of the source from which they proceed. It is not the inclination which the students and artists of our land show to put forth these claims on their behalf, which should make any religious man tremble. Just so far as they do this, they have taken a great step out of the infidelity of the last generation. What is alarming is the pretension which accompanies these claims; the loud talk about powers and faculties not derived but inherent; the practical evidence which our men of talent furnish by their scorn and contempt of others that they do rest upon these inherent powers, and do not recognise any sustaining, quickening inspiration."

53 For Maurice it is a grave misconception to believe that the necessity of the inspiration of the Holy Spirit made man passive. On the contrary, it is the Holy Spirit which makes men active. There is no contrast between the work of God and that of man, but the more vigorously God works, the more man is drawn freely and willingly into God's own work as His fellow-worker. Characteristically Maurice wrote in *The Prayer-Book*, 76: "It was an *Inspiration* – which belongs not to sounds, but to men; to conscious voluntary beings, to spirits formed in the image of God. It was an inspiration which went lower than the conclusions of their own understanding, than the determinations of their own wills; it found out that which lies at the root of these, their true essential humanity; that which they had not merely as David and Isaiah, not merely as living in this or that age; not merely as Jews, but as men. It was the inspiration of Him who had created them for this very end, that they might set forth his mind, not in the deadness and extinction or suspension of their own; but in its freedom, fulness, highest activity. The creature sinks into nothing before the Majesty of Him who has chosen it, but it sinks that it may rise; it becomes conscious of powers to which before it had been a stranger."

96

Spirit to the so-called religious sphere and to a specific group of people. Such an exclusiveness runs contrary to the Biblical message. The greatness of the Biblical authors stems from the very fact that, under the inspiration of the Holy Spirit, they proclaimed the truth about ordinary human existence. Like the prophets and the apostles, each man has his specific vocation which can be discharged only through the inspiration of the Holy Spirit.

Maurice's concept of vocation, therefore, further emphasizes the falsity of any attempt to distinguish between the holy and the profane, between a specific religious sphere and ordinary human life. Man is dependent upon God in all his doings, even in his daily life. God has appointed every man to an office or a ministry in the human fellowships of family and nation to render the service of love to his fellow-men. The Holy Spirit is ever near man, guiding and imparting love so that he can fulfil the purpose of his calling.

3. The Human Relationships as the Image of the Life of the Triune God

We have seen that, according to Maurice, every man is appointed to a divine office to serve his fellow-men as a minister of God in "that universal body politic of which Christ is the Head, because He is the Head of every man."[54] It is due to Christ alone that there exists a well-structured and harmonious Human Order, encompassing the fellowships of family and nation, to which every man belongs.[55]

Maurice's language very often left the impression that the Kingdom of God and the Human Order are identical. The reason for this is that he was anxious to oppose any separation between the heavenly and the earthly and to emphasize that all human life and all fellowship among men originate in God's creative activity.[56] However, a closer analysis makes it clear that his idea of the Human Order is more complex.

As previously demonstrated, Maurice held that the invisible and eternal world represents the ideas, or forms, according to which the visible world was made. The idea of the archetype and its image also applied to Maurice's interpretation of the Human Order and its fellowships. Thus, although there is the most intimate connection between the Kingdom of God and the earth, they do not coincide but are related to each other as the archetype is to the image. "What you want," Maurice

---

54 *Sermons* V, 241.
55 Cf. *Sermons* IV, 9: "And they did not dare – they did not find it possible – to think of human society except as constituted in Christ. It was the confusion, the unbelief of men, to regard themselves as capable of fellowship and existence without Him, to suppose that they would congregate merely because they found solitude inconvenient. It was the business of Christ's ministers to proclaim that there could have been no families, no nations, no social impulses, no laws, nothing to resist the selfish, self-seeking tendencies which each of us is conscious of in himself and complains of in his neighbours, if there had not been one living centre of the whole body of Humanity, one Head of every man."
56 Cf. *Christmas Day*, 78: "every privilege of your national life – all the order of society – all the fellowship among men – all kindness – all gentleness – all reverence – all courtesy – everything within us which is not brutal – everything around us which is not miserable, are the fruits of its [the Kingdom of God] establishment."

insisted, "is, not a heaven separated from earth, but one which shall explain its confusions and perplexities, instead of being constructed out of them; which shall show you how the forms of earth are the images of its forms, instead of being their archetypes. You want to have a door opened in heaven that you may not have an earth given up to oppression and cruelty."[57]

At times Maurice wrote as if there is a kingdom of archetypes in the invisible world in accordance with which earthly life is shaped. After all, his primary and basic idea is that the life of the Triune God is the archetype of all human relationships.[58] God created man in His own image but, as He eternally lives in fellowship with His Son through the Spirit of love, He has created human fellowships in the likeness of this Divine fellowship.[59] So Maurice could say that "all the orders and degrees among men rested upon relationships, ultimately upon the relation between the Father and the Son."[60]

It is characteristic of the life of the Triune God that the Father eternally exercises authority and the Son eternally renders obedience. However, it is not a question of capricious despotism and blind servile obedience, since both authority and obedience are exercised in mutual love – this constitutes their unchangeable order and unity. As the Human Order is created to reflect the life of the Father with the Son in the unity of the Spirit, it is not uniform, but hierarchically structured. Thus some are called to exercise power and authority, whereas others are appointed to subordinate positions of obedience. In spite of the richly varied character of the vocations there exists, however, a harmonious unity, since the law for every single vocation is the self-sacrificing love which causes all tyranny and rebellious self-will to wither at the root. As the Father does not use His power and authority to dominate and subju-

---

57 *The Apocalypse*, 58. Cf. also *Life* II, 242: "The necessity of confessing a kingdom of Heaven within – a kingdom of Heaven ever present with us now; different in kind from the visible world, but affecting it, and swaying its movements continually – has been with me an overwhelming one."

58 Cf. *Social Morality*, 231: "they were taught that He [Christ] had come to open or unveil that divine life, of which the human life in all its social conditions and circumstances was the image; to the end that the lower might be reformed by the higher, not the higher debased and darkened by the lower", and *The Prophets*, 206: "The cardinal doctrine of Hosea's prophecy and of his life, that without which one is as unintelligible as the other, is that man being made in the image of God, all human relationships are images of divine relationships; that through them God acquaints us with His character and government; that in them we are to show forth that character and government."

59 Because of his attachment to a Platonic idea of reality, Maurice sometimes made the invisible world with its ideas or forms the archetype of the visible world. Undoubtedly he was influenced by Plato's *Republic*, in which Plato dealt with the idea of the state in order to discover how the actual, existing state is to be ordered. But Maurice's main idea is that the Triune God is the archetype of human fellowships. This is borne out by the fact that he never attempted to give a detailed description of how we are to understand the invisible world of ideas. He confined himself to hints, which yield meaning when seen against the background of Plato's thought, but are of little practical significance to him. In fact these hints serve only to show that the visible world of time and space is not self-explanatory but must be referred to a divine cause and prototype. When it comes to a concrete description of this prototype, Maurice is always thinking of the Triune God.

60 *The Church a Family*, 14.

gate His Son but to bestow love upon Him, so he who is appointed to rule must use his power and authority to serve his subjects, and, as the Son submits in love to the will of His Father, so men must subordinate themselves and obey, in a loving spirit, those who are set over them.[61] Love is the bond which unites the different vocations in one harmonious fellowship, "the body politic of Christ".[62]

The working of this fundamental principle is well illustrated in the life of the family. To be a father means to be appointed to exercise authority over one's children, thus serving them and leading them to a true humanity. Conversely, to be a son or a daughter means to be placed in a relationship to a father with the duty of obeying him.[63] If the father fails in his responsibility of exercising authority or the children fail in their obedience, the human relationship is destroyed. The same is true of the life of a nation. National order and unity can only exist if those in charge of the various vocations act in self-sacrificing love towards each other.

Holding the idea of the Human Order as created and structured by God, Maurice, as previously indicated, rejected all schemes for changing the existing social order. A true reformation of society can never be brought about by transforming, or abolishing, the actual social structure. It is achieved only through the recognition that every man has been called to his particular task and that all the various vocations are equally necessary for the harmonious functioning of "the body politic of Christ". The task of the social reformer is to educate man to understand the God-given structure of society as it stands. He must also urge men to fulfil their callings in a spirit of loving service, since this is the sole condition of society's existence and well-being.[64]

61 Cf. *What is Revelation?*, 402: "A Son who perfectly delighted to do his Father's will, – who obeyed Him because His law was in His heart, – would seem to set forth the very meaning and nature of obligation, the sense in which it is the submission of a Will and the power of a Will."

62 Cf. *Sermons* V, 234: "There are members or limbs of the body politic, as certainly as there are members or limbs of the body natural. Each man is such a member or limb. Each man has a function or office assigned him in the body politic, as the hand or foot has in the natural body. One man may as little do the work of another, as the hand can do the work of the foot. One man may as little say to another, I have no need of thee, as the hand may say to the foot, or the foot to the hand, I have no need of thee. And here, too, the many members can never make us forget the one body."

63 A father must always discharge his office of exercising authority over his children in co-operation with the mother, whose relationship to the children is characterized above all by spontaneous care and love. The influence of the mother is just as necessary as that of the father, since it ensures that authority does not degenerate into despotism and force (see *Social Morality*, 27).

64 This is the fundamental idea behind Maurice's Christian Socialism. He completely repudiated the programmes of political radicalism and of socialism for the reformation of society, maintaining that these imply a denial of the fact that the given structure of society was created by God and was therefore perfect and good. It is futile to introduce changes in the existing order of things. Men must learn that they belong to the Kingdom of God and are to serve each other as brothers in their callings. So Maurice's remedy for the political and social evils of his own time was to make men realise the divine character of the Human Order in which they were placed and to make them see that all human relationships are constituted upon the law of love so that they might act accordingly. A more detailed and documented exposition of Maurice's idea of Christian Socialism may be found in my: *Origin and History of Christian Socialism 1848–1854 (Acta Theologica Danica* Vol. III, 1962).

Human relationships, being created and ordered in the image of the Triune God, are a ladder up which God guides man to a knowledge of Himself.[65] More than anything else the family, the basic human fellowship, leads man to a knowledge of God and to an understanding of the fundamentals of human existence.[66] By living in a family man learns that he is not his own master and is not able to shape his own life. As he is either a son or a daughter, he must trace his origin to something outside himself: a father and a mother to whom he must submit in trusting obedience.[67] A father's authority and a mother's love and care being a reflection of God's own being, the relationship between parents and children necessarily leads to a knowledge of God as the righteous and loving authority that awakens man's filial trust and obedience.[68] Because the earthly family has a divine archetype, family life leads man to realise the existence of a divine fellowship, that is, the fellowship of the Father with the Son in one Spirit.[69]

Once he has been educated to see a reflection of God's nature in the life of the family, man is also able to grasp the divine significance of the human relationships

65 Cf. *The Kingdom of Christ* (1838) II, 50: "Here [in the Bible] the circumstances and relations of ordinary life are exhibited as the ladder through which God is guiding man up to a knowledge of Himself;" *The Prayer-Book*, 96: "Human relationships were steps in a ladder, of which the top reaches to the throne of God," and *The Kingdom of Christ* (1838) III, 288: "-- human relationships are not artificial types of something divine, but are actually the means, and the only means through which man ascends to any knowledge of the divine, - and -- every breach of a human relation, as it implies a violation of the higher law, so also is a hindrance and barrier to the perception of that higher law, - the drawing a veil between the spirit of man and his God."

66 Cf. *The Kingdom of Christ* (1838) III, 11: "Most persons are constrained to admit, that family relationships are in some sense or other an ordinance of God; but only a few seem to acknowledge, that even these have a very distinct purpose in the Divine economy. Few seem to perceive, that the family order and constitution is the first great bulwark which God has provided against the dominion of the senses and of the outward world --; that it is the first step towards the acknowledgement of God." See also p. 284–5 and p. 317.

67 Cf. *Social Morality*, 22: "If -- you start from the indisputable commonplace 'We are Sons', such a way of considering the Universe [i. e. man as the centre of the universe] is from the first impossible. I cannot be the centre of the circle in which I find myself, be it as small as it may. I refer myself to another. There is a root below me. There is an Author of my existence." See also *The Prophets*, 264.

68 Cf. *Family Worship*, 216: "We have the signs and tokens of such a Father all around us, the earthly images of His Divine Nature. The earthly images and the heavenly Archetype will always sustain and illustrate each other"; *Country Churches*, 96: "He [God] has set over thee a father to remind thee of His justice and truth, a mother to remind thee of His mercy and gentleness", and *Sacrifice*, XXXIX: "Now this domestic life, grounded first on the authority of the father, and the example of righteousness which he afforded to his children, had its ultimate root in the belief that God was the righteous Father, and that each head of a household was to present Him in that character through his own acts."

69 Cf. *Sermons* II, 294–5: "Our Lord tells him that he is actually, really a child, not only of an earthly parent, but of a Father in Heaven. These relationships on earth are grounded on that celestial relationship; they exist because it exists; they are formed in its likeness."

which make up the life of the nation.[70] Thus, because the king does not rule in his own name and exercise an authority of his own, but is called by God to exert authority in the maintenance of law and order, the office of kingship reveals God as the true King and Lawgiver of man.[71] Similarly, the calling of the subjects to submit in loyal obedience to their king reveals that man's true state is that of dependence on God, from whom alone he can expect help and deliverance. Every vocation, regardless of its outward significance and the apparent importance of its tasks, bears witness to God and unveils His nature.[72] Because the fellowships of the family and the nation are created to reflect the life of the Triune God it is true that "the analogy between the human and the divine is not an imaginary one, but exists in the nature of things".[73] Therefore human relationships are the means through which God imparts knowledge of Himself and the true state of man.[74]

The fellowships of family and nation should never be considered in and for themselves. Then they will be regarded only as part and parcel of the changeable and transient world. Only when they are understood in their necessary relation to the Triune God, their creative Archetype, can their permanence, dignity and purpose be maintained. That is why Maurice could exclaim: "Oh! if there were no such visions [of God], brethren, what an utterly dark and weary and unintelligible place this world would be! How

70 Cf. *The Kingdom of Christ* (1838) III, 307: "If the ideas of husband and father, which must in some sense be acknowledged to be of divine origin, have not divine significance given to them, it is far less possible that we can see any significance in the idea of a king or lawgiver which we may plausibly enough suppose to be of more human origin."

71 Cf. *The Prophets*, 12–3: "Such kings – instead of intercepting the rays of His light, instead of putting themselves in place of Him – would continually remind their subjects of His presence; would impart to them a sense of divine government which they had never possessed before; would make them understand that a true divine government must also be a true human government; that man is made in the image of God; that the heavenly offices are represented in the earthly." Since the office of a king is a sign and witness of God Himself as the sovereign Lawgiver and Ruler, Maurice felt bound to preserve the monarchy and reject any idea of democracy or of the sovereignty of the people, which meant the abolition of monarchy to most of his contemporaries: "I begin – – in the acknowledgement of the divine sovereignty; thence I come to the Tory idea of kings reigning by the grace of God. This I hold to be the first of political truths historically, and the first fundamentally; that is to say, I do not look upon it only as belonging to the time in which it was asserted and developed, but as bequeathed by that time to all subsequent times" (*Life* I, 485).

72 Cf. *Country Churches*, 329: "Every act of mercy which our higher science is able to accomplish for sufferers from sickness, becomes a witness for God; so the work of every magistrate becomes a witness for Him equally; so commerce as it extends the bonds of fellowship between lands, and shows how one can give what another lacks, bears a witness no less mighty and effectual."

73 *What is Revelation?*, 100.

74 Cf. *Life* II, 563: "At the same time I know you will, more than ever, recognise with me the permanence and dignity of all human relations. God, it seems to me, has made and does make His revelation to us specially through them, though I own – – the great if the subordinate worth of the revelation through the outer world of nature," and *The Epistles of St. John*, 258: "God educates us by visible and imperfect parents – *fathers after the flesh* – to seek for Himself, the invisible and perfect Parent, 'the Father of our spirits'. Through brothers and sisters, through the love between sexes, through the marriage bond, we are prepared to apprehend the relations in which we stand to the Kingdom of Heaven."

completely we should be given up to the emptiest phantoms, to the basest worship of phantoms! What mere shows and mockeries would the state and ceremonial of kings, the debates of legislators, the yearnings and struggles of people, become! How truly would the earth be what it seemed to the worn-out misanthropical libertine, 'a stage, and all the men and women merely players'."[75]

The man who desires to perform the tasks of his vocation in accordance with its true purpose can never rest content with himself and his own abilities. He is forced to face the fact that his own sin and the sin of others is at work to destroy fellowship among men and will consequently see the need for God's guidance and the gift of love.[76] So, through their various vocations, God educates men to a true self-knowledge which makes them turn to God as the only one who can sustain their lives.[77] However, precisely because this desire for God arises from man's life with his fellow-men, it can never be a mere selfish quest for a Saviour of the individual soul. Through his vocational life man realises his need for God as the common Father for all men, and it is only in the life in the fellowships of family and nation that men discover the basic problems of human existence. This life provides men with a measure by which to test all the theories and systems for solving the problems of human life which have been offered them.[78]

75 *The Prophets*, 234.
76 Cf. *The Patriarchs*, 103: "The discipline which had raised him [Abraham] to a higher personal standard, which had enabled him to be truly a man, had been discipline through and for his family. His relations with his wife, his nephew, his children, had shown him what was petty and grovelling in himself, – had been the means of awakening the faith, hope, patience, which lifted him above himself, and made him act as the servant of God," and *Country Churches*, 336–7: "if the carpenter does neglect his tools, or the shoemaker his last, or the physician his patients, or the lawyer his clients, he will not find this home [Christ]; he will not know what need he has of it; he will not be able to abide in it. The harder a man works, the more he learns that he cannot let his thoughts go astray. They must be fixed somewhere. They must be turned to some one who will show him how he must pursue his business heartily, not lazily; honestly, and not like a rogue; as a freeman, not as a slave. Abide in this Lord of your hearts; set your heart upon Him and you will get this help."
77 Cf. *Sermons* III, 136: "it is in the common hard warfare of daily life that one becomes conversant with these secrets [i. e. that mysterious region wherein lie the roots of all our thoughts, feelings, purposes, acts]; in it one learns all the metaphysics that are worth knowing. In trying to do right, as husbands, brothers, fathers, citizens, we find the bands which hold us; the disappointments we meet with in our efforts to encounter the most ordinary temptations and provocations, to do the duty that lies nearest to us; the difficulty of being honest and truthful, still more, of being trustful and loving. Thus are we taught that we want an ever-present helper and deliverer, a daily absolution, a renewal of strength hour by hour." See also *Sermons* VI, 88.
78 Cf. *What is Revelation?*, 197: "But you and I are not schoolmen; we are roughing it in the world. We have to look upon all questions as they bear upon the actual business of life," and *The Apocalypse*, 182: "The arguments of doctors go very little way in settling controversies; generally increase them, and add to the perplexities of those who are suffering from them. But the earth swallows them up. They may be exceedingly sublime, heavenly speculations; who knows? But they do not meet the daily necessities, business, sufferings of earth. And after all, what we ask for is that which will do this. Opinions with the clearest warrants of antiquity, with the finest gloss of novelty, must be brought to this test. What can they do for us? You say, they are very probable: there is great evidence for them. No doubt;

The human relationships being the reality to which God has bound man, it is for Maurice obvious that it is the problems of ordinary daily life that the Gospel is meant to explain and solve. It does not at all deal with such so-called religious questions as the future destiny of the soul, but it does proclaim what the Human Order is and teaches men how to live in the human relationships with their fellow-men. Conversely, he who lives in the human relationships realises his own true needs and therefore opens himself to God's revelation.[79] The Gospel and ordinary human life are inextricably bound together.[80]

For Maurice the idea of man as a spirit warranted a deep respect for the common man. In contrast to the comfortable life of the rich, his hard life with its wants and sufferings sharpens his ability to distinguish the truth from its counterfeits and constrains him to seek the unchangeable reality which alone can sustain him and solve the riddles, perplexities and difficulties of his life. Now such clearsightedness is acquired only through life in the human relationships itself. The need to provide his family with its daily bread forces the common man to remain in his vocation. He has neither the time nor the means to escape the duties of ordinary daily life. He cannot take refuge in literary, philosophical and religious coteries and cliques in which only those who share the same opinions are considered as fellow-men. The common man rightly scorns all human systems and theories because they founder on the hard facts of ordinary life. He is brought to understand that only God's revelation of Himself can provide that sorely needed foundation on which he can rest his life.[81]

Created by God and reflecting His eternal nature, human relationships necessarily point to the Triune God as their ultimate foundation and explanation. He who sees

but I want something that I can rest upon; not something that is very likely, but something that is. Thanks to the good honest earth which in due time sucks up all watery notions, and only leaves that which has proved itself to be substantial."

79 Cf. *Family Worship*, VI: "I learnt that every layman, whatever his present confusions or scepticism, has in his domestic life a clue to the mysteries of the Gospel, as they are set forth in the history of the Bible, in the direct language of the Creeds, of which our teaching cannot deprive him. Theology and Family life are so closely linked together by God, that men cannot put them asunder. They must fall together; they may rise together," and p. 105: "the Father of our Lord Jesus Christ -- has made the family to supply that true *organon* of theology which all theories and schemes of divinity have tried to be, and failed to be."

80 Cf. *Sermons* II, 99: "What we have to desire is, that this faith should be no longer a mere blind faith, that it should be able to justify itself; as it will do, when the plain facts of human life are brought side by side with the express words of Scripture, and they are used to interpret each other," and *Christmas Day*, 282: "If certain truths, which you [the medical students] have been wont to call theological, have been thrust upon your notice, you will allow that they seem to be suggested by the facts which occupy you in your chambers, by the scenes which you witness in the sick-room, and instead of leading you into an unprofessional line of thought, you will begin to ask yourselves whether the voice of the preacher and the words of the Inspired Book are not guide-posts to principles which lie at the foundation of all you think, and speak, and do."

81 Cf. *Theological Essays*, 11: "Oh! let us give over our miserable notion that poor men only want teaching about things on the surface, or will ever be satisfied with such teaching. They are groping about the roots of things whether we know it or not."

the image cannot but ask for the archetype. This fact has prompted the rise of the various religions. Religion did not basically originate in primitive man's attempt to explain the phenomena of nature, as Comte asserted.[82] Admittedly, man lives in the Natural Order, but far more important is the fact that he belongs to the Human Order and is placed in relationship to his fellow-men. The desire to understand the Natural Order is quite subordinate to the necessity of understanding the human relationships with which his life as a personal being is bound up. Here he meets problems entirely different from those connected with explanations of the laws of the Natural Order.

Thus in his calling man is confronted by the demand to serve his fellow-men in love. Nonetheless, he can neglect and disobey the claims of his vocation and so violate his relationships to his fellow-men and destroy human fellowship. This situation raises the question as to the meaning of these human relationships and the nature of the "I" who, though placed in the Human Order together with his fellow-men, refuses to live in it. The religions represent the attempt to answer these fundamental questions. Their sole concern is to find a solution of the problems inherent in human life – they are interested in an explanation of nature only in so far as it is relevant to the interpretation of human existence.[83]

All specific religious ideas and problems arise from man's experience in human relationships. This is true of the origin of the idea of man as an immortal being. In the fellowships of family and nation man is bound to those who have preceded him and to those who are to succeed him. This makes the individual realise that his life does not belong to the transient moment and that it is not bounded by time and space.[84] Through human relationships man is carried beyond himself and made to see himself as part of an Order that lasts from generation to generation. It is furthermore significant that men refer the existence of human fellowships to divine powers

---

82 See *Social Morality*, 90.

83 Cf. *Social Morality*, 90–1: "But why ascribe these phenomena [of nature] to living agents at all? Why look at all beyond the tempest or the earthquake, the sunshine or the rain? If men bow down to powers above themselves, these are the powers. And such would assuredly be the tendency of men, such *is* their tendency now as much as ever it was. What counteracts this tendency? There are other facts more precious, more important than these, of which they *must* get the meaning if they can. They are sons, brothers, husbands; these relations are more serious to them than the tempests and the earthquakes; affect them more than the sun and the rain. They are with them at all times; at all times there is a disposition to cast them off. To be rid of this order is impossible; yet every father, son, husband, wife, brother, sister, master, servant can produce an effect upon it which he can not produce upon the fall of the rain or the heat of the sun. It was not then an impulse of mere curiosity which led men to ask what these relations signified, how they were upheld. The demand becomes inevitable for any people who have perceived their worth, who have become aware of the perils to which they were exposed."

84 Cf. *Social Morality*, 101: "With relationships is associated Memory and Anticipation; with them the thought of immortality is interwined", and *The Gospel of St. John*, 256: "But the reverence for ancestry, – the affection that binds us to a family and a nation, does not belong to time. It brings past and present into closest proximity; it leaps over distinctions of costume and circumstance, to claim affinity with the inmost heart of those who lived generations ago. For all family feeling, and all national feeling, has its root in a living God; therefore it defies death; it treats death as only belonging to the individual." See also *Social Morality*, 197 and *Theological Essays*, 40.

104

which, they believe, have created and defended them against all attempts to destroy them. Again, when men are seeking for the transcendent foundation of human relationships, they do not conceive of it in terms of natural forces but of living persons: "there seems to have been a strong persuasion among men that human relationships have something answering to them in that higher world from which they suppose their heroes to have descended."[85] Owing to the conviction that there is an intimate relation between the divine world and the human world, the gods are pictured in the personal categories proper to the vocations. They rule and give orders to man, and he shows trust, obedience and gratitude towards them. Although these beliefs are mixed with much falsehood, they represent true insights. However, this discovery is not man's work: it is the work of God Himself, who has imparted this knowledge through the human relationships.[86]

There is another respect in which religions have revealed a true understanding of the fundamental problems of human existence. The individual knows himself to be placed in an ordered fellowship with other men but, at the same time, he experiences how he can violate this order and how his selfishness and desire for independence isolate him from his fellows and from the divine powers. Man appears to be left to his own devices and, ultimately, to death.[87] Man is forced to ask whether life or death is the stronger power at work on earth and in his own life.[88] He cries out for a redeemer who can set him free from the sin which has been thrust upon him in his daily life. Motivated by a dim awareness that only an atonement can restitute broken fellowship and restore unity and harmony, man seeks to propitiate the divine powers, whom he feels that he has offended by sins committed in his relations with other men.

Since the various religions arose from the attempt to solve the problems of man's existence, they represent a true insight into man's basic needs. For this reason they can guide us to a clear understanding of the fundamental human problems and make us see that only God Himself can solve them – their beliefs must not be rejected as

85 *Theological Essays*, 20. Cf. also *Family Worship*, 73: "Did you ever consider how the gods of all countries were associated with the thoughts of fathers, mothers, husbands, wives, brothers, sisters?"; p. 83: "Religion and Domestic Life have some mysterious and inseparable connexion. You traced it in the Pagan mythology," and *The Kingdom of Christ* (1838) III, 291: "Paganism, considered as a mythology, exhibits the feeling that there is a meaning in these [human] relations; that they are the image of higher and more mysterious relations. But it explains none of these relations, it cries out for an explanation of them. The Pagan mythology says to every ear that is open to hear the words, says with the most affecting earnestness, We are sure that the bonds which bind us to each other here upon earth, need to be sustained, *are* sustained by other bonds, which connect us with the invisible world. We are sure that through these there is some way of ascending to the perception of those other bonds. Oh! tell us the secret, show us what this irresistible conviction means."
86 Cf. *Social Morality*, 102: "Accepting the belief that the God of all families does reveal Himself through the relations of the family I can appreciate the mythology which recognizes that belief, I can value every conception which men have formed about a union between the human and divine."
87 See *Theological Essays*, 40.
88 See *The Kingdom of Christ* I, 85–7.

simple falsehood as contemporary orthodox theology had done.[89] It was, on the other hand, quite clear to Maurice that the religions do not express the whole truth. Although they have laid bare the true problems of human life, they are deficient because they have attempted to solve them themselves and to find an answer of their own to man's quest for God. They assert man's need for reconciliation and atonement, but instead of believing that God Himself will come out to meet man as the deliverer and the atoner they try to propitiate Him by their own works and sacrifices.[90] The religions imagine God to be a distant power which man must seek out and establish fellowship with through his own endeavours. This false way of salvation is not only a denial of the living God, who is always near to His creatures, but it also leads men either to human pride or to hopeless despair. Similarly, although the religions rightly maintain that there is an intimate relation between the human and the divine, they do not wait for the revelation of Him in whose image man and the human fellowships are created. Instead they picture the divine in the image of the human,[91] transmitting to the divine powers the sin and mutability which they find in the external world and in their relationships to other men. It always will be true that "men cannot shake off the thought of *some* God, try as hard as they will. They may forget the good God, the true God, the Maker of heaven and earth – their deliverer and friend. But they will make to themselves a god; they will make him out of their own cruel fancies; they will make him like themselves."[92]

As man is created and upheld by God, he can never be satisfied with himself and with that which he himself achieves. Even when he is ignorant of God, or denies Him,

89 Cf. *Family Worship*, 78–9: "If I did not see so much meaning in the beliefs of the Heathen world, I might be ready to accept that modern and popular opinion. I might hold that there was no explanation of their truth, no exposure of their falsehood, to be found anywhere. I reverence and love the old Heathen world too much to entertain this opinion. The feeling of all nations after a Father, if haply they might find Him, is too sacred in my eyes to have nothing which corresponds to it. I cannot accept the horrible conclusion that the history and thoughts of so many thousands of years signified nothing, or that if they signified anything, He to whom they pointed, has given us no key to the signification."

90 Cf. *The Kingdom of Heaven*, XV: "We must treat it [religion] as an invention of men, as their substitute for the message of God. Those who hold the Bible not only to contain, but to be, the word of God, are especially bound to take this course. – – Men, by their religion, seek to establish some meeting-place or reconciliation between them and God. The Gospel is the news that God is reconciled to man in His Son, that in Him there is a meeting-point between God and man. A religion must always be affected by the local habits, by the individual temperaments of those who profess it. A Gospel is the unveiling or discovery to men of a common Head." See also *Sermons* I, 41.

91 Cf. *The Patriarchs*, 123: "They [all the heathen world] must have actual beings who could teach them; who could impart light and knowledge to them; who could see the past, the present, and the future in one. They tried to conceive of such Being. They could but shape their conceptions from the things and the persons which lay around them. Looking for a ground of their thoughts and experiences, their thoughts and experiences became the ground of those to whom they referred them", and *Social Morality*, 102: "I can see why those conceptions must become false when they assume the human as the ground of the divine."

92 *Religions*, 158–9. Cf. also *Christmas Day*, 139: "For men must worship something; if they do not worship an unseen Being who loves and cares for them, they will worship the works of their own hands; they will secretly bow down to the things that they see, and hear, and taste, and smell; these will be their lords and masters, these will be their cruel tyrants."

106

he is driven into a restless attempt to find the meaning of his life in something beyond himself. Mankind must always be searching for its creative and lifegiving archetype, which alone can enable it to understand itself and which alone can ensure and support human fellowship. In all its aspects human life is characterized by unrest until man finds the One in whom he is created to live. This is so because God has placed man in the Human Order and is educating him through its fellowships to understand that the only law of his life is to live with the Father through Christ, the Head of humanity and of every man.

II

SIN AND THE DIVINE ORDER

Chapter IV

SIN AND THE DEVIL

In the preceding chapters we have described Maurice's idea of the Divine Order. We have seen that the entire universe as created by God is always upheld by Him. This must necessarily be so, because it is decreed by the loving will of the eternal God. As the Head of all mankind, Christ is ever present to impart life and light to every man. Furthermore, God has through Christ established the Human Order with the fellowships of family and nation and through the vocations appointed men to serve each other in love. So the entire universe constitutes a perfect, harmonious whole. Because God is ever-acting creative love, it is an unchangeable fact that every man lives, moves and has his being in God.

However, we meet with a strand in Maurice's thought which apparently runs counter to the idea of an unchangeable, harmonious Divine Order. Maurice spoke strongly about the facticity of sin and its devastating effects. As already indicated, Maurice's description of the origin and nature of religions disclosed that man is possessed by sin and selfishness, which leads to an estrangement from God and his fellow-men and calls forth the cry for a divine deliverer and atoner to set things straight.

The necessity of treating Maurice's idea of sin seriously is further emphasized by the fact that his experience of the power of sin was an important factor in his final break with his father's Unitarianism. A deepened understanding of sin, and a desire to be delivered from it, forced him to reach out in new directions in order to satisfy his new spiritual need.[1]

During his spiritual crisis in the year 1828 the sense of man's sinfulness became an

---

1 Cf. *Life* II, 15: "When I began in earnest to seek God for myself, the feeling that I needed a deliverer from an overwhelming weight of selfishness was the predominant one in my mind." In a letter to his father, dated February 10th, 1829, Maurice wrote: "That there is such evil lurking at the root even of the conduct which seems most outwardly fair I have learnt even from the little self-knowledge I possess. And this conviction, I believe, occasions the principal difference between my opinions and yours. -- My heart was not sincerely devoted to God. I fancied so till I had searched it, but then I saw very clearly that self and the world had far the greatest part of it. If I could have conceived of God as anything less than perfect love, I might have found less difficulty in satisfying myself that I was conformed to the standard which He requires me to attain. But believing Him to be Love in the most absolute, unqualified sense, I felt the difficulty of approaching Him, or even of comprehending His nature, almost infinite, because love divided my heart with a thousand evil passions, and was itself tainted with evil and corruption like them" (*Life* I, 94-5).

111

overpowering reality for Maurice, and this profound consciousness of sin did not diminish with the years. It accompanied him throughout his life and left an indelible mark upon his preaching and writing. His words to his sister, immediately after his religious crisis, could have been written at any later point in his life: "I think I am beginning to feel something of the intense pride and atheism of my own heart, of its hatred to truth, of its utter lovelessness."[2]

This fact prompts the question as to whether Maurice, whilst acknowledging the fact of sin, could still maintain the idea of the harmonious Divine Order or whether he, in describing the created universe and the life of mankind, thought and argued along two different lines which, in the last analysis, defy reconciliation. To answer this question a closer examination of Maurice's concept of sin and its effects is required.

1. The Origin and Nature of Sin

Maurice regarded the power of sin and evil as an indisputable fact in the world and in the history of mankind. It enslaves man and destroys human life.[3] Man groans under the bondage of sin and strives to be set free from its chains.[4]

However terrible a foe, sin is not a power which meets man from without and irresistibly enthrals him. Its existence cannot be explained either from any imperfections in the created world or from the nature of man. Sin is man's own responsibility since it takes its origin in his will.[5]

---

2 *Life* I, 119 (January 4th, 1831).
3 Cf. *Family Worship*, 110–1: "The Apostles did not feel the difficulty which we feel in preaching deliverance till they had reduced sin into a theory and deduced it from an ancestor. They found men groaning under the burden of evil, they found nations under the hoof of an oppressor, families broken and divided by the sins of husbands and wives, fathers and children. They found them believing in false cruel gods, enemies whom it was a blessing to forget, who must be bribed to be merciful and just."
4 Cf. *Sacrifice*, 141: "the whole history of the world, of every portion of the world, for six thousand years, proclaims that the spiritual bondage is real; that this is the bondage from which men are seeking by all contrivances to break loose; that all material bondage is but the accident and result of it." See also *Theological Essays*, 12.
5 Cf. *The Apocalypse*, 289: "the source of evil lies in the will; – – our wills have set themselves in opposition to God's will", and *The Prophets*, 418: "In every case the cause of ruin would be not some weakness or flaw in the constitution of this race, not some adverse circumstances, but pride; a determination to exist for itself and by itself." Sin in the universe is not due to any imperfection in the creation, but has its origin in man, who is created to have dominion over all involuntary creatures: "we believe Him [God] to have given all things their right type and order; – – we believe them when in their relation to Him to be still very good; – – we believe their disturbance and incoherency to be the result of a voluntary renunciation of allegiance to Him, by the only creature which could commit such an act – –. Man – – is God's minister, acting for Him, able to perform His intentions towards His involuntary creatures; able, because he has a will, to set them at nought" (*The Kingdom of Christ* II, 32–3).

112

We have seen how important it was for Maurice to maintain that man was created by God as a spirit or voluntary being. Yet this did not imply that man was created to live independently. On the contrary, he was intended to depend entirely on God in trust and obedience.[6] This fellowship was not, however, forced upon man; by asserting that man had a will Maurice only intended to maintain that the relationship between God and man was a personal one, based on the freedom of love. That man, in contrast to all other creatures, has received the privilege of living in a personal fellowship with God, implied on the other hand that he was able by virtue of his will to refuse to live according to the law of his creation.[7] Now the simple fact is that every man, instead of choosing to live in dependent faith upon God and obey His will of love, has decided to live an independent life, loving himself and seeking only his own gratification and glory.[8]

By the rebellion of his will man attempts to make himself a god.[9] Because "sin consists in setting up a self, in refusing to own any other end beyond self",[10] sin is nothing but human pride and self-glorification. When man refuses to live in dependence upon God and His love, he denies Him as his Creator and Lord. The denial of God can therefore be said to constitute the very essence of sin.[11] Inasmuch as man refuses to trust in God and expect all good gifts from Him and instead relies upon himself,

6 As previously mentioned, the fact that man is created with a will signifies that he is meant to submit freely and willingly to God's will and to allow God to impart to his will its true freedom and power. Maurice therefore insisted that "the idea of the Divine Will was inseparably involved with the energy and activity of their own human will" *(The Kingdom of Christ* I, 124. Cf. also *The Faith of the Liturgy,* 40: "the source of all energy in men to do what is right and good, is from God; – – He originates the Will to do right, – – His Grace furthers that Will and enables its purpose to become acts.")

7 Cf. *The Kingdom of Christ* (1838) II, 107: "God has established an order among natural creatures, which these natural creatures cannot disobey. But God has also established an order among voluntary creatures, which voluntary creatures can, if they please, disobey."

8 Cf. *Sacrifice,* 230: "The sin of the world is its self-will, its self-gratification"; *The Epistles of St. John,* 54: "All sin – – is connected by the Apostle with the loss of fellowship. A man shuts himself up in himself. He denies that he has anything to do with God; he denies that he has anything to do with his brothers," and *The Prophets,* 107: "self-seeking and self-will have been rending asunder families, the nations, the Church, the world."

9 Cf. *The Gospel of St. John,* 157–8: "'Ye shall be as gods' was the first temptation presented to human beings, – the temptation to which they yielded. The ambition has never ceased in any age or in any man", and p. 298: "There *was* the greatest peril of men becoming Lucifers, – of their setting themselves up in the place of God."

10 *Sermons* I, 83.

11 Cf. *Sermons* II, 195: "The denial of that dominion [of God] over things, over other persons, over yourself, is Sin. The desire not to be under a Righteous Ruler, to break loose from Him, to be outside of Him – this desire cherished, gratified, fed upon, till the sense of government is gone, or till the government is supposed to be just the reverse of what it is, expresses the nature of Sin. Each man, in the depth of his own nature, is trying to be by himself, to live independently," and *The Epistles of St. John,* 305: "The sin is the denial of this relationship; the setting up to be independent of Him. The *truth* which the sin rebels against is, first, the truth that is in God Himself; secondly, the truth that we are born of Him, that we are His children."

Maurice could also describe unbelief as the true mark of sin.[12] Unbelief or distrust in God's love is the root from which all other sins stem.[13]

Maurice also asserted, however, that sin arises from man's ignorance of God. When men turn from God, the reason is that they do not know that God's only desire is to impart goodness; they imagine Him to be revengeful and malevolent towards them, and so seek their happiness in themselves or in the external, visible world. So ignorance generates unbelief, distrust and suspicion of God.[14]

Maurice did not see any contradiction between the idea of ignorance as the source of sin and the view that sin has its origin in man's rebellious will and his desire to make his self the centre of his life. Often he used these two ideas indiscriminately or combined them, as in the following characteristic statement: *"Not to see Him, not to know Him is the cause of sin. To see Him, to know Him, is the emancipation from it. -- sin and the sight or knowledge of Christ are antagonistic. The act of sin is the act of shutting our eyes to the true Lord and Deliverer; if we had kept our eyes open, if we had seen and confessed Him, we should not have sinned. This is a truth, and it is a universal truth."*[15] At other times Maurice stated that the consequence of the rebellion of the will is ignorance of God; they stand together as cause and effect.[16]

However hard man attempts to make himself the centre of the universe and forget the true God, he will, according to Maurice, never succeed. Man cannot undo the fact that he is created to live in fellowship with God. Rebellious man will always be haunted by the idea of God and compelled to ask for God and His relation to mankind. But his knowledge of God will be false, since sin has drawn a veil over the reason or the spiritual eye, by which man is intended to see God as He truly is.[17] He judges God by his own false standards and fashions Him in his own image. As self-

---

12 Cf. *The Prayer-Book,* 258: "Wherein had all creatures failed? Simply in this: they had not trusted God. They had not yielded themselves to Him, relying on His love, casting themselves unreservedly upon it; certain that in suffering and anguish, He was there and was the same, and that in death He would not leave them", and p. 365: "Because we depend and trust so little, we prove that we are still trying to be gods – *that* is our sin."

13 Cf. *The Kingdom of Heaven,* 46: "God wished to tear out their sins by the roots. He was not striking at some forms of evil, but at the great mother sin; at their trust in themselves, at their distrust of Him", and *Country Churches,* 360: "the sin of all is the same – unbelief in God, distrust in His Goodness and Truth."

14 Cf. *Sacrifice,* 299: "the destruction into which they fall through ignorance of Him, and of His purposes to them"; *The Kingdom of Christ* (1838) I, 198: "salvation is the deliverance from the sin, of which the cause at once and the penalty, is ignorance of him", and *The Prayer-Book,* 72: "A gracious Friend, ever nigh to us – ever persuading our hearts to trust Him – ever inviting us to give up that suspicion which has been the cause of our sin, and is the fruit of it; this is He of whom the Scriptures preach to us."

15 *The Epistles of St. John,* 182.

16 Cf. *The Unity of the New Testament,* 389–90: "Rebellion against a perfect Will which has been manifesting itself in acts of love to all creatures, which has been exhibiting its power, its redeeming power, over them and through them and in them, has been the misery of Jew as well as Gentile. This has been the cause of blindness, the incapacity of discerning the nature of that Will, which has come upon both."

17 Cf. *The Prophets,* 490: "It was their baseness and selfishness which made their eyes dim that they could not see, and their ears heavy that they could not hear. It was so then; it was so in every generation afterwards", and p. 468: "Ezekiel announces to them a great and

114

seeking man aims only at the gratification of his own selfishness, he necessarily believes that God is a capricious despot who, like himself, is dominated by selfishness. Unbelieving man sees God as a spiteful enemy[18] and imagines that he must seek to appease Him lest He should destroy him in His wrath.[19] The misconceptions of unbelief about God could for Maurice be "summed up in the thought, 'We have no friend to whom we may look up, none who will take care of us if we ask him, none to whom our cries will reach'."[20] He who denies God must necessarily conceive of God as a hateful and destructive deity.

Just as man can never escape the idea of God, so he can never be satisfied with making his own self a god. Because man, by his very constitution, is unable to create, he must always find something outside himself to worship and rely upon, as a divine being with power to gratify his desires. If man refuses to obey and worship the true God he must raise up new gods to serve.[21] Inevitably unbelief leads to idolatry.[22]

For Maurice, man consists of spirit and flesh, the former relating him to the eternal invisible world, the latter gravitating towards the transient changeable world. However, if man's spirit refuses to live in fellowship with its true Lord, it cuts itself off from Him who alone is able to bind it to eternal unchangeable reality. The result will by inner necessity be that his animal nature, having lost its counterpoise, drags him down into sensuality, and man, seeking his new gods in the changeable things of the world, will be dominated by them.[23] But as man is created to live with God in the eternal world, he can never be content with the idols which his unbelief has raised up and shaped in the image of the visible world. Sensuality can never satisfy man's true desires; they assert themselves even in the midst of his idolatry because he continues to be a spirit. Man is continually driven on from idol to idol, searching for his true good, a search that only leads to continual restlessness and despair. Man's rebellion

eternal moral law, one of the most varied application; God will answer you according to your idols. The truth which is presented to you, will be coloured, distorted, inverted, by the eye which receives it."

18 Cf. *Country Churches*, 359: "Do we not continually believe this God, this Father, this Deliverer to be our foe; One whom it would be well if we could banish from us for ever? Do we not act as if we wished that there were no such Being; as if we only acknowledged Him because we dare not deny Him?"

19 Cf. *Sacrifice*, 14: "Was not our sin that we *supposed* God to be an arbitrary Being, whom we, by our sacrifices and prayers, were to conciliate? Was not this *the* false notion which lay at the root of all our discontent, of all the evil thoughts and acts which sprung out of it? We did not begin with trust, but with distrust; we did not worship God, because we believed in Him, but because we wished Him not to come near us."

20 *Christmas Day*, 121. Cf. also *The Prophets*, 111: "to regard God as an object of terror or distrust contains the very essence of sin."

21 Cf. *The Prophets*, 172: "We can very easily get rid of that theology which recognises a Righteous Will, a Fatherly Will, as the ground of us and of the universe. We do get rid of that continually; we shake it off as a most inconvenient burthen. But we cannot get rid of *some* theology."

22 Cf. *The Prophets*, 122: "that God is indifferent to His creatures or hates them – – is the foundation of all idolatry."

23 Cf. *The Patriarchs*, 246: "They came into a region of transitoriness and change when they forgot Him, or began to draw their notions of Him from the vicissitudes of the world around them and the fluctuations of their own hearts."

against God and suspicion of Him thus leads him away from God and into the darkness of unbelief and ignorance, and makes him a slave to that nature over which he
was ordained to rule: "The evil is traced to its source when we are told that we have
not abided in Him."[24]

Man's decision to live in independence and selfishness not only isolates him from
God; it also divides him from his fellow-men.[25] By excluding him from fellowship
with God, his self-will cuts him off from the source of self-sacrificing love. Consequently he is no longer able to serve his fellow-men in love, but becomes filled with
hatred and selfishness and the desire to subjugate them to his own selfish ends.[26] Thus
sin destroys the Human Order, in which God has called men to live in the fellowship
of love.[27]

Sin may take many forms and appear in different guises but its essence is always
man's love of his own self.[28] Man will not live in accordance with the law of his
creation; he revolts against God and his fellow-men, forsaking fellowship with them
in order to live for himself in unbelief and hatred.[29]

Because man has no life in himself, the outcome of unbelief and selfishness must
always be death.[30] Death, as the wages of sin, destroys the life of man, as well as
the life of the entire creation.[31]

24 *The Gospel of St. John*, 387.
25 Cf. *Sermons* II, 169: "sin consisted in separation from his fellows as well as from God."
26 Cf. *Country Churches*, 54: "Sin is what separates us from each other. Sin is what prevents
us from understanding each other. Sin is what every man hugs in himself, and which keeps
him away from other people", and *Sermons* IV, 120: "the self-seeker has been separating
himself from his kind – from his race – or has only been using the members of it as instruments for obtaining his own ends."
27 Cf. *The Gospel of St. John*, 363: "Is not the spirit of selfishness that which has destroyed
human society, that which wars against the Son of Man, that which declares that man shall
not show forth the image of the perfect and unselfish God?", and *The Patriarchs*, 200–1,
where "the worship of visible things, Sensuality, Self-will, Selfishness" are described as "the
enemies of God's order".
28 Hence Maurice can neither admit any gradation of sins nor accept the possibility of sin
being merely external and moral: "For whence come the outward acts of unrighteousness,
but from the unrighteous heart and will? And what is an unrighteous heart or will but
a heart or will which has severed itself from a Righteous Being and is making another
object of worship for itself?" (*The Prophets*, 410).
29 Cf. *Sacrifice*, 187: "All sin is contradiction; if you speak of it, you must denote it by words
that cross and seem to confute each other. Unless men were spirits, you could not complain
of them for acting as beasts; unless they proved every moment that they were framed for
fellowship and mutual dependence, you could not blame their selfishness; if you were not
sure that they were intended to obey God's gracious will and to walk in His ways, you could
not accuse them of ruining themselves by determining, each one of them, to have a will and
way of his own."
30 Cf. *Moral and Metaphysical Philosophy* I, XXVII: "A creature sinking into itself dies; so
long as it is associated with a kind, it lives. I hold, as Christians generally hold, that man is
capable of that which we cannot impute to other creatures, – that he is capable of choosing
to desert the law of his kind, of choosing to sink into himself. I hold that a man cannot look
upon his death as he looks upon that of other creatures, for this reason, – though inevitable,
he must connect it with choice; he must accept it as a sentence of the law upon his choice."
31 Cf. *The Church a Family*, 122: "When they thought of death it was as of a mighty power
which had intruded itself into God's blessed order, and had broken up the fellowship, for

Speaking of death, Maurice is more concerned with spiritual death than with physical death. Real death does not occur with the coming of bodily death, but consists of man's separation from God and his fellow-men. The contrast between life and death is primarily a contrast between man's life with God and his separation from God respectively.[32] When man, through Christ as his Head, lives in fellowship with God he has true life, eternal life. But if he refuses to live in fellowship with God, he has given himself up to true death, eternal death.[33]

Maurice strongly asserted that, just as sin implies death, so it is inseparably bound up with bodily and spiritual miseries and evils. However, he fought the prevailing orthodox idea of his day which, in his view, stated that God inflicted these misfortunes upon man as punishment for his sins. When man, who is created to receive life and love from God, separates himself from the only source of life and love he brings himself, by this very act, into a state which is the deepest wretchedness, and from which flow all spiritual and bodily miseries and evils.[34] God has not cursed and condemned man; by his self-will man has inflicted on himself the greatest curse and condemnation, the state of being without God. Similarly, after physical death God does not condemn man to hell as a punishment for his wickedness and sin. Hell is simply "separation from God, – – the darkness into which those fall who love darkness rather than the light which has come into the world, and is shining into their

which He had formed His creatures. It was the great divider, that which took each person and thing apart, cutting the link between that and every other person and thing", and *The Patriarchs*, 201: "Would not Death, the breaker-up of family and national fellowship, present itself to him as the great intruder into Creation, which must be crushed before it could vindicate its true and original meaning?"

32 Cf. *The Patriarchs*, 57–8: "We may insist that it [death] shall mean the moment when the breath goes out of the body. And then we are disposed to say in like manner, that Life means the time during which the breath stays in the body. But this is not the *popular* use of the words. The common people feel that Life and Death are two powers struggling for them and in them; their superstitions show that they feel so. – – And most assuredly this is not the sense of the words in any part of *Scripture*. – – At that instant the creature loses its connection with surrounding things; it sinks into itself; it becomes a mere separate existence. That is Death. And therefore in the day Adam ate of the fruit, he died. That day he took his place as a creature formed out of the dust of the ground, as a mere Adam, and not as a creature formed in the image of God."

33 Cf. *Life* II, 415: "a spiritual being, created for a certain state without which its faculties and existence are unintelligible and contradictory, has [in the spiritual death] lost the possession or fruition of that state. It means that a creature which draws its life from the Eternal God is deprived of the Life that most directly, essentially, truly is His; the Life which Christ manifested to men, and of which He desired men to be partakers", and *The Conflict*, 188: "The eternal life must be the life of the Eternal God of which men are permitted to partake. The eternal death must be the separation from the Eternal God, whatever may be the length of that separation."

34 Cf. *Family Worship*, 214: "Eternal misery is in the separation from that Father and that Family. – – Into that misery I say my unbelief has brought me and does bring me. I carry about with me as you do, as every man does, an unbelief in the Father whom Christ revealed to us, a solitary self-seeking mind which cuts me off from His family. This is not a temporal misery; it can be measured by no minutes or hours. It is an eternal misery; it is the misery of a spirit; created for intercourse with Him who is and who was and who is to come; created to share His Life, and choosing Death instead of Life."

hearts."[35] The man who decides for a life of independence has already condemned himself to the confinement of hell, the state of unbelief and selfishness.

Death and hell, with all their misery and wretchedness, are simply different ways of describing the life of a sinner without God and His love.[36] As sin takes its origin in man's self-will, it is selfishness which is the true curse of human life.[37] It is not God man must fear as the One who punishes him with unspeakable misery and shuts him up in the prison of death and hell, but his own selfishness, which urges him to rebel against God and shuts him up in himself – this is man's real "prison-house".[38] God, on the contrary, does not leave man to his self-inflicted misery; His sole desire is to deliver him from his selfishness and lead him back to fellowship with Himself. God is continually struggling with men's selfish wills, urging them to give up their resistance and unbelief.[39] Once resistance and unbelief have been vanquished, the chains of death and hell are immediately broken, and then man enjoys eternal life, life with God through Christ as his Head.

3. The Devil and His Activity

But Maurice does not only talk of men's selfish wills. Behind man's sin stands the Devil, who is always seeking to subjugate God's creation and enslave it. Man is placed between God and the Devil and must submit to one of them.[40] The independence for his self that man thinks he will win through his revolt against God is therefore illusory; it only means that he has given himself up to the tyrannous dominion of the Devil.

Maurice knew perfectly well that any belief in the Devil as the enemy of God and of man is considered primitive mythology in so-called enlightened circles – a tale rendered obsolete by the progress of mankind and civilization. But this did not

---

35 *Sacrifice* XLVI. Cf. also *The Apocalypse*, 322: "Death and hell import a separation from God, a denial and contradiction of God. The bottomless pit is Atheism, the state of being without God", and *Sermons* V, 158: "the horror of the Kingdom of Hell consists in the absence of all knowledge of God's Righteousness and Truth and Love."

36 Cf. *Country Churches*, 304: "if they choose their sins instead of His righteousness and truth, they choose misery instead of peace, death instead of life, the kingdom of hell instead of the Kingdom of Heaven."

37 Cf. *Sermons* I, 306: "This great load of self, – of selfish thoughts, of selfish plans, of fears for self, of hopes for self, – is crushing us all, individuals, nations, Churches"; *Social Morality*, 409: "he feels his selfishness to be the curse and misery of his existence", and *The Commandments*, 148: "The secret that the self-will is itself the burden, that that is separating us from each other and from God, that it must be taken away before we can offer ourselves, and all our energies of mind and body, as sacrifices to God, dawns upon us at times."

38 *Theological Essays*, 18.

39 Cf. *The Prayer-Book*, 385: "He [God] is maintaining a conflict with the self-will which is the curse and dislocation of the world, and – – every plague, pestilence, insurrection, revolution, is a step in the history of that conflict, tending towards the final victory."

40 Cf. *Sermons* I, 150: "It is enough for us to understand who the combatants in all cases are. It is enough for us to know that it is the will in man which God and the devil are both claiming; and that it is the will which must submit to either."

weigh with him, because the actual facts of human life demanded the acceptance of the Devil's existence: "You will return – – to this mode of speaking, to this literal acceptance of the Divine record, not heeding or fearing those who may laugh at you for adopting an old fiction about the Devil; seeing that you know, from what you see and from what you feel, from the experience of heathens and your own, that it is not a fiction that there is a spirit who is a murderer and a liar; that he would lead you as well as them captive at his will."[41] Man has always felt himself to be oppressed by tyranny, and as it is primarily his will that is enslaved, this fact can be explained only by belief in the Devil and his enslaving activity. The universal conclusion of mankind is ratified by the Bible.[42]

The Devil existed as God's great adversary before the creation of mankind. Even before individual man had sinned, the Devil was striving to separate man from fellowship with God: "There is a mind, a will, a spirit, which from the beginning has been a man-slayer – has compassed the destruction of the man in each man. There is a mind, a will, a spirit, who has been from the beginning a liar, who would not stand in the truth."[43] This does not mean that the Devil has always existed, otherwise there would have been an evil principle eternally alongside God's goodness. The Biblical statement that the Devil sinned from the beginning makes it absolutely clear that he originally dwelt in God, but then revolted and refused to abide in the truth and to live in the fellowship of love.[44] Indeed the whole life and activity of the Devil is a negation of the will and work of God,[45] a fact further evidenced by the names given to him in the Bible: 'man-slayer' and 'the father of lies'. These names imply that the Devil possesses no creative powers; he is a destructive mind, a parasite existing only because God *is* and has imparted being to the entire creation.[46] His sole ability

---

41 *The Conflict*, 21–2. Cf. also *Family Worship*, 123–4: "You clever men, you great liberals, have found out that there are no evil spirits who hold the bodies and spirits of men bound in fearful misery and captivity. Every street and alley in every city of Europe laughs your wisdom to scorn. I must believe in a bondage which I feel myself, which I hear confessed in every cry that ascends from every human will against the foes who are crushing it and preventing it from being what it dreams of, happy, high, majestical."

42 Cf. *Theological Essays*, 12: "When, then, I speak of the belief in the existence and presence of an Evil Spirit as characteristic of the Gospels, I mean this: that in them first the idea of a spirit directly and absolutely opposed to the Father of Lights, to the God of absolute goodness and love, bursts full upon us." The Devil has always been active but the Incarnation makes the Devil, and his activity, stand out in such bold relief because it is the full revelation of God as absolute love and must, as such, expose the true nature of the Devil, whose work is aimed at the destruction of God's creation.

43 *The Gospel of St. John*, 252.

44 Cf. *The Epistles of St. John*, 189: "There *was* the Object then, there *was* the Law. Whoever sinned first, confessed Good to be; he said that a law was binding him, and that he wished to shake it off."

45 Cf. *The Gospel of St. John*, 252: "There was, then, a truth to stand in; there was a truth to revolt from."

46 Cf. *ibid.*: "The name 'murderer' implies a life to be taken away; the name 'liar' implies a contradiction of that which IS. – – it implies that the murderer is the author of *no* life; it implies that the liar has called nothing that *is* into existence." See also *The Apocalypse*, 171.

is to act as a destroyer and usurper, who lays hands upon another's property in order to lead it into destruction and death.[47]

The Devil refuses to acknowledge God and His love and seeks to involve all the rest of God's creatures in this rebellion and denial of God.[48] He is 'the Self-Will', entirely dominated by selfishness, always seeking his own glory.[49] Therefore he must hate God and be the implacable opponent of God's self-sacrificing love. Whereas God seeks to bind men to Himself and to each other and desires that they shall abide in life and love, the Devil tries to drive a wedge between God and man and between man and man, thus leading men into selfishness and death.

The Devil beguiles man into sinning. The true nature of his activity is indicated by the Bible when it calls him 'diabolos': the Slanderer.[50] The Devil fills man with slanderous lies, tempting him to rebellion. Being near to the spirit of man, he whispers a false and distorted idea of reality to his reason and conscience. He seduces man to believe that God is not a merciful Father, and that man is left to himself and has no right to trust in God as perfect love.[51] He attempts to sow contention among men by slandering them to each other and beguiling them into mutual hatred.[52] By attempting to make man believe that selfishness, sin, and death are the law of the universe, he wants to "persuade us that we belong to him, and

47 Cf. *Sermons* I, 280: "there being in him no creative energy; he having no right to claim anything or any person as his; it being our own part and duty to vindicate ourselves and all creatures from him; utterly renouncing his dominion; proclaiming that we are, one and all, the property of Him who is absolutely good and true," and *Christmas Day,* 196: "The evil spirit never has created anything, never can create anything. He is simply the destroyer, death is his only handy work, and Christ has taken that from him."

48 Cf. *Theological Essays,* 12, where the Devil is described as "a mere destroyer, a subverter of order, who is seeking continually to make us disbelieve in the Creator, to forsake the order that we are in."

49 Cf. *Sermons* I, 272: "There is an adversary of this Name, a self-seeking, self-concentrated, self-worshipping adversary, who is seeking to draw you out of communion with it, and therefore out of communion with each other", and *Family Worship,* 208: "To care only for self; to think only of self; to live only in self; is not that the condition of a devil?"

50 Cf. *The Epistles of St. John,* 185: "The word 'Diabolos' means Accuser or Slanderer. What he [St. John] says, giving his words their most literal sense, is, that one who sins or goes astray from God does so by listening to the voice of a spirit who accuses or slanders God."

51 Cf. *The Epistles of St. John,* 190: "there has been no period of the existence of human beings in which they have not been liable to the assaults of this Tempter; – – accusations against God, reasons for doubting and distrusting Him, have been offered to one man after another, to one generation after another. This is just what the Scripture affirms; just the assumption which goes through the book from Genesis to the Apocalypse", and p. 186: "Now there come to me every day whispers not received through the ear but heard in the heart, that God is not the Being whom Jesus Christ manifested; not a Righteous and True Being; not one whom I may trust; not one who means good to me and to my brethren; not one who cares that I should do right, or who will give me strength to do right."

52 Cf. *The Epistles of St. John,* 186–7: "With these whispers come others also very strange, against persons whom I know, persons, possibly, who have done me wrong, quite as likely persons who have done me nothing but good; suspicions of their kindness; doubts of their character; hints that they may be plotting something very evil. Then there are whispers more directly affecting oneself; incitements to think foully and to feel foully; to be malicious against those to whom one owes only forgiveness, affection, gratitude."

not to the God of truth."[53] To listen to, and accept, the Devil's slanderous lies against God and against one's fellow-men is to become fashioned into the likeness of "the father of lies".[54] By this means the Devil usurps power over men and establishes a rival kingdom, dominated by untruth, unbelief, selfishness, and hatred.

Man alone is created as a spirit, a voluntary being able to live freely in personal fellowship with God. This distinction marks him out as the highest being in God's creation, meant to rule over the involuntary creatures. Consequently, if the Devil is to subjugate the entire created world, his attack must be directed against man's will. Once it has been enslaved, the rest of creation will be dragged into slavery by the Devil: "This tempter speaks to me, to myself, to the will; – – over *that* he has established his tyranny; – – all things in nature, with the soul and the body, have partaken, and do partake, of the slavery to which the man himself has submitted."[55]

Maurice asserted that the fact that the human will can be led captive was the strongest argument that the Devil is a personal being; for only a will, the constitutive element of a person, can communicate with voluntary beings.[56] The same is implied when the Devil is called the Evil Spirit, since spirit, person and will are synonymous in Maurice's vocabulary.[57] Far from standing for an impersonal principle of evil in the universe, the Devil is a personal voluntary spirit, who rebels against God

---

53 *The Epistles of St. John*, 307.
54 Cf. *The Gospel of St. John*, 253–4: "I am able – – to look facts in the face, and confess that sin has entered into the world, and death by sin; that there has been from the beginning of man's existence on this earth, and that there still is, a murderer, who is seeking to sever him from his proper life; that there has been from the beginning of man's existence upon earth, and that there still is, a liar, who is seeking to persuade men that God is not all good; that He is not all true; that He is not the Father of their spirits; that it is not His will that they should know Him, and be like Him. I can admit that this liar has been listened to; and that men may enter into such communion with him – may become so penetrated with his false and mendacious spirit, that they shall become in very deed his children, entirely fashioned into his likeness, understanding no lessons but his."
55 *Theological Essays*, 12.
56 Cf. *Life* II, 21, where Maurice gave the following answer to F. J. A. Hort, who claimed that he had been unable to find a clear recognition of the personal existence of the Devil in Maurice's works: "I do not know what he [the devil] is by theological arguments, but I know by what I feel. I am sure there is one near me accusing God and my brethren to me. He is not myself; I should go mad if I thought he was. He is near my neighbours; I am sure he is not identical with my neighbours. I must hate them if I believe he was. – – I dare not deny that it is an evil will that tempts me; else I should begin to think evil is in God's creation and is not the revolt from God, resistance to Him. If he is an evil will, he must, I think, be a person. The Word upholds his existence, not his evil. That is in himself; that is the mysterious, awful possibility implied in his being a will."
57 Cf. *Life* II, 403: "Whenever I am told of a spirit, evil or good, I at once assume that that is like me, can hold converse with me, can tempt me to wrong, can encourage me to right. The Holy Spirit is the inspirer, as I believe, of all the energies by which my personal life manifests itself. He gives me the sense that I am a person; how can he be impersonal? The evil spirit speaks to me as a person, tempts me to think I am not a person, tries to reduce me into a thing. I never should dream of calling him a thing."

and so is able to speak to the spirit of man, enticing him into a denial of God and a refusal to live in the Divine Order.[58]

The ultimate cause of sin, then, is the Devil and his rebellion against God; he alone is in the last analysis responsible for all destruction and death in the universe. Therefore it is impossible to regard man or anything in man as being evil in itself.[59] His sin and misery are caused by the foreign dominion to which the Devil, God's great antagonist, has subjugated him. Accordingly, since man and the entire creation are good and perfect in themselves, there is nothing in them that needs to be destroyed in order that God's will may prevail.[60] God's redemption consists solely in the destruction of the Devil and his tyrannous dominion, so that men can live in accordance with the law of their creation. God's war against sin and death is not a war against the earth and mankind, but a war against the Devil with the sole purpose of delivering His creatures from the captivity into which the latter has brought them.

The recognition of the Devil and his destructive activity as the final cause of sin and death solves for Maurice the problem of evil, which has persistently haunted mankind. It enables man to regard "the whole universe as very good, even as it was when it came forth at the call of the divine Word," and, at the same time, "look facts in the face, and confess that sin has entered into the world, and death by sin."[61]

With this solution to the problem of the origin of sin it might appear that Maurice had discarded the idea of man's personal responsibility. This is, however, in no way the case. The Devil forces no one to sin. He is the tempter who lures man into sin, but sin only occurs when man decides to follow the voice of the Devil by assenting

---

58 Although Maurice acknowledged the Devil as a personal being, he did not like to speak of "the personality of the Devil", since this might create the impression that the Devil has "a bodily form" (cf. *Life* II, 402–3). Further explanation of Maurice's thought on this point is provided in the following quotation: "it is not among God's works one is to look for shapes and forms of evil; – – they are very good; – – I must think of evil as spiritual, as present, as appealing to my spirit, as appealing to me" *(The Epistles of St. John,* 198). Since it is anthropomorphic to conceive "that which is spiritual under a human shape" (see *The Unity of the New Testament,* 31–2), the Devil can have no human shape: "We feel that the personality which belongs to the opposing power has – – nothing to do with an outward shape or visible circumstances. We are led to feel that there is a deep, radical evil, a spirit of evil, underlying all the shapes and forms in which it presents itself to us on earth" *(The Unity of the New Testament,* 23).

59 Cf. *Theological Essays,* 12: "That there is a pravity or depravity in every man, and that this pravity or depravity is felt through his whole nature, the Gospel does not assert as a principle of Theology, but concedes as an undoubted and ascertained fact of experience, which no one who contemplates man or the universe can gainsay. What it does theologically with reference to that experience is this: as it confesses an Evil Spirit whose assaults are directed against the Will in man, it forbids us ever to look upon any disease of our nature as the ultimate cause of transgression. The horrible notion, which has haunted moralists, divines, and practical men, that pravity is the law of our being, and not the perpetual tendency to struggle against the law of our being, it discards and anathematises."

60 Cf. *Theological Essays,* 12: "And yet neither body nor soul can be in itself evil. Each is in bondage to some evil power. If there is a God of Order mightier than the Destroyer, body and soul must be capable of redemption and restoration."

61 *The Gospel of St. John,* 253.

to his lying accusations about God and his fellow-men and by pursuing his suggestions of living a life of selfishness. Sin and death prevailed in man because he submitted his will to the Evil Spirit and became his servant.[62]

Although man can never be discharged of responsibility for his sin, it is nonetheless true that the Devil is the ultimate cause of sin and death in the universe. He works to destroy God's creation and annihilate His love and truth, and as such he must be exterminated.[63] Love and selfishness cannot exist side by side but must wrestle with each other for dominion over the universe and mankind.[64] The Creator wages war against the Destroyer, Life struggles against Death.[65] This war has been going on ever since the Devil as the first of God's creatures revolted against God. There can be no neutrality in this battle. Every man is drawn into the conflict and must decide on which side he stands.[66] The struggle between God and the Devil encompasses all human life. It is indeed in the actual life of every man that the battle is fought which is to decide "whether humanity shall have its true and righteous king, or whether another power shall rule over it, and receive its homage."[67]

3. The Fall of Adam and the Depravity of Man

Maurice's strong language on the subject of sin and its devastating effects leaves the impression that the whole of mankind is involved in a rebellion against God and has chosen to live a life of selfishness. Similarly, Maurice's description of the Devil and his activities leads to the conclusion that man and the whole of creation have become subject to the Devil, God's great antagonist. The battle motif, which plays so promi-

62 Cf. *The Epistles of St. John*, 188: "St. John never for a moment says or dreams that he who commits sin, commits it because the devil or the accuser *obliges* him to do it. The thought of being obliged or forced is not only not implied in his words; it is contradicted by them. The names Tempter and Accuser do not indicate it; the word *Sin* excludes it. That must belong to man himself, -- it is connected with *choice* and *conscience*, i. e. with the man's own self. What the Apostle does say, is that sin comes from contact or fellowship between our spirit and a sinful spirit; that to commit sin is to become his liegemen, his bondsmen." See also p. 187.

63 Cf. *Christmas Day*, 86: "You will rejoice to think that he [God] is carrying on a deadly and exterminating warfare against your foes, and that he will not cease from that warfare until he has utterly destroyed them."

64 Cf. *The Apocalypse*, 61: "The perfect goodness and purity will wage war against all that is evil and dark."

65 Cf. *Theological Essays*, 7: "we do not thoroughly or heartily believe that there is that war of Life and Death, of Good and Evil, now in every man's heart, as there was of old", and *The Conflict*, 18-9: "We must read the whole Bible -- as the warfare of the Creator with the Destroyer, of Life with Death. The instincts of men in all countries have recognized such a warfare; only the recognition has been imperfect and confused."

66 Cf. *Sermons* VI, 53: "Every man was engaged in this battle. None could evade it. Every man must take his side. He must say, 'I submit myself to the Spirit of Good, of Truth, of Charity; I acknowledge myself to be His servant.' Or, 'I invite His enemy to come and reign over me; I promise to do his behests and work his will.' People might state the case differently, might prefer one nomenclature to another. But somehow or other they must come at last to this issue. Obedience to good or evil; this was the alternative."

67 *The Apocalypse*, 170.

nent a part in Maurice's theological thinking, might appear to emphasize that mankind and the universe no longer stand in God but live under the law of sin and death. Consequently God's redemptive work would appear to consist of an incessant and relentless struggle to destroy the Devil and restore mankind to fellowship with God.

There can be no doubt that in his conception of sin and the Devil Maurice was convinced that he had broken with the way in which the Enlightenment of the eighteenth century had interpreted human existence.[68] Nor is it an accident that by Maurice's account of the fact of sin and its nature one is continually reminded of that of the Reformers. Maurice was greatly influenced by their ideas and language, which coincided perfectly with his own personal experiences.

With this in mind it might be expected that Maurice would join forces with his orthodox contemporaries or at least have approved when in reaction to the Latitudinarian concept of Christianity they maintained the universal fall and depravity of mankind. But this was far from being the case. In fact Maurice openly opposed them, criticizing them for making the sinful state of man the pivot of their preaching and theology. Indeed their view of the fall and universal depravity of the human race was the very basis for their distorted view of the Christian faith. Therefore his opposition to the orthodox religious world of his day came to a head on this very issue.[69]

According to Maurice the prevalent orthodoxy taught that, since Adam was the head of humanity, his fall involved all men in sin and in death as the wages of sin. Adam's fall, then, prescribed the conditions for the life of every existing individual. Sin and death constituted the universal law of the life of mankind, whereas redemption only concerned that small number of men who believed in the incarnate Christ, who had died to rescue them from the world of sin and death.[70] Man's normal state

---

68 Cf. *Sermons* V, 259–60: "It would have surprised those excellent people [the Methodists of the eighteenth century] who had attained to their own sense of evil through the bitterest conflicts, to find how in our day this assertion of theirs has been accepted, apparently in all its fulness, – how it has now become an orthodox shibboleth, recognized as the fundamental dogma of the Bible, even by those who study it least and care least about its contents. The confession of universal depravity which was denounched in the eighteenth century as fanatical, is enforced by the public opinion of the nineteenth."

69 Thus Maurice wrote with respect to Dr. R. S. Candlish, the Scottish Evangelical: "I ought to say, that this writer has understood better than any I have met with, the real issue upon which the dispute between this school and me turns. It is the question whether the Fall or the Redemption is the ground on which humanity rests" *(Sacrifice,* XXXV). However, Orthodox Protestantism and Roman Catholicism formed a united front on this point: "Protestants and Romanists, even while they denounce and excommunicate each other, yet appear to recognize the fact of depravity, of Evil, as the fundamental fact of divinity" *(The Conflict,* 170).

70 Cf. *Sermons* V, 259: "But these tidings [of Redemption], however widely it might be their [the Methodists] duty to proclaim them, had reference to a small minority, who were not indeed in the least to boast of their privilege, – who were to ascribe it to the pure, undeserved grace of God, – but who must look upon themselves as exceptions to a rule. The rule was expressed by the assertion that man was a fallen creature. He might *become* something else; but he *was* a sinner. Everything that he did or thought had reference to that primary postulate; he could do nothing else till he had admitted that in the length and breadth of it."

124

is a life in selfishness and separation from God, whereas life in faith and obedience towards God merely denotes a break with and an exception from ordinary human life.

Although Maurice felt called to protest passionately against such views, he did not at all wish to contest the fact of Adam's fall. His concern was to explode the idea that from this event the law of human life could be deduced.[71] Adam was created in Christ as the image of God and was destined to have life, goodness and righteousness in Him. The law of Adam's life was to live in trusting dependence upon Christ, whereas his sin was his refusal to acknowledge this as the truth about his life. Adam attempted to live for himself and to act as though he was the centre of the universe. But even though he denied the law of his creation, he was not able to annul it. So Adam's fall did not bring mankind under the yoke of sin and death. Every man is created under the same conditions as Adam; sin always consists of a departure from, and a contradiction of, the immutable fact that man stands in Christ.[72]

The account of Adam's sin only tells of his personal denial of the law of his creation. It has, on the other hand, a universal validity because it faithfully describes how sin enters every man's life.[73] It is, however, inadmissible to use the term 'universal depravity'; it is only meaningful to speak of 'individual depravity' because this term denotes that sin always consists of man's denial and departure from the Divine Order in which he has been placed.[74]

It is important to note that Maurice's polemic against the orthodox doctrine concerning Adam's fall and the universal depravity of mankind is in no way prompted by any desire to assert an inherent goodness and integrity in man. This is ruled out by his idea of man as created to receive his life and being from God through Christ.[75] Maurice opposed the orthodox doctrine of Original Sin because it implied that man's sinful will and the work of the Devil were able to frustrate God's purposes and expel Him from His creation. If Adam's fall had been capable of bringing sin

---

71 Cf. *Sacrifice*, 294: "The Fall is a fact in history, just as the Bible presents it to us; but it is not a fact from which we can dare to deduce the Law under which we are living and acting."

72 Cf. *The Patriarchs*, 55: "The principle that man was made in the image of God, is not a principle which was true for Adam and false for us. It is the principle upon which the race was constituted and can never cease to be constituted. Adam's sin consisted, if we are to accept the Scripture account, in disbelieving that law, in acting as if he were not under it. He would be a God; he was not content to be in the image of God."

73 See *ibid*.

74 Cf. *Sermons* V, 267: "It is far better, safer, truer language to speak of individual depravity than of universal depravity. By individual depravity I mean my own. I find it out in myself; or rather, He who searcheth me and trieth my ways, finds it out in me. That sense of depravity implies the recognition of a law which I have violated, of an order from which I have broken loose, of a Divine image which my character has not resembled. It is the law and order which are universal."

75 The attempt to mitigate the Reformers' understanding of Adam's fall and its consequences by maintaining that a vestige of the image of God still remains as inherent moral and religious qualities in man only met with Maurice's contempt and blunt rejection. These were empty phrases which resolved themselves into nothingness when closely scrutinized, that is, when tested in real life (see *Theological Essays*, 13).

and death upon him and all posterity, thereby achieving a separation between mankind and God, then a human will would have had the power of deciding the question of God's relation to man. As the Devil had also been at work in Adam's case and instigated him to his rebellion, the orthodox view of Adam's fall made out the Devil to be stronger and more powerful than God and able to determine the life and destiny of God's creation. In fact both Roman and Protestant preaching and theology made sin and the Devil the victors in the battle for the universe, dictating the law of its existence. Even if it is maintained that God has sent Christ to save and deliver some men out of the sinful mass of humanity, this does not alter the fact that sin and the Devil remain the true masters, forcing God to leave mankind, and the entire creation, under their power.

The very fact that both man and the Devil are created by God proves the untenability of this blasphemous idea. They have received all their being from God and do not therefore possess any creative powers in themselves. Their rebellion against God is simply a denial of 'He Who Is', an act of separation from the source of all being. Consequently, since their sin is void of being, they are powerless in their revolt against God and in their attacks against His creation. As God alone is true Being and His will, always desiring to communicate being, is unchangeable, His created universe must necessarily continue to exist. Therefore Maurice could exclaim: "I ask you not to believe that a man [Adam] was able to frustrate the purposes of God; not to think that the world was created in Adam, or stood in his obedience; for the Scriptures of the New Testament, illustrating those of the Old, teach us that it stood and stands in the obedience of God's well-beloved Son; the real image of the Father, the real bond of human society and of the whole universe."[76]

Just as Adam's unbelief and selfishness were powerless to destroy the law of God's creation, so the sin of the rest of mankind is unable to impair the Divine Order.[77] Man can refuse to recognize that the universe and mankind stand in God and are created to be the continuous object of His love, but he cannot change this fact as it is decreed eternally by God.[78] Even though man decides to forsake God and live a life of selfishness in independence of God, he will never succeed. God does not leave man

76 *The Patriarchs*, 66.
77 Cf. *The Patriarchs*, 140–1: "The order which God created is very good. The order which He preserves and upholds is very good. There was no flaw in it before man fell, there is no flaw in it since men fell. That fall had actually no power to subvert it, or derange it. That fall was precisely the refusal of man to recognise his own glorious place *in* this order; an effort to make for himself an independent place *out* of it. He wants to be something in himself; he will not act and live as one made in the image of God. The history goes on, the disbelief and disorder multiply. But the eternal order goes on asserting itself, – calmly, uninterruptedly. God treats man according to the law which He laid down for him on the Creation-day", and *The Prophets*, 207: "the fallen nature itself, or the most actual and terrible result of that nature in the most depraved society, [do not set] aside the order which God has established, or [make] the exhibition of that order impossible."
78 Cf. *The Patriarchs*, 63–4: "His Will cannot change; let other wills set themselves against His as they may. His must remain the absolutely good Will, which from eternity it was. His order cannot be changed or repented of, let men transgress it as they may. It stands firm and unshaken. No other can be substituted for it."

to himself, nor does He cease to have fellowship with him.[79] In His love He continues to deal with man as His child.[80] Though men may refuse to recognize Christ as the Head of humanity, He remains the Head of every man and constitutes his life by giving him of His own life.[81]

Against this background the significance of a number of Maurice's favourite expressions for describing the nature of sin can be clearly understood. Thus, Maurice can define sin as 'that which is not'.[82] This implies a denial of *that which is,* but as this denial is void of being in itself, it can have no power to destroy that which has being, God's created universe. In the sense of life and being sin has no reality and can be described as 'the unreal', 'a falsehood', 'an untruth'.[83] It may, indeed, have a powerful hold on the minds of men, leading them into a false knowledge of God and His created Order, but it is unable to mould existing reality according to its desires.

Similarly, when Maurice pictured sin as a denial and refusal of God, his aim was to demonstrate that sin is a mere negation, incapable of changing *that which is*; sin can say 'No' to God, but it can never establish anything that thwarts God's purposes and limits His acts of love towards His creatures.[84] Maurice accordingly spoke frequently of sin as 'a lie'. When man sets up his own self as his only god and attempts

79 Cf. *The Patriarchs,* 141: "But how are these inhuman, disorderly creatures regarded by their Creator? Have they succeeded in establishing that place for themselves outside His universe which they seem to covet? No! they are within the circle of it, they are under His discipline and education. He is teaching them by their own disorders; by all that they are doing to set at nought His government, and to canonize their own self-will. He claims them as belonging to Him. They may resist the claim, they may choose a way of their own. They may try to shut themselves up in their separate Adam nature. But they cannot do it. The divine order is hemming them in, forcing them in their most inconsistent acts to acknowledge its presence, and to pay it homage."

80 Cf. *Sermons* VI, 28–9: "We try to ignore the presence of God, we deny our relation to Him; that it is the secret of our evil. Every act becomes contradictory, because this huge contradiction is at the root of it. God treats men as what they are, not as what they try to be when they yield to the spirit of lies. He affirms them not to be independent of Him, not to be outcasts from Him."

81 Cf. *The Patriarchs,* VIII–IX: "In these discourses [on *The Patriarchs and Lawgivers*] I have had to encounter that which I believe to be the great denial of our time, – the one which is most at variance with the express letter of the Bible, and with its whole object and history, – the denial, I mean, that man continued to be in the image of God after the Fall, with the denials which correspond to this, and grow out of it, that man was originally created in the Divine Word, and that apart from Him, neither Adam nor any of his descendants either had, or ever would have, any righteousness or any life."

82 Cf. *The Patriarchs,* 167–8: "And now that Moses is going forth to encounter the unrighteousness of the world in its high places, – now that the chosen people are called to this higher stage of their history, now that they are not only to witness for good on the earth but to fight with evil, – that Name is proclaimed which tells them that their calling is to struggle for that which IS against that which is NOT; for the Absolute and Eternal Truth against every thing that is counterfeit and false."

83 Cf. *The Gospel of St. John,* 401: "And the Spirit would convince the world also of this, that the untruths to which it bows down can have only a brief dominion; that that which is, must prevail over that which is not."

84 Cf. *The Prayer-Book,* 118–9: "St. Paul speaks of the Mystery of Christ as the *ground* of all things in Heaven and Earth, – – this is that true Original Foundation which sin has been concealing, and denying, and seeking to destroy."

to live without God, he is doomed to failure. He is living in, and acting on, a lie by not realizing that he is created to live in Christ as his Head. He can never escape this unchangeable fact of life.[85]

Furthermore, Maurice was consistent in describing the Devil as 'the father of lies'. The Devil was the first to deny God and His love, and he is always seeking to instil in man a false idea of God and His attitude towards mankind. Likewise, when Maurice wanted to indicate the nature of the work of the Devil as a destroyer, it was with good purpose that he termed him 'the Slanderer' and 'the Accuser'. The Devil whispers a false idea of reality to man, inducing him to believe that he is not a child of God, living in His kingdom as the subject of His love, but under God's revengeful wrath and subject to the dominion of the Devil and sin. Thus the Devil's destructive work ends up by leading man into a false knowledge of reality.

By subscribing to the Devil's slanders, man gives himself up to lies and falsehood. His spiritual eye becomes veiled so that he can no longer know reality as it is.[86] To be a sinner is therefore to have a false conception of reality and to build one's life on untruth. Sin is a contradiction, since the man who sins acts on a false knowledge of reality instead of being governed by the true knowledge of God and His created Order.

4. Education and Punishment

To all appearances our previous analysis has revealed two different trends in Maurice's conception of sin. On one hand he describes sin, being unbelief and selfishness, as a terrible power which separates man from God and his fellow-men and subjugates him to the dominion of the Devil, the great Destroyer, in such a way that sin and the Devil truly appear to have wrought disorder in God's created universe. On the other hand Maurice conceives of sin as the false knowledge of God and His creation. It is capable of denying and refusing to receive God and His love, but it cannot cause God's work to cease or limit it in any way, just as it cannot destroy or overthrow the Divine Order.

These different views, which even occur alongside each other in Maurice's writings, leave a rather perplexing and even contradictory impression with the reader. Yet we also meet many statements in which Maurice is obviously anxious to maintain both the reality of sin and the integrity of the Divine Order. This concern is reflected in Maurice's mode of expression. He very often used a rendering which rather indicates the purport of sin and the Devil with respect to God's creation than describes what they have actually achieved. Thus Maurice asserted the existence of a terrible and inexorable conflict between God and the powers of evil. However, it is significant that he frequently merely says that sin or the Devil 'is seeking to destroy', but carefully omits to say that they have destroyed God's created Order. Maurice vividly depicted how owing to the attacks of the evil powers the creation is constantly

---

85 Cf. *The Kingdom of Christ* I, 256: "this mystery [that men were created in Christ before all worlds is] the true constitution of humanity in Christ, so that man believes and acts a lie who does not claim for himself union with Christ."

86 Cf. *The Kingdom of Christ* I, 281: "we believe that there is an eye in all men which can be opened if the evil will do not keep it closed."

threatened with death and destruction, but he refrained from saying that death and destruction have prevailed. The words are carefully chosen to make it clear that the Divine Order remains inviolate despite the destructive purpose of sin and the Devil.[87]

Maurice certainly wanted to stress both the power of sin and its devastating effects, and also the sovereign power of God and His love. In the idea of God's education of mankind he found a means of reconciling these two apparently contradictory positions. Maurice had asserted that man is created as a spirit, a will, which can decide in freedom and responsibility whether to live in dependence upon God, or whether to defy and deny Him. As sin consists in the decision of the will to refuse to acknowledge God, it follows that evil can be removed only when the will relinquishes its opposition and freely and willingly decides to trust in God.[88] Since the disobedience of the will cannot be eradicated by force, God's loving care for man's recalcitrant will therefore assumes the form of an education, in which He makes man experience the dreadful consequences of his rebellion against God, so that he turns from his selfishness and once more trusts God by his own free decision. God makes man's sin and misery the means by which He leads him to the realisation that he is powerless in himself and cannot live without God.

The continued existence of sin, then, does not prove that sin with its disunity and disorder is the strongest force in the universe. Sin exists as long as the will of man decides that it shall. But man has succeeded neither in setting up a separate self, independent of God, nor in thwarting God's purposes. God still encompasses man in His love and urges him to give up his selfishness.[89]

87 Such an observation can be verified from almost every page of Maurice's writings – and therefore from many of the previous quotations. A single example will suffice to demonstrate that his apparently loose and imprecise terminology stems from deliberate consideration and is prompted by the desire to affirm the actual power of sin without making sin the actual master of man: "We are told that the very first man *forgot that he was made in the image of God; yielded to the temptation of an inferior creature; came under death.* He *denied the law after which he was created.* And each of his descendants is shown to have *the same propensity to obey that which he was meant to rule; to disbelieve in Him whom he was meant to obey.* But neither the first man nor any of his successors could make *this degradation and disobedience* anything else than *an anomaly and contradiction.* The worst man in Scripture is never represented as *evil in any other sense than because he fights against the law under which he exists, and of which his very transgression is the continual witness.* And therefore in the Bible God is ever represented as addressing Himself to the creature whom He had formed, as awakening in him by His voice *a consciousness of his right condition.* – – In each case it is assumed that *the creature* addressed *stood in a direct relation to the Creator, however he might be denying it, and determining to shut himself out from it*" (*Religions*, 192–3. Our italics).

88 Cf. *What is Revelation?*, 432: "no man can be rescued out of the state of sin and suffering without the co-operation of his own will; because Sin is the very revolt of man's will from the true will, and because to speak of being delivered from a disease in the will without the will itself being set right, is more monstrous than to speak of being cured of a disease in the liver without the liver being set right."

89 Cf. *The Patriarchs*, 63: "And why could He not make it [the earth] fulfil them [the ends of His creation], by a fiat of His omnipotence? Because, brethren, He had made man in His own image; because He had given him a will; because He could only restore and regenerate him by restoring and regenerating his will. Hence we have to read all the Bible through, of

Instead of limiting God's love man's sin only shows that the Divine love is sovereign and is the foundation of the life of mankind and the universe. The experience of sin makes man cognizant of the greatness and awful responsibility involved in being created for personal fellowship with God. At the same time man also discovers that the independent life which he had desired and decided to establish is without substance. The pursuit of it makes him a restless victim of the transient world, unable to satisfy his deepest longings.[90] The same lesson is taught through the human relationships when man attempts to base them upon selfishness.[91] This experience of the futility of all the endeavours of selfish man is the instrument that teaches him that his entire existence is founded upon God and His love, and that God never forsakes him despite his unbelief and selfishness. Therefore Maurice exclaimed: "How can we lament the fall of Adam, if we believe it has led to the manifestation of the glory of God, and of His Kingdom over earth and over the spirits of men?"[92]

That God continually loves and upholds sinful man does not mean that he overlooks his sin. God is truly a holy and righteous God, who must wage war against sin. But this does not imply that God's holiness and righteousness demand that those who have sinned against Him must be punished with death and perdition, as the contemporary orthodoxy asserted. God's righteousness has nothing to do with retaliatory vengeance – it means quite simply that God is the righteous One, whose sole aim is to make man righteous.[93] Nevertheless it would be just as wrong to conclude that wrath and punishment have no place in God on the grounds that He, being perfect love, is bound to forgive man.

To speak of God's loving forgiveness without admitting His wrath and punishment

floods, famines, pestilences, earthquakes, anarchy, tyranny. It is throughout, the history of an actual government, – throughout, the history of an actual education; a government of voluntary beings to teach them subjection; – an education of voluntary creatures to make them free. And He who carries on this government and education, is seen, the more He makes Himself known to us, to be not a hard despot, but a loving Ruler; with that heart and sympathy in perfection which He requires in His creatures." See also *The Epistles of St. John*, 289.

90 Cf. *The Patriarchs*, 60–1: "for the Divine Order has not been interrupted because a man [Adam] has refused obedience to it; – it is only made more evident by that violation. It is seen to stand, not in the will of a creature, but on some deeper, safer ground, which would be more and more clearly revealed. And since God's order is not destroyed, His purpose that man should be in His own likeness, cannot be destroyed. Man has set up a self-will, has fallen under the dominion of the nature which God had given him. This very act is a step in his education, – a means by which God will teach him more fully what he is, what he is not, what he was meant to be, and what he was not meant to be; how he may thwart the purposes of his Creator, how he may conspire with them."

91 Cf. *The Gospel of St. John*, 258: "When all schemes of human policy crack and crumble; when we discover the utter weakness of the leaders and teachers we have trusted most; when we begin to suspect that the world is given over to the spirit of murder and lies; He says to us, 'The foundations of the universe are not built on rottenness; whatever fades away and perishes, I AM'."

92 *Sermons* V, 205. Cf. also *Sermons* I, 78: "Must they not bless God that He suffered men to eat of that tree, of which the fruit was death? Did not life lie behind that death, – a diviner life than any which Adam could ever dream of?"

93 Cf. *The Prophets*, 276: "A righteous Being seeks to act righteousness on the earth. If men will hear His voice and submit to be made righteous, He has no pleasure in destroying them."

is to cut oneself off from a genuine understanding of its true character. Such forgiveness would be no more than a tolerant benevolence towards men which winks at their sins. In fact it represents the greatest cruelty since it leaves man in the dreadful state of sin.[94] True love can never rest satisfied by leaving man in the sin and death which he has inflicted upon himself.[95] It must always oppose wickedness and seek to destroy it.[96] So there exists a burning wrath of love, which struggles to consume evil.[97] God's wrath is not revengeful, the very opposite of love, but is as a cleansing and purifying fire the expression of love towards sin. Wrath is an inherent part of that true love which does not permit evil to rage and triumph.[98]

The Divine wrath manifests itself as a punishment which aims, not at "the perpetual prolongation of evil", but at "the cure of evil".[99] Punishment opens men's eyes to the misery they have drawn upon themselves so that they can see the necessity of turning to God and receiving true life from Him. "What we want," Maurice was convinced, "is to know the barrenness and hollowness of our own selves,"[100] and it is just this insight which punishment will impart to men. By letting them taste the fruits of their selfishness and experience the results of their rebellion against God punishment destroys men's complacency about their sins. Punishment breaks down that false idea of reality which selfishness and unbelief have produced and makes men see their true situation so that they may abandon their resistance to God and turn to

94 Cf. *The Conflict*, 83–4: "The sins which he has committed have darkened the face of God to him. He dreams of a God like himself, good-natured, tolerant of evil, so kind as to let us destroy ourselves and our neighbours without any interference, a feeble magistrate, a murderously indulgent parent," and *Country Churches*, 212: "Suppose he desires God to overlook his sins; to let him go on in them, not to let him be punished for them, he certainly cannot expect that God in His justice and faithfulness will do that. – – There is no mercy in letting a man go on in a course of villany; there is no mercy in letting him get worse and worse, and therefore more miserable – *that* is cruelty." Se also *The Apocalypse*, 349 and *The Epistles of St. John*, 51.

95 Cf. *Sermons* I, 99: "It [the Will of God] was not a poor paltry benevolence, which wishes all creatures happiness, and will perhaps take pains to give them the outward animal ease and felicity which some men crave for, which no man is ever content with. It is not a Will to save them from toil or suffering, or rightful punishment. It is a Will to impose and inflict these, so long as they contribute to the purification and elevation of the will, the spirit within; so long as they helped to remove clogs and impediments from that, so long as they tend to bring the man to the state in which he alone is a man, renewed in the Image of God."

96 Cf. *Sermons* II, 213: "To make the forgiveness of God – and we are to forgive as He forgives, and only as He forgives – into tolerance of evil, is to pervert its nature fatally. The forgiveness which does not hate crime and seek for the extinction of it, which shrinks from the punishment of the crime, is devilish forgiveness, not Divine."

97 Cf. *The Apocalypse*, 228: "the fire of love – – will consume what is hostile to love", and p. 224: "God's fires are not for the ruin of the earth, which is the work of His hands, but for the ruin of those who defiled it by the work of *their* hands."

98 Cf. *The Gospel of St. John*, 79: "For he had learnt that a gracious Being must be intolerant of that which is ungracious, that a true Being must seek to destroy falsehood – –. He felt that this wrath must have reached its highest point in the most gracious, most true Being, in Him from whom all had received their portions of grace and truth."

99 *The Kingdom of Heaven*, XXVI.

100 *The Prophets*, 253.

Him as their merciful Father.[101] Consequently, punishment is not to be feared; it is an inestimable good which serves man's true welfare.[102] What is really to be feared is a life of sin free from punishment, for this is to be without God.[103]

There can be no harmony between God's love and sin. But God's education of man by means of punishment makes it clear that sin is incapable of separating man from God or thwarting His purposes. Even sin is made subservient to God and is compelled to bear witness to the fact that mankind and the universe always stand in God's love and that His will must be done and shall be triumphant. With this understanding the pitfalls of both monistic Pantheism and dualistic Manichaeism are avoided, or as Maurice put it with flowing eloquence: "Deep and unfathomable mystery, worthy to be meditated on by those who are fighting with evil upon earth, and by those who have won the victory; the key to all the puzzles of history, the comfort and consolation amid the overwhelming evils which we see around us and feel within us; the deliverance at once from the debasing Pantheism which teaches that sin is only another form of righteousness, – wrong only an aspect of right, – and from the Manichæism which would lead us to think that evil may at last triumph, or hold a divided empire with God. The wrath of man has praised Him and will always praise Him. Sin and Death and Hell must do Him continual homage now, and will be led as His victims and grace His triumph, when His glory is fully revealed. But neither now nor then will they ever blend with His works, or be shown to have their origin in Him, or be known as anything but the contradictions of His nature."[104]

101 Cf. *Life* II, 470: "Punishment, the Bible teaches me, is always God's protest against sin, His instrument for persuading men to turn from sin to righteousness;" *Sacrifice*, XV: "There [in Holy Scripture] I find God using punishments, to make men sensible of the great misery of being at war with His will," and *What is Revelation?*, 435: "Punishment is one of God's blessed instruments for making us aware of sin, and for making us feel that it is from *that* we need to be delivered."

102 Cf. *The Apocalypse*, 230: "You must stumble at every passage in the Apocalypse if you discover any contradiction in the idea of the highest blessings being revealed through punishment, which look only like curses."

103 Cf. *Country Churches*, 108: "And I am well convinced that the murderer and adulterer to whom He [Christ] has given repentance would be very sorry if they did escape it [the punishment]. They would feel that He was not the great God such as they believe Him to be. They would feel that He was not the Saviour such as they believe Him to be, seeing that He did not keep them in mind of the evil which had separated them from Him, and did not compel them to turn away from themselves and seek Him. – – Understand that a man cannot have any curse so terrible as to be left in his sin, or to be allowed to go on without punishment; and that he cannot have any such great blessing as to be raised out of his sin, and to have it treated as his blackest and bitterest enemy," and *Theological Essays*, 121: "Punishment, I believe, seems to most men less dreadful than death, because they cannot separate it from a punisher, because they believe, however faintly, that He who is punishing them is a Father. The thought of His ceasing to punish them, of His letting them alone, of His leaving them to themselves, is the real, the unutterable horror."

104 *The Prophets*, 100. Cf. p. 99–100: "Not as if He [God] were the author of those acts which have their source in the evil will. They are by their very definition and nature, resistances to His Will, rebellions against it. But as they work out their own sentence and condemnation, they become the reluctant servants of Him with whom they are fighting; they are not only foils to His righteousness, – they actually help, as Scripture expresses it, to turn righteousness into judgment, to make the truth which they are denying, manifest for their own age and for all ages to come."

5. The Adam-nature and God's Judgment

Following St. Paul and the XXXIX Articles,[105] Maurice spoke of man as "condemned in Adam" and "justified in Christ".[106] However, he was anxious to point out that this must not be taken to mean that the whole of mankind had been condemned until Christ came in the flesh and justified men through His expiatory death upon the Cross. On the contrary, it represents a truth which is valid for every man.

At times Maurice appears to understand this contrast as two different ways of regarding man: considered in himself as an independent being, he is evil, dead and condemned, but considered in relation to Christ, he is righteous.[107] Accordingly the condemnation in Adam stands for the life of unbelief and selfishness while the justification in Christ stands for man's union with Christ, his life-giving righteousness. Far more frequently, however, Maurice maintained that every man has a relation to the corrupt Adam-nature as well as to the justifying Christ.[108] This means, in reality, that there is in each man an Adam-nature which inclines towards evil, and that which aspires towards Christ, in whom alone it finds its true being.[109] Although the true man within each individual always protests against sin and desires to live with Christ, this part of him is always threatened by the danger of being overcome by his sinful Adam-nature. Now the corrupt Adam-nature is simply man's fleshly, animal nature; it is condemned because it drags the spirit of man down into sensuality and prevents it from fulfilling its true destiny. The justification in Christ, on the other hand, means that Christ has fellowship with the spirit and imparts righteousness to it.

105 Especially Article IX which states that Original Sin is "the fault and corruption of the Nature of every man, that naturally is engendered of the offspring of Adam", wherefore man "is of his own nature inclined to evil, so that the flesh lusteth always contrary to the spirit."
106 *Sermons* V, 265.
107 Cf. p. 265–6: "If He [God] pronounces or adjudges us sinners, it is because we are sinners; if He justifies or pronounces us righteous, it is because we are righteous. St. Paul declares both facts as facts for all men, just as we have discovered them to be in our experience. But he does not leave us in the bewilderment in which that experience leaves us. He clears the contradiction; he shows how that which is true if we look upon Man in one aspect, is false if we look upon him in another. He is depraved, utterly depraved, in himself. Find the man who is utterly shut up in himself, who never rises out of himself, and I say, 'In that man is no good thing; he is buried in his lost Adam-nature; by the conditions of the universe, by the eternal law of God, he is simply, nakedly evil.' – – we cannot find him. In every one we perceive a struggle to get out of this selfish Adam-nature; a repudiation of it, an acknowledgement of some other law and standard than that which it gives."
108 Cf. p. 265: "But if that [Christ's death and resurrection] was the manifestation of an eternal truth, – if that showed Who holds the race in one, while the act of Adam showed what rends it in pieces, – we must be wrong when we speak of a universal Fall without speaking also of a universal Justification. We must be departing from the lesson of Scriptures, if we teach that each man comes into the world with a nature that is ready to sink into selfishness and death, without adding that he is related to a righteous and living Lord who would raise him to righteousness and life."
109 Cf. Sermons I, 149: "on the road to Damascus he [St. Paul] learnt for the first time to know that there was *perpetually* in him an old Adam which sought to hide itself from the presence of God, and that there was *perpetually* in him a second Adam, who turned to that presence as to its only deliverance. At any moment he might yield to the one; at every moment he required the help of the other to raise him and renew him."

The essential feature in this interpretation is that Maurice conceived of man as made up by the two opposing forces of spirit and flesh.[110] Man's spirit, his true self, does not stand in sin but remains inviolate and struggles for deliverance from the fleshly, animal nature which binds him to the sensual finite world.[111] Indeed, the struggle between the spirit and the flesh is so violent and is carried so deep into man's inner being that the question arises to whom man's own self belongs. Is his 'I' identical with selfishness and the fleshly nature so that it belongs to death and condemnation, or does it belong to life?[112] To the man who has painfully experienced how his own 'I' has become a riddle, God's judgment appears as an act of mercy.

God's judgment has nothing to do with a condemnation to death and destruction. Etymology clearly proves that the word signifies the act of sifting, discriminating and separating. Consequently, God's judgment means that He distinguishes and separates between true and false, between that which belongs to Him and that which opposes His will.[113] God's judgment of man is an act of enlightenment which scatters the darkness of ignorance so that he may see his true state. By this very act of judgment

110 Cf. *The Kingdom of Christ* (1838) I, 310: "No one could be more anxious than he [Fox] to assert that a spiritual life is intended for man, – that a fellowship with a Being above us is one of the conditions implied in our very constitution; nor could any one proclaim more fully than he the mighty obstacles which our nature opposes to the attainment and enjoyment of this, the great end of our being."

111 Thus, we see why idolatry, in the sense of worship of sensible things, plays such a dominant part in Maurice's account of the consequences of unbelief. Only through fellowship with Christ can man's spirit rise above the tenacious grasp of sensuality (cf. *The Prayer-Book*, 287: " He [God] has not left us to be fleshly creatures, to be animals, as we are naturally inclined to be, and would be altogether, if He were not upholding us", and *The Kingdom of Christ* II, 1: "man is a creature prone to sense, rising above it by virtue of a union with an invisible Teacher"). Man's refusal to acknowledge this truth issues in the ascendancy of the flesh and the enslavement of the spirit. In this way Maurice tried to reconcile the idea of a rebellious will as the root of sin with the opposition between spirit and flesh in man. At times Maurice even appears to identify the animal nature with selfishness. This is due to the fact that for him the possession of the animal nature means to be a concrete individual, who for this very reason is liable to self-seeking and refuses to see himself as a member of the human race with Christ as its Head. Individuality, the fleshly nature, and selfishness are so closely interrelated that Maurice often used the terms almost as synonyms (see, e. g., *Sermons* I, 71–2: "And the encouragement which is given us is, that we cast off the slothful, cowardly, self-seeking nature, which belongs to us as individuals, and may be clad with that enduring, self-sacrificing nature of Him who died and lives for all," and *The Kingdom of Christ* II, 27: "that very evil of selfishness, of individuality").

112 Cf. *The Kingdom of Christ* I, 85–6: "Here are two powers struggling within me, one good, one evil; sometimes one prevails, sometimes the other; sometimes the darkness seems about to be scattered, sometimes the light seems almost quenched; but I, who am I, in the midst of all this awful struggle? Do I belong to the light, or to the darkness? Of which have I a right to call myself the child now; of which shall I be the child for ever?" and p. 87: "Is this evil and accursed nature which belongs to me, my own self? Are not its evils imputed to me? Are not they counted a part of me? Will not Death destroy that nature; and when he destroys it, shall I be spared?" See also *Theological Essays*, 15–17.

113 Cf. *The Apocalypse*, 240–1: "Judgment means, in its ordinary use, discrimination, the assigning to each thing its real worth, the separation of that which is real from that which is merely apparent or counterfeit. Mean *that* when you speak of God's judgments. Mean nothing whatever which is inconsistent with that." See also *Theological Essays*, 77.

the spirit, man's true self, which desires fellowship with God, is separated from the fleshly, animal nature. God's judgment gives man a true knowledge of reality and assures him that his spirit as the child of God shall live, while his evil and corrupt flesh shall perish.

Since God's judgment is an act of love, Maurice strongly urged men to desire it.[114] However, they must not imagine that it will only take place at the end of the world. God is always near to man, judging him by carrying on a Socratic dialogue within him that enables him to perceive the real and distinguish and separate it from the unreal.[115] God must always be the judge because He, in His love, never permits man to be content with his own imperfect knowledge, but desires to impart a true knowledge of reality.

Maurice's understanding of God's judgment presupposed that there is that in man which is righteous and true and that which is evil and false. At times he describes the righteous and true as though it were an inherent quality in man, a personal possession. Nevertheless Maurice's real concern is to show that man's spirit is righteous because, by virtue of its fellowship with Christ, it partakes of His righteousness.[116] The ambiguity simply arises from the fact that this idea is fused with his Platonically conceived contrast between the spirit and the flesh.

6. The Problem of Sin in Maurice's Theology

Our previous analysis has revealed various lines of thought in Maurice's treatment of the problem of sin and evil. These lines do not converge to provide a consistent pat-

114 Cf. *The Apocalypse*, 362: "Brethren, no real tenderness can be apart from judgment and scrutiny. We need to have the precious and the vile separated in each of us."

115 Cf. *The Unity of the New Testament*, 66: "they had a Lawgiver and King always with them, who was seeking to separate the chaff from the wheat, that in them which desired right and truth from that which was cleaving to earth and nature, the divine seed from the evil seed which an enemy had sown in their hearts", and *Theological Essays*, 16: "When a man knows that he has a righteous Lord and Judge, who does not plead His omnipotence and His right to punish, but who debates the case with him, who shows him his truth and his error, the sense of Infinite Wisdom, sustaining and carrying out Infinite Love, abases him rapidly."

116 Thus Maurice saw Job as the true pattern for every man: "Sin cleaves very close to him; it seems as if it were part of himself, almost as if it were himself. But his righteousness belongs to him still more entirely. However strange the paradox, it is more *himself* than even that is. -- Job is shown, and we are shown, by an *experimentum crucis*, what in him is merely accidental, what beongs to him as a man." *(Theological Essays*, 15–6). But this righteousness is Christ Himself, who is near to man: "we say boldly to the man who declares that he has a righteousness which no one shall remove from him – 'That is true. You have such a righteousness. It is deeper than all the iniquity that is in you. It lies at the very ground of your existence. And this righteousness dwells not merely in a law which is condemning you; it dwells in a Person in whom you may trust. The righteous Lord of man is with you – not in some heaven to which you must ascend that you may bring Him down, in some hell to which you must dive that you may raise Him up, but nigh you, at your heart'" (p. 17).

tern, and the confusion increases when different, apparently contradictory conceptions are juxtaposed – often in one and the same passage.

It is, then, hardly surprising that students of Maurice have entertained highly divergent opinions as to the place and significance of sin in Maurice's theology. Thus Dr. Jens Nørregaard was of the opinion that Maurice's idea of justification by faith – which he equated with Luther's – was derived from "eine tiefe Empfindung des Ernstes und der Macht der Sünde", and that this was to be understood just as radically as Luther understood it.[117] In contrast John McLeod Campbell believed that for Maurice "all sin is reduced to ignorance", for "there is nothing real in the nature of things answering to this sense of guilt" in man's experience.[118] Maurice's son vigorously rejected this accusation as a complete misunderstanding and misrepresentation of his father's thought.[119] His plea did not, however, convince the judicious Richard H. Hutton. "For my own part," he remarked,[120] "I have never been able to reconcile Maurice's profound and deep sense of the awful reality of sin – expressed hundreds or thousands of times in these volumes [*Life* I–II] – with his language as to the absolute completeness of redemption even as regards those who have not been rescued from a life of sin; nor with his language here and there – – as to the purely negative and unreal character of sin." A. M. Ramsey also found a tension, and even an inner contradiction in Maurice's conception of sin, which could not be smoothed out or harmonized. Although there is much in Maurice's thought that rightly makes us ask whether sin is not unreal and the result of ignorance, Dr. Ramsey is nevertheless of the opinion that Maurice used ignorance in the Biblical sense, as something related to, and having its origin in, selfishness.[121]

These divergent interpretations of Maurice's views on the nature and power of sin can in a way all be substantiated from Maurice's own words. However, all of them are inadequate since they have either adhered too closely to one trend of thought, disregarding other trends, or are not based on an exhaustive examination of the material.

It must readily be admitted that Maurice's understanding of sin and evil is a most thorny problem to tackle. Our analysis should have demonstrated that although it is impossible to find a governing idea in Maurice's various statements on sin, we can nevertheless see the concerns which prompted him. Maurice was genuinely anxious to emphasize sin as a terrible, destructive power, cutting man off from God and his fellow-men and leading him and the entire creation into death. At the same time he maintained energetically that sin is powerless in its rebellion against God. It cannot thwart God's purposes nor derange or destroy the Divine Order. All that sin can achieve is to lead man into a false knowledge of God and His created Order.

Any description of Maurice's conception of sin must take equal account of these

117 See *Frederick Denison Maurice und das Luthertum* in *Zeitschrift für systematische Theologie* 15 (1938), 507–9.
118 *Memorials of John McLeod Campbell, D. D. Being Selections from His Correspondance. Edited by His Son, the Rev. Donald Campbell* (London 1877) II, 343.
119 See *Life* II, 537–540.
120 *Essays on Some of the Modern Guides of English Thought in Matters of Faith* (London 1887), 318–9.
121 See op. cit., 70–1.

two concerns. For this reason it is true that his statements betray tensions and even contradictions.[122] Yet, by means of the idea of God's education of man as a voluntary being, Maurice attempted to demonstrate that the recognition of the fact of sin and the Devil as God's incalcitrant foes does not imply any diminution of God's sovereign love nor any frustration of His purposes for mankind. In addition Maurice used the Platonically conceived idea of the opposition between the spirit and the flesh in order to allow for sin without jeopardizing the fact of man's unbroken fellowship with God.

However unsatisfactory Maurice's treatment of the problem of the existence of sin and the Devil in God's created universe may appear, it does demonstrate that he never finished wrestling with the problem of man's rebellion against God. His own personal experiences, undoubtedly strengthened by the influence of the Bible and of the Reformed Theology, made him speak strongly of the extent and gravity of evil. He even described how man and the universe lived in a state of unbearable slavery under the tyrannous dominion of sin, death and the Devil. But then he, so to speak, recoiled by modifying and even nullifying what he had asserted regarding the power of evil.

The explanation of this fact is to be found in his basic conception of God as "He Who Is". In this concept the Platonic idea of reality was merged with the idea of God as perfect love. What God in His love decreed must of necessity be, just as *that which is* can never change nor be destroyed. The universe, created and imbued with being by God, must stand forever. To believe that sin introduces a separation between the Creator and His creation and to speak of a fallen, disorderly universe, given up to the dominion of the powers of evil, is to attribute constitutive significance to the decisions of God's creatures, acting in the changeable world of time and space. As God alone is the ultimate and unchangeable reality, the earth and mankind are nothing in themselves; everything which man achieves on his own account is void of being and consequently unreal and powerless against God, the Supreme Being.

As a result of our analysis of Maurice's views on sin and its relation to the Divine Order we can conclude that, for all his strained and even contradictory statements, he considered sin as unreal and unable to subjugate God's creation and lead it into death and destruction. Despite indications to the contrary, God remains the sovereign love which alone is the foundation of the life of the universe and of mankind. Despite every assault of sin and the Devil Christ remains the Lord of the universe and the Head of all mankind. Always God is the One in whom every man lives, moves and has his being.

---

122 Later on we shall repeatedly observe an incongruity between the face-value of the terms Maurice employed and the sense which he intended to convey. Thus, he often made use of words and phrases from the Bible and traditional theology but gave them a significance, different from any literal interpretation. Most probably this is also the case in his description of the destructive work of the powers of evil although it is difficult, not to say impossible, to arrive at any definite conclusion. The reason is that Maurice earnestly wished to assert the awful power of sin and the Devil and so went a long way to impress it upon his readers, and at the same time felt bound to stress God's love as the conquering and triumphant power in the universe. The tensions and contradictions in Maurice's statements on sin cannot always be explained by referring to his use of an imprecise terminology.

The final proof of the correctness of this interpertation can, however, only be given after an examination of Maurice's understanding of the Biblical history of revelation. Only then can a decision be made as to the real place and significance of sin in Maurice's theology.

III

THE MANIFESTATION OF THE DIVINE ORDER

Chapter V

ETERNITY AND HISTORY

1. The Basic Problem in Maurice's Theology

Our previous account of Maurice's idea of the Divine Order has in fact been an exposition of his conviction that theology must start from God and not from man. Man must begin with God and His eternal world in order to arrive at a true understanding of the earth and mankind. As "He Who Is", God is unchangeable, motivated only by perfect self-sacrificing love, which is the very nature of His being. His creative acts originate in His eternal decision to call the universe and mankind into existence. Eternity constitutes the world of time and space – not *vice versa*. Hence God's relation to His creation is always the same. Since Christ is the One in whom God's will is expressed and carried out, He always remains the Creator and Lord of the universe. He is the Head of mankind and of every man, thus constituting an all-embracing human fellowship, the Body of Christ. A universal and necessary order and harmony characterize God's creation. True, the existence of sin and the Devil did seriously threaten the Divine Order, but they did not succeed in accomplishing their destructive purposes. The bond between God and His creation could not be torn asunder. The Triune God and His love continued to be the foundation of the universe and the life of mankind. This is the result to which our inquiry has so far led us.

Yet, at the same time Maurice's writings provide a body of ideas which apparently run counter to his basically clear and consistent view of the Divine Order. Thus Maurice spoke of the Bible as "a Divine history, a history of God's manifestations of Himself".[1] It represents "an orderly historical revelation".[2] It is the account of how God is seeking man in order to save him.[3] It describes God as the Deliverer of man.[4] The Bible is not a collection of opinions and doctrines, but the witness to God's acts in history.[5] God's saving acts are described as a war, in which the Creator wrestles

---

[1] *The Patriarchs*, 60.

[2] p. XVI.

[3] Cf. *Sermons* II, 50: "One all-important contrast suggests itself, the moment we open the Scriptures. They do not set forth the history of a man seeking for God, but of God seeking for man."

[4] Cf. *Life* I, 517: "And what is the Bible after all but the history of a deliverer – of God proclaiming Himself as man's deliverer from the state into which he is ever ready to sink, a state of slavery to systems, superstitions, the world, himself, – Atheism?"

[5] Cf. *Sacrifice*, 158: "the Bible is a record of actual doings, of actual intercourse between a living Being and His creatures upon earth, not a collection of notions and opinions, about which we are to dispute and to tear each other in pieces."

with the destroyer of His creation;[6] indeed, the Bible is "the book of the wars of the Lord".[7]

Similarly Maurice described how the incarnation, death and resurrection of Christ constituted the focal point in the Biblical history of revelation. These events inaugurated man's salvation and the foundation of the Church.[8] The Incarnation presupposed that man was in a fallen state and was unable to break the dominion of sin: "We could not confess a Saviour at all, if we did not believe that men had fallen into an evil condition, out of which they needed to be raised. We could not confess such a Saviour as Jesus, if we did not believe that the worst part of the fall was voluntary; that men had themselves to blame for their greatest calamities. That principle is involved in the idea of an Incarnation. It is carried out in the minutest details in the acts of Christ."[9] The Incarnation has ended the state of mankind in which it lived without God and without fellowship with his fellow-men: "Christ, by taking the body of man, united men to each other; – – by offering it up to God, he united them to God."[10] Through Christ's coming into the world men have been made children of God[11] and partakers of His life;[12] by the sending of the Holy Ghost they have been fashioned into the likeness of Christ.[13] Christ has joined heaven and earth, God and man.[14] As this could only be accomplished through a struggle with the Devil which had enslaved the creation, Maurice could write that "Christ has come to destroy the works of the Devil, and has not failed in the purpose of His coming."[15] Through Christ's victory over the powers of evil man has been redeemed from sin, death and the De-

---

6 Cf. *The Conflict*, 18: "We must read the whole Bible as the record of – – the warfare of the Creator with the Destroyer, of Life with Death."

7 *Life* II, 347.

8 Cf. *The Kingdom of Christ* (1838) I, 295: "The Incarnation of Christ – Christ becoming perfect man – is the central point of ours; this is the ground of our idea of humanity; this is the foundation of our church," and II, 121: "We charge you with not understanding in what respects our condition is changed by the incarnation of Christ, and the descent of the Spirit."

9 *Sermons* III, 75–6.

10 *The Kingdom of Christ* (1838), 205. Cf. also *The Gospel of St. John*, 271–2: "Christ did not merely stoop to our condition. He stooped to us that He might raise us. – – And as this was the ultimate object of His Incarnation and Humiliation, so far as we are concerned – it appeared in every part of the work which He did while He was clothed with our mortality," and *Sermons* V, 171: "They were sure that He had united His divine nature to the human, that the human might share the divine."

11 Cf. *Christmas Day*, 167: "he [Christ] came into the world for this very end – – that he might make us the children of God in Him."

12 Cf. p. 161–2: "fulfilling the purpose for which he came down from heaven which was to make men partakers of his own joy and love."

13 Cf. *Country Churches*, 11: "And now that God has given His Son to take our flesh and to die for us, He deals with us as sons. He says, I will send the Spirit of my Son into your hearts, that you may be like Him."

14 Cf. *The Gospel of St. John*, 56: "For the Son of Man, who joins earth to heaven, the seen to the unseen, God and Man in one, He is with you; through Him your spirits may arise to God, – through Him God's Spirit shall come down upon you."

15 *The Epistles of St. John*, 278. Cf. also *Sermons* V, 275: "He [Christ] was engaged in a conflict to blood against evil, in a death-struggle whether it should put out the light of the world, or whether that light should prevail against it," and *Religions*, 178: "A divine Incarnation is affirmed to be the great instrument for redressing the evils of the world."

142

vil;[16] He is "the Restorer of Humanity to its true condition".[17] By His incarnation Christ has become the Head and King of the human race.[18] Accordingly Maurice maintained that "Christ came to establish a universal dispensation, which did not exist previously; that this dispensation is grounded upon a manifestation of God as absolute, universal love; upon the fact that He has entered into relations in the person of his Son with man as he is, and that to men so united to his Son, he gives his Spirit."[19]

Although we have only adduced a few examples – they could be supplemented almost *ad infinitum* – they should be sufficient to demonstrate that Maurice expounded a consistent view of the Bible as bearing witness to God's saving and redeeming acts in history, culminating in the Incarnation. That this body of ideas must be taken seriously in any comprehensive study of Maurice's theological thinking is emphasized by the fact that his view of the Incarnation as the pivot of God's revelation to man was the outcome of his spiritual crisis in the year 1828. Thus, in a letter, dated February 10th, 1829, to his Unitarian father, Maurice indicated the nature of the new insight which the experience of his own sin had brought him: "The perfect spirituality of God's character I found I had no idea of – –. Hence the necessity of that perfect spirituality being embodied to me in a human form; hence the necessity of being able to contemplate Him, in whom and through whom only I could contemplate God, as the pardoner and remover of that evil in my heart which prevented any spiritual idea of God being entertained by it; and hence the necessity, when that obstacle, that disease, was removed, of the Spirit of God dwelling in my heart to enable it to think rightly of and pray rightly to Him."[20] In other words, sin makes it impossible for man to contemplate God as truth and love, and so God Himself must be manifested in the flesh and remove the evil separating man from God.

Maurice's view developed further under the influence of Edward Irving and his exposition of the decisive importance of the Incarnation for the salvation of all mankind. Thus Maurice's own experience of the power of sin and his ensuing under-

16 Cf. *Country Churches*, 274: "He [God] sent His only begotten Son to deliver those who had rebelled against Him from sin; to deliver them from death and from him who had the power of death," and p. 346: "Our spirits have fallen under the power of sin; our bodies have fallen under the power of death. Christ, our true king, has shown that he is mightier than both; that He is the Deliverer from both."

17 *Theological Essays*, 64. Cf. also *Religions*, 221: "the true estate into which Christ, by taking your nature, has redeemed you," and *Sermons* I, 32: "All the purposes and revelations of the different ages had been converging to one point. The Son of God, the express image of the Father, had been revealed in the nature of man. He had brought that nature through death and the grave, and had exalted it to his Father's right hand."

18 Cf. *Christmas Day*, 76: "Christ has justified your race before God, and – – he is now the Head and King of that race, the everlasting Mediator, by whom your spirit may ascend up to God, and his spirit may come down to you."

19 *The Kingdom of Christ* (1838) I, 58. Cf. also *Christmas Day*, 188: "And now there was one – –, who had entered into the world that he might glorify the name of God, – that he might do the will of God – and that he might establish the kingdom of God',, and *The Apocalypse*, 146: "the glorious purpose for which the Jewish nation had existed was brought to pass; – – because a dispensation was to begin which was grounded upon the regeneration of humanity in the Son of Man; because a Divine Spirit could abide with men and make His temple in their hearts and bodies."

20 *Life* I, 95.

standing of the necessity of the Incarnation were the decisive factors in his break with his father's Unitarianism and his acceptance of the doctrinal beliefs of the Established Church.

Not least recent studies have stressed the significance of Maurice's concept of the Bible and the Incarnation and maintained that it is here the inner core of his theological thinking is revealed. Thus A. M. Ramsey put Maurice's position in the following way: "The uniqueness of the Bible as inspired lies in the uniqueness of the Biblical history as the history of a Kingdom of God in the midst of the world. – – The *Biblical history* is therefore the crux of Maurice's theory. Upon the uniqueness of history the special character of Scripture rests. – – all depends not upon the Bible as a special sort of book or upon the writers as possessors of a special sort of inspiration, but upon the history as a special sort of history."[21] Maurice was prophetic, because he had, despite all his limitations, grasped the Bible's own conception of revelation and "was laying bare that foundation in a remarkable way"[22], which leads beyond the barren contrast between orthodoxy and Biblical criticism. H. Hodkin maintained that for Maurice "the centre of his mind and teaching, 'the master light of all his seeing', was the Incarnation" – it was for him "the constitutive belief of the Christian Faith and the cardinal event in the history of mankind."[23] The same view is expressed by H. G. Wood[24] and A. R. Vidler.[25] Although Dr. Ramsay pointed to the Platonic influence, even he was convinced that the essence of Maurice's theology is a Scriptural insight into the significance of the Incarnation: "He pleaded for the light that lighteth every man, against theologies which virtually denied it – but he never lost sight of the uniqueness of the Word-made-flesh."[26]

As already suggested there is ample evidence to support an assessment of Maurice as a theologian of the Incarnation, firmly rooted in the Biblical history of revelation. It must, however, then be added that in Maurice's theological thinking we meet with two entirely different sets of ideas. On one hand he maintained that theology must start from God and the eternal world. On the other hand he pointed to the Scriptures as the record of God's saving acts in history, culminating in the incarnation, death and resurrection of Christ.

In the first instance the created universe and the life of mankind are seen as the image and reflection of God and His eternal world. Just as the archetype is always essential to the image, so Christ must of necessity be near to every man as his constitutive principle. Through Christ man is always a child of God. The Divine Order remains always the same, being upheld by God's love. Universality and unchangeableness characterize God's relation to the universe and mankind.

---

21 Op. cit., 85.

22 p. 90. For Dr. Ramsey Maurice's understanding of the problems of Biblical criticism and natural science was very limited (see p. 96).

23 *Theology* XL, 10.

24 Cf. *Frederick Denison Maurice* (Cambridge 1950), 38: "So Christ is not only the head of a new humanity: he has changed the moral situation for all men. This conviction inspires Maurice's book on the Kingdom of Christ."

25 Cf. op. cit., 113–4: "But the regeneration that Maurice always had in mind was that of the race by the finished work of Christ."

26 op. cit., 113. See also p. 20.

In the second instance it is God's acts in a particular history in the world of time and space that constitute His relation to mankind. In this case history is not the reflection of God's eternity, which excludes the categories of time and space. That which takes place in history now acquires constitutive significance. God's acts in history are the basis of man's salvation and fellowship with God.

Thus, we apparently find in Maurice two sets of ideas, both of which are characterized by an inner consistency, their distinctive features being the Platonic idea of reality and the Biblical idea of reality respectively. We should even be justified in maintaining that both complexes of ideas exercised a powerful influence upon Maurice and gave his thought its characteristic shape. Hence arises the fundamental question as to whether Maurice's theology is in fact made up of two basically different bodies of thought, which he expounded without any attempt at integration. An affirmative answer to this question would provide a natural explanation of that obscurity and mistiness of which Maurice has so often been accused. It would also account for the highly divergent ways in which the fundamental character of his thought has been interpreted.

However, careful examination of Maurice's interpretation of the Bible, the Incarnation and the Church will – to anticipate its result – demonstrate that the impression of Maurice's theology as a *complexio oppositorum* is merely apparent. His thinking displays far more inner unity and consistency than scholars have assumed. At the same time it will be demonstrated that Maurice's thought represents a highly original fusion of the message of the Bible and the Platonic idea of reality.

2. The Idea of Revelation

We have seen that according to Maurice man is created with reason as the faculty through which he arrives at true knowledge of himself, of the universe, and of God as the supreme Being. Yet the reason by itself is unable to attain to knowledge, since it is created to receive what God reveals to it. Thus the very existence of the reason implies man's need for a revelation. This is accomplished through Christ, the Word of God and the Light that always lighteneth every man. By contrasting the reason with the understanding, which with its logical deductions based on sense-perceptions arrives only at appearances and opinions, Maurice's conclusion appears to be that, by communicating with the reason of man, Christ imparts knowledge directly without the mediation of anything belonging to the visible world of time and space.

We also meet the idea, however, that the created universe, being an image of the eternal world as its archetype, is a means through which God reveals Himself to man. This applies to the Natural Order and, more especially, to the Human Order.[27] Here facts are the starting-point for arriving at knowledge. Once they have been grasped by the senses, man must pierce through their outward, visible shape and discover *that which is* – their constitutive principle. This is achieved by the reason or rather by Christ, who illuminates the reason so that it can perceive true being.

27 Cf. *What Is Revelation?*, 388–9: "It is the belief of an Unseen God that he has clung to amidst all difficulty; a God exhibited to him, in some degree, in the Order of the Universe, in some degree in the Order of human life."

Thus the law of man's existence is always to receive the knowledge which God reveals. Now, in his description of how man receives knowledge through the Natural Order and the Human Order Maurice treats them as an imperfect means of revelation. The knowledge which is revealed through them is incomplete and can, therefore, do no more than lead men to expect a full revelation of God Himself. There is another respect in which man is in need of a perfect revelation which can impart true knowledge of God and man. Having closed his spiritual eye to Christ's light of revelation, man gropes blindly in darkness, dominated by a false knowledge of reality. The actual state of man demands a specific act of revelation on God's part to dispel this gloom and falsehood by giving him a complete knowledge of God and the Divine Order.

Maurice saw no difficulty in maintaining Christ to be the inward Light which directly imparts the knowledge of revelation to man's spirit and at the same time asserting that man has an imperfect and even false knowledge of reality and therefore needs a new and complete revelation. The explanation is to be found in his firm conviction that God had revealed Himself in a particular history, to which the Bible bears witness, in order to impart true and perfect knowledge. Maurice never felt the need to argue or to prove why only the Biblical history of revelation can satisfy man's longings for true knowledge. He simply assumed this to be an indisputable fact. His task was to let the Bible speak for itself and thus reveal the perfect truth to man.

Because Maurice accepted the Bible as the book of God's history of revelation, he could establish the principle that God reveals Himself only through facts.[28] It is not at all surprising for him that God's revelation takes place through visible things since God Himself had created the visible world of time and space.[29] It is indeed with good purpose that God reveals Himself through the forms of sense. Revelation, which is meant for all, can then address itself to everybody because every man, created with the organs of sense, understands the language of the senses.[30] Furthermore, God's revelation of Himself through concrete, visible facts which meet man from without

28 Cf. Life II, 411: "Nevertheless, I do not undervalue legends. They contain man's attempts to feel after God's ideas; they bear witness that no idea can be represented to us without some vesture. But the vesture of God's own ideas must be facts. If He reveals His ideas to us, the revelation must be through facts. I accept the revelation recorded in the Scripture as a revelation of the Divine mind through facts."

29 Cf. Sacrifice, 307: "To some, the language of symbols may seem unsatisfactory; some may even denounce it as idolatrous and profane. They may speak as they like; but if they will have the Bible, they must have symbols; they must be content to let God speak to them through the forms of sense, because they are His forms, and because no others could convey His meaning to the hearts which He desires to take it in, so well as they do," and What Is Revelation?, 467: "The realities which are behind the veil express themselves through the forms of sense, because that is the order and principle of God's universe."

30 Cf. What Is Revelation?, 467: "the Bible –– is written in the language of the senses, and with such an absence of logical formulas as is to be found in no other book. ––. Beginning from the Eternal, and descending to the Temporal, proceeding from the Infinite to the Finite, the forms of logic, which are abstractions from the Finite and the Temporal, have no place in it," and The Apocalypse, 347: "The language of the senses is the only real language – the only language – which presents spiritual things to us as they are, not modified and disturbed by our understandings, not as if our perceptions of them were the grounds of their existence. So it has been throughout the Scriptures."

demonstrates that revelation must neither be confounded with nor identified with man's own notions and feelings.[31]

Although God reveals Himself through the forms of sense it was just as important for Maurice to point out that man must never rest satisfied with these.[32] This would chain man to the outward and transient, to the concrete and individual. On the contrary, revelation addresses itself to the spirit or reason of man, which is created to know the universal and unchangeable.[33] Confronted by God's acts of revelation in history, man must penetrate their outward forms and grasp the universal truth. Thus revelation, expressed in visible facts, becomes the instrument through which God leads man to the knowledge of true reality.[34] Consequently Maurice wrote: "the revelation is a progress from the comprehensible to the incomprehensible, a gradual, orderly, scientific progress from those manifestations of God which are apprehensible to the affections, and in some measure to the understandings of man, to those which we require for the satisfaction of the deepest and most awful longings of our spirits. The last discoveries of the book [the Bible] are, as they should be, the most transcendent and wonderful, – those which the mind can least take in, those in which it is most content to be lost."[35] Far from binding men to anything specific in history the purpose of God's revelation is to raise them above the sensible and finite and guide them to eternal reality.[36] Thus, in the last analysis,

31 Thus, Maurice wrote of Colenso's criticism of the Bible: "He was robbing us of the *facts* of God's revelation, and so throwing us upon religious ideas, the 'God consciousness', and all that talk which means something to Germans, but to an Englishman is the substitute for a meaning" *(The Claims,* 76. See also *Religions,* 55).

32 Cf. *The Unity of the New Testament,* 406: "The forms of sense are therefore the best, nay, if we follow Scripture, the only forms which can express spiritual truths; all attempts to translate them into intellectual propositions weaken their force. But on the other hand, the longing of men for deliverance from mere sensible material things, from idols, is a most genuine longing, one which the true preacher seeks to awaken. It is connected, though it must not be identified, with the longing for deliverance from moral evil. That arises when the man is conscious that he himself is his tormentor, that he has bowed to outward things, because he has wandered from some higher centre."

33 Cf. *The Word Revelation,* 18: "For it is not an outward Revelation, a revelation to the eye of the flesh. It will be as it has been, a Revelation to the man within," and p. 35: "Speech and letters would only impart any wisdom in so far as He discovered to that eye the objects which it was meant to behold, without which it could not be satisfied."

34 Cf. *What Is Revelation?,* 280–1: "Is not your Gospel a message concerning the Infinite, the Absolute, the Eternal? Is not your Bible a book of Facts by which men are led gradually on to know what the ground is at their feet; to feel, through the actual finite, for the Infinite, – through the actual temporal, for the Eternal?" and *The Word Revelation,* 26: "the discovery of God himself, of His inmost being, of His own love, constitutes the Revelation; – – this Revelation is of that which is *invisible* and *infinite* – beyond the grasp of the senses, beyond the grasp of the intellect."

35 *The Kingdom of Christ* (1838) II, 22. "Comprehensible" denotes the knowledge gained by the understanding on the basis of sense-observations. On the other hand, that revelation leads man to the "incomprehensible" means that it takes him beyond that which is limited by time and space and brings him to a direct knowledge and vision of the eternal God. See also *The Kingdom of Christ* I, 282.

36 Cf. *The Kingdom of Christ* (1838) III, 404: "he [Christ] has taught us that we are spiritual beings, and that all sensible forms and images may illustrate the mysteries of this kingdom, but can never be substituted for them, or made a part of them."

the Platonic idea of reality determined Maurice's concept of revelation. Although man must begin with facts, with the visible and concrete, he must never content himself with their outward shape, for then he would become dependent upon the finite world of time and space and be forced to regard it as essential. The outcome would be idolatry, the worship of visible things.[37]

A corollary of this view was Maurice's rejection of the concept of revelation, held by contemporary orthodoxy. It considered revelation to be a series of divine acts which established a new order of salvation in the history of mankind. Such a view contradicted the Biblical idea of revelation. This is evident from the fact that the Bible most often described revelation as 'apokalypsis'. As this term, quite literally, means the removal or lifting off of a veil, God's revelation consequently signifies that He removes the veil which conceals true reality from man. Revelation does not create a new reality nor inaugurate a new situation in God's relation to man. It imparts true knowledge of *that which is*. Through revelation God removes the false idea of reality in which man is ensnared because of his sin; He dispels the darkness of ignorance so that man can truly know God and the Divine Order in which he is placed.[38] By revelation God makes known to man that the universe and all mankind unchangeably stand in Him.[39]

As another precise term for the Biblical idea of revelation Maurice employed 'discovery', as the word clearly signifies that God 'dis-covers' the veil of ignorance and imparts true knowledge of reality.[40] Other terms which Maurice found adequate to convey the true meaning of revelation were 'manifestation', 'proclamation' and

37 Maurice's interpretation of the facts of revelation fits in with his understanding of the significance of facts for science. Indeed Maurice called the Biblical revelation 'scientific' and compared the purpose of revelation to Newton's discovery of the law of gravitation: "It is to the spirit within that God makes any of His discoveries. Only with this spirit can a man seize any truth, or enter into communion with it. Newton might have seen a thousand apples fall from the trees on which they hung; there was one which led him to perceive the law of the universe. The object that was presented to his outward eye became the instrument through which an idea was presented to the man himself. A universal truth shone through that special instance" *(What Is Revelation?, 2).*

38 Cf. *The Epistle to the Hebrews,* XXIV: "He [the reader of Scripture] may be inclined to say: Does that word [revelation] mean 'creation'? Suppose Revelation does create, is there nothing else that it does first, and more characteristically? Does it not signify 'lifting off a veil'? Does it not seem to intimate the disclosure of that which is; *this,* rather than the formation or production of anything which previously was not? – – the Lord of all was Himself lifting off the veil; was disclosing Himself to a creature formed in His image; was thereby awakening that creature to know what it is; to understand itself in its relation to Him." See also p. XXXIV.

39 Cf. *Introduction to William Law's Remarks on Mandeville's Fable of the Bees* (Cambridge 1844), XXVII: "the very word *revelation* imports the making known that which is, to the persons who are most interested in knowing it; and – – *this* revelation proclaimed itself to be a light to the feet and a lamp to the path: not professing to supply a set of portable rules or maxims, but offering to lead the humble disciple into the apprehension of the laws and mysteries under which he is himself living."

40 Cf. *The Word Revelation,* 34: "If we like that word [discovery] better than revelation, let us use it, only remembering that the sense is not the least different," and *Theological Essays,* 114: "In both [Testaments of the Bible] He is discovering Himself to men; in both He is piercing through the mists which conceal Him from them." See also *Sermons* IV, 212–3.

'declaration'.[41] They all demonstrate that through revelation God manifests, proclaims or declares to man that which has always been true and which will always remain so. The choice of terms is of secondary importance as long as it is clear that the sole purpose of revelation is to impart an unambiguous knowledge of reality. Revelation throws light on and explains actual existence but otherwise it changes nothing in the life of the created universe and of mankind.

For Maurice St. Paul's account of his own conversion is most instructive in this respect. It illustrates how God, through a particular event directed towards a particular individual, revealed and manifested a universal law which is unchangeably valid for every man. St. Paul did not regard his conversion a break with the past, transferring him from the old realm of sin and death into the kingdom of God, inaugurated by the incarnation, death, and resurrection of Christ. Nor did it signify that it was only at that moment that St. Paul entered into fellowship with Christ. Since Christ had always been the One in whom Paul stood and upon whom he had been dependent for his entire life, his conversion consisted of "his awaking from ignorance of this foundation to a full, clear apprehension of it".[42] A divine revelation made St. Paul realise that the secret of his own life had been that Christ, as his Lord and Deliverer, had always been near to him and had fought against that which sought to separate him from fellowship with Christ: "God has opened his eyes to see that he could not exist if this Lord, this Son of God, were not sustaining his existence."[43]

However, St. Paul's conversion did not merely reveal the truth about his own life. It also proclaimed what was true of every man. His own conversion became to him the concrete example which revealed the unalterable truth about the relation between God and mankind.[44] It manifested that all mankind and all human fellowships exist in Christ. This revelation became the burden of St. Paul's proclamation of the Gospel to the Gentiles: "St. Paul's special work was to carry this message to the nations, to tell men that the Son of God was IN them, that He was the real head and root of their

41 Cf. *Sermons* III, 102–3: "He [St. Paul] had no hope from his own rhetoric, from his powers of persuading men to adopt a new opinion. His hope lay in this, that he came to declare the thing as it was, – that which was from the beginning, but which God was now making manifest, through the birth and death and resurrection of His Son," and *Sermons* IV, 26: "It had not yet been declared that He [Christ] is moving at the heart of humanity, that all nations have a common fellowship in Him."

42 *Sermons* V, 210. Cf. *Theological Essays*, 78: "Whenever he gives the story of his conversion, he describes it as an unveiling of Christ to his bodily eye; when he lays open the principle and meaning of his conversion, he represents it as the revealing or unveiling of Christ *in* him," and *Sermons* II, 226: "That vision, he says, was the revelation that Christ was in him, that the King Whom he had looked upon as far off was the Lord of his heart and reins, was claiming the dominion there."

43 *The Acts of the Apostles*, 133. See also *The Conflict*, 77–8, 96–7 and *The Commandments*, 141–2.

44 Cf. *The Acts of the Apostles*, 135: "Could they speak too warmly of such moments [of conversion]? Could they prize them too highly? Only if the momentary was substituted for the permanent truth which was revealed in that moment, only if it was more thought of than the God who is present in that moment, and in every moment of our lives; who is always fighting with us and for us against ourselves; who is always speaking to our wills and drawing them out of their own ignorance and perverseness; who would always be converting them to Himself."

humanity, that apart from Him they had no life, or righteousness, or unity at all; to bring out this fact in relation to the experiences of their own minds, to the facts of history, to the calling of the chosen people, to their law, to the order of Society, to the past, present, future condition of the world. He was to shew how our Lord's Incarnation, His death, resurrection, ascension, bore upon and explained His relation to human beings, expounded the riddle of their own existence, confuted the innumerable evidences, which outward and inward facts seemed to oppose to a belief in His actual fellowship with them and dominion over them."[45] Sin had not blotted out the fact that Christ is the Head of every man; it had merely obscured man's spiritual sight so that he could not see reality as it truly is.

The significance of the Platonic idea of reality for Maurice's understanding of revelation is further illustrated by his comparison of Socrates and St. Paul. Both were true philosophers seeking *that which is,* the ultimate foundation of existence. Both used the same method in debate, seeking to lead men away from "speculation about all things in heaven and earth to seek for the ground of their life; for a Substance that lay beneath them."[46] The difference between them was that Socrates only had glimpses of true reality whereas St. Paul, because of the revelation of Christ, could clearly and unambiguously declare Christ to be the Lord and Deliverer of every man.[47]

According to Maurice, then, revelation imparts to man knowledge of the unchangeable reality which constitutes the life of the creation. Revelation does not bind man to specific events in history; these are only manifestations of eternal truth. Man must ascend through that which is concrete and particular in order to apprehend the universal and the permanent, which alone can be the object of true knowledge.[48]

45 *The Unity of the New Testament,* 353–4. Cf. also p. 536–7: " Here was the foundation of a Gospel, *the* Gospel with which St. Paul was entrusted; good news to men, not of something which was coming to them, but of their actual state, of that state which belongs to them, but which they do not recognize," and p. 410: "The foundation *is* laid. Christ is at the root of humanity. The preaching of Apollos, the preaching of Paul, can but declare things as they are, cannot change facts in the least."

46 *The Acts of the Apostles,* 284.

47 Cf. *ibid.:* "He [St. Paul] told them of a Lord of their spirits – One who would guide them out of wrong to right. It had pleased God, he said, to reveal His Son in him, that he might preach Him among the Gentiles. God had shown him who that Guide and Teacher was, to whom Socrates, in his conscious ignorance and weakness, had turned; whom he had asked to keep him from the snares of sense, and to show him the thing that is. St. Paul could speak out the name of this Divine Teacher," and *The Kingdom of Christ* II, 15–6: "It was the great glory of the greatest philosopher of antiquity [Plato] to affirm, What man wants is a knowledge of that which *is;* he cannot be content with opinions and notions about that which *may be.* His being will not rest upon this. Society will not rest upon it. The ground of both must be a reality, an invisible spiritual reality; not any scheme or theory about this matter or that. The first Fathers of the Church had the strongest sympathy with this philosopher, precisely because he affirmed this. They felt that he was asking for the very thing which a revelation, if it were a revelation, ought to give. They felt, We have a revelation not of certain notions and dogmas about certain thngs, but a revelation of God Himself."

48 Cf. *The Unity of the New Testament,* 186: "The universal is seen in the individual, according to the Scripture method, which is also the method of nature, the method of reason, in short, the divine method in all its manifestations."

Reality, then, is always the same for every man, regardless of when and where he lives. Revelation does not mean that God now establishes His Kingdom or a new state of salvation in the midst of the world of sin and death. The new element introduced by revelation is the perfect knowledge of God and of humanity as being created in Christ and always living in Him.[49] Revelation is an illumination and explanation of man's existence. Thus, Maurice's idea of revelation presupposes that the Divine Order remains inviolate despite the assaults of sin and the Devil – these have merely succeeded in inculcating in man a false knowledge of reality.

3. The Biblical History of Revelation and its Veracity

Maurice accepted the entire Bible as true. He was convinced that it narrates how, through His acts in a particular history, God revealed Himself to be the Redeemer and the Deliverer, the One who seeks man to save him and wars against the foes of His creation. The Bible is truly the witness of "a Divine history, a history of God's manifestations of Himself." The Bible is, without reservation, the account of the history of the Kingdom of God and of God's rule of love, being "throughout, the history of an actual government, – throughout, the history of an actual education; a government of voluntary creatures to teach them subjection, – an education of voluntary creatures to make them free."[50] Maurice's assertion that the Bible contains God's revelation to man was the expression of his deepest conviction, and he saw it as his essential task to bring its message home to his contemporaries. Repeatedly he penetrated so deeply into the Biblical texts that his interpretations were filled with a spiritual force and originality capable of making the Bible existential.

While unreservedly accepting the authority of the Bible, Maurice opposed the view that it witnesses to an exclusive history of revelation. He could assert and use everything the Bible records on the sole condition that every intimation of the exclusive and particular is discarded. Dr. Ramsey was, therefore, mistaken in maintaining that the characteristic feature of Maurice's view of the Bible is that he considered it a record of "a special sort of history", which in its uniqueness may be contrasted with the history of the rest of the world.[51] It is indeed this very attempt to maintain "the uniqueness of the Biblical history"[52] that Maurice so vigorously opposed: "It has been a miserable part of our apologetic system to set up Sacred History as a kind of rival to Profane; to treat one as if it concerned God, and the other as if it were merely of the earth."[53]

Despite sin and the Devil the whole universe stands in Christ and lives by virtue of His creative acts. Hence it is false and meaningless to distinguish between a history

49 Maurice accepted the difference between 'the old man' and 'the new man'. However, that difference must not be seen in terms of 'life without Christ' and 'life with Christ'. 'The old man', because of his sin, lives without knowing that Christ is the foundation of his life, whereas 'the new man' has received this knowledge through God's revelation (see *The Unity of the New Testament*, 541–2).
50 *The Patriarchs*, 63. See also p. II–III.
51 See op. cit., 85.
52 *ibid.*
53 *What Is Revelation?*, 462–3.

under the wrath of God and subject to the law of sin and death and an exceptional history of salvation characterized by a special intervention on the part of God which may only benefit a small section of mankind. All history is the history of God's salvation, since the life of all men is founded upon God's self-sacrificing love. Since, in the face of man's disobedience and ignorance, God's dealings with man take the form of an education, all history is the history of God's education of mankind, the purpose of which is to make every man know God and the Divine Order and to urge him to give up his selfishness and defiance towards God and live according to the law of his creation.

Although the Bible must not be considered the account of a unique history of salvation, it nonetheless possesses a marvellous and unique character. It is truly marvellous because it records how God in His love deals with men, but it is marvellous in no other sense than all history is marvellous on exactly the same grounds. Similarly, the uniqueness of the Bible is that, through its account of the particular history of a particular nation and particular men, it reveals the unchangeable reality constituting the life of all other nations and of all other men. Consequently Maurice contended that "the Bible is remarkably a book of laws, a book explaining the Divine order of the universe; if it be not this, it is nothing."[54] In the Bible God, through concrete historical examples, teaches how He always acts towards every man.[55] The Bible contains "lesson books for mankind, teaching by experiment what is incompatible with the order of human existence, gradually discovering the principles which are at the root of it."[56] Its sole function is to give man a true knowledge of himself and of his relation to God and his fellow-men.[57] The reality God has created remains the same always, but through a specific history God removes man's ignorance and imparts a full and perfect knowledge, which enables man to act in accordance with His purpose.[58]

54 *The Kingdom of Christ* II, 156. Cf. also *Christmas Day*, 6: "the whole Scripture is a discovery and revelation to us, of the laws according to which God has made the universe and made man"; *The Prophets*, 136: "the Bible is a revelation of permanent laws and principles," and *The Patriarchs*, 213: "the Bible is a revelation of laws, not of anomalies; it unfolds to us unvaried and eternal principles of the divine government."

55 Cf. *Theological Essays*, 90–1: "If Science concerns that which is fixed and absolute, *that which is*, then to believe that God has declared Himself, that He has withdrawn the veil which hides Him from His creatures, that He has in a wonderful and orderly history enabled us to see what He is, and what He is to us, what those eternal laws and principles are which dwell in Himself and which determine His dealings with us, is to believe that there is a divine and human *Science*, that we are not left to the anticipations or guesses of one age or of another."

56 *Social Morality*, 52. Cf. also *Sermons* III, 100: "the records of Scriptures [are] instances and exemplifications of a law, of the course of the Divine working," and *Theological Essays*, 46: "I accept the Scriptures as teaching me laws by instances, and so correcting my theories, and dispossessing me of them."

57 Cf. *The Epistle to the Hebrews*, XXVI–XXVII: "this function [of the Bible is] to interpret to them themselves, their relation to their fellow-men, their relation to God, and the course of his dealings with our race," and *The Kingdom of Christ* (1838) I, 49–50: "Scripture is not merely a *collection of texts*, but the exhibition of a grand and coherent scheme, by which God has trained man to the knowledge of his true position, and of Himself."

58 Cf. *The Epistle to the Hebrews*, XXXVI–XXXVII: "This, I think, is the principle of the

152

This view of the Bible placed Maurice in opposition to the advocates of the orthodox view of the Scriptures who, to his mind, believed that they were exalting the Bible and safeguarding its sacred character by maintaining that its subject matter is a life of salvation in which men may be partakers but which has nothing to do with their actual lives.[59] By raising up a barrier between the Bible and common human life, however, they only succeeded in making its message meaningless for ordinary men.[60] Maurice emphasized that the Bible deals precisely with "the ordinary stuff and material of human existence."[61] It is concerned with "the great commonplaces of humanity" and tells of "those events in which one man has the same interest as the other."[62] "The marvel of the history," Maurice wrote,[63] "lies in the *absence* of the peculiar, the grotesque; in the homeliness of all the details; in the inherent littleness of the personages, who are the subjects of it." The Bible takes up, explains and throws light on the ordinary life of all men.[64] It reveals that human life is created and sustained by God's love: "That *is* a strange history which teaches us to look upon the familiar as most wonderful; upon the every-day order of existence as a divine order; which connects God not with exceptional acts, but with the habitual course and current of existence. The Bible is unlike other books, precisely on this ground."[65] It is as "the human book" which interprets human existence that it manifests its unique, divine character.[66]

In the demand that the Bible must not be subjected to a critical examination in

Bible, the principle which goes through every part of it, that the unseen God is actually ruling over men; that all orders of men are appointed by Him, and are ruling under Him; that just so far as they know this, and live and act in the faith of it, they are doing their right work in the world, are helping to expound the laws and principles of the Divine Government, are helping to bring man into that service which is freedom."

59 Cf. *The Kingdom of Christ* II, 201: "You know I have told you very often that the Bible is not a show-book, written about things which have nothing to do with you, but one that concerns all your common business and tells you how to set about it in a right way," and *The Prayer-Book*, 221: " 'The Bible', we are told sometimes, 'gives us such a beautiful picture of what we should be.' Nonsense! It gives us no picture at all. It reveals to us a fact; it tells us what we actually are; it says, This is the form in which God created you, to which He has restored you; this is the work which the eternal God, the God of truth and love, is continually carrying on within you."

60 Cf. *Introduction to Julius Hare's Charges*, LXXXV: "Both [Evangelicals and High Churchmen] degrade it [the Bible] into a mere document – a book which is divine because it is not human – although all its statements are grounded on the assertion that man is made in the image of God; although the centre of its revelation is the God-man."

61 *The Patriarchs*, 73. See also p. 77.

62 p. 103.

63 p. 103–4.

64 Cf. *The Kingdom of Christ* (1838) II, 64: "the Bible is essentially a human book – rather say *the* human book, – and this not in spite of its being divine, but *because* it is divine; – – the rising of the sun in the heavens necessarily makes every tree and hedge-row about us clear and distinct; – – all the conditions of persons, as related to each other, become manifest, just as their common relation to God becomes manifest."

65 *The Patriarchs*, 104.

66 Cf. *The Kingdom of Christ* (1838) II, 8: "The book is most recognised as divine, when it is most felt to be human; the acknowledgment of its being delivered by real men, is at the same time the acknowledgment of its origin from God."

accordance with the rules which apply to all other literature Maurice saw another dangerous attempt to isolate the Bible from actual human life.[67] Instead of furthering respect for its divine authority this demand only degrades it. Only if the Bible is treated on a line with any other book will it be able to manifest its true power. The more it is allowed to bear upon the problems of human life, the more it will demonstrate itself to be divine, because it alone is able to solve the riddles of human existence.[68] Similarly, due respect is not shown to the Bible by fencing it in with theories of divine inspiration and infallibility. The Bible asks to be allowed to speak for itself: "If the facts, contained in the books themselves, do not interpret to us the facts of our own life, and the constitution and history of the world, they are not what they profess to be; if they do, this will be the highest evidence they can produce of their divinity; the most satisfactory witness that they are what we want."[69] The only right way of asserting the infallibility of the Bible is therefore to let it bear its own testimony and leave it to prove itself as a divine revelation by shedding that light on human life which men so eagerly desire.

As a corollary to this view of the self-authenticating power of the Bible Maurice bluntly rejected the apologetic work which had been carried out since the 17th century to prove the veracity of the Bible.[70] However good the intentions which had prompted the attempt at establishing the integrity and authenticity of the Biblical

67 Cf. *The Kingdom of Christ* II, 144: "Are we then to say – – that criticism is wholly inapplicable to this particular set of records; that they must be taken for granted upon some authority or other, be it that of primitive antiquity, or of the Church in the present day; and that, being so taken for granted, all further inquiry respecting them is to be discarded? – – There comes a time, however, when other books are subjected to this trial; it has been the will of God that the book which we consider pre-eminently His should be subjected to the same. It is a solemn inquiry for us, whether we shall dare to pretend that we will take better care of His book than He has taken care of it; whether we shall affirm that it cannot bear the application of tests, which we believe that ordinary literature will bear."

68 Cf. *Sermons* II, 234: "the Bible should be treated, not as a book which stands aloof, frowning upon these inquiries [as to the problems of human life], but as the *key* to the meaning of them," and *Life* II, 229: "I believed the Bible did serve as a key book which enabled us to understand the histories and legends of various nations, to justify the true beliefs which were in them, to show what false beliefs or unbeliefs had mingled with these, to explain how they had become confounded. I have called for the application of this most severe test to its records; I have said that they ought to bear it if the book is what it assumes to be, and that Christians have wronged and degraded it by severing it from all other books instead of manfully evincing their confidence in its veracity and its strength by trying whether it will not throw light upon all."

69 *Introductory Lectures Delivered at Queen's College* ("Queen's College, its Object and Method"), 25. Cf. also *The Claims*, 101: "Priests and doctors in all ages – – have looked upon the Bible as a feeble, tender plant, which was committed to their nursing, which they were not to let the winds of heaven visit too roughly. And the great proof of its vitality is, that it has lasted through all this nursing; that *they* have not been able to kill it; that their fencing-rooms and hot-houses have been thrown down by the winds which they dreaded for it; that it has thriven and put forth fresh leaves and richer fruits in the open air."

70 Cf. *The Kingdom of Heaven*, XXXII: "If the Gospel is a Divine message to mankind, it *cannot* depend for the proof of its veracity, for its influence over men, upon any theories about the composition of the books which contain it, upon any arguments about their authenticity or inspiration, upon any definitions which we can give of the words 'Authenticity' and 'Inspiration'."

writings in order to guarantee the truth of their contents, such a preoccupation with the question of external evidence is nevertheless tantamount to disbelief in the Bible. It is no longer believed to contain a divine message, capable of demonstrating its own truth.[71] Furthermore, the use of human arguments and theories to prove the veracity of the Bible leads men in fact to trust in human authorities rather than in the Bible itself.[72] Therefore, all apologetic endeavours on behalf of the Bible are blasphemous, as they interpose human theories between man and the testimony of the Bible. They are even absolutely pointless. If the Bible itself does not carry the convincing power of truth, all man's attempts to prove it to be the truth are of no avail.[73]

We have seen that through the human relationships man is led to that self-knowledge which makes him see his true needs and realise that he can only be satisfied by a perfect revelation of God Himself. Accordingly Maurice maintained that the evidence for the truth of the Bible lies in the longings and aspirations of the spirit of man, trained in the hardships of human existence.[74] This must, however, not be taken to mean that the spirit itself is the judge of the veracity of the Bible; it is God

71 Cf. p. XXXIV: "The awe of the Word, the power of the Word, has departed, while we are in the very act of asserting its awe and its power. The Word no longer convinces us, governs us. We are its masters, we are to enforce it on the acceptance and obedience of men."

72 Cf. *Life* II, 510: "This worship of mere testimony has been the disease of our theologians and historical students for more than two centuries. – – We believe, because credible people – that is, people whom we think credible – tell us we ought to believe; that it is dangerous not to believe."

73 Cf. *Tracts for Priests and People. 1st Series No. 2* ("The Mote and the Beam: a Clergyman's Lessons from the Present Panic"), 69–70: "Then if people ask us, – Where did you get the books which tell you of this Revelation? we can answer them, – Is it a Revelation to you? Does it tell you of yourselves? Does it tell you of Him whom you are feeling after, if haply you may find Him? If it does, you will receive it as God's Revelation of you and of Himself, through whatever hands it comes to you, wherever we found it, whether we are beasts or true men. If it does not come to you as a revelation of God, no evidence which we can bring to convince you that it is, will have any power over you," and *Introductory Lectures Delivered at Queen's College* ("On Theology"), 260: "The natural philosopher, and the musician, and the mathematician, begin with no evidences. Those truths which they have to communicate are the evidences; as they present them in one form or another to your minds, they are confident that they *will* carry *their* own light with them." Maurice believed that Biblical criticism had served a useful purpose by exploding all human theories on the divine character of the Bible, thus making room for the Bible to assert itself: "the student of theology must – – confess that a number of hard, dogmatical abstractions respecting spiritual objects, and, not least, respecting the books which treat of these objects, were darkening the face of the heavens, and making men's path along their common earth less clear. That some fiery process would be necessary for the destruction of these, we might conjecture. Of what kind it should be, we could not be judges. God ordained that it should be this destructive analysis. We cannot doubt that what He appointed was best" *(The Kingdom of Christ* II, 146).

74 Cf. *Christmas Day*, 300: "I come to say to you, that so far as you are brought into contact with real life and real suffering, just so far have you an evidence of the truth which we preach: we ask for no other. We announce to you certain things as true – we believe we have commission to announce them; the proof of them is in your hearts and consciences, and daily experience," and *Religions*, XIV: "For do *we* not need – – to be taught that the Gospel is not a dead letter, by discovering what living wants there are in us, and all men, which it meets and satisfies?"

Himself who, by means of the Socratic dialogue, has educated the spirit to recognise the truth intuitively when it is revealed to it.[75] Inasmuch as the Bible solves the problems of human existence which man demands to have solved, it is in its encounter with the spirit of man that it proves itself to be a living truth of divine origin.[76]

Maurice's rejection of any attempt at proving the truth of the Biblical narratives was not merely due to a firm belief in the self-authenticating power of the Bible. He repudiated all apologetical work whatsoever because it involved the exaltation of the understanding at the expense of the reason. This is disastrous because the Bible directly addresses itself to that faculty in man which is created to receive knowledge of *that which is*.[77] As the function of the reason is to penetrate the external visible shapes of things in order to discover eternal laws and principles, this implies with respect to the Bible that it is the task of the reason to perceive the eternal truth revealed in the historical events to which the Bible bears witness. To concentrate on the outward concrete circumstances accompanying the Biblical history of revelation only means submitting to the yoke of the senses and the thought-forms of the understanding. When this happens the Bible becomes a dead book in which only an outward, particular and contingent history counts at the expense of *that which is,* the unveiling of which is the core of the Biblical revelation. The essential point in any interpretation of the Bible is to grasp the eternal necessary truths which are embodied in the Biblical history of revelation.

75 Cf. *The Prayer-Book,* 103: "We tell you that it [the Bible] will interpret yourselves to you and the world to you. And again, that the world and yourselves will interpret *it* to you." The Bible is "at once a voice speaking to them from heaven and a voice echoing the most secret longings and groans which they have uttered upon earth" *(The Kingdom of Christ* (1838) II, 7).

76 Cf. *Introductory Lectures Delivered at Queen's College* ("On Theology"), 260–1: "The kind of evidence which I hope will commend itself to the minds of my pupils is this. They will learn, I trust, to look at the Bible in its simplest form, without any elaborate expositions, or ingenious inferences, as containing the history of the Divine government and education of our race. It will give them a view of the growth of human thought and of human society, which I think explains wonderfully both the facts we meet with elsewhere and the elaborate theories respecting them, which seem to stand out in fierce opposition to each other. It is busy with all common things, with the transactions of daily life; in them, not apart from them, men learn that they are mysterious beings. How God awakens the discovery, how He guides those to whom He has made it, the book declares in the clearest and simplest language – language, however, which would not be plain to us, if there were not the like processes going on in ourselves. – – We ask *it* to interpret what we see and feel, and the different partial notions respecting itself; gradually a light dawns upon us; we feel that it is from above, because the ground at our feet is made clear by it; we feel that it proceeds from that Life which is the light of men."

77 Cf. *The Epistle to the Hebrews,* LXXXV: "But [the reason] is that which justifies a Revelation, petitions for a Revelation; confesses that it has in itself no substitute for a Revelation. You need not meet it with arguments to prove the Revelation; it will not care for them or listen to them. Meet it with the thing itself," and *Introductory Lectures Delivered at Queen's College* ("On Theology"), 259: "If we are honest in our profession of believing in a revelation, we must suppose that it is addressed to human beings; that they need it; and that they have consciences and hearts which were created to receive it; surely then we are safer in speaking directly to these, than in taking a long round-about course to convince their understandings that they ought to be convinced; to shew them why they should bow to that, which we believe has a greater power in it to make them bow than anything else has."

156

Since Maurice saw the essence of the Bible to be its revelation of universal and unchangeable laws and principles, it might have been expected that he would have had no difficulty in accepting the results of Biblical criticism and in admitting that even legends and myths might proclaim eternal truths. This position was adopted by Colenso, who had entirely accepted Maurice's theology. Colenso applied the methods of historical criticism to the Bible and was not troubled by its findings because of his firm conviction that *quaestio facti* is irrelevant: eternal truths may indeed become manifest in historical events, but are always valid – regardless even of their manifestation in history. But Maurice refused to draw Colenso's entirely consistent conclusions from his own idea of revelation. Indeed, he denounced Colenso vehemently. However important it is to emphasize that the core of the Biblical history of revelation is the manifestation of necessary, universal truth, Maurice was nevertheless anxious to maintain that the revelation of eternal laws and principles cannot exist independently nor be separated from its external, visible embodiment – they stand and fall together.[78] Maurice stressed the historical reliability of the Biblical narratives, since to consider them as mere legends and myths makes it impossible to know the eternal truth revealed through them. *Quaestio facti* is, then, vitally important to him. It is, however, also evident that Maurice tried to deal with this problem in accordance with his fundamental idea of revelation.

The reason alone, Maurice asserted in refutation of Colenso, is able to decide the question of the veracity of Biblical history. When a particular history manifests laws and principles, the truth of which is intuitively perceived by the reason, it must follow that this history is true. The truth of an idea establishes the historical validity of its outward embodiment. The reason knows for sure that when the Bible records a historical event, it must have taken place because it grasps the eternal truth, manifested through it. Consequently the problem of the veracity of the Biblical history of revelation can only be solved by proclaiming it as a manifestation of universal truths, and when the reason has recognized and received it as such, the truth of its historical embodiment stands firm.

Maurice's polemics against all theories on the divine character of the Bible are severe and often expose obvious weaknesses in the attitudes and arguments of their proponents. Apparently he was opposing all human efforts to guarantee the Bible as

---

78 Cf. *Life* I, 251–2: "Coleridge belonged to another generation than ours – one of which the business was to indicate the preciousness of truths as distinct from facts. This function he performed marvellously well. – – But I believe also that we are come upon an age in which truth without facts will be as impossible as facts without truth; and that the attempt to set either up exclusively must be conducted in quite a different spirit from that which animated either Coleridge or the good men of the preceding age, however the results may at times correspond. – – I believe, so far as I am able to keep my end in sight of reconciling the facts of Christianity with its principles, and of showing how both are required to satisfy the wants of men now, and explain those which history makes known to us, and how they can only co-exist and co-operate in a church, I shall do some good to persons in a certain state of mind," and *The Kingdom of Christ* I, 213: "The doctrine that systems, religions, churches, are dying out, but that they have been the clothing of certain important ideas which will survive their extinction, and which it is the business of wise men to note, preserve, and perhaps furnish with a new vesture, is one which I cannot be expected to entertain; nay, to which if this book mean anything I must be directly opposed."

the Word of God, demanding only that it be allowed to assert itself by speaking for itself. He appears to be protesting against the attempt to reduce the Bible to a compendium of divinely inspired dogmas and moral rules on the basis of a static view of revelation. His criticism of the orthodox view of the Bible seems to be prompted by the desire to clear the way for a conception of the Bible as bearing witness to a living, personal God and His acts of revelation in history.[79] It might seem as though Maurice was speaking from a new and profounder understanding of the Bible's own message than his contemporaries.

Although a later age has been inclined to take this view, our analysis should have demonstrated that Maurice's polemic stand was ultimately founded upon an idea of revelation, which sought to unite the fundamentally ahistorical Platonic idea of reality with the Biblical concept of history. In the resulting fusion, however, Platonism became the decisive factor. H. G. Wood's contention that Maurice is "the convinced exponent -- of Biblical realism"[80] is due to a misconception of Maurice's theology. Equally unfounded is A. M. Ramsey's view of Maurice as a prophet whose "Biblical teaching points -- to the recovery of the Bible which is happening to-day."[81] Admittedly, the Biblical history of revelation has a central place in Maurice's theological thinking, but it is interpreted and understood on the basis of a Platonic conception of reality.[82]

This fact is further illustrated by Maurice's protest against any identification of the Bible with the Word of God. Christ alone is the Word of God. Though the Bible

79 Cf. *Queen's College,* 14: "Our -- great desire therefore has been to present the Revelation of God to those who learn from us, as the Bible presents it, in a living history, to set forth Him to them as the Bible sets Him forth, livingly, personally; not by those words and names which the religious fashion of our day recognises; such as 'the Deity', 'the Divinity', 'Omnipotence', 'Providence'."

80 op. cit., 35. For an understanding of the significance of this term Wood refers to H. Kraemer's *The Christian Message in a Non-Christian World.* In connection with Maurice's controversy with Mansel, Wood remarks that "the two controversialists were more nearly at one than either realised. Both accepted what has been called the scandal of particularity" (p. 127). This view of Maurice is wrong. With all the means at his disposal he combated "the scandal of particularity". It had to be rejected as incompatible with his Platonic idea of reality. Leslie Stephen, who has been denounced by so many modern students of Maurice, recognized this clearly when he wrote: "The general difficulty which Mr. Maurice intends to meet, and the result to which he would lead us are clear enough. Men object to a theory which gives to certain historical facts or to special observances a character entirely disparate from that which belongs to all other history and to all natural operations. -- Mr. Maurice would retain the divine character of the history whilst removing these limitations; and retain the full significance of the facts, while denying them to be exceptional" *(The Contemporary Review* XIX (June 1874. "Secularism and Mr. Maurice's Theology"), 610–1.

81 op. cit., 96–7.

82 James Martineau, who clearly realized the problem of the relation between eternity and history in Maurice's thought (see *Essays, Reviews and Addresses* I, 264–5 and II, 433, 465), rightly indicated how Maurice sought to establish the connection between them (see I, 262). He has, however, not sufficiently stressed how earnestly Maurice sought to bring about a union between them. The two trends of thought are not as discrete as Martineau apparently thought (see I, 264).

bears witness to Him, it must never be conceived as being the Word of God itself.[83] This is simply bibliolatry, another expression of idolatry. It was nonetheless precisely such a bibliolatry which was carrying the day because of the prevailing orthodox theology and preaching.[84]

Bibliolatry does not only mean that man puts his trust in the Bible instead of the living God Himself; it implies that God speaks only in the Bible, so that His revelation is limited to its pages. It enslaves man to the letter and binds him to a specific history of the past that can have no relation to the lives of men of a later age.[85] In other words, bibliolatry is a blunt denial of the fact that Christ as the Word of God is always related to man and is the foundation of the life of every man. The Bible reveals this reality. Therefore neither the Bible nor the proclamation of the Biblical history of salvation is a means of grace with any constitutive significance for man's fellowship with Christ.[86] Just as a distinction must be made between the eternal truths and their historical manifestation, so it is necessary to distinguish between Christ as the Word of God and the Bible as the witness of this truth.

Our examination of Maurice's idea of revelation has demonstrated that he did not rest content with the knowledge which Christ as the eternal Word of God directly

83 Cf. *Life* II, 499–500: "When 11,000 clergymen declared – – that the Bible not only contains, but *is,* the Word of God, the position struck me not as an exaggeration, but as a perilous *denial* of the truth. *The* Word of God, I believe, as St. John taught and as George Fox taught, to be very much above the Scriptures, however he may speak by and in the Scriptures."

84 Cf. *Life* II, 501: "The Bible becomes dearer and more sacred to me the more I read it; I have no sympathy with its arraigners, even too little with its critics. Yet I feel compelled often to stand with both against those who turn it into a god, and so deny the living God of whom it bears witness. That idolatry is so fearful, and the numbers who are rushing into it so great and respectable, that I fear we ought to bear any reproaches and any suspicions, rather than be the instruments of promoting it," and *The Gospel of St. John,* 169: "we are likely not to search the Scriptures, because they bear witness of the Word of God, but to turn them into idols, because we have not the Word of God abiding in us." See also *The Apocalypse,* 2–3.

85 Cf. *The Gospel of St. John,* 213–4: "His [Christ's] testimony is to the world. It is borne at this time to a letter-worshipping world, – to a world which believed that certain letters had come long ago from God, but which utterly disbelieved that God could hold converse with men in their day. Such people have lost all sense of the meaning of letters. They are no longer the blessed media of intercourse between soul and soul, witnesses of spiritual communication."

86 Cf. *The Prayer-Book,* 242: "numbers who have been treated by others, and have learnt to look on themselves, almost as outcasts from the fold of Christ, may find that He has never forgotten them, and that they stand in the nearest and closest relation to Him! It is not in a book they hear first of Him. It is not only with those who can read the book, or are possessed of it, or believe in it, that He holds converse," and *Life* I, 510: "The Gospel is, "Christ is with you, and in you, and He is in me." I cannot live except it were so, nor can you. I can live because it is so; and you can do the same. But the preaching of Christ out of a book, as if He whom we read of in the Gospels was not actually our Lord, the Lord of our spirits, is very poor work. Let the phrases which describe Him be as Evangelical or as Catholic as they may, the hungry sheep look up, and are not fed; there is no real approach made to the centre and citadel of men's hearts. I feel more and more the importance of the history in its simplest, most direct form. But I believe we cannot read the Gospels simply and directly, except we consider them the revelation of Him upon earth who is the light that lighteneth us and all men, whether they walk in His sight or dwell in the darkness."

imparts to man's reason. The Bible as the record of a particular history of revelation is likewise of the greatest importance to man's knowledge of reality.[87] Through historical events God has revealed the eternal laws and principles constituting the life of the universe and mankind. Because the purpose of God's revelation is to impart knowledge of *that which is,* it addresses itself to man's reason, which is capable of grasping the eternal truths behind their historical embodiment. In this way Maurice maintained the significance of the Bible without in any way abandoning the idea of the continued and unbroken existence of the Divine Order, rooted in God's own being.

It now remains to be seen whether Maurice was capable of carrying out this fundamentally clear and consistent view throughout a detailed interpretation of the Biblical history of revelation.

87 These two roads leading to knowledge of reality appear side by side and complement each other, even though it is the knowledge given in the Biblical history of revelation which obviously appears to be the more important. This is partly due to Maurice's dependence upon the Bible, and partly to the fact that sin and unbelief have obscured man's spiritual eye so that it cannot apprehend true reality except by means of a specific historical revelation on God's part.

Chapter VI

THE CALLING OF A NATION

1. Israel

For Maurice the fundamental and leading principle of the Old Testament is the idea of God's covenant with Israel. This idea is presupposed in all the Old Testament writings and is their bond of unity.[1]

The covenant was first established with a family. After having chosen and called forth Abraham as the head of a family among all the other families on earth, God made His covenant with him and his family.[2] God's calling was, however, not an arbitrary act, nor did His covenant place the Patriarch and his family above all other families as though He had no fellowship with them. Admittedly, God's covenant with Abraham was exclusive, but this exclusiveness consisted in their separation from "sensuality and sensual worship" by which all were enslaved.[3] These sins had raised barriers between families and prevented them from realizing that they all belonged to an unchangeable Order. By being separated from the true causes of exclusiveness, Abraham and his family could serve all the other families of the earth: "the Abrahamic family, though cut off by their covenant from the other families of the earth, was so cut off expressly that it might bear witness for the true order of the world; for that order against which all sensible idolatry, and all independent choice or self-will, is rebellion; for that order in which alone man can be free, because to abide in it they must sacrifice those inclinations which make them slaves; for that order, in and through which, as we might have guessed from the Gentile records, the idea of God can alone be imparted."[4] Through His covenant with Abraham God declared what is true of every family; through the history of the Patriarchs He warned men of the dangers threatening the life of the family and taught them that family order can only be preserved if men subordinate themselves to God and trust in Him.

From the family of the Patriarchs Israel arose as a people and a nation. This new

---

1 Cf. *The Kingdom of Christ* I, 239: "Everyone who reads the Old Testament must perceive that the idea of a covenant of God with a certain people is that which presides in it. In plain history, in lofty prayers and songs, in impassioned denunciations of existing evil, and predictions of coming misery, this idea is still at the root of all others. Take it away, and not merely is there no connexion between the different parts, but each book by itself, however simple in its language or in its details, becomes an incoherent rhapsody."

2 Cf. *The Kingdom of Christ* I, 239: "This covenant is said to be with a *family;* with a man doubtless in the first instance, but with a man expressly and emphatically as the head of a family. −− It is impossible to look upon the patriarchal character of Abraham as something accidental to his character as the chosen witness and servant of the Most High."

3 *The Kingdom of Christ* I, 241.

4 *ibid.*

human fellowship did not, however, destroy the family; family life remained an integral part of the life of the nation.[5]

The very existence of Israel as a national fellowship was founded upon a divine act. God elected Israel by delivering it from its tyrants, its sensual and evil nature and its worship of sensual things.[6] He established a covenant with the nation in which He revealed Himself as I AM THAT I AM. At the same time God revealed the law for the life of the people of Israel. This law proclaimed God to be Israel's invisible Lord and King.[7] Having received the knowledge of God as love and thus learnt the nature of His dominion, Israel now knew whom it was to worship and honour as its Creator and Sustainer.[8]

God's covenant with Israel was entirely due to His will and initiative; it represented "a union of Love; a divine Lord seeking His human bride, binding her to Himself, bidding her trust in Him and depend upon Him for all things."[9] But just as Israel had been received into the covenant without any merit of its own, so its continued existence was based entirely on God and His loving acts. Israel's obligation was therefore to submit to God and put its trust in Him.[10] Only in obedience to God's covenant could the Israelites maintain their national unity. Disobedience to the covenant meant lawlessness and the dissolution of national fellowship.[11]

5 Cf. *The Kingdom of Christ* I, 244: "But we are not to suppose that the family relations had less to do with this stage of the history than with the former. As they were embodied in the national institutions, as the existence of these institutions depended upon them, so their meaning in connexion with national life and national sins, and with a Being of whom both witnessed, became continually more apparent."

6 Cf. *The Prophets*, 243: "the very idea of a convenanted people is of one raised above these impulses [of nature], brought into the true human condition, the condition of dependence upon God which He intends for the creature whom He has made in His image," and *Sacrifice*, 92: "Did they not know that His purpose in taking them into covenant with Him was to reform them; to separate them from their evil; to deliver them from the adulterous, deceitful, slanderous tendencies of their own nature?"

7 Cf. *The Patriarchs*, 244: "the highest mercy God could confer upon men was to make them conscious of His presence and of His order; – – want of belief in that Presence, want of submission to that order, were *the* curses of human beings, – from which all slavery to men and to natural things, all division, all suffering, proceeded. – – Moses teaches his countrymen that God *has* conferred upon them the highest prize which man can conceive, freely and without any merit on their part."

8 Cf. *Christmas Day*, 127: "He [Moses] describes this, as the primary benefit of God having chosen them, and united them to himself, that, thereby, it became possible for them to have a distinct knowledge of him who created them. – – The privilege of the Israelite is said to be that he worships the Lord, and *none else* – that is to say, that he does not confound the unseen Being of whom his conscience and his heart speak, the Being of whom he feels himself to be the offspring, with the works of his hands; that he looks upon all things in nature as inferior to himself, and to God as above himself; that he feels himself the lord of creation and the servant of *the lord*. This was the great privilege of the Jew, and it was a privilege which rested wholly upon his being in covenant with God."

9 *The Prophets*, 437.

10 Cf. p. 209: "the nation – – was brought into an order. The unseen Lord had declared that it was in an actual relation to Him; that it stood while it acknowledged Him and depended upon Him; that when it ceased to acknowledge Him it would fall under the dominion of its own instincts and appetites; that these instincts and appetites would assuredly make it the slave of visible things."

Israel, however, constantly forgot God's covenant, and so God raised up the prophets, whose sole task was to bear witness to the nation that the covenant was the foundation of its existence.[12] The prophets were not exceptional men standing in a unique relation to God. It is true that it was their constant temptation to regard themselves as different from, and superior to, their fellow-citizens because of their prophetic calling, but if they succumbed to this temptation they only proved themselves to be false prophets.[13] The true prophets lived the ordinary life of their fellow-countrymen and participated entirely in the life of the nation.[14] In fact, they were "Politicians; — — men who were profoundly concerned in the well-being and continuity of their nation."[15] Only in this way could they fulfil their office to lead their countrymen to a clear knowledge of the Divine Order in which they lived. At times they had to withdraw from the national fellowship but this was only in order that they might bear strong and telling witness to the people of Israel concerning the foundation of their national existence.[16]

The purpose of the prophetic office was to reveal and to proclaim an already

11 Cf. *Christmas Day*, 129: "it is in virtue of this covenant they could be a nation at all. They owed to it he feeling of union among themselves, or of being connected with their forefathers or their posterity. He [Moses] shows them that the acknowledgment of one God over them was the only security of their being one people. The moment they forgot that they were related to this God, that he was their Lord and King, and that he had taken them to be a people unto him, that moment they would become divided and helpless, losing all respect for each other, and a prey to their enemies."

12 Cf. *Sermons* III, 88: "They [the prophets] assume a Divine order of the world. They start from a God Who has made a covenant with the Nation, Who bids all the members of it fear Him and trust Him; Who gives them commandments; Who promises them a right heart, that they may keep His commandments"; *The Prophets*, 183: "the prophet — — is the witness for the true God; for the divine order. — — It was the special vocation of the prophet to declare the meaning of his country's order and thereby to prevent his brethren from mistaking it for routine," and p. 336: "the prophets tear off the masks which hide the true condition of a people."

13 See *The Patriarchs*, 235–6 and 343–4.

14 Cf. *The Prophets*, 146: "It would have been the most glaring contradiction to all his [the prophet] professions if he had regarded the prophetical power as something bestowed for his honour, a gift to separate him from the rest of the people. — — in a prophet of the Lord God of Israel it would have been most detestable. God had given His law to the whole nation. All were under it; therefore all might study it and delight themselves in it. It was a law which imported a government over the inner man, over the conscience and heart and will. The conscience and heart and will of every man might be awakened to know the nature of this government, to receive light from the source of light. And since light is given that it may be communicated, since it shines into a mind that it may shine forth from that mind, there was no reason why any one of the Lord's people should not be a prophet."

15 p. XVI. See also p. 203.

16 Cf. p. 147–8: "The man of God might have been looked upon as a mere separate being, cut off by the awfulness of his character and dignity from the rest of his countrymen; an object of distant admiration or dread, not an example of what they ought to be. These men [the sons of the prophets], taken from among themselves, and associated with him, declared that he was only withdrawn from their communion, that he might the better claim privileges for them which they were in hazard of losing; that he was only chosen out by the Lord God of Israel, that he might the more clearly understand, and help them to understand, their national calling."

existing reality which constituted the life of Israel.[17] By pondering upon the riddles and contradictions, displayed in the life of the nation, the prophets had come to realise that God, because of His covenant with Israel, continued to uphold its national fellowship despite its unbelief and sin. As genuine seekers after truth they took their point of departure in the concrete facts of the life of the nation, that is, the institutions and events and crises which befell it, endeavouring to penetrate to the eternal principles which were embodied in them; they "proclaimed it to be their task to strip off outsides and take away varnish that they might show the thing as it really was."[18] Through this truly scientific method they were able to demonstrate the nature of the Divine Order and the eternal laws which constituted the life of Israel.

With this view of the prophetic office Maurice found himself in opposition to the traditional interpretation of prophecy according to which the essence of the prophetic calling was to foretell Christ's coming and the establishment of the Kingdom of God. This idea had to be rejected because it implied a denial of the Divine Order as an existing reality. In the prophets, Maurice maintained, we find no fictions or superstition as if they were dealing with the future, contingent acts of an arbitrary God.[19] Their entire concern was to witness to God as the ever-present Lord and Ruler and to the unchangeable laws and principles of His dealings with man. This was not to deny that the prophets made predictions, but these were not fortuitous since they were founded upon and deduced from the divine laws which were manifesting themselves in the actual events of the moment.[20]

Thus the office of the prophets was to interpret and explain the unchangeable

17 Cf. *The Apocalypse*, 138: "the Scriptural idea of prophesy – – is an unfolding or discovery of the meaning and purpose of the eternal God. It explains the principle of an unchangeable government. It exhibits a law working in the very vicissitudes and caprices of self-will," and *The Prophets*, 120: "the office of a prophet in Israel [is to say]: 'There is an eternal order which cannot be violated. Whosoever defies it, will bring ruin upon himself and upon his house. God is; a power which sets him at naught and substitutes changeable things in His place, cannot abide'."

18 *The Prophets*, 185. Cf. also p. 145: "All facts were to him [the true prophet] signs of a divine purpose, solemn indications of truth which they could not themselves make known, but which nevertheless lay in the heart of them, and which God could discover to the patient and faithful seeker," and *The Apocalypse*, 262: "The prophecy is to deliver us from slavery to shapes and apparitions."

19 Cf. *The Prophets*, 145: "If his [the prophet's] utterances seem to be fortuitous, they could not bear the witness which he desired they should bear of a permanent ruler," and *Sermons* VI, 177–8: "We shall find in these ancient seers no superstition, which later science desires to be rid of. Rather we shall find them witnesses for Eternal Truth, and against the several counterfeits of it which science craves. We shall find them no pleaders for any priestly abuse or pious fraud; rather a continual assurance that God is Himself present in all events that befall nations or individuals."

20 Cf. *The Prophets*, 485: "The true prophet – – is a witness for Him who is and was and is to come. If he taught that the future were to be unlike the past, that there was no common root out of which they both grew, he would be faithless to his vocation, he would be forgetting the permanent and eternal Being," and *The Apocalypse*, 8–9: "Prophecy, according to their use and understanding of it, is the utterance of the mind of Him who is, and was, and is to come. Events, days of the Lord, crises in national history, were manifestations of His everlasting mind and purpose. The seer was to explain the past and the present; only in connection with these did he speak of the future."

reality that encompassed Israel as a nation and a people. The prophets were to expound what was implied in God's covenant with Israel. They were to proclaim how, through kings and priests, God had given the people signs of His invisible government and guidance of them. Indeed, the entire history of Israel is the record of how God, through all the vicissitudes of its life and despite its unbelief and sin, educated the nation to know Him and the true character of His relation to it. Consequently Maurice contended that there is "a principle which goes through the whole of the Jewish polity and of Old Testament history. God is throughout spoken of as bringing His people into a true and right state, a state of fellowship with Himself."[21]

It was important for Maurice to establish that Israel had not been favoured at the expense of other nations, even though God had elected it, made His covenant with it and given it the law and the temple with its priesthood. To be sure, Israel repeatedly prided itself on the covenant, the law, and the temple as exclusive privileges, indicating its unique position as God's chosen people. Yet this was a complete misunderstanding. God's election and covenant with Israel did not mean that He had arbitrarily taken mercy on a single nation. Seeing that an unchangeable fellowship between God and man has always existed, founded upon God's eternal will, God's covenant with Israel cannot constitute His fellowship with it.[22] The true significance of the covenant is that it is the visible expression, or sign, of God's relationship with all men.[23] Thus, the very nature of the covenant and the institutions granted by God to the Jews implied the eradication of all exclusiveness on their part. Israel did not possess a privileged relationship to God in contrast to that of any other nation.

It is true that Israel had been separated from the rest of mankind through God's election but, as in the case of Abraham and his family, this setting apart meant a separation from sin and from worship of visible things.[24] Israel's election was nothing but a calling to serve all other nations by bearing witness to the truth concerning their own existence.[25] Through His covenant with Israel and through its entire history God had given a visible demonstration of how He is always the self-sacrificing, loving

21 *Sermons* II, 62.
22 Cf. *Sacrifice*, 274: "both Jews and Gentiles wanted to be told whether there was an actual, original, eternal relation between God and them; or whether it was an artificial, legal, formal relation, which institutions had created, and which would perish if they perished. – – Those who put the Law and the Covenants, and the Sacrifices and the Priesthood, for the God who had appointed the Law and the Covenants, and the Sacrifices and the Priesthood, or supposed that they created the bond between Him and His creatures, of which they bore witness, were hastening towards the deepest unbelief."
23 Cf. *The Gospel of St. John*, 105: "the people whom God had chosen, and with whom He had made a covenant, were those whom they [the prophets] taught to regard themselves as united in this eternal bond, of which covenants were but the outward expression, which existed long before Abraham or Noah."
24 Cf. *Religions*, 169–70: "in that call [of Israel] was involved the idea of distinction, of separation. – – A gross animal taste, a disposition to honour visible things and bow before them, is characteristic of men generally; the elect people are taken from the surrounding nations, that they may be emancipated from this slavish tendency," and *The Kingdom of Christ* I, 243: "the exclusiveness of the Jews – – excluded the idea of choice and of self-will."
25 Cf. *What Is Revelation?*, 118: "It was the election of a people to know what are the rights of men, that they might be witnesses to all men of *their* rights. It was the election of a people to testify that God Himself is leading His creatures out of darkness to light, out of

Creator, who has founded and sustained the life of every individual nation.[26] Israel did not only illuminate and interpret all national existence when it lived in the covenant in trust and obedience to God. Even in the midst of its unbelief and disobedience, it was forced to bear witness to the fact that despite the rebellion and sins of a nation God is ever triumphant, executing His will and upholding the nation and its people. The very human history of Israel is the most telling proclamation of the truth that it is to God alone that every nation owes its existence and continued life.[27]

The testimony of the Old Testament concerning the covenanted life of Israel proclaims that a nation is not a fortuitous association of individuals but a spiritual being, created by God and existing in Him.[28] God has called forth every nation, established His covenant with each of them and given it national institutions which fulfil the same functions as those appointed for the Jews.[29] His dealings with every nation follow

vague notions and conceptions of what is right and holy, to the knowledge, and so to the possession, of His righteousness and holiness"; *The Unity of the New Testament*, 385: "Israel [was] called out by God to represent the true state of man, to declare man's relation to God, to declare that the relation is a spiritual and not a carnal one," and *The Kingdom of Christ* (1838) I, 293–4: "the history of the people which declares that it was chosen for the express purpose of leading men to the knowledge of their invisible Lord, of their relation to him, of themselves, is the clue by which the mazes of other histories are threaded."

26 Cf. *Sermons* VI, 241–2: "For the Israelites – so the prophets tell them – were chosen by God to be a holy Nation, that they might be a witness to all Nations concerning Him and His character and His purposes. The Israelites were to let all know that a self-willed Power was not ruling over the Universe; that they must not attribute evil to an Evil Creator," and *The Prophets*, 417: "The prophets uniformly take Israel and its polity as a sample of God's dealings with His creatures, as a witness to them of all what He is, and what He is doing with and for the children of men. This was their high calling; it was their privilege and their glory to proclaim by their words, their acts, their very existence, the God who executes righteousness and judgment *in the earth*."

27 Cf. *The Patriarchs*, 262: "If this people were represented as a particularly exalted and virtuous people in themselves, their history would throw little light upon that of others. They would be merely rare exceptions, from whose successes or failures no inference could be drawn. But being throughout affirmed and proved to be a hard-hearted, stupid, stiff-necked people, we perceive whence all their strength, vitality, courage proceeded," and *The Prophets*, 47: "the nation of Israel was the witness for the nothingness of man in himself, for the might of man when he knows that he is nothing, and puts his trust in the living God."

28 Cf. Sermons II, 57: "We speak sometimes as if the Jewish history were unlike all others, because it refers all the common transactions of the world, all ordinary offices, all the statutes and ordinances of civil life, to God as their ground and author. I believe that we must come to understand that it is the rule of all other histories because it makes that proclamation; that we shall be less able to explain what a nation is, or how it can exist, if we refuse to think of Him as the present King and Lawgiver of it," and *The Prophets*, 415: "But the time is come, – let us say it boldly, – when the Bible must be thrown either into the fire as an old worn-out document, or when a nation must be felt to be not a formal corporation but a spiritual reality, a society of which we *can* predicate spiritual conditions and spiritual emotions, which can repent and can be reformed as truly as an individual can."

29 Cf. *Sermons* IV, 45: "And he [St. Paul] vindicated the truth of the history of his own nation, by showing how it helped to explain the history of all nations. Each one had a calling from God, each one had in its national laws and institutions a testimony in behalf of a righteous, living, and true God; each one had in these institutions and laws a testimony against divided and evil and visible Gods." See also *The Epistle to the Hebrews*, 61–2.

the same laws and principles as those which are unveiled in the history of Israel.[30] The Old Testament will therefore never become obsolete.

All nations belong to the Divine Order and have God as their loving Creator and invisible Lord, but not even Israel's election to be a witness of this truth to all other nations implies the possession of a unique position. Every nation has been similarly elected to perform specific tasks in the service of the universal fellowship of nations.[31] Thus the Greeks were chosen to bear witness to man as a spiritual being, whereas the Romans were called to show that men are created to live in a fixed order and to obey the laws which constitute this order. No nation has the right to exalt itself above other nations. All the tasks which the nations have been appointed to perform are equally necessary if mankind is to know and understand the significance of the Divine Order.

Thus we see that Maurice's interpretation of Israel's history is consistent with his conception of revelation. Israel does not occupy an exclusive position among all the nations. Every nation stands in God and is upheld by Him. Israel's special calling is, through its history, to be a visible demonstration of the true constitution of every nation and of the eternal laws and principles in God's dealings with a nation. All the nations constitute a universal fellowship within the Divine Order.

2. The Incarnate Christ as the Desire of Nations

It has been repeatedly noticed that Maurice's interpretation of the Bible is monotonous. No matter what text he expounded, it always appears to be expressing the same basic ideas.[32] This is, however, the necessary consequence of his concept of revelation:

30 Cf. *The Commandments,* 78: "[Israel is] a particular nation, which He [the living God] chose out of all nations to be a witness of Him, a specimen of His ways and doings, and of His relation to every people under heaven. – – the principles of that history are unchangeable principles, – – the code which embodies these principles is a code for all kindreds and peoples."

31 Cf. *What Is Revelation?,* 39–40: "God hath formed the nations of one blood, of one family. God hath watched over the bounds, the circumstances, the destiny, of each nation upon the face of the earth. The Jewish nation had existed to be a witness for this universal fellowship among the nations. It had existed as a witness against that which tended to divide them and set them at war. It had existed also as a witness for the special work of each one of those bodies which had its definite geographical limits, its sympathies of kindred and race. It existed to say, 'The one living and true God has created you all to be one. The one living and true God has assigned you your tasks. He has never left you alone. No one fact of your history has lain beyond the circle of His providence. No one thought has been awakened in your minds without His teaching and guidance. I [St. Paul], the Jew, the child of Abraham, stand forth to make that claim on behalf of the God whom I worship. I stand forth solemnly to repudiate the doctrine that any nation whatever has a right to deny connection with any other. I, the Jew, the child of Abraham, stand forth to declare that you, the men of Athens, have had a divine vocation, that the God of all has appointed you to play a distinct and very remarkable part in His great drama'."

32 Cf., e. g., A. R. Vidler, op. cit., 173: "his general tendency was to discover the highest level of insight at any and every point and to make the Biblical testimony consistent from beginning to end. Thus there is a certain monotony in his exposition of Scripture in spite of the range and variety of the ground he covers and of his desire to let the Bible always speak for itself. He makes the authors of Scripture speak too much a common language."

the world of time and space is always determined by the eternal unchangeable world, and revelation imparts knowledge of this fact; Israel and its prophets were taught to recognize the nature of the Divine Order and its implications for the life of their nation; the prophets even attained to the knowledge of Christ as the Head of every man and of every nation and people.[33] For Maurice the essential thing is always the unveiling of the Divine Order as an existing reality which encompasses all human life, and hence the monotony of his exposition.

At the same time Maurice spoke of the Bible as the record of "a progressive Revelation".[34] The Old Testament represents the history of Israel as a preparatory step in God's history of revelation: "The history is always pointing to a completion, and that completion in a Person. The Prophets have a vision of a King, who shall be the manifestation of God – the perfect image of Him – *the* Man – the Deliverer of the called nation, the ruler of all the nations: who should establish righteousness, should open the unseen world, should unite earth and heaven. For such an one, these Prophets say, David and his line were the preparation – He would really establish a universal kingdom."[35]

It would seem that with the idea of a progressive revelation Maurice had now introduced a different view from that which dominated his interpretation of the prophecies of the Old Testament. The presupposition no longer appears to be that the Kingdom of God, the Divine Order, always constitutes the life of mankind, so that the only issue is the attainment of true knowledge of this fact. We are apparently now faced with a view that takes God's revelation in the history of Israel to imply the expectation of a universal kingdom which is to be established at the appointed time by Christ's coming in the flesh. According to this concept revelation does not signify the manifestation of eternal truths, of *that which is,* and history acquires constitutive significance. Everything points to a decisive event as the centre of the history of mankind: "All things from the beginning of the world had been advancing towards the revelation of Him in whom heaven and earth are united."[36]

The prophets, Maurice argued, were led to expect the establishment of a universal kingdom by realizing the limitations of a national fellowship in which the people was only bound together in common responsibility and duty to each other, but had no

33 Cf. *The Gospel of St. John,* 9: "The 'word of God' is the favourite expression in the writers of the Old Testament, because they are testifying of an invisible Lord who speaks to man's spirit," and *The Prophets,* 301: "To know the actual living centre of the nation was – – the great gift which the prophet had derived from the teaching he had received hitherto; all new trials and disappointments were to bring this centre more clearly before him; he could not but contemplate this as the great end and interpretation of them to the whole people."

34 *Tracts for Priests and People, 1st Series. No. 6* ("Morality and Divinity"), 33. Cf. also *Introductory Lectures Delivered at Queen's College* ("On Theology"), 252: "The unveiling is not instantaneous, but gradual. The Bible I have taken as a history of the steps of that unveiling. The revelation is to a creature formed in the Divine image, who reflects that image so far as he sees it and no further."

35 *Religions,* 148. Cf. also *The Epistle to the Hebrews,* 4: "This fulfilment then would seem to be the accomplishment of a purpose or idea which had been latent in earlier times; which had been gradually making itself manifest to the divinely instructed Teachers; through them to as many as profited by their teaching."

36 *The Apocalypse,* 346.

bond of fellowship with other nations. This insight called forth the wish, indeed the need, for a universal fellowship embracing all nations.[37] This longing was, however, intertwined with the expectation of a new and more perfect revelation of God's mind and will in the same way as the establishment of the fellowships of the family and the nation had been accompanied by a divine revelation.[38]

The prophets arrived at a deeper understanding of the character of this coming manifestation of God by pondering upon the significance of the covenant, the national institutions such as kingship, priesthood, and the temple-service. These were visible signs of God and His eternal Kingdom, the means through which God educated men to a knowledge of Himself.[39] But since they were merely signs, man could never rest satisfied with them. They necessarily called forth the hope and the expectation that He whose nature they reflected would manifest Himself clearly and unambiguously, thus explaining their true meaning.[40]

The kings, the priests, and the prophets of Israel had been called by God, through their offices, to be the image and instrument of His self-sacrificing love for the people. However, they often rebelled against God and abused their offices by using them to assert themselves at the expense of the nation and of God. The harmonious co-operation which God had intended to exist between king, priest and prophet for the sake of the people was then replaced by dissension and disunity. Yet this abuse only strengthened men's longing for a life under the authority of a king, a priest, and a prophet from whom selfishness was banished. The hope was even awakened that He, from whom these offices had proceeded and who must therefore be the true King, Priest, and Prophet, would make Himself known.[41]

When men performed acts of love and truth in the fellowships of family and nation, such acts were intuitively felt to be the reflection of perfect love and truth and the

---

37 Cf. *The Kingdom of Christ* I, 246: "The wish for fellowship with other nations was a true wish – –; the dream of a human polity was one which the true God had sent to the Jew – –. To bring out the true idea of such a polity, to show how it lay hid in all their own institutions, and how it would at length be brought out into full manifestation, this was the great office of the Hebrew seer."

38 Cf. p. 247: "And as each new step in the history of the covenant – the first call of the patriarch which made them a family, their deliverance under Moses which made them a nation – was connected with a fresh revelation of the Divine King through these different relations, neither displacing the other but adopting it into itself; this glorious vision would have been utterly imperfect, if it had not involved the prospect of such a discovery as had not been vouchsafed to any former age."

39 Cf. *The Epistle to the Hebrews*, 56: "the living God had actually made Himself known to the Jewish people; – – He was their King and Teacher; – – their institutions were His institutions; – – through them, and through every event of their history, He was educating them to the knowledge of Himself."

40 Cf. p. 71: "Each institution is shewn to be imperfect, in so far as it was merely an institution; till the eternal ground of it in the relation of Man to God, in the relation of the Divine Son to the Father, in the self-affirming Being of God, was manifested, its truth and meaning were still hidden. When this ground had been declared, that converse of the spirit of man with God for which He had been educating it, would be in the fullest sense possible."

41 Cf. *The Kingdom of Christ* (1838) II, 64: "the idea of the office should be gradually brought out through the acts of imperfect men, and partly by means of their imperfections; and – – the full realization of each character, should be in the God-Man."

expression of true humanity. Nonetheless, as love and truth were only displayed in an imperfect and fragmentary way, men longed to see the manifestation of perfect love and truth. They desired to see the revelation of perfect humanity so that they might know that what they acknowledged as right and true in their own and their fellow-men's lives actually had an eternal foundation and thus be assured that the sin and evil which constantly threaten to annihilate goodness and truth would be vanquished.[42] Furthermore, no man had ever been able to give up the idea that he belongs to a world beyond time and space and that he is created in the image of another Being. This conviction kindled in men the hope for the manifestation of Him in whose image they were created so that they would not need to grope blindly for the ground and root of their own lives.[43] By considering actual human life with all its vicissitudes and contradictions, men were led to hope that the True Man, the archetype of mankind, would manifest Himself and distinguish between what is true and false in their own lives, between that which derives its origin from the eternal world and that which is due to the power of sensuality and sin.

The desire for a perfect revelation of God and the establishment of His Kingdom was formed against the background of man's experience of sin, suffering and distress. Struggling with the question as to how the eternal, spiritual and holy God could reveal Himself to men prone to sin and sensuality,[44] the prophets were gradually led to realize that only by becoming man and by identifying Himself with man in his sin, suffering and distress could God reveal Himself completely, lead man away from idolatry and bind him to Himself.[45] The expectation that God would stoop to man-

42 Cf. *Theological Essays*, 27: "Men have declared, "The actual creatures of our race do tell us of something which must belong to us, must be most needful for us. A gentle human being does give us the hint of a higher gentleness; a brave man makes us think of a courage far greater than he can exhibit. Friendships, sadly and continually interrupted, suggest the belief of an unalterable friendship. Every brother awakens the hope of a love stronger than any affinity in nature; and disappoints it. Every father demands a love, and reverence, and obedience, which we know is his due, and which something in him as well as in us hinders us from paying. Every man who suffers and dies rather than lie, bears witness of a truth beyond his life and death, of which he has a glimpse." Men have asked, "Are all these delusions? Is this goodness we have dreamed of all a dream? this Truth a fiction of ours? Is there no Brother, no Father beneath those, who have taught us to believe there must be such? Who will tell us?" "

43 Cf. *Sequel*, 93: "He must reveal Himself to us who are made in His image if He would not have us make Him in our image; – – the revelation must be a moral one in a perfect Man, and not through any physical or logical or mathematical part of creation."

44 Cf. *The Kingdom of Christ* I, 247: "How these two longings could be both accomplished; how idolatry could be abolished by the very manifestation [of God] which would bring the object of worship more near to all human thoughts and apprehensions; how the belief of a Being nigh to men could be reconciled with that of one dwelling in His own perfection; how unceasing action on behalf of His creatures consists with eternal rest; how He could be satisfied with men, and yet be incapable of satisfaction with anything less pure and holy than Himself; these were the awful questions with which the prophet's soul was exercised, and which were answered, not at once, but in glimpses and flashes of light coming across the darkness of his own soul, and of his country's condition."

45 Cf. p. 248: "they felt that the God-man, in whom the fulness and awfulness of Godhead should shine forth, might *therefore* have perfect sympathy with the poorest and most friendless, and might at the same time enable them to enter into that transcendent region which their spirits

170

kind and make Himself one with men was further nourished by the testimony of the lives of those in Israel who had truly been God's servants. Because they had sacrificed themselves for their fellow-men in the performance of God's will, the prophets perceived the intimate relation between God's mind and will and self-sacrificing love. This strengthened their conviction that only he who completely sacrificed himself for man, could perfectly reveal God.[46]

The longing for God's perfect manifestation in a man who wholly shared the life of all men was in no way restricted to Israel alone. The Incarnation was the hope and desire of every man and every nation: "The union of the Son of God with our nature seemed to them the great blessing of all. None which God could bestow could exceed that; every other was interpreted by it. All the dreams of men in all nations and ages had pointed to this Marriage; whether they were dreams of a perfect emancipation from evil, or of a perfect union among men, or of a perfect fruition of God, they could have no other realization than this."[47] It is true that this longing appeared in widely divergent forms and was often distorted, being mingled with much that was false and originated in man's sin and sensuality. Nevertheless, behind all the variegated religions and philosophical systems lay mankind's expectation of an Incarnation as its sole hope and rescue.[48] All men desired that God should reveal Himself as the One who exerted His loving rule over them and in whom they might

had ever been seeking and never been able to penetrate," and *Religions*, 195: "The Jewish Prophet, when he is most overwhelmed with his own evil and with the evil of his nation, obtains most apprehension of the truth that God will exhibit His perfect Image to men, in a Man, and will so confound all images they have made."

46 Cf. *Christmas Day*, 292–3: "the Jews had been taught, in the persons of their two great teachers [Moses and David] – of these two whom all their scriptures and all their traditions taught them to regard as God's most favoured servants, and most resembling the future Deliverer – that the fullest participation in the sorrow which his subjects endured was the test and criterion of the highest and divinest ruler," and p. 294–5: "It became the teacher to unfold this great principle to his hearers, to show how every act of God towards man had been an act of condescension, a stooping to meet his ignorance and satisfy his wants; to show how every one of his messengers had been permitted to exhibit more of the divine character the more he identified himself with the poorest and most wretched of God's creatures. The teacher was to do this, the really inspired teacher did it, and in this way prepared the chosen nation to expect that any one who perfectly manifested the divine character, must be one who more completely and wonderfully than all who had preceded him entered into the depths of human grief."

47 *Sermons* I, 173. Cf. also *The Kingdom of Christ* (1838) I, 42–3: "the yearning in the hearts of men before the coming of Christ was not for a light, since that they had already, but for that to which the light pointed – for a personal manifestation; for some one who should bind men together in one commonwealth, by binding them to God – one who should appear as the Head of the race – to establish a communion between the race and its Father, and by doing that, should bind the members of the race to each other."

48 Cf. *Theological Essays*, 25: "The Sons of the Gods in Greek mythology can scarcely be separated from human forms, from actual flesh and blood. Those mysterious emanations from the Divinity which the Oriental spoke of, and which became closely connected with the later Greek philosophy, shrank from this contact. But the hearts of the people, as much in the East as in the West, demanded Incarnations; no efforts of the more spiritual and abstracted priests could resist the demand," and *The Gospel of St. John*, 179: "A Son of Man, – a King who was yet a Brother, – they secretly longed for; half their wild acts were done in the struggle to find such a one."

trust, and at the same time they knew that this revelation only could embrace them if God Himself stooped down to them and shared the conditions of their lives.[49]

Furthermore, the desire that God would come near to man in human shape was linked with the idea that it would then be made manifest what man really is. Like the Jews all men had experienced acts of truth and goodness in everyday life and felt that truth and goodness were meant to rule over them. They could, however, not apprehend these qualities clearly and distinctly and were unable to see how they were to gain the ascendency over mankind, since it was being constantly dragged down into the transient world by sin and sensuality. All men desired these ideals to be embodied in a person, the true Man, and felt intuitively, at the same time, that this would only be possible in a man who wholly and fully reflected God.[50]

Bound up with this expectation was the conviction that the manifestation of Him who was truly God and truly man would solve the contradictions and riddles of human life. Men's experience taught them that they could never rest satisfied with themselves and their own endeavours. They found that their lives had a deeper foundation than themselves, that what was human in them was of divine origin, and they desired the manifestation of that Divine Humanity which they, however dimly, felt that they were related to. Only in this way could they be assured of the truth about human existence. Maurice summed up these ideas as follows: "Christ is that Cornerstone of Humanity, of Whom all nations had been dreaming, Whom they had been conceiving under different forms, Whose manifestation in His own true and proper nature all had been desiring."[51]

49 Cf. *Sermons* I, 6: "What was the desire of nations? What was it that the different tribes of the earth, so far as we can gather their longings from the different songs, mythologies, complaints of philosophers who scorned the people, complaints of those who represented the people, were seeking for and could not find? Surely it was a Son of Man. It was One higher than men, Who could govern them. It was One acquainted with men, Who could feel as they felt, suffer as they suffered. To unite the two sides of the character seemed impossible. But each presented itself with mighty force and attraction to one and to another. To *that* ideal it was felt there must be some reality corresponding," and *The Gospel of St. John*, 46: "Those who were suffering from a burden might desire to cast it upon God, might doubt if any one but He could sustain it. But who could understand their grief, who could feel its pressure, except a Man? All their sympathies and wishes pointed to a Man."

50 Cf. *Sermons* I, 132–3: "And did not the same revelation justify the assurance of the philosopher, that there must be somewhere and somehow an Ideal of truth, and righteousness, and beauty, which men did not create for themselves, which is no image of theirs, but which is the image of the perfect and eternal Substance, which He can enable them to apprehend and embrace," and *Religions*, 220: "The Greek asked for one who should exhibit humanity in its perfection; he was told of a Son of Man. He felt that whoever did so exhibit Humanity must be divine."

51 *Sermons* V, 32. Cf. also *The Kingdom of Christ* II, 11: "the belief of a divine humanity has existed in all ages, – – it has taken innumerable forms. I have maintained that all these forms have presumed the existence of some more perfect form; that they never have compassed the end at which they aimed; that they have not revealed THE MAN, the head of the race, while nevertheless they have testified, one and all, with more or less distinctness in proportion as the light which they endeavoured to concentrate was more or less clear, that such a one there must be," and *Sacrifice*, 103: "their hearts said also, God leading them to the conclusion, 'Such an One there *is*, and such an One will be manifested. His existence is implied

172

Thus, by means of a gradual revelation, God had educated and led all mankind – Jews as well as Gentiles – to expect the Incarnation. God had awakened and exposed men's deepest longings, which only the Incarnation could satisfy, and the Gospel of God Incarnate is, therefore, no strange and incomprehensible message. On the contrary, when men hear it proclaimed, they recognize at once that here is the truth for which they have always been seeking, the fulfilment of all their hopes and expectations.[52]

in all we are thinking, feeling, doing. Some day he will make it clear by a transcendent act, an act pregnant with the mightiest consequences *to the world,* that He is'."

52 Cf. *Christmas Day,* 299: "his incarnation and passion would have seemed to them most deep and wonderful mysteries indeed, but mysteries without which everything they saw around them, everything in the future, was incoherent and unintelligible," and *Theological Essays,* 29: "I wish to put that doctrine of the Incarnation, which is so often denounced as an outrage upon reason, conscience, and experience, to every possible test of reason, conscience, and experience."

Chapter VII

THE INCARNATION

1. The Inward Christ and the Incarnate Christ

Maurice considered the incarnation of Christ to be the centre of God's history of revelation.[1] He even appears to make it the pivot of his theological thought: "First, We accept the fact of the Incarnation, because we feel that it is impossible to know the Absolute and Invisible God as man needs to know Him and craves to know Him, without an Incarnation. Secondly, We receive the fact of an Incarnation, not perceiving how we can recognise a perfect Son of God and Son of Man, such as man needs and craves for, unless He were, in all points, tempted like as we are. Thirdly, We receive the fact of an Incarnation, because we ask of God a Redemption, not for a few persons, from certain evil tendencies, but for humanity, from all the plagues by which it is tormented."[2]

As previously mentioned, the immediate impression of many of Maurice's statements on the significance of the Incarnation is that it marks the turning point in the history of mankind. Thus, Maurice described how God had revealed Himself fully and completely in the incarnate Christ. Sin, death and the Devil, as the enemies of creation, have been conquered by Christ's assumption of human flesh. In the incarnate Christ mankind has been reconciled to, and united with, God. By His acts of redemption and recreation Christ has become the Head of the new humanity. Owing to the Incarnation the Kingdom of God has been established, in which men live with God and with each other in the fellowship of faith and love. Thus the life, death and resurrection of Christ appear as the events which have wrought the salvation of the human race.

Upon closer examination, however, Maurice's interpretation of the significance of the Incarnation is seen to accord completely with his concept of revelation. This is apparent in his strong warning against any attempt at contrasting Christ as the Head of every man with the incarnate Christ in history.[3] To maintain an inward Christ

---

1 Cf. *Sermons* I, 32: "All the purposes and revelations of the different ages had been converging to one point. The Son of God, the express image of the Father, had been revealed in the nature of man. He had brought that nature through death and the grave, and had exalted it to His Father's right hand," and *The Apocalypse*, 292: "The union of Humanity with her true Husband – the overthrow of the idolatry that had separated them, and had degraded her – to this all the hopes of the creation, to this all the revelations of God, have pointed."

2 *Theological Essays*, 26–7.

3 Cf. *Sermons* IV, 170: "For I cannot help finding the secret of our lukewarmness, and of our self-conceit, in the attempt which men are making to divide what He has joined together – the testimony of the Conscience, from the facts of the History; the voice of Christ at the door of the heart, from the voice of Christ in His acts upon earth, or in the Book which

without His historical manifestation paves the way for an interpretation of Christ as a symbolic expression of man's spiritual nature and powers and results in pantheism, in which the distinction between God and man is blurred.[4] Only by realizing that the inward Christ is none other than the historical Christ is it possible to make it absolutely clear that Christ is a living person who always speaks to the spirit and reason of man. It is equally harmful to adhere entirely to the incarnate Christ, excluding any idea of Him as the light and life of every man. This inevitably leads to the conclusion that Christ had no existence or, at least, no relation to men before His coming in the flesh,[5] thus compromising the idea of the necessary union between Christ and mankind. Christ's fellowship with men will be seen to be artificial and fortuitous because it only encompasses that small section of mankind which happened to have the opportunity of seeing Him or hearing about His life and work in history. On such a view Christ may indeed be considered a great and even important founder of a religion, but His religion is destined to sink into nothingness.[6] This must be so, since to found man's relationship to Christ upon His outward fleshly appearance is to build upon that which has no substance. Anything which takes place in the history of time and space participates in its mutability and transience. Historical events can demonstrate and manifest eternal truth, *that which is*, but they can never have creative significance. It was, therefore, vital for Maurice to establish the fact that "there was a relation between Christ and men which did not depend upon flesh and blood, which did not commence when He assumed our nature, which was the reason of His assuming it."[7]

The same concern is evident in Maurice's criticism of the orthodox view on the place of the Incarnation in God's economy of salvation: Christ as the Son of God had to become man in order to reconcile man to God and destroy sin and death. Such a view is nothing but to "confound time and eternity".[8] If the Incarnation only

records these acts. If one of these voices is treated as figurative, so will the other be; if one of these voices is supposed to be only for a select class, so will the other be," and *The Conflict*, 99: "We may make artificial distinctions between an inward Christ and an historical Christ, a Christ for ourselves and a Christ for the world."

4 See *The Kingdom of Christ* I, 151–4.

5 Cf. *Theological Essays*, 31: "They will lead people to suppose that the Image of the Holy One had no reality till it was presented through a human body to men, or at least that till then this Image had no relation to the creature who is said in Scripture to be formed in it. By this means the whole of the Old Testament economy, instead of being fulfilled in the revelation of the Son of God, becomes hopelessly divided from it. But what is worse still, by this means the heart and conscience of human beings become separated from that revelation. It stands outside, as if it were presented to the eye, not to them; as if those who saw Christ in the flesh must really have known Him for that reason."

6 Cf. *Sermons* IV, 53: "The head of a religion, the chief of a society, the founder of a set of institutions, may be great through one or many generations, and then may sink into nothingness. Whatever depends for its reality upon human faith [i. e., that which is related to time and space] must be exposed to all the accidents and fluctuations of that faith. But if Jesus Christ was the root and ground of human society in the days of Claudius and Nero, He is the root and ground of human society now."

7 *Sacrifice*, 232.

8 p. 107.

occurred because it was necessitated by man's sin, then God becomes dependent upon that which takes place in time and space. However, God can never act otherwise than He has eternally decreed. "I grant you," Maurice exclaimed, "that the fall did not in the least frustrate the scheme of God. I grant you that it is very wrong to speak as if He had merely devised a scheme as a remedy for the consequences of the fall. Christ was before all things, and by Him all things consist. In Him He created men, and His Incarnation, though it came later than the fall, was really in God's purpose before it."[9]

Maurice agreed with the orthodox that man is elected in Christ and has his life in Him, but he denied that this was due to the fact that Christ came into the world and accomplished His work of redemption. God's election of man in Christ did not take place "in time, but in the strictest sense, in Eternity."[10] On the other hand, that which is fixed in eternity is destined to be revealed in time.[11] Thus, Christ's life and work in the flesh did not create a new order of salvation; it was the visible manifestation in the history of time and space of God's eternal purpose.[12] In the incarnate Christ man is not confronted with something contingent, exceptional, and surprising; in Him man finds a demonstration and proclamation of that which is immutable and necessary because it is founded upon God's eternal will. Instead of binding men to history, the Incarnation leads them to see and know God as the Supreme Being, whose will must of necessity be carried out.

In strict accordance with his concept of revelation Maurice interpreted the Incarnation as a manifestation in history of an eternal reality. In Christ's life and work on earth that which has always been true is unveiled.[13] That Christ is the Creator and Lord of the universe and mankind is the truth that is made manifest in His Incarnation. Through His earthly life Christ unveils Himself "as the root of humanity, as the ground of their personal and their social life, as the only bond of their unity."[14] The fact

9 *Life* I, 375–6.

10 *The Unity of the New Testament*, 522.

11 Cf. *The Kingdom of Christ* I, 256: "St. Paul tells them that they were created in Christ before all worlds, and – – he speaks of the transcendent economy as being gradually revealed to the Apostles and Prophets by the Spirit," and *The Unity of the New Testament*, 236: "the *eternal* mystery, which at the appointed *time* is to be known to men."

12 Cf. *The Unity of the New Testament*, 518: "a divine purpose which was to be executed in time, but which was not formed in time, which cannot be contemplated in reference to it and under its conditions."

13 Cf. *The Gospel of St. John*, 309: "He did not come into the world to show special favours, but to assert and manifest universal truth. He did not come into the world to break God's laws; but to establish them, and to show forth the will which was at the foundation of them," and *Theological Essays*, 17: "Do we not really believe that Christ was, before He took human flesh and dwelt among us? Do we not suppose that He actually conversed with prophets and patriarchs and made them aware of his presence? Or is this a mere arid dogma, which we prove out of Pearson, and which has nothing to do with our inmost convictions, with our very life? How has it become so? Is it because we do not accept the New Testament explanation of these appearances and manifestations; because we do not believe that Christ is in every man, the source of all light that ever visits him, the root of all the righteous thoughts and acts that he is ever able to conceive or do?"

14 *The Unity of the New Testament*, 216. Cf. also *The Gospel of St. John*, 432: "He [St. John] had spoken of a Word by whom the world is created, who is the Source of its life, though

176

that Christ displayed his healing power on certain individuals and addressed Himself to a tiny body of men and elected them to be His disciples does not imply that He was acting arbitrarily and dealing only with a privileged group. Christ's acts were visible signs, imparting a true and perfect knowledge of His unchangeable relationship to mankind and of the work He performs invisibly in all men at all times: "what He was on earth must be the explanation of what He is."[15] Hence the Incarnation can never be made the basis of a new form of religious exclusiveness. On the contrary, it effectively counteracts all such attempts by revealing the eternal laws and principles that constitute Christ's relation to the universe and to the life of every man.[16]

The Incarnation, then, has not changed the reality in which man is placed; it merely illuminates and explains that which has always been true of human existence. Yet the Incarnation can be said to have introduced something new, since it conveys a true and clear knowledge of reality.[17] The Incarnation has changed man's situation in this sense that he now no longer needs to grope in darkness, ignorant of the basic conditions of human life. The Incarnation has removed the veil which on account of man's unbelief and sin had blurred and obscured his understanding of true reality.[18]

To grasp the full significance of the Incarnation it is, however, necessary to consider it as the twofold manifestation of Christ as the Son of God and as the Son of

it knows Him not. He had spoken of this Word as the Light of men. He had shown how the Word, being made flesh, proved Himself by all His acts and discourses to be the same who had taught the hearts and consciences of men in all ages."

15 *Theological Essays*, 24. Cf. also *The Gospel of St. John*, 428: "he [St. John] regards every act done by our Lord, to effect ever so temporary a redemption, for ever so small a body, or so insignificant an individual, as a sign of what He is, of the work in which He is always engaged, of the blessing which He has wrought out and designs for the universe."

16 Cf. *Sermons* III, 72–3: "Either the Incarnation means nothing, and we should pay no heed to it, or it determines what our thoughts and deeds should be, all our lives through. We should go to it, not to find exceptions from the laws by which men are governed, but to learn what those laws are. It will not, I am sure, encourage or tolerate in us any sentiment which is at variance with this principle."

17 Cf. *The Gospel of St. John*, 19: "I wished you to feel that there was, in one sense, no novelty in his [St. John's] proclamation, because he was saying that which was implied in all the past history and literature of his people; yet that there was, in another sense, the most important novelty, because that which had been implied could now for the first time be expressed," and p. 25: "the especial grandeur of the new time [is] this, that it reveals that which had been of old, that which had been from the beginning."

18 Maurice frequently expressed himself as though the sin and ignorance of men had necessitated the Incarnation. Thus he wrote: "believe that every creature with whom you are brought into contact, is connected with Him by the same bond that unites Him to you, believe that to make us conscious of that bond, to deliver us out of our misery and ignorance, that Lord thought it not too great an ignominy to bear our flesh, to die our death" *(Christmas Day*, 180–1. Cf. also *Sermons* II, 255: "If the love of God could have been content with anything less than this redemption and reconciliation, with anything less than the imparting to men the full rights and condition of Sons of God, the Word would not have been made flesh, the life on earth which the Evangelists set forth to us would not have been lived"). Maurice apparently adopted here the orthodox explanation of the necessity of the Incarnation. His real concern is, however, to maintain that the Incarnation took place because of God's eternal decree. The imparting of true knowledge of reality is a consequence of the Incarnation, but does not provide the motive for Christ's assumption of human flesh.

Man. Since this implies that Christ has been revealed as the Image of God as well as the Head of humanity,[19] the Incarnation is able to impart true knowledge of both God and man.[20]

Our next task will be to give a detailed analysis of Maurice's interpretation of these two aspects of the Incarnation.

2. The Incarnation as the Manifestation of the Son of God

Maurice was anxious to maintain that Christ lived the same life on earth as He eternally lives with His Father. Only when it is understood that it is the eternal relationship of the Son to the Father which was manifested in Christ's earthly life can it be claimed that Christ revealed absolute and necessary truth.

In His life on earth Christ was, as always, subordinate to the Father and yet was at one with Him through obedient trust and love.[21] That is why Maurice wrote: "the Will of the Father in Heaven, the Obedience of the Son, take precedence of other principles in the Revelation of Christ."[22] The incarnate Christ did not speak and act in His own name; He did not wish to glorify Himself and desired nothing but "the privilege and glory – – in all things to obey – in all things to do His Father's will."[23] Freely and willingly He performed only what the Father charged Him to do.[24]

By virtue of His obedience to the Father Christ, even in His earthly life, remains "the perfect image and reflex of that which is the Nature and Essence of God",[25] and the Incarnation could, therefore, impart true knowledge of God to man. In Christ's

19 Cf. *The Word Revelation*, 14–5: "But if He unveils God to men, He will also unveil men to themselves. – – The whole Evangelical history is but an exposition of the double aspect which it presents to us," and *The Contemporary Review* XIV ("Grammar of Assent"), 172: "The revelation of Christ – – professed to be the discovery of the Son of Man, the Head of every man – of the Son of God, the perfect image of the Father."

20 Cf. *The Worship of the Church*, 37–8: "Still we ask, 'Is there no fact in the history of mankind, standing out at once as a revelation to Man of what God is, and of what he himself, what his own humanity is – –?' Assuredly, says St. Paul, there is such a fact; – – the fact of Christianity itself."

21 Cf. *Christmas Day*, 160–1: "the life of the Son of God was the life of obedience. Proud men cannot understand how He, who is one with the Father, yea, equal to the Father, should yet be obedient to the Father. They do not enter into this mystery of love – they cannot explain in their carnal hearts, how the Almighty Father commands because the Son obeys, and the Son obeys because the Father commands; and how there would be no command if there were not obedience, and there would be no obedience if there were not command. And they do not see how the Son came to carry on the same life here on earth which He had in heaven, to show forth this same blessed obedience in his human life and human death."

22 *Social Morality*, 309. Cf. also *The Gospel of St. John*, 131: "the relation of a Son to a Father, with all trust, obedience, communion which it implies, is the subject of the new revelation."

23 *Christmas Day*, 161.

24 Cf. *Sacrifice*, 109: "His acts here, plain and palpable, done among men, done for men, have shown forth that perfect filial obedience to the Creator of all things, that entire filial union with the Eternal Father, which is the ground of the universe and the ground of our humanity," and *Christmas Day*, 160: "That life which he had with the Father before all worlds was a life of love, of confidence, of rest. The life which he came to lead upon earth was the same life, a continued resting upon the love of the unseen Being, a continual listening to his voice that he might utter it forth to men."

25 *Sacrifice*, 287.

words and acts God is revealed as perfect love, only desiring to perform acts of love towards men.[26] As Christ did nothing by Himself but only spoke and acted that which His Father gave Him,[27] men receive the assurance from His words and acts that God has always embraced all men in His love.

Christ's perfect revelation of God as the universal Father dispelled man's false thoughts of God as a revengeful and capricious despot.[28] Similarly, Christ vanquished the Devil, who sought to erect a barrier between God and man by insinuating that God is a vindictive and malicious deity desiring man's downfall and destruction: "He revealed the Father, and so in human flesh He destroyed the great calumny of the devil, that man has not a Father in Heaven, that He is not altogether good, that He does not care for His creatures."[29] Men no longer need to grope in the dark, for the God whose true nature they have ever been striving to know has in the incarnate Christ revealed Himself as the loving Father in whom they may trust since He only desires to bestow His love upon them.[30]

Christ's coming in the flesh is not merely the revelation of God's mind and will towards man; it also implies a manifestation of the true structure of the universe. From eternity the Father has been well-pleased with the self-sacrificing love of the Son, and so He has made Him the Creator and Lord of the universe. Christ has always been invisibly present, imparting life to the universe and upholding its order and harmony. Men have, however, not perceived Christ as the lifegiving centre of the creation because of the false idea of reality which sin and the Devil have instilled in them. But this false knowledge is dispersed through the miracles which Christ performed during His earthly life. They manifest Christ as the Creator and Lord of the universe and reveal the nature of His rule.[31]

26 Cf. *Sermons* III, 73: "the Incarnation of Christ [is] the revelation of God's mind and character to men"; *Sermons* I, 301: "He is bringing down into this nature of man that love which had created man," and *The Apocalypse*, 229: "The Lamb of God, the perfect image of the Father, reveals not His works only, but His ways; He shows Him forth as He is. -- He strips Himself of all power, that the eternal love of God may be seen through His emptiness. He clothes Himself with power that it may be seen that all the power of the universe is the power of love."

27 Cf. *The Gospel of St. John*, 247–8: "Jesus had spoken of His Father as the root of all His loving acts, – of the wisdom, and truth, and love which were expressed in His words and in Himself."

28 Cf. *Country Churches*, 55: "He [Christ] said that God was not a tyrant, but a Father; and that in Him they might see the Father, and only in Him. And it is in Him, brethren, that you and I must see the Father, and only in Him. If we try to think of God without thinking of the Son of Man, we shall get all astray, and suppose Him to be another Being altogether from what He is."

29 *Theological Essays*, 29. See also *The Epistles of St. John*, 190–1.

30 Cf. *The Apocalypse*, 287–8: "Whether the Author of the universe is the Oppressor or the Deliverer, the Enemy from whom men have to escape, or the Friend in whom they may rest the burden of all their doubts, their dreads, their hopes – this was what all the past ages were striving to know. What we say is, that the revelation of Jesus Christ was the solution of that question."

31 Cf. *What Is Revelation?*, 62: "Here is then not a King now for the first time installed in that office, now for the first time expressing its noblest functions. Here is the manifestation of Him whose goings-forth have been from everlasting; a revelation of Him from whom all powers and methods of healing have been derived."

That Christ is "the revealer and assertor of the Divine order"[32] is, however, contradicted by the orthodox conception of miracles. Thus, the orthodox assertion that Christ proved His divinity by performing startling and unique miracles, violating the laws of nature,[33] necessarily entails that His rule over creation will be considered arbitrary.[34] Fortuitously He displayed His power over nature and took pity on individuals and helped them through miracles at random. Apart from the fact that not even His living contemporaries could rest assured that Christ would offer them His miraculous help it was in any circumstances necessary to meet Him in the flesh to receive benefit from His miracles. Furthermore, the orthodox view of miracles chains man to the concrete and sensible by fixing his attention to the individual miracle and the outward circumstances accompanying it. The result is an exclusive interest in the outward, historical Christ, whose life and acts stand for the contingent and the particular and appear as a violation of the harmonious order of the universe. Man is forced to take his point of departure in time, and not in eternity, thus forfeiting the possibility of a true understanding of the significance of the Incarnation.[35]

Maurice had no more sympathy with the rationalist interpretation of miracles, which merely regarded them as phenomena originating in immutable natural forces. Admittedly, it represented a most needed protest against the orthodox conception, since it acknowledged an unbroken order and harmony in the universe. Nonetheless, this interpretation must be rejected since it implies that man is subject to impersonal natural laws, and is, therefore, enslaved by sensuality.[36]

Thus, the orthodox and the rationalist positions force men either to assume that in a specific place and at a specific time Christ had arbitrarily performed exceptional

32 *The Kingdom of Heaven*, IX.
33 Cf. *The Epistles of St. John*, 154–5: "There is a disposition in many of us to hold that Jesus proved Himself to be the Christ by doing great and startling miracles, by showing that He had power to break through laws which men generally are obliged to obey. This, we affirm, was the sign that He came from God."
34 Cf. *The Acts of the Apostles*, 39: "Do I regard them [the miracles] as direct attestations of the power and presence of One who is the King and Lord of men, the giver of life and health to men, the enemy of disorder, irregularity, disease, death? Or do I only regard them as witnesses to the fact that a certain man was born in Palestine at a certain time, who is entitled to be called a Messiah or the founder of a religion? And do I think their force as witnesses lies in the fact of their being irregular, unusual, – in fact departures from the method according to which God governs His world?" For Maurice the latter alternative represented orthodox theology.
35 Cf. *The Gospel of St. John*, 482: "Those who wish to think and speak of Him as not only born at a certain time into the world, but as living before the world, and as the founder of it, find themselves perpetually embarrassed by the notion which has worked itself into the minds of our people and of ourselves, that He established His claim to be an extraordinary person by doing extraordinary acts in the towns of Galilee and the city of Jerusalem, instead of showing by signs what He is and always has been. The Catholic doctrine is more undermined than we are at all aware by the feeling which this deviation from the original has sanctioned and promoted. We assume Christ's simple humanity as the ground of our thoughts, and then add to it an indefinite notion of divinity."
36 Cf. *The Kingdom of Christ* (1838) II, 72, where it is stated that when the rationalists see in the miracles "the effects of natural causes", they are virtually making man "the passive slave and victim of a set of natural agents, moving by a blind mechanism". Their concept of miracles implied that they "wish to make man the creature and slave of sense, – wish him

180

miracles in violation of the laws of the universe, or to assert a universal but godless and impersonal order of nature. Although both views express a vital aspect of the truth, both equally fail to fathom the significance of Christ's miracles.

To prove this Maurice resorted to the Gospel of St. John. Its prologue, which tells of Christ as the Creator of the universe, provided the key to a true understanding of the nature and purpose of Christ's miracles.[37] When He was manifested in the flesh He proved Himself to be the Lord who had established a harmonious order and governed and directed the life of creation according to fixed laws. To demonstrate this truth He performed His miracles.[38] It is true that Christ's miracles might seem surprising and exceptional, but this is only because men have become so blind and insensitive that they do not see that the Natural Order and the Human Order are wonders, because they are created and upheld by Christ. The purpose of the apparently surprising element in His miracles is simply to shake men out of their dull apathy and awaken them to a true knowledge of the created universe.[39]

Since "God may perform wonders to break the chains of sense, to make us aware that He is always at work,"[40] miracles have no significance in themselves. They are important because they are concrete examples of the unchangeable and universal laws and principles according to which Christ exercises His dominion over the universe and mankind.[41] The miracles are, in other words, signs, bearing witness to Christ as the eternal Lord and King.[42] Consequently, when Christ changed water to

to feel that sense has never been led captive, – wish to make him feel that there is no order in the world but what they call natural order; that is to say, an order of appearances and accidents."

37 Cf. *The Gospel of St. John*, 70: "if we make St. John's first chapter the expounder of his object in every subsequent narrative, we shall be delivered from innumerable difficulties by which the study of miracles generally, and of each particular miracle is beset."

38 Cf. p. 64: "If Jesus was the Word made flesh, if the order of the world was established by Him, then His acts upon earth would be done for the purpose of vindicating this order. By them He would claim it as His."

39 Cf. *Sacrifice*, 28: "Apparent breaches in the regular course of events, surprising visitations, prove at times what the evenness and persistency of nature proves habitually – that the just God, of whom man is the image, against whose laws he is so continually striving, is the Author and Ruler of all things." See also *The Prophets*, 247–8.

40 *The Gospel of St. John*, 71.

41 Cf. *Sermons* V, 118: "It is in little things, in particulars, that the laws of a universe reveal themselves. The unfolding of a flower may teach us more of the birth and growth of all things than we can obtain by reflecting on the whole Cosmos. And in this one act of changing the water into wine at the marriage-feast, the sense of all good things coming down through a Brother, from a Father, may have been more profoundly awakened in the minds of those fishermen, than it had been awakened in all kings and prophets before them. From what material conceptions of Creation may it not have delivered them! How they may have risen to the perception, if not at once, yet through the discipline of after-years acting upon that one event, of a Word who giveth life!"

42 Cf. *The Gospel of St. John*, 70–1: "The Scriptures teach us to care for no miracles except so far as they are signs. Of what are your miracles signs? Do they signify that the Word who was made flesh is not continually acting in the affairs of men now? If so, they contradict those signs which we confess to be true signs, those which have signified to us and to our forefathers that all life is in Him, that all light is from Him. Or *do* they say this? Then they

wine, fed the multitude in the wilderness or healed the sick and the lame, He was demonstrating that it is He alone who always imparts joy, upholds man's bodily existence and heals disease. Through His miracles Christ proclaimed that His work always consists of giving life to men, and that He alone is the giver of all good gifts, even when He employs other men or the natural forces as His agents and instruments.[43] Thus, Christ's miracles reveal that all human life is miraculous because it has Christ as its author. By teaching that all men live under Christ's dominion and are always the objects of His love, they give a new significance to everything in man's daily life. All gratification of hunger, all healing of disease, all joy experienced become sacraments which bear witness to Christ as man's ever present lifegiver.[44]

At the same time the miracles are a clear demonstration of Christ's rule over the natural forces. Men falsely believe that they are subject to impersonal and mechanical natural laws.[45] This false knowledge was dispelled by Christ when through His miracles He showed that the natural laws are subject to Him and obey His commands. Thus, when Christ stilled the storm on the lake, this act proclaimed that He is always master of the powers of the sea.[46] When Christ changed water into wine, this event was "an instance of the working of a universal law. We shall conclude that all living processes – be they slow or rapid, be they carried on in the womb of nature or through the intervention of human art – have their first power and principle in Him, that without Him nothing could become that does become."[47] Because of Christ's miracles man attains to a perfect knowledge that there exists a harmonious order in the universe and that the forces of nature are destined to serve God and man as created in His image.[48] This not only eliminates all superstitious belief in, or fear of, a blind

say what every marriage is saying just as clearly; what our ordinary food and wine, what the growth of trees and flowers, what the plough of the husbandman and the laboratory of the chemist are such pledges of as your miracles can never be."

43 Cf. *Christmas Day*, 416: "And if we can say to every lame and sick man – 'It is Jesus Christ who maketh thee whole, whether he works through the physician or without him', why is our condition worse because in our day it rather pleases God to put honour upon his subordinate agents than to dispense with them," and *Sequel*, 258: "Then the war with sickness and sorrow and all forms of misery which Christ carried on in His miracles, will be felt indeed to illustrate His words, 'The Father worketh hitherto, and I work', and to vindicate every brave and true effort of men for the extirpation of sickness, sorrow, and misery, as prompted and inspired by Him."

44 Cf. *The Gospel of St. John*, 71: "if we receive the beginning of signs which Christ gave us in Cana of Galilee, all common things will become sacraments of His presence."

45 Cf. *The Prophets*, 187: "the sense of mere sequence in outward phenomena dulled the mind as to the invisible cause, the inward order which they betokened. When that effect had been produced, – and who knows not how soon it is produced, – the chain of custom and association must be broken through, or it will bind the spirit in an Atheism the more fatal, because unsuspected."

46 Cf. *What Is Revelation?*, 65: "To realize, by one special instance, in whose hand was the trident of the seas."

47 *The Gospel of St. John*, 66.

48 Cf. *The Kingdom of Christ* (1838), 78: "the stories of those signs – – have demonstrated that spiritual power is superior to mechanical; that the world is subject to God, and not to change or nature," and *The Gospel of St. John*, 146: "All natural powers are felt to be angels of God, because they are under the direction of an intelligent and righteous Ruler."

arbitrariness in nature, but also provides the most powerful motive for the exploration of the created universe for the benefit of mankind.[49]

As the miracles are visible signs of eternal truths, it was obvious for Maurice that they cannot "draw men away from the invisible to the visible, – from the object of faith to an object of sight; but just the reverse of it."[50] Man must penetrate the concrete external shape of a miracle and discover the eternal law and principle which is manifested through it; indeed he is bound to penetrate still further to a knowledge of the eternal God in whom the immutable law and principle has its origin and whose will it serves. When this method is followed it becomes evident how senseless it is to ask for new specific miracles. As the miracles which Christ performed during his earthly life were not "breaches of laws", but "assertions of laws against irregularities and disturbances",[51] they were a vindication of that Divine Order which always constitutes the life of every man. They demonstrated that human existence is dependent upon Christ and His acts of love. As Christ continually performs miracles towards every human being, the demand for new miracles is nothing but a denial of the fact that He is the ever present Lord and Lifegiver of the universe and mankind.

This view appears to be contradicted by Maurice's description of the miracles as acts by which Christ wrested dominion from the Devil and redeemed and restituted the creation by expelling sin and death.[52] A more thorough analysis, however, reveals a strange incongruity between what Maurice actually said and what he intended to convey. On occasions Maurice spoke strongly of the Devil's dominion over

49 Cf. *The Gospel of St. John*, 264–5: "If Christ's other signs testified that there is an invisible power at work in all the springs of our life, – that there is a Fountain of life from which those springs are continually refreshed and renewed, – did not this sign [St. John 9,1–7] testify that there is a potency and virtue in the very commonest things; that God has stored all nature with instruments for the blessing and healing of His creatures? The mere miracle-worker who draws glory to himself wishes to dispense with these things, lest he should be confounded with the ordinary physician. The great Physician, who works because His Father works, who comes to show what He is doing in His world, puts an honour upon earth and water as well as upon all art which has true observation and knowledge for its basis. He only distinguishes Himself from other healers by showing that the source of their wisdom and renovating power is in Him." – To prove that the Natural Order and the Human Order originate in God was, in Maurice's view, also the purpose of Christ's parables: "Our Lord spoke to His disciples in parables; through them He declared the mysteries of the kingdom. The fact of outward nature, the ordinary transactions of men, He recognized as a sacred writing, in which God had expressed part of His meaning, a meaning which He did not will to remain hidden, but which His Son unfolded" *(Religions, 222)*.

50 *The Gospel of St. John*, 302. Here "faith" is used synonymously with "reason". According to Maurice the Biblical miracles are distinguished from prodigies and portents in that "the one is the assertion of man's superiority to sense and nature, and the other of his subjection to them. One is imparting to him the feeling of his connection with a Lord of his spirit, and thereby of his dominion over that which is merely external and material; the other is laying him low before everything most gross and material" *(The Kingdom of Christ* (1838) II, 70–1).

51 *The Epistles of St. John*, 155.

52 Cf., e. g., *Sermons* V, 234: "We must believe that health is the law of the world; sickness, the anomaly. Reason says so. We must suppose the anomaly will some day be removed. Our Lord's miracles of healing bear that testimony," and *The Kingdom of Heaven*, X: "They [miracles] are directed against the confusions of the world, against the plagues and torments which distract human life."

the earth and vividly described bodily and mental disease and evils as the result of the Devil's tyranny; similarly, he represented the incarnate Christ as engaged in a great war against the Devil to deliver the enslaved earth.[53] But when it came to the point, Maurice just stated that Christ achieved the victory by manifesting Himself and declaring Himself as the true Lord of the universe, from which it follows that the law of the entire creation has always been life and not sin and death.[54] In effect, the activity of the Devil consists in his claiming to be the ruler of the universe, but this is an empty assertion, which he has no power to implement.[55] For man to believe that he is enslaved to the Devil, therefore, simply denotes that he is enslaved to a false idea of reality. When Christ through His miracles proved that the creation had always stood under His loving rule, Maurice might indeed maintain that Christ had vanquished the Devil and delivered mankind from its bondage to him, but this, plainly stated, meant that Christ had proved the assertions of the Devil to be delusions and had thereby delivered mankind from a false knowledge of reality. Maurice was consistent, then, in his interpretation of the miracles as visible signs of the eternal laws and principles which constitute God's created Order.

To conclude: for Maurice the Incarnation as the manifestation of the Son of God implied that, because of His eternal Sonship to the Father, Christ has revealed God as perfect love, whose will it is to impart His love to every man. Furthermore, the In-

53 Cf. *Country Churches*, 31–2: "St. Paul came to these men, saying 'God, who created all things, hath sent forth His only begotten Son, the express image of His person, into this world of ours, to deliver it, and them who dwell upon it, from the enemies which are tormenting it. You are not mistaken; the evils of the world are as great as you take them to be. They are about you, tormenting you every hour. You do need to be set free from them. And you are not mistaken that these evils, the very worst of them, come from yourselves. – – While He was on earth He was freeing men from plagues of body, hunger, leprosy, palsy, fever, and their minds from plagues of rage and madness, and confusion.' All these, he said, were proofs that an evil spirit, a tyrant, had got dominion over men and that they were acknowledging his dominion. These things were not the will of His Father, they were contrary to His will. He came to do His Father's will by making His creatures straight and well, by breaking the yoke of the oppressor."

54 Cf. *Religions*, 179: "Yet never for an instant did He speak of the claim which He put forth for the dominion of the Gracious Preserver and Father, as a new claim. Never when He spoke of setting up His Kingdom did He admit that He was not King of kings and Lord of lords before," and *Sermons* I, 216: "He Who gave signs, when He was upon earth, of that dominion over Nature, and over the wills of men, which has been His always; which He is putting forth over us who are here – over all men in every section and corner of God's Kingdom, – shall vindicate that dominion against all which defies it, and would establish a tyranny that is hostile to it."

55 Cf. *Religions*, 179: "The Incarnation – – affirms the Preserver to be the Lord of all; affirms Him through the whole course of His government to have been upholding this earth and those who dwell upon it; to have been interfering for their rescue. Here, in this very Incarnation, and that which follows from it, is the assertion of His complete dominion; the answer to the Destroyer's claim to be in any sense the Creator, to have any dominion whatsoever over that race which has paid him such fearful homage," and *The Kingdom of Christ* I, 286: "men of all countries, languages, customs – – have a common friend and a common enemy; but – – the enemy has been vanquished, has been declared to have no right or property in any human creature, in any one corner of the universe; – – his power is conferred by our faithlessness; – – while we are claiming our true position we may despise and defy him; – – it is only by making a lie that we come under the dominion of the father of lies."

carnation demonstrated that Christ, by virtue of His obedience to the Father, is the Creator and Lord of the universe and mankind and manifested the nature of the rule and power He is ever exerting in His creation. By His incarnation Christ has given man a true knowledge of reality, thus solving the most profound problem of human life, the search for God and the desire to know His mind and will towards men.

3. The Incarnation as the Manifestation of the Son of Man

Man yearns not only for perfect knowledge of God; he also desires true knowledge of his own existence as a human being. He feels that he belongs to a higher world and is united to a Being from whom he has received everything that is true and genuinely human in his life. Yet this feeling is vague and continually seems to be contradicted and dissolved in an illusion, as man sees himself held back by sin and the Devil from fulfilling that which he feels to be his true destiny. The fundamental problem haunting man is to gain a clear understanding of what it is to be a man. He desires a manifestation of true humanity which will prove that the profoundest dreams of mankind are no mere fancies. And at the same time he longs for a vindication of the existence of a relationship between every individual and perfect humanity.

The Incarnation is the answer to these desires and longings. Thus Maurice has Christ say: "I find you in darkness, in ignorance of yourselves, of your relation to each other, of your relation to God. I am come a Light into the world, – a Light to show you what you are, where you are, what you have to do with your fellows, what you have to do with Him apart from whom you have no life."[56] In the Incarnation Christ is manifested as perfect humanity, and so the truth about every man has been revealed.

If Maurice has to succeed in affirming Christ to be the manifestation of true humanity and of the truth regarding every individual, he must repudiate the orthodox interpretation of Christ's manhood. The assertion that the Son of God renounced His life with the Father in eternity so that He might become man and live a human life on earth, limits His manhood to the historical Christ. This view interprets Christ's manhood as contingent on the fallen state of mankind: it was necessary for Christ to become man in order that he might save the human race from sin. Thus sin is regarded as the ultimate cause of Christ's manhood. Time is made dominant over eternity – and this is bound to have dire consequences. It becomes impossible to say what humanity truly is since Christ's manhood, necessitated by sin and limited to the history of time and space, does not originate in eternity, in God's eternal will. It also becomes impossible to perceive any necessary relation between Christ's manhood and each existing man. If His manhood is a reality only at a definite point in history, it cannot be constitutive for all mankind, nor can it interpret and shed light on the actual life of man. As a unique and exceptional fact it stands out as a glaring violation of ordinary human life.

In other words, the traditional interpretation of Christ's manhood bars man from

56 *The Gospel of St. John*, 346.

any understanding of the Incarnation as a manifestation of eternal necessary truth.[57] If, however, eternity is taken as the starting-point for an interpretation of Christ's manhod, then it becomes clear that through His assumption of human flesh Christ was manifested as He who has always been the true Man, in whom God and mankind are united.[58] Even with respect to Christ's manhood the Incarnation must be understood as the historical event through which eternal truth is revealed to man.[59]

Consequently, when Maurice spoke of Christ's manhood, he was thinking of His eternal Divine Humanity. As previously mentioned, Christ, because of God's eternal decree, is from eternity the perfect man, the Man, in whom God elected and created mankind. Being the "Archetype of man", "the perfect ideal of humanity",[60] Christ is the creative and life-giving idea of man. Christ is, therefore, the Head of mankind and of every man, and it is this fact that has been revealed in the Incarnation.[61]

If the Incarnation is the manifestation of Christ's Divine Humanity, the life of the incarnate Christ can in no way be regarded as a departure from the life Christ lives eternally. That Christ by assuming human flesh stoops down to man in order to serve him is only the visible demonstration of the way He, as the Head of the human race, has always dealt with every single man.[62] Christ's eternal manhood, His perfect humanity, has been fully revealed and manifested in an actual human life.

57 Cf. *Tracts for Priests and People, 2nd Series. No. XIV* ("Letter to the Writer of the Foregoing Letter" [i. e. R. H. Hutton: "The Incarnation and the Principles of Evidence"]. London 1862), 62–3: "the perfect image of God cannot be merely *a* man. He must be *the* Man; the Head of the Race; the Person in whom the race is created; by whom it stands. Such a Person, I think, the Evangelists set forth to us. The powers which they say that Jesus exercised, the sufferings which they say He underwent, belong to such a person. You, I suspect, feel the need for such a one as much as I do. But you feel, as I did, that, *contemplated from the human ground,* a universal man is merely the fiction of an antiquated realism."

58 Cf. *Theological Essays,* 75: "But – – the Creed has been declaring Him to be the Son of God our Lord; – – it has been exhibiting Him, first, in the closest relationship with God, secondly, in the closest relationship with man, – this relationship not being created by any acts which are recorded afterwards, but being the ground and explanation of those acts; not being the consequence of His Incarnation, or Death, or Resurrection, or Ascension, but the cause of them."

59 Cf. *Sermons* V, 155: "For if once we perceive that fact of God's union with our race in the Person of a Mediator as the interpretation of all other facts, – as the kernel mystery of the Universe, – we cannot suppose that we rise to conceptions of God through the things of time and sense, we cannot help supposing that through these things He is speaking to us."

60 *The Prophets,* 421.

61 We have previously pointed out that Maurice cannot make out any distinction between Christ as the Son of God and as the Son of Man (see p. 37 note 69). It is merely a question of looking at two different aspects of Christ. In His relation to the Father He can be described as the Son of God, inasmuch as He reveals God and carries out His will; in His relation to mankind He can be called the Son of Man, the perfect man, because He is the life-giving principle of every man. As Christ in His earthly life merely unveiled what He eternally is, there can be no conflict between the divine and the human: "All is consistent from first to last; all has been divine, and all human. No clashing of the one with the other; but the human showing forth the divine as the perfect light from which it has been derived; the human leading on to the divine as that in which it is satisfied" *(The Gospel of St. John,* 417).

62 Cf. *Sacrifice,* 220: "Christ, being the perfect image of the Father, was the image after which

Maurice accepted that at His incarnation Christ, who has always been "the original man", "the type of all creation", "assumes the condition of individual men; – – puts on the fleshly accidents which belonged to them as He had before stood to them in the closest spiritual relation."[63] Only on one occasion did Maurice admit that the fact that Christ had assumed "that earthly mortal mould",[64] which belongs to every man as an individual, involves a limitation of the life Christ has had from eternity. He gave, however, no hint as to the nature of this limitation and, indeed, this idea had no practical consequences for his interpretation of the Incarnation.[65] For Maurice there must exist a perfect identity between Christ's eternal life with the Father and His earthly life. This point is central, since only if it is accepted does the Incarnation clearly and distinctly manifest Christ's eternal Divine Humanity.

Because He is the archetype of man, the incarnate Christ demonstrated in a concrete historical life what it means to be created in the image of God. His earthly life represented the embodiment of the idea of man in its perfection,[66] thereby revealing God's purpose in creating man and vindicating all men's dreams and aspirations concerning the high destiny of man.[67] But the Incarnation as the visible manifestation of Christ's Divine Humanity has deeper implications than this. It also reveals the truth about the actual life of every human being.

At first sight it appears puzzling that the Incarnation affords men a clear and unambiguous knowledge, not of what they are to become, but of what they truly are. This is, however, quite in accordance with Maurice's basic convictions. Man is created to live in Christ. This fellowship can never be broken as it is not based upon man's will and acts but upon Christ's self-sacrificing love. Although men may refuse to recognize this fact, Christ always remains the archetype of man, the Head of every man. Thus, the truth about every man is that he only exists because Christ lives and works in him. When He became incarnate and triumphed over sin in a human life,

men were created. The relation between Him and our race was implied in its existence. – – To become one of the race when He was the Head of it – to become a servant when He was the Lord – this was an act of deep and loving condescension; but there was nothing in it irregular and anomalous; the glory of it is, that it is the fulfilment of an original and divine purpose."

63 *Sacrifice*, 221.

64 p. 222.

65 Cf. *Tracts for Priests and People, No. XIV*, 63: "The fact that Christ must have been born in some time and some place – that He must have been actual child, boy, and man – will remain. These are essential to the idea of an Incarnation. There may be, there must be, limitations involved in that birth, childhood, boyhood, manhood." Undoubtedly this statement must be considered as a concession to R. H. Hutton who maintained that a kenotic christology was the only possible solution to the problem of how that which is eternal can be united with that which takes place in the history of time and space. Although Maurice concedes to Hutton that the Incarnation must imply a limitation, he will not hear of a doctrine of kenosis. He simply rejected Hutton's theory without replacing it with an alternative.

66 Cf. *Sequel*, 246–7: "If there is such a manifestation as this, I can understand the words that Man is made in the Image of God; I can understand how it is possible for men to show forth that Image."

67 Cf. p. 256: "it is the manifestation of the *Divine* excellence, of the excellence of that Nature of which the human Nature is the Image, of all that men had dreamed of as necessary to Divine perfection, of all that they had felt was demanded for their own perfection."

death and the Devil, this was a manifestation of His Divine Humanity which is always at work asserting itself in the life of men. As the life lived by the historical Christ is completely identical with the life He lives in every man, the incarnate Christ reveals the truth of man's actual existence. The Incarnation imparts true self-knowledge to man by proclaiming that he always stands in Christ and lives by His work in him.

There occur, however, in Maurice's writings a number of statements which appear to offer a different interpretation of the significance of the Incarnation. Thus he asserted that, by becoming man, Christ entirely identified Himself with mankind and took upon Him its sin and death as His own.[68] Christ assumed the nature of mankind in its totality in order to lead it back to God.[69] The incarnate Christ is the meeting-point of God and man because in His own body He has "actually conquered death and hell – –. He has actually united our nature to God's nature; – – has actually glorified our nature at God's right hand."[70] The purpose of Christ's assumption of human nature was that He might redeem man from his sin and make him a partaker of His divine nature.[71] Christ has achieved "the perfect reconciliation of divinity and humanity".[72] Since He has assumed the sinfulness of all mankind and annihilated it in His own body, all men are now pure and holy, so that every man because of Christ has both the right and the duty to regard himself as righteous and holy.[73]

For this presentation of the significance of the Incarnation Maurice was indebted to Edward Irving's *Orthodox and Catholic Doctrine of Our Lord's Nature* (1830). Irving maintained that Christ had truly assumed man's sinful and godless nature and had thereby, in His own flesh, conquered all human sin and all the enemies of human life, thus redeeming and delivering mankind and uniting it with God. The striking similarity between Irving and Maurice is no coincidence[74] since, as previously men-

68 Cf. *Country Churches,* 54: "He has everything which belongs to a man. He enters into everything which there is in every man. And that is the reason He is called the Son of Man. He is *The* Man; the Head Man, the King of Men."

69 Cf. *Sermons* III, 77: "Christ did not merely stoop to our condition, He stooped to us that He might raise us. – – And as this was the ultimate object of His Incarnation and Humiliation, so far as we are concerned – it appeared in every part of the work which He did while He was clothed with our mortality."

70 *Sermons* IV, 72–3.

71 Cf. *The Conflict,* 54: "Yes, this is our Gospel, the Gospel of Him who took our nature, that He might redeem us from all iniquity"; *The Gospel of St. John,* 439: "the evidence of Christ's actual relation to our nature is the assurance that He cleanses it of its defilement, that He endues it with a new and higher life", and *Sermons* III, 8: "The Father had exalted Him, and in Him had exalted the race with which He had identified Himself."

72 *The Prophets,* 289.

73 Cf. *The Epistle to the Hebrews,* 29–30: "In Him we find how humanity has been a holy thing, though each man felt himself to be unholy. For the moment He clothes Himself with all its vilest accidents it becomes actually holy; the sinfulness which belongs to each man's separate nature is *purged* out of human nature when He inhabits it, and takes it unto Himself. In Him it is proved that man is meant to have his dwelling with God; for He having purified the soul and body which he had taken, *"sat down on the right hand of the Majesty on high"*, claiming for men the privileges of spiritual beings, the power of rising above the limitations of space and time – of entering into fellowship with Him who filleth all in all."

74 A few passages from Irving's remarkable book will be sufficient to demonstrate the similarity between Irving and Maurice. According to Irving the purpose of the Incarnation was

tioned, it was Irving, who had given Maurice a deepened understanding of the Incarnation as the pivot of Christian faith.[75] Maurice even appeared to make Irving's concern entirely his own: "He [Irving] found that he could not maintain the Incarnation in its reality and power if he shrank from the assertion that evil in all its ghastliness, in all its attractiveness, offered itself to the mind and will of Christ. That it was rejected by that mind and will no one could affirm more vehemently than he did. But to adopt any shift for the sake of making the conflict a less tremendous one than it is in the case of any son of Adam, seemed to him to be dishonouring Christ under pretence of asserting His purity, and to be depriving human creatures of the blessing and victory which He took flesh to give them."[76] Maurice's constant use of Irving's terms and ideas seems only to emphasize his desire to carry out his intentions.

Yet, Maurice could not follow Irving entirely in his interpretation of the Incarnation. Although Irving's idea of Christ's manhood contained a vital truth, Maurice was of the opinion that he had committed a fundamental error in interpreting the Incarnation in the light of *Confessio Scoticana*, which – in Maurice's version – maintained that "the race stood in Adam, and had fallen in Adam", for which reason "a scheme of salvation of which the Incarnation formed a step was necessary to rescue certain persons from the consequences of the fall."[77] Maurice's observation is certainly accurate, since Irving maintained that the purpose of the Incarnation was to conquer and abolish sin and the powers of evil in man. Indeed, it is the acceptance of sin as a truly life-destroying power that makes Irving's account of the Incarnation meaningful. He believed that the Incarnation introduced something radically new by achieving the redemption and regeneration of sinful human nature, and that Christ

"to reconcile, sanctify, quicken, and glorify this nature of ours, which is full of sin, and death, and rebellion, and dishonour unto God" (op. cit., VII). This work was effected through Christ's assumption of sinful flesh: "All creation is sinful, being in a state of alienation from God; it has one law in it, the law of sin; and through all its parts this law binds it in one great sinful operation. The Person of the Son of God was born into it; he restrained, withstood, overcame, this co-operation of a sinful creation, conquered the conqueror, and won it back to God; obtained power over all flesh. This is the great theme which we maintain" (p. X. Cf. p. 114: "if Godhead in the person of the Son did not embrace our nature, as I and all men possess it, that nature, which I and all men possess, is not yet embraced by God. It is not stooped unto; it is not lifted up; it is not redeemed; it is not regenerated; it is not raised from the dead; it is not seated on the throne of God"). Christ conquered the enemies of human life: "in his body, he strangled them there [all sin, and all weakness, and all mortality, and all corruption, and all devils, and all creature-rebellion], he did judgment upon them there, he resisted, he overcame, he captured them. They are no more valid, they are no more potent, they are no more valiant in the creation" (p. 8. Cf. also p. 151: "His Son the Christ became flesh of our flesh, and bone of our bone; that is, he came into the experience, and the obligation, and the suffering which all flesh is heir to; and by the power of the Godhead he took this flesh out of the hands of all his and our enemies, and presented it unto God at all times, and in all ways, pure and spotless, whereby was shewn the grace and power of our God").

75 This has been overlooked by many students of Maurice, although Maurice has himself acknowledged the debt and always referred to Irving's views with great sympathy despite some criticisms (see *Sacrifice*, XVIII–XIX; *Tracts for Priests and People*, No. *XIV*, 64–7 (= *Life* II, 406–8) and *The Kingdom of Christ* I, 155–7).

76 *Tracts for Priests and People, No. XIV*, 64.

77 p. 65.

had, therefore, become "the great Head of the regenerate race, the Base of the regenerate world. He was the great prototype of redeemed manhood."[78]

Maurice protested against this interpretation of the Incarnation as implying a denial of the fact that Christ is "now and always the Head of the race".[79] The Incarnation has changed nothing in Christ's relation to mankind, nor did the incarnate Christ perform any other work than that which He has always performed for the salvation of man. When Christ by assuming human flesh became an actually existing man who defied the enemies of man, He demonstrated that our own manhood, which originates in and is sustained by His Divine Humanity, will not be destroyed despite sin and the Devil. To give an unambiguously clear illustration of this fact it was, however, necessary for Christ to live His life under exactly the same conditions as all men. This is what Maurice wanted to point out when he said: "I could believe that the Head of man had entered fully into the condition of every man, had suffered the temptations of every man, had wrestled with the enemy of every man; and that he had brought *our* humanity untainted and perfect through that struggle."[80] Because Christ is "the root of humanity", all mankind is included in that which He is and does. Thus Maurice appreciated Irving's idea that Christ's life and work are related to the entire human race, but he refused to acknowledge that this relationship was established when Christ, the eternal Son of God, became man on account of sin. The union between Christ and mankind is eternally realized in Christ's Divine Humanity. The Incarnation only manifested this truth.

Maurice's criticism of Irving stemmed from a concept of the Incarnation which was entirely consistent with his idea of revelation.[81] Therefore he knew precisely

78 op. cit., 110–1. Cf. also p. 60: "The Christ-form of being God and man, in one person, was only an idea and a purpose till the Incarnation, when it became a fact. The person of the eternal Son, I mean, did not become the Christ in very deed, until he took human substance of the Virgin."

79 *Tracts for Priests and People, No. XIV*, 65.

80 p. 66.

81 What is so confusing and is even apt to lead to a false understanding of Maurice's true concerns is partly that he seldom elaborated and indicated the presuppositions for his own statements, and partly that he used terms and ideas derived from a chain of reasoning, the premises of which he repudiated. Maurice's treatment of Irving's interpretation of the Incarnation is an illustrative example of the way in which he always dealt with the philosophical and theological ideas he encountered. He reproduced Irving's thought without further ado, thus creating the impression that the Incarnation had accomplished something decisively new in God's relation to mankind: sin, death, and the Devil have been conquered, and the human race has been redeemed, regenerated and reunited with God. At the same time he rejected the basic assumptions which gave Irving's interpretation coherence and made his terminology meaningful. Maurice adopted Irving's terms and ideas but interpreted them in the light of his own basic convictions; hence the incongruity between what Maurice wanted to say and the face-value meaning of his words.

Maurice was never concerned to weigh the terms and the concepts he used; nor did he analyze the ideas and arguments he borrowed. The reason is that the views and arguments of others acted as catalysts upon him. If they either awakened a certain association of ideas in him or enriched his own basic convictions and furnished him with new arguments, he found it appropriate to use them as a means of expressing his own thoughts. This meant, in reality, that Maurice wrenched these terms and ideas from their original context, supplied them with his own interpretation and then assumed that others would understand his meaning

what he could accept and what he had to reject in Irving's interpretation of the Incarnation. Thus, after having disposed of the idea that the Incarnation was a unique and decisive event in God's relationship to man, Maurice was nevertheless capable of emphasizing that Christ had wholly and fully become man and assumed the nature of all men – an emphasis, dictated by his understanding of Christ's Divine Humanity. To demonstrate that men are not enslaved to the powers of evil, but stand in Christ and are the children of God, Christ as "the root of humanity" had to become man so that in and through the life of an individual He might raise up a sign of what is valid for all men.

To make this demonstration valid for all men it was, however, necessary that Christ lived a life which identified Him with the meanest, most despised and most hopeless state of man. If Christ had indeed appeared in human flesh but had lived a life devoid of temptation, sorrow and distress, He would have lived under conditions different from the hard, burdensome life of ordinary men. The result would have been that they would have been unable to see that Christ's life demonstrated the truth about their own lives. For this reason Maurice strongly asserted that Christ "claimed – – a position which identified Him with *all* men, with the lowest men, instead of one which raised Him above any."[82] Indeed, He took upon Himself man's unbelief and selfishness as His own.[83] Christ was "a man of sorrows": "He was really, and not

without any further explanation. And so we find time and again that Maurice expressed his own views by means of terms and ideas which, when analyzed critically, suggest an entirely different meaning than the one he wished to propound. Because Maurice neglected to work out a precise terminology which could convey his own thought unambiguously, his actual phraseology must not be taken at its face-value. It is especially important to pay attention to his critical hints and guarded *caveats* – they usually provide the clue to a true insight into his ideas. It will then become evident that Maurice's fundamental position is clear, and that the incongruity and apparent contradictions in his thinking are very often due to the fact, that he expressed his own consistent views with the help of concepts belonging to different bodies of thought, the ultimate presuppositions of which he contested.

82 *Sacrifice*, 222. In this way Christ proved Himself to be the true shepherd: "The false shepherds wish to find out a way for themselves, which is not the way that the sheep take. They do not like the thought of stooping – beings of another and higher race as they are – to the conditions of these silly creatures. *He* identifies Himself with them. – – His claim to be the Shepherd of the people was, that He would not be above them; that He would bear what they bore, and sink as low as they had sunk. And this not from some great effort, – in virtue of some arrangement, – but because He had the most intimate and original sympathy with them, because they had always been His, and because He had made Himself one with them in all things" *(The Gospel of St. John, 284–5)*.

83 Cf. *The Gospel of St. John*, 287–8: "If you would think rightly of the Son of Man, think of the Person who knows thoroughly everything that each one of you is feeling, and cannot utter to others or to himself, – every temptation from riches, from poverty, from solitude, from society, from gifts of intellect, from the want of them, from the gladness of the spirit, from the barrenness and dreariness of it, from the warmth of affection and from the drying up of affection, from the anguish of doubt and the dulness of indifference, from the whirlwind of passion and the calm which succeeds it, from the vile thoughts which spring out of fleshly appetites and indulgences, from the darker, more terrible, suggestions which are presented to the inner will. Believe that He knows all these, that He knows *you*. And then believe this also, that all He knows is through intense, inmost sympathy, not with the evil that is assaulting you, but with you who are assaulted by it."

apparently, the poor suffering man. He had not seemed to become like the poorest of you. He had become so. Think of the poorest, saddest state in which you have been – think of the poorest, saddest creature you have ever conversed with, and say, 'Christ was poorer and sadder than I or than that man'. And do not, for an instant, fancy, that, in his mind within him, there was some compensation for his outward contempt and humiliation. Do not think that he could say in himself, 'All this is nothing; it will last but a few days; then triumph will follow'. No! He poured out his *soul* unto death. He gave up the power of having such thoughts as these, they were crushed by his agony. The contempt which was poured upon him was felt within; down in the very depths of his being."[84]

For Maurice Christ's assumption of the nature of all men signified His solidarity with men and His identification with all their experiences of sin and suffering. All that moves man and draws him away from God was felt by Christ as something He personally had to struggle against in order to remain in trusting and obedient fellowship with God. [85] But this does not imply that, by identifying Himself with men in their sin and distress, Christ had to give up His eternal life with the Father, since it was precisely His fellowship with the Father which enabled Him to bear the sorrows and sufferings of men. As God, being pure love, finds His sole pleasure in caring for that which is mean and despised and giving to it of His own abundance, so Christ, in obedience to His Father, had to stoop down to and identify Himself with those who are tormented by sin and the Devil.[86] It is true that He has always borne men's burdens, but in His Incarnation this fact was made manifest. Christ did not, then, become a sinful man in order that He might bear the sins of mankind. On the contrary, it is His sinlessness that enables Him to take them upon Himself and experience them as His own personal responsibility and burden. Solidarity with others originates only in self-sacrificing love. A man who is weighed down by his own sin can never attain to fellowship with others and bear their sins as his own – sin, being selfishness, shuts man up within himself and cuts him off from others. Only the man who lives the life of perfect love is able to sacrifice himself, to renounce all personal claims and to dedicate his life entirely to the service of others. This was the life Christ lived. His solidarity with mankind did not clash with His eternal life with the Father, but was simply its consequence.[87]

84 *Christmas Day*, 219–20.
85 Cf. *Sacrifice*, 191: "The evangelist says, speaking of His healing the sick, *Himself took our infirmities and bore our sicknesses;* as if every cure He wrought implied an actual participation in the calamity. He endured in this sense the consequences of sin in *particular* men; He endured the death which is the consequence of sin in *all* men."
86 Cf. *The Gospel of St. John*, 291–2: "there was a Man in whom the Father was perfectly satisfied, and –– the ground of His satisfaction was that this Man entirely loved men – entirely gave Himself up for men. He could be satisfied with nothing less than this; for nothing less than this was the expression of His own mind and will. In no act of less love than this could His love declare itself ."
87 Cf. *Country Churches*, 54: "Sin is what separates us from each other. Sin is what prevents us from understanding each other. Sin is what every man hugs in himself, and which keeps him away from other people. The Son of Man had no sin, and therefore He felt for all, and cared for all," and *The Prayer-Book*, 261: "Every one feels that the Son of Man is entering into this grief – knowing the inward source of it – penetrated by the sense of it, as he never

Thus, when Maurice spoke of "His taking the nature of you and of all men upon Him",[88] he meant that, through His intense love and sympathy, Christ identified Himself with all that affects man. And so men learn from Christ's earthly life that God's love reaches out to and encompasses every man, just as they know that in Him they find the truth about their own life.

Maurice's interpretation of the account of the temptation in the wilderness provides a good illustration of his concern. The Devil sought to draw Christ out of fellowship with God and tempted Him to live for Himself. As the struggle between Christ and the Devil differed only from the struggle that is waged between every man and the Devil in that it was far more radical,[89] it can impart knowledge of the true nature of that struggle with evil in which every man is always engaged.[90] In this respect, too, Christ was subjected to the same conditions as all men in that He overcame the Devil through the same trust in and obedience to God that every man is created to live by. Because Christ had entirely identified Himself with the state of man, every man is bound to understand himself as included in Christ's victory over the Devil.[91] The demonstration that the Devil has no power over Christ – the import of Christ's victory – gives man the certain knowledge that he does not belong to the Devil.[92] With this knowledge he can take heart when he is assaulted by the Devil, who tempts him to deny that he lives in Christ and receives his life from Him. Because Christ has demonstrated in His struggle with the Devil that He is the stronger, man knows that He, being the Head of every man, will also triumph over the Devil in man, and hence he can effectively reject his lying slander.[93]

Christ's victory over the Devil solves, therefore, the agonizing riddle which besets human existence. Men always have felt, like Job, that they have a friend as well as

can be. All that we feel weakly, imperfectly – all that we wish to feel and do not, we are sure was part of His sympathy and agony. What in us is mixed so consciously with selfish retrospections, indignations, apprehensions, we are sure was in Him the perfect sorrow of Love; possessing the most exquisite intenseness, just because it had no alloy; because it found no compensation or relief in hard or vengeful thoughts of any creature. He bore the burden alone."

88 *The Worship of the Church*, 39.
89 Cf. *Christmas Day*, 148–9: "if there was one in the world who entirely hated evil, who had never entertained it in his heart at all, would not you think that he would have the greatest fight of all? – – Do you not see that he would be able to feel fully what each one had felt imperfectly, that he was fighting the *common* enemy – fighting an enemy who was entirely separate from him, who was the most entirely unlike him, and who, therefore, was assaulting him more directly than he had ever assaulted any other being?"
90 Cf. p. 178–9: "by these temptations of our Lord we are to understand our own temptations, – – we kan only know what the spirit of evil is saying to us by knowing what he said to him."
91 Cf. *The Epistles of St. John*, 113–4: "our Lord's Temptation – – was a victory over the power of evil, not for Himself only, but for those whose nature He had taken."
92 Cf. *Theological Essays*, 29: "If we suppose that the Son of God had any advantage in that trial, any power save that which came from simple trust in His Father, from the refusal to make or prove Himself His Son instead of depending on His word and pledge, we shall not feel that a real victory has been won. And thence will come (alas! have come) the consequences of supposing our flesh to be accursed in itself, our bodies or our souls to be subject to a necessary evil, and not to be holy creatures of God, made for all good."
93 See *Tracts for Priests and People, No. XIV*, 65–6.

an enemy close to them. Yet they did not know who was the stronger, nor could they perceive to whom their own being truly belonged. These clouds obscuring men's knowledge have now been dispersed by Christ. Now men need neither belittle the powers of evil nor believe that they are enslaved to them. They know for sure that evil attacks them, but they also know that Christ is stronger than evil and that they will triumph through His victorious Divine Humanity.[94]

Maurice's anxiety to assert that Christ's incarnation unveils the truth about every man is also seen in his interpretation of the Virgin Birth. Maurice wished to uphold the doctrine of the immaculate conception of the Virgin Mary. Yet he insisted that Christ's birth was not "strange and anomalous", but "the most perfect carrying out and exhibition of the divine law and order".[95] The agency of the Holy Spirit in the conception of Christ finds its necessary explanation in the fact that it is "the Universal Man" who is coming into the world;[96] hence the Virgin Birth is "the most reasonable account of the entrance of the Head of Man into the ordinary conditions of humanity".[97] Nor does the fact that Mary gave birth to Christ imply that she occupies a unique position among women. She is merely a representative of the female sex.[98]

94 Cf. *The Kingdom of Christ* (1838) I, 25: "For I say, that when the Word was made flesh, and dwelt among us; when, in that flesh He passed through the trials, and troubles, and conflicts of man; when in that flesh He died a real death; when He rose again triumphant over that death; that he answered these dreadful doubts and questions of the spirit of man at once and for ever; and that no other answer whatsoever could have satisfied them. Then was that question, Who am I? – am I to account myself the child of light, or the child of darkness? – am I to believe that God looks upon this evil nature as myself, or as my enemy? – am I to believe that He regards me as His child, or merely as His servant – as one whom He wishes to save from death or sin, or one that He is only content to save if I please Him? – at once resolved by the most wonderful demonstration that men or angels ever saw." Because Christ's victory over the temptations of the Devil is a demonstration of an unalterable fact, the past, too, is interpreted and understood rightly: "Christ's conflict with the Spirit of Evil and His victory will be looked at, not as a solitary event, or great exception in the world's history, but – – as a witness that God had been resisting the Evil Spirit through every one of His fighting servants; as a consummation of their struggles; as a discovery of the strength in which they had prevailed; as a pledge that the fight shall not cease till the Divine purpose has been fully accomplished" *(Sequel, 258–9).*

95 *The Church a Family*, 97–8. Cf. also *The Unity of the New Testament*, 172–3: "Suppose – – that St. Matthew set out from the belief – – that Jesus was the eternal Son of God, would it seem to him strange that His incarnation should take place in what we call a miraculous way? Might it not seem to him, if I may use the expression, the most *natural* way in which such a person could be brought into this world? Might he not look upon this birth as rather explaining the law of other births than being merely an exception from them?", and *The Kingdom of Heaven*, 28: "he [St. Luke] was not recording a miracle which had interrupted the course of history, and deranged the order of human life, but was telling of a divine act which explained the course of history and restored the order of human life."

96 *The Church a Family*, 97: "the received doctrine respecting the way in which the Son of God became man, and was manifested as man, was the simplest that we could adopt. Any other contains something which shocks the heart and conscience, something which limits the Universal Man to narrow, partial conditions, something which interferes with the full and clear recognition of Him as the only-begotten of the Father." See also *Tracts for Priests and People, No. XIV*, 68.

97 *Tracts for Priests and People, No. XIV*, 68.

98 Cf. *The Church a Family*, 96: "her glory consisted in being a woman, that, and nothing

194

Being fundamentally a birth like any other birth, Christ's birth can explain human life. It demonstrates that marriage belongs to "a gracious economy; that it, in an especial manner, embodies and presents a divine Mystery."[99] Because Christ, the Creator and Upholder of mankind, has been born man, "each marriage, each birth, under the new dispensation, has a higher worth, a deeper signification, a more perfect sanctity, than could have belonged to it under the old."[100] Christ being the archetype of man, "an awful dignity has been put upon every child born into this world by the fact that He was actually born of a woman."[101]

Thus, for Maurice, the decisive point in the manifestation of Christ as the Son of Man is that the Head of the human race, "the root of humanity", assumed human flesh. As it is Christ's Divine Humanity which is constitutive both for the life of the incarnate Christ and for that of every man, it necessarily follows that the Incarnation imparts a true knowledge of the unchangeable state of all human beings. That man stands in Christ, and that man's life is entirely founded upon Christ are truths which are not propounded through notions and propositions, but are proclaimed through a historical fact, the earthly life of the incarnate Christ. This enabled Maurice to maintain that "He who was without sin showed forth to us in Himself what is the true normal condition of humanity."[102] In the incarnate Christ man sees "humanity in its orderly state, in its perfect harmony."[103] By sharing the conditions of the meanest and most despised of men, Christ demonstrated through His earthly life as a concrete example of a universal law that He is always working in man in order to impart His Divine Humanity.[104] It is only in the incarnate Christ that "we know what we are, and why we are created".[105] Therefore those who deny the Incarnation "are doing an injury to their fellow-men, – – they are robbing them of the truth which is the one great barrier against a cruel conception of God, against a degrading conception of humanity."[106]

more. – – Her song shows that she felt it as a benediction conferred upon her sex and upon herself as the lowly representative of it."

99 p. 98–9.

100 p. 98. When the Church proclaims the birth of Christ by a woman, "it discards the Manichæan dogma once and altogether. It claims the whole region of human feelings as a sanctified region. The higher mystery is not introduced for the sake of refinement, but for the sake of justifying God's laws, and man's conformity to them" (p. 99).

101 p. 96.

102 *Theological Essays*, 43.

103 *The Prayer-Book*, 367.

104 Cf. *Sermons* VI, 260: "It is the true essential humanity, God's original creation, now manifested in Christ, into which the man may enter, which he has a right to claim. – – He is not to ask for something novel and rare. He wants the permanent, the eternal, which was always with him"; *Christmas Day*, 247: "– – Christ hath made himself so entirely one with us, He is so completely the head of our race, that whatever befel Him must befal us," and *Sermons* II, 293: "He came to declare, and in His Own person to manifest, the truth that God and man are not divided, but eternally united."

105 *The Epistles of St. John*, 61. Cf. also *Sermons* I, 116: "only in that Image [Christ] can we know Him [God] or know ourselves; – – apart from Him we have an animal birth and an animal death; – – apart from Him, we have that death of sin, which only spirits can know; – – in Him we are raised, redeemed, united to God and to each other."

106 *The Epistles of St. John*, 330.

We have seen that, according to Maurice, the Incarnation did not denote a new and decisive turning-point in God's relationship to man, since the created universe and the human race have always stood in Christ. On the other hand, when Maurice maintained that the Incarnation was a decisive event in the history of mankind, it was in the sense that the incarnate Christ imparted the true knowledge of reality to men. Men experience the power of sin and the Devil so strongly in their own lives and in the created world, that they are liable to regard themselves as being without God, at the mercy of evil. This false understanding is rooted out by the Incarnation, which assures them that "their crimes and sins have not destroyed them yet, because Christ is on their side; because Christ is the advocate and supporter of that in them which He has Himself created; because it is not His will or His Father's will that that shall perish."[107] Through His coming in the flesh Christ satisfied the deepest longings of humanity by giving assurance that man, created in His image, belongs to the eternal world and has fellowship with God in Christ.[108]

Our analysis should thus have shown that Maurice interpreted the Incarnation as the visible manifestation of Him who has eternally been "the God-man", "the Son of God and the Son of Man." In the incarnate Christ man sees Him who, as the Image of God, has always revealed God and performed His will. At the same time he sees Him who, as the archetype of man, constitutes the life of every individual man. Thus in the incarnate Christ man attains to the true knowledge of reality.

107 *The Epistles of St. John,* 61. Maurice could write that Christ can "save thee from all thy enemies by saving thee from thyself" *(The Acts of the Apostles,* 265), implying that Christ reveals that He is always near to men, dispelling their false self-understanding which is the result of their sin and sensuality. To prove that the life given by Christ Himself cannot perish is to impart a true knowledge of the fact that the enemies men imagined to be invincible are in reality impotent. Hence Maurice could conclude that mankind has been saved from them. So man's salvation from sin, death and the Devil signifies that he is delivered from a false view of them as his victorious tyrants. The same thought is expressed in the following: "We are members of Christ's body. He is with every one of us. To believe that He is; to believe that we have Him as our Helper and Deliverer; to believe that He is stronger than all the enemies that are mightiest whithin us, this is infinite comfort and joy; this assures us that the sin which seems so near us is really divided from us; that it is not our master; that we shall be able to trample it under foot" *(Country Churches,* 59–60). True knowledge of reality delivers us from the powers of evil which give us a false insight into the nature of the Divine Order.

108 Cf. *Sermons* III, 90: "The Gospel of Jesus Christ – – does profess to show both why the life of man is not a vanity, and how it becomes vanity. The life of man, so the Gospel declares, is not vanity, for it is derived from the life of the Son of God. He is the Lord of every man. In Him is life, and His life is the light of men," and *Sermons* II, 234: "the revelation of Christ was the interpreter of the thoughts which He Himself had awakened in them; – – He Himself was the satisfaction of them."

Chapter VIII

CHRIST'S DEATH ON THE CROSS

1. The Problem of Maurice's Doctrine of the Cross

In Maurice's interpretation of the life and work of Christ the idea of redemption plays a prominent part. Thus, he tells us – to cite one typical statement – that "a redemption of man, a redemption of all that had been lost or disorderly in creation, was equally assumed in the preaching to Greeks, Romans, and Goths. It was set forth as an accomplished fact; as laying the only right and reasonable ground-work for human life; as that of which the Church, by its very existence, bore testimony."[1] Maurice frequently described redemption as a deliverance from the evil tyrants of mankind.[2] The entire life of the incarnate Christ he could consider as an act of redemption and deliverance from the powers of evil, culminating in His death: "The Cross gathered up into a single transcendant act the very meaning of all that had been, and all that was to be. God was there seen in the might and power of His love, in direct conflict with Sin, and Death, and Hell, triumphing over them by sacrifice."[3]

Because Christ's death upon the Cross constitutes the very essence of the Gospel, Maurice stated: "there is no subject upon which I desire more to be explicit. Every year and day convinces me more that our preaching will be good for nothing if the main subject of it is not the atonement of God with man in Christ – if we may not proclaim His sacrifice as a finished work; if we may not ground all our sacrifices upon it; if we stop short of the Eucharistic proclamation that God of His tender mercy hath given us His Son to be a full, perfect, and sufficient sacrifice, oblation, and satisfaction for the sins of the whole world. Any notions, theories, practices,

---

1 *Religions*, 224. Cf. also *Hope for Mankind*, 11: "God is Himself the Redeemer of mankind in that Son in whom He originally created man. The Redemption is from the power of death, and of the grave, from the power of all invisible tempters who draw our spirits into malice, falsehood, despair. The Redemption extends to the whole man, to the animal frame which is so curiously and wonderfully made, to the thoughts, counsels, purposes of the mind, to the desires, apprehensions, longings which carry us above ourselves; which must create ever new visions of bliss or of terror for us if we cannot grasp what is solid and not visionary."

2 Cf. *Theological Essays*, 78: "His [St. Paul's] Gospel to men was a manifestation or revelation of Christ to them, as one who had proved Himself to be their Lord, by entering into their death, and by redeeming them from their tyrants."

3 *Sacrifice*, 262. Cf. *Life* II, 383: "I think the only begotten Son, the Head of the race, has by His sacrifice redeemed us out of the power of the devil, the spirit of selfishness, and that this redemption is the necessary groundwork for that operation of the Spirit of love and sacrifice on our hearts to raise us above the power of that enemy," and p. 348: "the agony and bloody sweat of Christ – – was – – the battle of God with that which is resisting His nature."

which interfere with the fulness of this Gospel deprive men, it seems to me, of a blessing which has been bestowed upon them and to which they have a right – deprive them of the only effectual foundation for social and individual reformation."[4]

Maurice was convinced that he had expressed himself clearly on the significance of Christ's sacrificial death. His contemporaries, who thought otherwise, found him obscure. It was clear to them, however, that he was definitely opposed to the idea of Christ's death as a penal substitution for the sins of mankind, a view powerfully held by all the orthodox inside and outside the pale of the Church of England.[5] But they found it impossible to make out Maurice's own doctrine of the Cross. Many felt convinced that he was merely giving vent to Socinian and Unitarian ideas by teaching an exemplarist or Abelardian view of the atonement. Nevertheless, it was difficult to maintain this interpretation since Maurice obviously used terms and ideas characteristic of the "objective" doctrine of atonement. His contemporaries were simply unable to grasp his concept of Christ's sacrificial death.[6]

On the whole the next generation of Maurice students welcomed his strong criticism of the "objective" theory of atonement and inclined to see him as a representative of a "subjective" view of the atonement. More recently, however, there has been a growing feeling that this interpretation failed to grasp Maurice's true concern. It has been suggested that he had in fact expounded the "classic" idea of the atonement.[7] Most important is A. M. Ramsey's brilliant attempt at arriving at a fresh evaluation of Maurice's teaching on atonement. "Nowhere," Dr. Ramsey contends,[8] "did his contemporaries misjudge him more than in his doctrine of the Cross; and

4 *Life* II, 364–5. Cf. also *Sacrifice*, XLVI–XLVII: "That doctrine [of sacrifice] I hold, as our forefathers held it, to be *the* doctrine of the Bible, *the* doctrine of the Gospel. The Bible is, from first to last, setting forth to us the meaning of Sacrifice. If we cannot preach that that meaning has been accomplished, that the perfect Sacrifice has been made for the sins of the whole world, that God has made peace with us by the death of His Son, I do not see that we have any gospel from God to man."

5 Only Maurice's views on eternal life attracted greater attention from his critics. His fierce rejection of the "objective" doctrine of the atonement aroused them into their denunciation of him.

6 Even the astute James Martineau found himself unable to find any coherence in Maurice's statements: "In our author's doctrine, then, on this ancient subject [Christ's sacrifice], we find the old phenomenon repeated: it is clear and sound in what it removes; confused and incomprehensible in what it retains" (*Essays, Reviews, and Addresses* II, 452).

7 The first indication of this view is found in the preface to the English translation of Gustaf Aulen's "Den kristna försoningstanken", in which A. G. Hebert writes: "in spite of the prominence of the idea of the Incarnation in English theology, we have so far had only hesitating approaches towards the 'classic' idea of the Atonement. To this generalization, however, there is at least one exception to be made: the great name of F. D. Maurice" (*Christus Victor*, 1931, VIII). Hebert does not pursue the subject. – H. G. Wood makes the same suggestion by writing: "Another aspect of the Cross, which meant much to St. Paul and is neglected by us, appealed to Maurice. In the Cross, Christ vanquished principalities and powers, stripped them of their dominion over the minds and lives of men. Maurice, like present day Lutheran theologians, reaffirmed belief in a personal Satan. He thought we judged men too harshly, by refusing to recognise the power of the adversary. Likewise, we underrate the salvation Christ has brought, because we discount the victory of the Cross over the powers of evil" (op. cit., 110–1).

8 op. cit., 58.

nowhere, in my own belief, was his constructive achievement as a theologian higher. He saw beyond the ruts into which the doctrine had fallen, and anticipated a synthesis which has only in very recent years come into sight." Dr. Ramsey admits Maurice's obscurity and failure to set out his thoughts on the atonement clearly. Nevertheless Maurice's position was perfectly clear: "He was pointing the way beyond the false nineteenth-century dilemma, 'penal substitution or exemplarism', and anticipating the recovery of a more comprehensive doctrine. *The Doctrine of Sacrifice* brought back the unity of atonement and creation; it linked together the idea of sacrifice and the doctrine of the Trinity; it gave to many their first glimpse of the classic conception of the Cross as the divine victory."[9]

It must be readily acknowledged that these recent attempts to make Maurice an exponent of the "classic" doctrine of the atonement can point to many statements in his writings for substantiation. But if this interpretation is valid, then Maurice's doctrine of the Cross introduces a tension, indeed a contradiction, in his theological thinking, since the "classic" doctrine of atonement presupposes that sin, death, and the Devil are cosmic powers which have actually brought disorder to God's creation and have held men in bondage apart from God, the only source of life and love; against this background it asserts that through His life and death Christ has vanquished the powers of evil and restored the fallen creation. Consequently the Incarnation is the radical turning-point in God's history of salvation. We have, however, seen that this is exactly what Maurice denied, the Incarnation being, for him, a visible manifestation of eternal truth, an unveiling of unchangeable reality. Quite apart from the fact that Maurice's doctrine of the Cross has never received an exhaustive treatment, this issue makes it imperative that his interpretation of Christ's sacrificial death be examined afresh.

2. Maurice's Attitude to Previous Theories of Atonement

Maurice left no doubt about his view of the essential features of the "objective" theory of the atonement: "God had condemned all His creatures to perish, because they had broken His law; –– His justice could not be satisfied without an infinite punishment; –– infinite punishment would have visited all men, if Christ in His mercy had not interposed and offered Himself as the substitute for them; –– by enduring an inconceivable amount of anguish, He reconciled the Father, and made it possible for Him to forgive those who would believe."[10] This theory was insidious poison in Maurice's view: it destroyed the Gospel that God had entrusted to His Church. To oppose and reject this theory did not imply an attack on the Bible as the religious world angrily asserted; on the contrary, it was necessary to combat it since it rested upon premises which were entirely alien to the Bible.

The idea of penal substitution was based on an un-Biblical conception of God, because it presupposed "a Divine justice delighting in infinite punishment."[11] God

---

9 op. cit., 68. See also p. 62.
10 *Theological Essays*, 35.
11 *Theological Essays* (1853), 140. Reference to the first edition indicates that the quotation in question is limited to that edition.

was "the offended Sovereignty" because man had broken His law. He is pictured as a tyrant, a destructive deity, who finds pleasure in man's condemnation and death. In fact, God is identified with "an Evil Spirit".[12] Moreover, the reasoning behind the contention that God was induced to relinquish His will and intention to punish and destroy sinful men by the fact of Christ's penal death[13] was founded upon a heathen conception of sacrifice. The pagans viewed sacrifice as a means both of propitiating and also of obtaining special benefits from a divine power,[14] because they assumed it to be an arbitrary and selfish being whose favour they must win for themselves by offering it their sacrifices as an act of barter.[15] This notion of sacrifice inevitably makes selfishness the essential feature in man's relation to God. Man sacrifices in order to save and safeguard his own self; the purpose of his sacrifices is simply to appease the deity and make it connive at his will and wishes.[16]

12 *ibid.*

13 Cf. p. 140–1: "the Son of God has delivered His creatures from their Father's determination to execute His wrath upon them." – Maurice agreed with those who protested against the idea of God's vindictive righteousness and against the idea of the vicarious suffering and punishment of the innocent as an outrage against the moral sense of mankind: "We can forgive a fellow-creature a wrong done to us, without exacting an equivalent for it; we blame ourselves if we do not; we think we are offending against Christ's command, who said, *'Be ye merciful as your Father in Heaven is merciful'*, if we do not. We do not feel that punishment is a satisfaction to our minds; we are ashamed of ourselves when we consider it is. We may suffer a criminal to be punished, but it is that we may do him good, or assert a principle. And if that is our object, we do not suffer an innocent person to prevent the guilty from enduring the consequences of his guilt, by taking them upon himself. Are these maxims moral, or are the opposing maxims moral? If they are moral, should we, because God is much more righteous than we can imagine or understand, suppose that His acts are at variance with them? Should we attribute to Him what would be unrighteousness in us?" *(Theological Essays, 35–6)*. In protesting against the idea of vicarious suffering and punishment, Maurice followed Coleridge, who in his criticism of the "objective" theory of atonement maintained that it transfers what is valid in the non-personal world of things to the spiritual world, which is constituted by men with personal responsibility for their acts (see *Sacrifice*, 194).

14 Cf. *Sacrifice*, 69: "According to the heathen notion of sacrifice – – the offerings – – must be always experiments to obtain some benefit, which the power to whom they are presented can bestow, or to remove some evil which it is likely to inflict."

15 Cf. p. 34–5: "sacrifice may be the expression of the two most contrary feelings and states of mind; – the most contrary, and yet lying so close to each other in every man that only the eye of God can distinguish them, till they disinguish themselves by the acts which they generate. Sacrifice may import the confession of a child, who feels that he has nothing, and is a mere receiver. It may import the sense in a man that he has something to offer which his Maker ought to accept. It may import the trust of a child depending on One from whom it believes all good comes, aware that what is not good is its own. It may import the hope of a man – an uncertain sullen hope – that he may persuade the power he supposes is ruling, to give him some benefit, – to avert from him some danger. It may be an act of simple giving up, of surrender; it may be an act of barter, – a bargain to relinquish a less good on the chance of obtaining a greater."

16 Cf. p. XLVII: "I find from the history of the world expounded by the Bible, that there has been always a tendency in the corrupt heart of man to make Sacrifice itself the minister of man's self-will, self-indulgence, self-glorification. Instead of giving himself up to God, man seeks to make his God, or his gods, give up to him; he offers sacrifices, that he may persuade

200

When, as is the case in the "objective" theory of atonement, this heathen idea of sacrifice is fused with the Biblical teaching on Christ's sacrifice, the consequences are damaging. If Christ is regarded as He who, on behalf of mankind, brings His life as the only adequate sacrifice that can appease the vindictive wrath of God,[17] then He is not seen as leading men to God. On the contrary, He is seen to be protecting them from the living God and His will, because by His penal death He accomplishes "the deliverance of man out of the hand of God, the procuring a change in His purpose or will."[18] Furthermore, the idea of God being compelled by Christ's sacrifice to give up His punishment and condemnation of sinful mankind involves a conflict in the very nature of God between justice, which demands that righteousness be done, and mercy which forgives sin. Christ is no longer He who performs God's will; His task is, through His sacrifice, to induce God to give up His justice and let mercy prevail.[19] Finally, this conception of Christ's sacrifice as a penal substitution implies that it is conceived as "a provision that is contingent upon human events and human will."[20] Christ's sacrificial death, then, cannot manifest eternal necessary truth but represents an exceptional and unique act, necessitated by the sins of mankind. From these premises it even follows that Christ, by virtue of His death on the Cross, has gained a position in the Divine economy different from that which He had occupied from eternity. Far from being an act of obedience to God's will, His sacrifice must be interpreted as an attempt to deserve a position, not rooted in God's eternal will and decree, as the protector of man against God's wrath. Christ no longer lives by God's will and love, but has claimed an independent status because of the merit acquired through His sacrifice. Christ has become the chance founder of a religion.

The "objective" theory of the atonement only endorses and strengthens man in his selfishness. His self-centeredness directs him to seek deliverance not from sin, but only from the punishment of sin. He believes in Christ in the expectation that He, because of His penal death, can protect him from God's vindictive punishment of his sins. The only thought animating man is to save himself from the wrath and the

the power which he thinks he has wronged, to exempt him from the punishment of his wrong. This is man's theology; this is what has produced all the hateful superstitions under which the world groans."

17 Cf. p. 99: "We may build up for ourselves a notion of some one who has come to offer a great and gorgeous present to the Lord of all, which has changed His mind towards His creatures; we may unawares thrust into our Christian faith those heathen notions of sacrifice – –."

18 p. 141. Cf. also p. 134: "He redeems us from the curse which God Himself had denounced, and was prepared to enforce, against His creatures; – – He stepped in, as their Advocate, to shield them from His Father's indignation; – – He offered His blood which was an adequate purchase-money or ransom from it."

19 Cf. *Theological Essays* (1853), 139: "All notions respecting a conflict in the Divine mind between the claims of justice and mercy; all notions of the Son winning from the Father that which did not proceed from His own free gracious will; all notions which substitute the deliverance from punishment for the deliverance from sin; all notions which weaken the force of the words, or make them anything less than the classical words on the matter, "Lo, I come to do thy will, oh God", are it seems to me, of this kind, subversive of the Divine Revelation, Rationalistic in the worst sense of that word, not to be countenanced or tolerated."

20 *Sacrifice*, 109.

judgment of God. This theory prompts men to be interested only in their own salvation and security without any concern for their fellow-men and without caring for deliverance from their sins which constantly threaten them with destruction.[21]

However harsh, one-sided and even unfair Maurice was in his criticism of the "objective" doctrine of the atonement, it is not difficult to see why he considered it so abominable that it had to be refuted at all costs. This theory denied that perfect love is the true expression of God's unchangeable nature and will. Likewise, it made Christ's sacrifice a contingent act which took place only because of the existence of sin. It bound men to the history of time and space and excluded any understanding of Christ's sacrifice as the manifestation of His eternal life with the Father.

From Maurice's fierce criticism of the theory of penal substitution his orthodox contemporaries generally concluded that, with the Latitudinarians, Maurice was advocating an exemplarist theory of the atonement. There certainly appeared to be a good deal of justification for this interpretation. Maurice had not been afraid to use rationalistic arguments taken from the Unitarians in his criticism of the "objective" doctrine of the atonement.[22] Moreover, he did not openly and directly repudiate the contemporary liberal theologians who expounded what was virtually the Abelardian view of the atonement.[23] That it was wrong to lump Maurice together with them became apparent, nevertheless, when in 1862 Francis Garden published an article: *The Atonement as a Fact and as a Theory* in *Tracts for Priests and People*,[24] a series which Maurice himself had started with the purpose of demonstrating that the fullnes of the Gospel transcended the narrowness of both orthodox and liberal theological thought.

In his article Garden maintained that the teaching on the atonement of the Early

---

21 Cf. *The Gospel of St. John,* 338: "the Atonement by the blood of One who has taken the manhood into God, – who has raised, purified, redeemed, glorified the earthly nature by joining it to the Divine, – is changed into a cold, formal arrangement for delivering certain men from the punishment of a sin which has itself not been purged away. – – Nay, the cross of Christ – of Him who gave up Himself – is actually so presented to men, that they suppose it is the instrument by which self-seeking men may secure the greatest amount of selfish rewards." Thus Maurice characterized the "objective" doctrine of the atonement as "a scheme for persuading God to be at peace with that evil against which He has declared eternal war; a scheme for proving that He is still at enmity with a great majority of that race with which He has made peace in the blood of His Son" *(Sacrifice,* 212). When it is asserted that only those who believe in Christ's atoning death are acquitted from the wrath and punishment of God, Maurice understood this to mean that a barrier has been erected between the saved and the damned.
22 When Maurice was accused of being rationalistic in his treatment of the atonement, he rejected the accusation emphatically. He retorted that it was the "objective" theory that was rationalistic! It represented a "theology of consciousness", partly because it was based on "the sin-stricken conscience" and its false idea of God conditioned by mistrust and fear, and partly because it was systematized by means of "carnal conceptions and notions" (see *Theological Essays,* 33–4).
23 Although his silence was interpreted as approval, Maurice felt unwilling to launch a direct attack upon these liberals, since they were already under fire from the powerful orthodox religious world. Instead he thought it right to oppose their misconceptions indirectly by simply propounding the Biblical teaching on the atonement (see *Life* II, 367–8).
24 *1st Series, No. III,* 1–24.

Church, according to which Christ's death was a ransom to the Devil in order to deliver mankind from its thraldom under him, was completely out of date and no longer had any adherents. Garden also disapproved of St. Anselm and advocated the view that Coleridge's exemplarist interpretation of the atonement opened the way for a true understanding of its nature.

Maurice obviously found that Garden's article did not fulfil the purpose of his *Tracts.* He felt it his duty to remedy its deficiencies by publishing *Comments by Another Clergyman* in his series.[25]

Maurice was anxious to vindicate the position of the Early Church: "I cannot abandon so readily, as the writer [Garden] seems to do, that doctrine respecting the Redemption from the Evil Spirit which he says was overthrown by Anselm. – – To myself this belief of a Redemption out of an usurper has been one of quite unspeakable comfort. I know that I have been ready to use the very language, in hours of conflict and oppression, which appears so unreasonable. 'Tyrant! thou hast been paid thy full price. Thou hast had better blood than mine since thou desiredst it. Thou hast no right over me!' "[26] The idea of the atonement as a deliverance from the bondage of the Devil was more than merely a great comfort to Maurice personally; he asserted that it was a fundamental idea in the Bible and consequently must have an integral place in any genuine interpretation of Christ's work of redemption.[27] The reason why Maurice found fault with Coleridge's exposition of the atonement was precisely that it left no room for the idea that through His death Christ had achieved the victory over the Devil and the deliverance of mankind from the powers of evil: "Holding that belief, I maintain that the word Redemption points to the greatest of all divine and human realities, and is not, as Coleridge seemed to think, a metaphor drawn from earthly transactions; this Redemption could only have been effected by the death, burial, and descent into hell of the Son of God."[28]

Yet the "classic" theory of the atonement expressed only one aspect of Christ's redeeming work, though a most important one. Maurice found that even St. Anselm had pointed to a vital truth in emphasizing Christ's death as a satisfaction to God – it was "a witness against the notion that anything can satisfy God but a perfection, a holiness, a love which is the image of the only-begotten Son."[29] Coleridge,

---

25 *Ist Series, No. III,* 25–37.

26 p. 26. Oddly enough the students who consider Maurice a representative of the "classic" theory of the atonement have not called attention to this article, which seems to support their contention.

27 Cf. p. 27: "And though I would never speak of Christ's blood as Redemption money paid to the devil, I do maintain that a deliverance of men by their true Father from an evil power who had claimed him as his subjects, underlies all the lessons concerning Redemption in the Bible, and explains the passage in St. Peter, and a thousand others, which, as the writer of the Essay truly says, startle the modern reader. Any idea of Redemption but that which imports that it is the purchase of a creature out of bondage by a Creator who cares that it should be free, seems to me feeble, self-contradictory, impractical."

28 *ibid.*

29 p. 32. Maurice argued that the reason why St. Anselm had abandoned the teaching on the atonement held by the Early Church was that he had not experienced the true situation of man's life as one of bondage: "Living in an organized Christendom, he did not understand the import of Redemption as clearly as those who had seen men enslaved to false gods. Living

too, had an important contribution to make, representing a necessary protest "against all attempts to resolve the union of Christ with men and with God into artificial arrangements, and against the notion that the act of reconciliation can be anything less than a divine and transcendent act."[30]

In his *Comments* Maurice did not develop his own view on the significance of Christ's death upon the Cross. He limited himself to hinting that the various theories which had been expounded throughout the history of the Church all pointed to important aspects of Christ's redeeming work – none more so than the "classic" theory of the atonement.[31] Nevertheless, the article reveals that Maurice was not just an uncritical eclectic, borrowing from various doctrines of the atonement. His criticism appears to be rooted in a clear understanding of the significance of Christ's death.

3. Christ's Sacrifice

It was with good purpose that the series of sermons which Maurice published in 1854, dealing with "the might and efficacy of Christ's Cross",[32] was given the title: *The Doctrine of Sacrifice Deduced from the Scriptures.* Maurice wished to indicate that the idea of sacrifice is basic to a real understanding of Christ's death upon the Cross, and that it provides the key to the correct interpretation of the various aspects under which the Bible expounds the significance of the Cross.

Maurice in no way denied that Christ, by dying on the Cross, offered Himself as a sacrifice to God and that this act had a direct bearing upon the sins of man. But this was not to be taken to mean that Christ's sacrificial death occurred as necessitated by sin – this would involve regarding Christ's death upon the Cross as an exceptional event which was not rooted in God's eternal nature. To understand Christ's sacrifice "we must not start from the assumption of discord and derangement, however natural to creatures that are conscious of discord and derangement such a course may be; we must begin with harmony and peace, and so understand why they have been broken, how they have prevailed and shall prevail."[33]

We have previously pointed out that for Maurice sacrifice constitutes the life of the Triune God. That the Father eternally lives with the Son in the Spirit of love

in a cloister, he did not understand the meaning so well as preachers addressing men who were sunk in lusts and baseness" (p. 27–8).

30 p. 33. Maurice also spoke approvingly of the interpretation of Christ's death as "the bearing of sin, the endurance of the chastisement for sin", being "a witness against the notion that anything short of an actual endurance of human sorrow, an actual endurance of human evil by the Son of God can content creatures who are conscious of guilt, or can relieve them from the burden of it" (p. 32–3).

31 Cf. p. 25–6: "All of these are, I confess, very inadequate; each taken by itself will be merely the contradiction of some other; each may interfere with that great principle of Sacrifice, for which the writer of the Essay [Francis Garden] demands, and I think most rightly, the central place. But each may indicate some aspect of that all-embracing verity, which is above us, and yet in which we live; which none of us can speak of except most feebly and imperfectly, but which we must, nevertheless, make the main subject of our preaching."

32 *Sacrifice*, **XLIX**.

33 p. 110.

means that He is ever sacrificing Himself for the Son, and that the Son is ever sacrificing Himself to the Father to perform His will. Because God's nature is self-sacrificing love He from eternity decided to impart being to a universe and a mankind, and as Christ sacrificed Himself to carry out the will of the Father, the creation is grounded in the sacrificial life of the Trinity. Since man is created in Christ as the image of God, he is created to sacrifice himself for God and for his fellow-men. Sacrifice being the law of human life, it is not the state of sin that makes it necessary for man to sacrifice himself and lose his life. On the contrary, sacrifice and sin are diametrically opposed. Where the sin of selfishness exists, men refuse to sacrifice themselves for God and their fellow-men.

The fact that self-sacrificing love is the very essence of God's nature and that Christ's eternal sacrifice constitutes the life of the universe and of mankind, has, however, been gradually revealed and made manifest in time. The Bible is the account of how step by step God educated men to this knowledge.[34]

For Maurice it is a complete misunderstanding of the Old Testament sacrifices to see them as a means of propitiating a God who would otherwise punish and condemn man because of his sin. On the contrary, God appointed the sacrifices in order to make manifest that sacrifice is part of His being and to bear witness that it is His self-sacrificing love which has called Israel into existence and will always prove triumphant over human disobedience and unbelief.[35] At the same time the sacrifices served to demonstrate that man's true life consists in his sacrificing himself in faith

34 Cf. p. 113: "This wonderful truth [that obedience and sacrifice belong to man who is made in God's likeness, because they are involved in the very character and being of God Himself], so utterly contradictory to all the notions which men had formed to themselves of their Creator when they had supposed Him to be a mere power, who might exercise capricious vengeance upon them, and whom they were to conciliate by their sacrifices; – and yet which was implied in those very sacrifices, and in every act of real obedience and devotion, by parent, friend, warrior, sage – in every act which had been acknowledged as truly acceptable to the gods – in every dream of gods who themselves deigned to be deliverers of men; this truth, I say, had been unfolding itself gradually to the seers and sufferers among the chosen people. The Bible is a history of the discovery. – – The manifestation of this perfect Son of God, – of this Lamb, in whom dwelt the very law of sacrifice, whose whole mind and heart were fashioned into conformity with it, who never swerved, or broke loose from it – this manifestation was reserved for the latter days."

35 Cf. p. 87: "these provisions [of the Levitical law] asserted the divine doctrine that Sacrifice must proceed from the Will of God, and is perfected when the will of man is subdued to it;" p. 57: "By this earliest token [the offering of the first-born at the Passover], God signified that He had constituted a society upon this divine basis; a society which would stand as long as it confessed this basis – which would fall as soon as it tried to establish itself upon any other. What was true of the nation as a body, was true of each member of it. He was at once adopted into the covenant; he came in under this law of sacrifice," and p. 71: "A whole scheme of services, ordinances, institutes, is arranged and appointed under the most awful sanctions, by the Divine King – for what end? That He may re-establish an intercourse between Him and His subjects which has been interrupted; that He may bring back those whose hearts tell them they have wandered." Maurice's idea was that the sacrifices proclaimed that God always stood in fellowship with the Israelite, though, because of his sin, he might believe that he had cut himself off from God. The testimony of the sacrifices dispelled man's false understanding of God.

and trust to God. The visible acts of sacrifice are simply the outward token of the fact that man throws himself completely upon God as his loving Father.[36]

However, the revelation which the Old Testament sacrifices impart is imperfect. Therefore they awaken in man the expectation of One who will come and fully reveal God as self-sacrificing love and establish that sacrifice is the foundation and law of the universe. Because man experiences the imperfect character of all his sacrifices to God, this expectation also includes the hope that He who is to come will offer the perfect sacrifice of faith and obedience to God on behalf of all mankind.

These expectations were fulfilled by Christ's sacrificial death upon the Cross. Because of His obedience to His Father, Christ as the Son of God perfectly reflected His Father's inmost nature. Consequently, when He sacrificed Himself upon the Cross in fulfilment of His Father's will, God was revealed as self-sacrificing love.[37] Thus man sees God as He really is in Christ's sacrifice, and the false idea of God as a vengeful, destroying tyrant is dispelled.

The crucified Christ is, however, also the Son of Man, the Head of humanity, the life-giving principle of every man, and hence all mankind is embraced in Christ's sacrifice. When the Father was well-pleased with the sacrifice of His Son and accepted it as good and holy because it sprang from obedience to His will, He was, therefore, bound to consider every man righteous and holy.

On the Cross Christ is revealed as the One who unites and reconciles God and man. Christ did not, however, become the Mediator through His sacrificial death on Calvary. That event was merely the visible demonstration of what is eternally true. From eternity Christ has sacrificed Himself to fulfil the will of His Father, and, as the Father is eternally well-pleased with His sacrifice, He has always considered mankind good and holy seeing that Christ's sacrificial life is the sole foundation of its existence. So God and man are eternally united and reconciled in Christ's sacrifice, and it is this fact which is made manifest in Christ's death upon the Cross.[38]

4. The Cross as the Victory over Sin, Death and the Devil

For these reasons Maurice asserted that Christ's sacrificial death on Calvary is a visible demonstration of an eternal truth. Nevertheless we have seen that he described the significance of Christ's death in such a way that he seemed to consider it a deci-

36 Cf. p. 35: "Trust in a righteous and life-giving Being was, in his [Noah's] case, as much as in that of Abel, the meaning of his offering," and p. 14–5: "Must not all its [Abel's sacrifice] worth have arisen from this, that he was weak, and that he cast himself upon One whom he knew to be strong; that he was ignorant, and that he trusted in One, who he was sure must be wise; that he had the sense of death, and that he turned to One whence life must have come; that he had the sense of wrong, and that he fled to One who must be right? Was not his sacrifice the mute expression of this helplessness, dependence, confidence?"

37 Cf. *The Unity of the New Testament*, 404: "That Word – – has proved Himself in this act of dying to be the expression of God; for in his death has come forth the very innermost meaning of God's character, His essential love; yea, and His essential power."

38 Cf. *Sacrifice*, 109: "He has appeared in our world, in our nature; He has sacrificed Himself. In that sacrifice we see what He is – what He always has been. His acts here, plain and palpable, done mong men, done for men, have shown forth that perfect filial obedience to the Creator of all things, that entire filial union with the Eternal Father, which is the ground of the universe and the ground of our humanity."

sive and all-important act in God's history of salvation. On the Cross Christ is said to have conquered sin, death and the Devil and thereby delivered mankind from the bondage of its tyrants. In other words, Maurice appears to have expounded the "classic" view of the atonement. Whether this is actually the case, only a close examination of the relevant material will decide.

In a sermon on 1. Pet. 1,18–19, entitled *Christ's Sacrifice a Redemption*,[39] Maurice described how God delivered both the Jews and the Gentiles from the captivity into which they had fallen: "The sacrifice is a means to this end; the means which God uses; the power by which He ransoms the enslaved captive."[40] Mankind was in bondage because it lived and acted as if God did not exist. In their unbelief the Jews lived in subjection to visible things and in dread and horror of God as an evil and malignant despot.[41] The Gentiles, too, were enslaved "because they were living as if He [God] were not, as if some other than He were, their Ruler, and the Ruler of the universe."[42] A false knowledge of God is the essence of the captivity and tyranny under which men are groaning: "Do you not know that there has been an oppression on your conscience, a tyranny which you could not shake off? Do you not know that this oppression arose from a sense of separation from God, of being at war with Him? Do you not know that, while you have that sense, you cannot pray to Him as a Father, you cannot serve Him as a living God? And can any one emancipate his own conscience from this bondage?"[43] Just as slavery consists of a false knowledge of God, so redemption consists of the deliverance of men from these false conceptions by leading them to a clear knowledge of God and of His loving will. Through the Cross God accomplishes this deliverance, because "He proclaims His gracious will in that Son, who perfectly does His will, by offering up Himself."[44] God has manifested Himself as the self-sacrificing love that always regards and deals with men as His children. That is how the chains of bondage have been broken, and how men can now approach God "in the faith that He had owned them, accepted them, delivered them."[45]

So, for Maurice, deliverance from sin does not mean deliverance from a tyrannous power that holds men in real slavery. Sin is ignorance of God's true nature and of His relation to mankind. This spiritual blindness, which may well be called a tyrant enslaving man, is driven out by the perfect knowledge of God given by Christ's sacrificial death on the Cross.

In *Theological Essays* Maurice wrote that Christ "became subject to death, *"that He might destroy him who had the power of death, that is, the Devil."* Here are

39 *Sacrifice*, 115–30.
40 p. 119.
41 See p. 124.
42 p. 126.
43 p. 127–8.
44 p. 128.
45 p. 123. Cf. also p. 127: "He who vindicated for us a right to enter into the presence of God, and enabled us to enter into it – – He has found the redemption for us." This deliverance from a false knowledge of God can also be expressed by saying that Christ "took away the sins of the world" because He "lifted you out of your miserable subjection to visible things, out of your dark and slavish notions concerning God, out of your dread and horror of Him" (p. 124).

reasons assigned for the Incarnation and the death of Christ. He overcame death, their common enemy, by submitting to it. He delivered them from the power of the Devil."[46] But what Maurice meant by Christ's victory over the Devil is demonstrated clearly in a sermon on Hebrews 2, 14–15: *Christ's Death a Victory over the Devil*.[47] Here Maurice described the Devil as the slanderer and accuser, who seeks to beguile man into false ideas about God, his fellow-men, and finally about his own "I".[48] To support his accusations the Devil refers to sin and misery as evidence of God's ill-will towards man, but the strongest argument he employs in his lying campaign is death.[49] Because men consider death to be something final, putting an end to all life and making annihilation the fate awaiting the entire creation,[50] the Devil attempts to show that the very fact of death proves that God is either indifferent to His creation or wills its destruction, or, if man still insists on God's mercy, that God is powerless to prevent death from thwarting His purposes.[51] Thus, the Devil's power lies in false accusations and in the distorted picture of reality that he seduces man to accept by working on his fear of death.

However, from the Cross "came forth an answer to his [the Devil's] whispers; – – the answer is a complete one; – – the moment we accept it, his chain is broken for us; because God has in truth broken it for our race."[52] In Christ's sacrificial death God has been manifested as self-sacrificing love, always upholding His creation and treating men as His children; by this act the accusations of the Devil have been shown to be false and so the power he has held over men has been wrested from him. In this way Christ's death conquers the Devil.

Similarly, on the Cross Christ defeated death and broke its power.[53] Maurice could describe death as the cruel enemy of mankind, separating man and God, and isolating

---

46 *Theological Essays*, 37.

47 *Sacrifice*, 232–47.

48 Cf. p. 250: "The Accusing Spirit – – misrepresents the mind and will of God towards us, the acts and dispositions of our fellow-creatures, our own moral condition. He leads us to suspect an enemy in our Father, an enemy in every brother, an enemy in our own heart." See also p. 237–9.

49 Cf. p. 240: "The words of my text point to the greatest and most decisive argument of all, by which this accusation is supported. That Devil, it boldly says, was he who had the power of *Death*."

50 Cf. *ibid*.: "Whatever reasons some higher and better teacher might suggest to men for trusting God, for believing that He intended good to them, and not evil – whatever rains from heaven and fruitful seasons might tell them, Death was the answer to them all. That was the great ordinance for the whole race, for the whole creation. That stopped all the projects of the individual man; that made all purposes of improvement abortive – –. That cut off all the bonds of family, of tribe, of nation. – – That said, Talk of your freedom as you please; there is this death always waiting to crush it at the last."

51 Cf. p. 241: "This was one part of the argument; one demonstration that God meant nothing by the universe He had formed, or that He meant destruction by it; or that His purpose, if it was a gracious one, had been defeated."

52 *ibid*.

53 Cf. *Country Churches*, 181: "Whatever difference there was between Jews and the other people of the earth, there was one thing that was common to them – Death was common to them, they all died. And Death said to every man, 'I am coming to thee because thou hast done wrong; if all were right with thee, thou wouldst live and not die. I shall take thee away from thy neighbours, and thy family, and from all thy plans and purposes. Thou mayest

men from each other.[54] Yet his view was that it is not the mere fact of death but man's distrust of God that creates fear of death.[55] Since man, in his unbelief, regards God as an oppressor and destroyer, he believes that it is God Himself who has sent death in order to destroy the universe and mankind. When, therefore, Maurice wrote: "Thanks be to that God whom we have counted our enemy, who we supposed had pleasure in our death, for conquering the very enemy we accused Him of sending among us,"[56] his meaning is that Christ by His death proclaims God as perfect love, sacrificing Himself to bestow life, and thus imparts the knowledge that God desires His creation to live in fellowship with Him.

Furthermore, Christ conquered death in the sense that He unveiled the true nature of death and thereby proved that man's horror of death is without any foundation. When Christ gave Himself up to death, He was not forced to do so by the fact that death is an irresistible and cruel enemy. He took death upon Himself in obedience to the will of His Father. That Christ by His sacrificial death gave Himself up to His Father means that He died from self in order to live for Him only. Christ's death is simply the consummate expression of the obedience of faith towards God, and so, by this very act, Christ demonstrated that death, far from being an enemy which separates and destroys, unites man with God and therefore leads him to life. Consequently Maurice could assert of Christ: "He had solved the mystery of death. He had changed it into a Sacrament of fellowship."[57] In Christ man can see the essential nature of death. Death, being a renunciation of and dying from self, is precisely the bond uniting God and man. Death does not mean the destruction of man but is God's means of raising him to a new life.[58] Christ's death dispels the fear of

have friends and helpers above and below, but who will help thee against me? Who will take thee out of my hands? And if I once get thee, dost thou think that I shall ever lose hold of thee?' So Death spoke to each man; so Death claimed each man as his prize and his slave. Who could answer him? St. Paul says Christ has answered him. The Son of God became a man. He conquered Death for other men. He bade Death do his worst on Him. He did this not in obedience to Death, for He was not Death's servant; but in obedience to His Father, the everlasting God."

54 See, as another typical instance, *Sacrifice*, 243-4.
55 Cf. p. 244: "Death is utterly horrible as long as it is linked to that distrust of God which is Sin, and the root of all sins; so long as it keeps that up in our minds; so long as it teaches us that our safety is in flying from His presence." See also *Christmas Day*, 251-2.
56 *Sacrifice*, 245.
57 *Sermons* V, 197. Cf. *Sacrifice*, 242: "God perfects His only-begotten Son through death. That which was said to be the clear declaration that men are regarded by God as enemies, becomes the sign which Christ gives of His Sonship − −. Christ bears death not in obedience to an inevitable fate, but to a loving will; not because the tyrant has conquered the earth and those who dwell upon it, but as an eternal testimony that he has not conquered it − that it belongs to the Creator, not to the Destroyer. Death seems to make the great and final chasm, − of which all other separations were but dim prophecies, − the chasm between the Father and Him in whom He delighted. Death is made the pledge of Their eternal union; the pledge of Their infinite satisfaction in each other."
58 Cf. *Christmas Day*, 331: "death changed its nature when it passed upon Christ, and became a new birth," and *Sequel*, 258: "Then, too, all pain and anguish and death will be regarded as receiving their interpretation from His Agony and Passion and Death, that Death being the vindication of the goodness of His Father in permitting it to His Creation, and showing

death and thereby removes its sting. His victory over death signifies, therefore, that He imparts a true understanding of the fact of death in contrast to the false conception which the Devil seeks to impress upon men.[59]

It is true that in his account of the significance of the Cross Maurice makes use of terms and ideas which might suggest that he was propounding the "classic" view of the atonement. But our analysis has demonstrated that he used them in his own way. Man is truly enslaved but the bondage and the tyranny under which he suffers are ultimately due to a false understanding of reality. Man imagines God to be a vengeful and malignant tyrant and believes that sin, death and the Devil will succeed in destroying the universe and mankind. True redemption and deliverance from the foes of man can be achieved only by a full and perfect knowledge of reality. Because Christ by His sacrificial death upon the Cross has revealed that God in His love always sacrifices Himself for men, it can be said that He has broken the power of sin, death, and the Devil and delivered mankind from its bondage.

5. The Cross as the Manifestation of the Eternal Mediator

We have said enough already to show that Maurice's interpretation of the Cross is determined by his basic conviction that God's revelation imparts perfect knowledge of unchangeable reality. That Christ is the eternal Mediator between God and man and that mankind is always united and reconciled to God through Christ's eternal sacrifice is the truth which is manifested upon the Cross. This truth cannot be expressed effectively through dogmas and intellectual propositions but must be proclaimed through the actual death of a real person, since revelation takes place only through facts which can speak directly to all men, without the mediation of the understanding or the intellect.[60]

To an astonishing degree students of Maurice have failed to see that for him the Cross is the visible manifestation of the eternal truth that God for Christ's sake is always reconciled to mankind, forgiving its sins and dealing with every man as His child. This is undoubtedly because they have been misled by the emphatic way in which Maurice spoke of the Cross as "a Reconciliation", as "an Atonement",

that there is a birth to which all its travail and groans are leading. Then that sorrow and agony and death will be taken to interpret, sanctify, and fulfil all that men have endured anywhere or in any time for truth and right."

59 Cf. *Sacrifice*, 245: "we can now answer the Accuser with these words: 'We know what death is, for Christ has died. We know that His death is the proof of God's eternal love, the pledge that He has reconciled the world to Himself; the encouragement to draw nigh to Him; the assurance that a new and living way is opened into His Presence, and that in that Presence is fulness of joy'."

60 Cf. p. 205: "St. Paul knew how poor words were as a translation of all the secret love-messages and pledges which the blood of Christ carried to the wanderer. He resorted to explanations when they were necessary; he always joyfully returned to the language which implied an act, sufferings, a person. The Spirit who governed him would not suffer his explanations to put themselves in place of that which they were to explain, or to hinder the direct communion which the living symbols expressed and kept up."

"a Sin-Offering" and "a Propitiation". By exploiting every term or idea to be found in the Bible in his interpretation of the Cross, he gave his readers the impression that he ascribed the same constitutive significance to Christ's sacrificial death as the New Testament writers do. The untenability of this interpretation becomes apparent as soon as his statements concerning the Cross and its implications are considered in their context and in the light of his polemics against other theories of the atonement.

That Maurice made use of Biblical terms and ideas in his interpretation of the Cross as the visible manifestation of Christ as the eternal Mediator was not due to any intellectual confusion. Nor was it, as J. H. Rigg suggested, a question of a *disciplina arcani* as though Maurice deliberately veiled his own interpretation behind the phraseology of the Bible and the doctrines of his Church so as to make it more palatable to his contemporaries. Maurice was sincere in his belief that what he proclaimed was simply to be found in the Bible and in the doctrinal standards of his Church. Not for one moment did he suspect that there was any contradiction between the teaching of the Bible and his own interpretation of the significance of the Cross. As he was convinced that the Bible proclaimed the full and perfect truth, he could reproduce its ideas on Christ's sacrificial death without any reservations. Furthermore, he feared that to depart from the Biblical presentation of the Cross would imply the advancing of one's own theories of Christ's sacrificial death instead of letting this event speak for itself and convey its own message to "the hearts and consciences of mankind." The Bible's proclamation of the Cross must not be spoiled by the dogmas and concepts of the understanding, since the Bible follows the principle of merely presenting concrete facts as the means of demonstrating eternal truth.

Maurice appeared to be justified in seeing no disparity between his interpretation of Christ's sacrificial death and that of the New Testament writers in that he, too, accepted it as the crowning event in God's revelation to mankind. The Cross manifested so clearly and unambiguously the truth about God's relation to man in Christ that it completely dispelled man's ignorance and distrust of God. Only on Calvary does man see God's love victoriously revealed. In Christ's death man meets God as "the Reconciler", "the Redeemer", "the Atoner", "the Deliverer" and "the Conqueror", who wars against everything that prevents men from attaining to fellowship with Him, that is to say, against the false idea of reality which is the fruit of man's unbelief and selfishness. Because these hindrances were destroyed by the Cross, Christ's sacrificial death has changed man's situation, for man has now received a perfect knowledge of God and of himself as living in fellowship with God. The Cross has truly removed sin, because it has vanquished man's fear and distrust of God.[61]

61 Cf. *Sacrifice*, 178: "the Mediator, He of whom all covenants and sacrifices had been testifying, for whom all periods had been waiting, had been manifested once in the crisis or winding up of the ages to put away sin by the sacrifice of Himself"; p. 183: "The sacrifice of a Son who came to do His Father's will, who entirely gave Himself up to do it, did reach the conscience, it did take away sin. How rightly then may this sacrifice be called a Sin-Offering!", and p. 182: "the revelation of God is the revelation of a Sacrifice. And though I have maintained that sacrifice is entirely independent of sin – that the most pure and perfect state we can conceive, is the state of which sacrifice is the Law – I have contended, as strongly, that nothing but sacrifice can take away sin."

The Cross has really reconciled and united man to God, for the true knowledge of God makes man trust Him as His loving Father.[62]

Maurice's only desire was to expound the Bible as containing the true and perfect revelation of God. For this reason he felt bound to adopt into his own teaching all the aspects under which the New Testament regards the Cross. Although he was apparently successful in this endeavour, a closer analysis always reveals a radical reinterpretation of the Scriptures. Maurice had an amazingly deft, and often ingenious, way of making the Biblical texts say precisely what his Platonic conception of reality demanded that they say. This was done in such a way that the reader hardly notices that Maurice is twisting the Biblical texts to make them the vehicle of his own views. His sermons in *The Doctrine of Sacrifice* are illuminating in this respect!

The reason why his readers often fail to recognize this drastic reinterpretation is that Maurice appears to have accepted all the aspects under which the New Testament considers Christ's sacrifice. Thus, he assented wholeheartedly to the idea of Christ as the Mediator between God and mankind, in whom men are reconciled to God and have been justified and sanctified. However, in contrast to the New Testament, this is not based on the fact of Christ's death on the Cross, but on Christ's eternal sacrifice. The events of salvation, which are recorded in the Bible, are relegated, so to speak, to eternity and regarded as eternal, unchangeable truths, which are subsequently revealed in time and space through a specific history of revelation. Maurice could accept everything in the Bible on the condition that all that is contingent, particular and unique is excluded. Not for a moment did he cast doubt upon the fact that Christ truly became man and died upon the Cross. But whereas the New Testament writers understood this event as the entry of the new order of redemption and salvation into this world living under the bondage of sin, death and the Devil, Maurice saw it as the manifestation of an eternal reality. The Platonic conception of reality was such a self-evident truth for him, that, with intuitive, almost somnambulistic mastery, he redrafted the Biblical history of salvation by eliminating all traits of uniqueness.

As already mentioned, Maurice's own contemporaries were usually in doubt as to his own understanding of the significance of the Cross. It was evident that he was violently opposed to the "objective" doctrine of the atonement, but the purpose of his criticism was not at all obvious, since he himself used terms and ideas characteristic of this doctrine. This observation provoked J. B. Mozley to make the following comment on Maurice in a review of his *Theological Essays:* "He appears to regard established forms of belief as things to be knocked down; as so many incrustations, harsh and artificial, which surround the essential truth, and exclude the mind from access to it. But after knocking down the established formulas, when he comes to give his own, we find that it does not, substantially, so much differ from the establis-

---

62 Cf. p. 174: "The alienation must be removed; the man himself must be atoned with his
   Maker." It is not God who must be reconciled, but the reconciliation is accomplished in the
   removal of man's feeling of being separated from God. This is achieved in Christ's death upon
   the Cross which proclaims God's love, and hence it may be said that "the new world exists
   to testify of the atonement of God and His creatures, of their union and fellowship with
   each other, on the ground of the Sacrifice that He has made" (p. 215).

hed one."[63] To substantiate this statement Mozley referred to the following passage by Maurice: "Supposing all these principles gathered together; – supposing the Father's will to be a will to all good; – supposing the Son of God, being one with Him, and Lord of man, to obey and fulfil in our flesh that will by entering into the lowest condition into which men had fallen through their sin; – supposing this Man to be, for this reason, an object of continual complacency to His Father, and that complacency to be fully drawn out by the Death of the Cross; – supposing His death to be a sacrifice, the only complete sacrifice ever offered, the entire surrender of the whole spirit and body to God; is not this, in the highest sense, Atonement?"[64] Mozley commented on this as follows: "If this passage means, what it appears to do, that the life and death of our Lord, regarded as one sacrifice, are perfectly pleasing and acceptable to the Father, and that for the sake of that life and death He is reconciled to or forgives the sins of man, we must confess we do not see the great difference between Mr. Maurice's doctrine and that which he has been so strongly impugning; nor can we see exactly the reason why this Essay [on the atonement] has been written."[65]

Mozley's strictures, as might be expected of such an observer, are not wholly without foundation. Considered by itself the essay on the atonement in *Theological Essays* is perplexing, but considered in the light of Maurice's theological thinking as a whole and with due regard being paid to his peculiar way of arguing and expressing himself, the matter becomes quite simple. Maurice had to oppose the orthodox doctrine of the atonement not only because it asserts God to be a *justitia distributiva,* but also because it presupposes that man's sin had destroyed the fellowship between God and men, making a new divine act of salvation necessary for the restoration of that which man had forfeited. Maurice's arguments were intended to dispose of the assumptions involved in any interpretation of the Cross as a constitutive and unique event. Having eliminated them Maurice was perfectly free to speak of Christ as the Mediator and of His work of reconciliation and atonement through His full and perfect sacrifice to God on the Cross. Thus the fact that Maurice ruthlessly knocks down "the established forms of belief" was not due to morbid querulousness, as Mozley suggested; he had a definite purpose: the repudiation of the idea of the uniqueness of the divine act of redemption. Once this had been achieved, and Maurice, in Mozley's word's, had removed "the harsh and artificial incrustations", then the way had been opened for an understanding of "the essential truth"; it became possible to see the Biblical history of salvation as the manifestation of an eternal reality.[66]

---

63 *Essays Historical and Critical* II, 279. Cf. p. 272: "He appears to us sometimes more unsound as a destroyer than as a constructor. He has a bias against all existing forms of opinion, all doctrines, in which they are actually held and received, and seems to consider it his special vocation to assail them. But allow him to construct the doctrine himself, and put it out in his own formula, and it will not be very unlike the original one."

64 *Theological Essays,* 38.

65 op. cit., 280.

66 A. M. Ramsey appears to admit the force of Mozley's criticism of Maurice in the following comment: "he [Maurice] denies that the death of Christ is rightly regarded as penal and that the satisfaction consisted in the death. Having made this denial *(Theological Essays,* 3rd edition, p. 117), he goes on to affirm something not unlike what he denies. 'Since nowhere is the contrast between infinite Love and infinite Evil brought before us as it is

Both as a polemist and as a constructive thinker Maurice was extremely consistent. He knew with intuitive certainty what to accept and what to reject; he was always well aware what he was aiming at. Once it has been realized that a Platonic idea of reality is at the core of his interpretation of the Bible and of his attitude to the various theological systems, everything becomes lucid. All his expositions and polemical remarks, however fragmentary and casual they may appear, will be seen to stem from a theological totality of view, marked by consistency and coherence.

6. The Cross as the Manifestation of "the True, Sinless Root of Humanity"

We have seen that Maurice regarded the Incarnation as a revelation not only of God, but also of man. This is also true of his understanding of Christ's sacrificial death. In Christ crucified man sees not only the Son of God, but also the Son of Man, "the Man", "the Head of humanity", and therefore the Cross reveals the truth concerning man's own existence. While it is true that this aspect does not appear to occupy the same prominent position in Maurice's writings as his interpretation of the Cross as the proclamation of God's self-sacrificing love, its crucial importance is evident

there, we have the fullest right to affirm that the Cross exhibits the wrath of God against sin, and the endurance of that wrath by the well-beloved Son. For wrath against that which is unlovely is not the counter-acting force to love, but the attribute of it. Without it love would be a name, and not a reality. And the endurance of that wrath or punishment by Christ came from His acknowledging that it proceeded from love, and His willingness that it should not be quenched till it had effected its full loving purpose. The endurance of that wrath was the proof that He bore in the truest and strictest sense the sins of the world, feeling them with that anguish with which only a perfectly pure and holy Being, who is also a perfectly sympathizing and gracious Being can feel the sins of others. Whatever diminished His purity must have diminished His sympathy. Complete suffering with sin and for sin is only possible in one who is completely free from it.' In the paragraph just quoted Maurice expressed what he felt to be the heart of the matter" (op. cit., 59–60). Quite apart from the question of how we are to understand this passage, it is not correct to say that it expresses the essentials in Maurice's doctrine of the atonement. Maurice expressly stated how the exposition in question was to be interpreted, and the six caveats which Ramsey enumerates (see p. 60–1) clearly show that Maurice understood these terms differently from the adherents of the "objective" doctrine of the atonement. Furthermore, Maurice introduced the passage under consideration with a statement clearly indicating that we are dealing with a subordinate line of thought: "I do not deny that besides these leading convictions which take possession of the heart as it contemplates the Cross of Christ, there are others apparently of a different kind" (p. 117). Finally, a weighty argument against attributing any crucial significance to the ideas in the passage, quoted above, is the fact that it does not occur in the first edition of *Theological Essays,* the section on pp. 139–42 having been subjected to a thorough revision involving the insertion of the passage in the later editions, to which Ramsey refers. The reason is undoubtedly that critics had maintained that Maurice did not speak of Christ bearing God's wrath and punishment, and that he wished to avert this criticism by demonstrating that he was quite capable of interpreting the Cross from this angle as well. However, Maurice did not mean to say that by His sacrificial death Christ had satisfied God's wrath and thus averted His punishment; his point was that, by His sympathy and solidarity with men, Christ felt Himself subject to the divine wrath which is the reaction of love against sin, and so He endured the punishment which rightly must be meted out to sin. Thus the Cross proclaims that God's love is always opposed to sin, and that sin always entails its own punishment – and this must be so until love ultimately triumphs.

214

from Maurice's discussion with John McLeod Campbell on the subject of his *The Nature of the Atonement and its Relation to the Remission of Sins and Eternal Life* (1856).[67]

In this book Campbell had rejected the idea that Christ endured sufferings and death on behalf of mankind in order to satisfy the divine righteousness so that man might be saved. By way of contrast he argued that the atonement is the revelation of a loving God who desires the salvation of all men. Maurice declared himself perfectly in sympathy with Campbell's concern: "I think I entirely accept your idea of the atonement so far as it bears on the relations of God with each individual soul."[68] However, Campbell had so confined himself to this one aspect of the atonement that he had failed to see how, according to the Bible, the Cross is related to the state of all mankind. Maurice illustrated his criticism by pointing out the deficiencies in Luther's understanding of the relation between the atonement and justification by faith. Maurice certainly assented to Campbell's description of Luther as a man who had "surely entered into St. Paul as no one else has done".[69] Nevertheless, Luther and his disciples had introduced an individualism into their doctrine of justification by faith which was completely foreign to the teaching of the Bible concerning the Cross. They had begun with the individual's consciousness of sin and guilt and had thus been led to lay an exclusive stress on the significance of the atonement for guilt-stricken consciences. On these premises the relevance of the atonement must be exhausted with the justification of the individual sinners.[70] The Bible, however, does not start with the sinner but with God, and for this reason it views the atonement first and foremost in its significance for the human race and only then for the individual.[71] This is clearly seen in the preaching of St. Paul and St. John: "while St.

67 See *The Gospel of St. John*, 492–8 and *Life* II, 297–8.
68 *Life* II, 298. Cf. *The Gospel of St. John*, 492: "I cannot feel too thankful to the pious and excellent writer for the light which he has thrown upon this subject; for his exemplary charity to those with whom he is at variance; for his successful effort to reclaim the doctrine from the region of hard scholasticism to the region of practical life and holiness; above all, for his vindication of the character of God as a Father, and for his determination to assert, that likeness to His character, and communion with Him, are the ends which God is seeking for us, and which we are to seek from Him. In every one of these respects, I wish to be a learner from Mr. Campbell."
69 *The Gospel of St. John*, 494.
70 Cf. p. 496: "They start from evil, from the conscience of evil in themselves, and then either each man asks himself, – 'How can I be free from this oppression which is sitting so heavily upon me?' or the schoolman asks, 'What divine arrangement would meet the necessities of this case?' Of course, the results of these two inquiries are very different; and Mr. Campbell has done an immense service to Christian faith and life by bringing forth the former into prominence, and throwing the other into the shade. His book may be read as a great protest of the individual conscience against the utter inadequacy of the scholastic arrangements to satisfy it."
71 Cf. *ibid.*: "We need not begin with the sinner; we may begin with God. And so beginning, that which speaks most comfort to the individual man may not be first of all contrived for his justification. God may have reconciled the world unto Himself; God may have atoned Himself with mankind; and the declaration of this atonement, the setting forth the nature and grounds of it, and all the different aspects of it, may be the real subjects of those Epistles [of St. Paul], in which the individual man has found the secret of his own blessing, of his own restoration; but which he mangles and well-nigh destroys when he reconstructs

Paul's main work was to set forth the fact of atonement, laying its groundwork always in the righteousness of God manifested in Christ, and ascending, in the Epistle to the Ephesians especially, to the purpose which He purposed in Christ before the worlds were; St. John's calling was to trace this last idea to its source in God Himself; to exhibit the original consitution of man in the Divine Word; to set forth atonement as the vindication of that constitution, and the vindication of the right of all men to enter into it; to set forth the union of the Father with the Son in one Spirit, as the ground of the reconciliation of man, and of his restoration to the image of his Creator."[72] By following the theological method of St. Paul and St. John one not only attains to a full understanding of all the implications of the Cross, but even theological ideas such as the substitution of Christ and imputed righteousness, which Campbell rejected as illegitimate, will be seen to express vital truths.[73]

In his criticism of Campbell Maurice did not elaborate upon this aspect of the Cross. He did, however, employ his characteristic key-words which clearly indicated what he was driving at. Thus, when Maurice maintained that the atonement is the vindication of "the original constitution of man in the Divine Word", he wished to point out that Christ's sacrificial death implied the revelation of Him as the Head of humanity and, therefore, of "the whole mystery of man". Once it is realized that this concept forms an integral part of his interpretation of the Cross,[74] a number of statements, which at first sight appear puzzling, fall into place and will be seen to be a consistent expression of his basic convictions.

In his essay on the atonement in *Theological Essays* Maurice wrote that "Christ was actually the Lord of men, the King of their spirits, the Source of all the light which ever visited them, the Person for whom all nations longed as their Head and

them upon the basis of his individual necessities, and makes them utter a message which has been first suggested by them," and p. 497: "My great complaint of the oracles of the English religious world is, that they do give a most unusual and unnatural sense to the word Atonement; that they give it a most contracted signification; that they lead their disciples to form a poor opinion of its effects; that they do not follow Apostles and Evangelists, in connecting it with the whole revelation of God and the whole mystery of man."

72 p. 497.

73 Cf. p. 498: "On many points I believe I could adopt forms of language usual among Calvinistical divines, to which Mr. Campbell, looking at them from his point of view, rightly objects as involving fictions," and *Life* II, 298: "Perhaps I hold more strongly than you [Campbell] do a reconciliation of the whole of humanity with God in Christ, which would enable me to use some of the expressions which you would reject; though I should be very careful of using them, lest I should convey a dishonest impression, and be suspected of differing with your great axiom."

74 In a review of Campbell's book in *The National Review*, 1856, R. H. Hutton briefly made the same critical point as Maurice. This is not fortuitous, since Hutton had been influenced by Maurice and was one of the very few who had grasped the importance of the idea of Christ as the Head of mankind for Maurice's interpretation of Christ's incarnation and death upon the Cross. Besides Hutton only J. Scott Lidgett has seen that for Maurice Christ's sacrificial death implies a manifestation of the true nature of man. He indicated this in his treatment of Maurice's teaching on the atonement in *The Spiritual Principle of the Atonement* (1898) and in greater detail in his *The Victorian Transformation of Theology, Being the Second Series of Maurice Lectures Delivered at King's College During the Lent Term 1934* (London 1934). His analysis is, however, unsatisfactory for the reason that he interpreted Maurice in the light of his own Neo-Hegelian position.

216

Deliverer, the root of righteousness in each man. The Bible speaks of His being revealed in this character; of the mystery which had been hid from ages and generations being known by His Incarnation. If we speak of Christ as taking upon Himself the sins of men by some artificial substitution, we deny that He is their actual Representative."[75] The central idea in this passage is that Christ crucified is none other than the Head of humanity, the One who truly represents mankind because it is created by Him and lives in Him alone. It is therefore an inherent part of the very constitution of man that Christ acts on behalf of man and represents him before God. As Christ by God's eternal decree is "the Man", the root and ground of the life of every existing man, God can only look at man in and through Christ. This enabled Maurice to maintain that God imputes Christ's righteousness and holiness to man. On the same premise Maurice could assert that Christ laid down His life and died on the Cross for the sake of mankind. His death was truly a vicarious death on behalf of man. Only, Maurice emphatically repudiated the idea that because of man's sin Christ was bound to die on his behalf. If this were so, it would not originate in God's eternal decree that Christ as the representative of man acts on his behalf – it would then simply be "an artificial substitution". Thus, it is not the idea of Christ's vicarious death on behalf of man that Maurice opposes in the "objective" doctrine of the atonement; the point at issue is whether this is an eternal fact, or whether it only became true because of Christ's death upon the Cross.[76]

God was well-pleased with Christ's sacrificial death because, as the expression of love, it reflected His own perfect character. But as He who sacrificed Himself was none other than the One who, as the Head of humanity, always represents man before God and always acts on behalf of man, all mankind is included in His sacrifice. Therefore God was well-pleased with every man for Christ's sake. Hence Maurice could maintain that on behalf of mankind Christ had brought the only sacrifice which could satisfy God and had by this act reconciled God to man and effected the "at-one-ment".[77] Admittedly, Maurice's language may easily leave the

75 *Theological Essays*, 37.

76 J. H. Rigg was wrong in maintaining that Maurice rejected the substitution of Christ: "to the whole school of Coleridge there is no greater horror that this doctrine of substitution, however taught; though it is so inwoven in the Scripture phraseology and so craved for by the guilty conscience of men" (op. cit., 100. See also p. 101). Although Maurice did not use the term – apparently he felt it too akin to the false idea of penal substitution – he clearly wished to maintain that Christ stands in man's stead before God and that man is acquitted of his sin and guilt and counted righteous in God's sight because of Christ as his *justitia aliena*. He only wanted to establish it as a fact that by virtue of God's eternal will and purpose this is always the truth about humanity.

77 Cf. *The Prayer-Book*, 258: "If the idea of a satisfaction as the fruit of Love, as the image of Love in the Son, answering to the archetype of it in the Father, were filling our minds, there could be no difficulty in admitting the assertion that the Son reconciled the Father to us. He presented that perfect reflex of His own character to the Father with which alone He could be satisfied. In Him alone could He see Humanity as He had formed it, with all its powers in full exercise, free and glorious – free and glorious, because entirely submissive to love; exercising dominion over all Nature, because surrendered to its true unseen Lord," and *The Kingdom of Christ* (1838) I, 44: "By never committing one act of selfishness – by identifying Himself perfectly with the meanest of the race, He proved Himself to be the Head of the race; and He was perfectly acceptable and well-pleasing to God, in that He

impression that it was only through His death on Calvary that Christ reconciled God to man, but the purport of his argument is simply that Christ's death upon the Cross is a manifestation in time of His eternal sacrifice, with which God is ever well-pleased and thereby ever reconciled to all mankind. Because the Cross reveals Christ as "the true, sinless root of Humanity" it has been manifested in whom God by His eternal decree has elected and loved mankind, so that men now may know in whom they are always united and reconciled to God.[78]

This theme is dealt with at some length in a sermon on Eph. 2,11–18: *Christ's Sacrifice the Peace-Offering for Mankind* in *The Doctrine of Sacrifice*.[79] For St. Paul, Maurice explained, God's covenant with Israel meant that God had elected it and surrounded it with His love despite its disobedience. The Cross revealed that it was Christ in whom Israel was elected and that this election was not exclusively restricted to the Jews, but also encompassed the Gentiles.[80] By His death Christ broke down the barrier between Jew and Gentile because in this very act he was manifested as the Head of the human race.[81] All barriers and divisions between men have also been destroyed in this respect inasmuch as it has been demonstrated that the basic conditions are the same for the life of every man. Everybody is subject to the temptation to live for himself and deny the law of his creation, but it is equally true of every man that Christ remains his Lord and that because of Christ he is always embraced by God's love. Since this has been revealed through Christ's sacrificial death, the Cross can be said to have established peace, union and fellowship among all men upon earth.[82]

was the perfect image and express likeness of His own love. The only sacrifice with which God could be pleased – the only suffering that could satisfy His righteousness and His love, was made upon Calvary, and by that act, we say, God is reconciled to mankind – mankind is shown to be constituted and established in Christ, and through Christ it is possible for God to maintain a perfect fellowship with man."

78 Cf. *Theological Essays*, 38: "supposing His death to be a sacrifice, the only complete sacrifice ever offered, the entire surrender of the whole spirit and body to God; is not this, in the highest sense, Atonement? Is not the true, sinless root of Humanity revealed, is not God in Him reconciled to man?"

79 *Sacrifice*, 199–216.

80 Cf. p. 205–6: "Now when he [St. Paul] had seen in the cross of Christ the full revelation of the God of Abraham, he perceived also the deep and true foundation of that divine election, which he had taken to be artificial and arbitrary. The Cross told him in whom it was that God had elected them, in whom He had blessed them with all spiritual blessings. It showed him the Eternal Mediator, the Living Word, in whom God had created the worlds, in whom He had held converse with the sons of men. It unfolded the mystery of the past; the Law, the Prophets, the Priesthood, the Sacrifices. But it took away the exclusiveness, the merely Jewish character, of them all. They were witnesses of the *Man*, in whom God looked not upon the sons of Abraham, but on the sons of men."

81 Cf. p. 209: "recollecting that the aim of St. Paul, in all his letters, has been to trace the whole economy of the universe, and of the redemption of men from their wicked works and the enmity which they had caused, to God's original purpose, to His creation of man in the eternal Son – we gain a glimpse of the nature of Christ's peace-offering, and of its effects on mankind, which illuminates all the past history of the world, as well as all the saddest experiences of individuals."

82 Cf. p. 210–1: "One Man is proclaimed as the King and Saviour of both. The signs of His royalty, the marks of the Victor, are the prints of the nails. – – These are the sure testimo-

It is important for Maurice to stress the necessity of seeing in the Cross the manifestation of Christ as the Head of mankind, "the true, sinless root of Humanity". Every man is prone to deny that he is created to live in fellowship with Christ and receive life from Him. Indeed, the experiences of human life with its distress and misery appear to belie this fact. The accusations of the Devil, the feeling of separation from God and one's fellow-man and of the overwhelming power of sin enslave humanity and seem to condemn every man to perish in darkness without God. It is only by looking to the crucified Christ as the revelation of "the whole mystery of man" that all this is proved to be false. Then man knows for certain that he stands in Christ, and that having fellowship with Him he shall not perish because Christ upholds him and repulses his enemies. Because Christ eternally is the representative of man, "the Man", the revelation of Him in this capacity implies the revelation of the truth about the life of every man.[83]

Since this knowledge is imparted through Christ's death upon the Cross, Maurice could assert: "we are all raised to a new and regenerate condition in Christ, – and – – this is our true human condition, – and – – it is one which we may all of us claim, – and – – we shall only claim it when we believe that there is a Son of God, and a Son of Man, who has delivered us by dying for us."[84] It is this fact that must determine

nies that God has atoned MAN to Himself; that there is no distinction of favoured and neglected race. *He is our Peace;* the centre of union and fellowship between the tribes of the earth – –. Humanity, which had heretofore stood in these apparently hopeless divisions of Jew and Gentile, – while yet it was evincing itself, by the most undoubted proofs, to be essentially the same in both – the same in its conscious evil, the same in its certainty that this evil was the strife against a good, for which it was created – humanity henceforth stands united in Him. – – Henceforth, to treat any man as an alien from God, as cut off by any legal sentence from Him, was to deny Christ's death; to say that God had not made the great Peace-offering; that the Cross had not removed all which gave one advantage over another," and p. 212: "this Atonement is the fulfilment and manifestation of His original purpose, when He created all things in Christ."

83 Cf. p. 314: "the Cross of Christ makes known to us Him, in whom we are created, Him by whom we consist, Him who is the source of righteousness, of strength, of life to every man, because He is Himself the Eternal Son of God, and because by His acts He declares to us what God is working in us, to will, and to be, and to do."

84 p. 298. Cf. also *Theological Essays* (1853), 226: "every great article in the Church's Creed presumes the revelation of a Son of God, as the root of righteousness in every human being, as the centre and corner-stone of humanity itself. Supposing such a Person to have been actually revealed – supposing He has come, and that we do not look for another, it would seem as if the Regeneration of man in the most radical sense one can dream of it – – has not been commenced only, but effected, not for a few of us, but for all. If it can be said that God has manifested His Son, made of a woman, that we might receive the adoption of sons – – the idea of Regeneration as the restoration of human beings to their true filial position in Christ, of mankind to its unity in Him, is fulfilled." The terms "regeneration" and "restoration" are misleading, for in themselves they indicate the recreation and restitution of fallen humanity by Christ's incarnation and death. But this is not what Maurice meant. Christ has always been "the Head of every man", "the corner-stone of humanity", but as the life and death of Christ incarnate has revealed this truth and delivered man from a false understanding of reality, it may be said that humanity has been "regenerated" and "restored". That nothing more is meant by "regeneration" is quite apparent from the Essay on regeneration in *Theological Essays*, 55–65. In this essay Maurice not only rejected the idea of a

men's attitude to each other: "since that life [of Christ] must be for our brethren as well as for ourselves, for men of every caste and character, we ought to know how we have a right to regard them; what we have a right to tell them, respecting themselves and respecting Him who created them. While we are uncertain about that point; while we do not know whether we are to fly from them as devils, or to recognise them as children of one Father; whether we are to esteem them as creatures whom He has doomed to destruction, or creatures whom He seeks to rescue from the destruction into which they fall through ignorance of Him, and of His purposes to them; I cannot understand how we can think one hopeful thought or speak one helpful word."[85]

Our analysis of Maurice's interpretation of the Cross has demonstrated that he understood it as the visible manifestation of Christ's eternal sacrifice, by virtue of which He is the eternal Mediator between God and man. As the Son of God, Christ has revealed God as perfect unchangeable love, and as the Son of Man, He is revealed as the Head of humanity, in whom God has elected and loved mankind. The Cross unveils the reality which always constitutes the life of every man. The decisive significance that Maurice apparently ascribed to Christ's sacrificial death with respect to the relation between God and man and the way in which he described it as the victory over the powers of evils and the redemption and deliverance of mankind from its bondage were due to his desire to be faithful to the Bible. That Maurice, however, used the Biblical ideas and terms in his own sense is a fact evidenced by his strenuous opposition to any view which implied the idea of the uniqueness of the Biblical history of redemption. Christ's death upon the Cross has decisive significance only in the sense that it imparted the clear and unambiguous knowledge of reality which dispels man's false understanding of God and his own existence. Maurice's interpretation of Christ's sacrificial death on Calvary has proved to be in full accordance with his basic idea of revelation.

restoration of the fallen creation (p. 58); he based his entire argument on the assumption that the Bible and the Incarnation merely unveil an actually existing reality, "the spiritual constitution of man", that is to say, man's life in fellowship with Christ.
85 *Sacrifice*, 298–9.

Chapter IX

THE RESURRECTION AND ASCENSION OF CHRIST

For Maurice it was essential to maintain the belief in Christ's resurrection and ascension. They were not merely to be seen as events which necessarily followed from His life and death on the Cross; it was even necessary to insist on them, since they alone could safeguard a true understanding of the Incarnation.[1] The significance of the Resurrection and the Ascension were, however, distorted when they were taken to be "merely extraordinary, anomalous events".[2] This fatal misinterpretation had to be removed and Christ's resurrection and ascension understood "as events which could not have been otherwise, which exhibit eternal laws, which vindicate the true order and constitution of human existence, – while, at the same time, – – they must in some way be *pattern* events – examples of that which men were to be and to do."[3] Here we find, in a nutshell, Maurice's idea of revelation applied to Christ's resurrection and ascension. It remains to be seen how far Maurice was able to carry out this fundamental principle in his interpretation of Christ's resurrection and ascension.

1. The Resurrection

Maurice's understanding of the significance of the Resurrection can only be truly grasped against the background of his conception of death.

According to Maurice, the history of mankind testifies that men fear death as the great enemy which destroy both their spirits and their bodies. Although death appears to be the inevitable fate of every man, men feel its existence as "utterly monstrous, anomalous, – something to which they cannot and should not submit."[4] They can never regard death as a comfort and deliverance[5] and cling to the conviction that their true destiny is to be in communion with life, whereas death is the destructive power waiting to strip them of everything.[6] What especially makes death so terrible for man is the fact that it is inextricably bound up with sin. Sin, the refusal to live in

---

1 Cf. *The Prayer-Book*, 118: "His Resurrection and Ascension are not strange, perplexing additions to the narrative, but the orderly carrying out of its meaning, events without which all that goes before would be incomprehensible."

2 *Theological Essays*, 70.

3 *ibid.*

4 p. 40.

5 Cf. *Christmas Day*, 323: "the verdict of mankind is not in favour of the notion which some sentimentalists seek to encourage; – – men everywhere, when in their right senses, are seeking for some deliverance from death, not looking to death as if it were itself a deliverer."

6 Cf. *Sermons* VI, 70–1: "Is he [death] the great King of all kings? Why do we fight him to the last? Why do we not quietly yield to his supremacy, since he has established it by the evidence of centuries? Why this clinging to life? Why this dream of immortality?"

fellowship with God and his fellow-men, inevitably leads man into isolation, and as "death, nakedly considered, is nothing but the being left by ourselves and to ourselves,"[7] it is the ratification of that state which man has chosen for himself. Even if man realises that death is his due because of his sin, he nevertheless desires to be delivered from it. At the same time this horror of death is mixed up with a feeling that death might be a blessing because it sets man free from his self, his restlessness and misery.

Thus, the fact of death is the great riddle of human existence. Both the desire to escape it as the common foe of mankind and the attraction towards it are equally genuine and demand to be explained and satisfied.[8] No theories are, however, of any avail. Only the death of Him who is both the Son of God and the Son of Man can interpret the death of every man: "Here is the Universal Death – the death of the Head and Brother of mankind; that is the only test and explanation of its nature; that is the only one to which we dare refer when we would understand the meaning of the universe and God's purposes to it. When we fall back upon our thoughts and experiences, and reason and speculate upon them, we fall back into the hands of the Accuser."[9]

As previously mentioned, Christ's death has proved that man's conception of death as a tyrannical, destructive enemy is false. When Christ gave Himself up to death as an act of sacrifice to fulfil the will of His Father, His death meant the consummation of the fellowship of love. Therefore Christ, through His own death, revealed that death does not involve separation from God and the cessation of life, but, on the contrary, fellowship and the beginning of life.[10] Because Christ of His own free will gave Himself up to death, He demonstrated that death is not man's irresistible fate. He has made death the bond of communion with God.[11]

7 *Christmas Day*, 329–30.
8 Cf. *Sermons* II, 186: "it required no evidence to convince men that death was a fact with which every child of Adam has to do. But men did need to know what this fact signified. It was as strange and monstrous as it was indisputable. Through it was the great commonplace of the world, each new case exhibited some new variety of it; it was essentially individualizing, though it was universal. – – Men have always wanted to know, men do want to know, what Death is, as well as what Life is; and they have always felt that the finest, sagest, divinest definition, if it proceeded from the lips of God Himself, could not tell them."
9 *Sacrifice*, 243. Cf. p. 244: "when they turn from their miserable attempts to solve the mystery for themselves, to Him who entered into the mystery for them, that He might bring light out of darkness; when they determine to learn there what death is, and what man is, and what God is, there and only there; then they find their bondage turned into freedom."
10 Cf. *Sermons* II, 189: "It seemed scarcely right, scarcely consistent with the sense they had of evil and punishment, not to regard it as a horrible separation, a deep abyss, as something into which the light of God's countenance did not penetrate. Our Lord's Death is the one termination – need we fear to say it? – the one possible termination, of such a state of feelings," and *Christmas Day*, 331: "death changed its nature when it passed upon Christ, and became a new birth."
11 Cf. *Christmas Day*, 253: "For when Christ, the sinless One, walked through death, then were these two divided, never to be united again; Christ is now the Lord of death as well as of life," and *Sermons* II, 188: "His Death was a voluntary sacrifice. Herein its holiness, its perfectness, its power consists. Death had been felt to be a dark necessity, the submission to a power which was not human, not divine, and yet which must be obeyed."

222

Christ's death must, however, not be understood as a unique event, different from the death of ordinary men. If this was the case, His death could not interpret the death of every man. Maurice strongly emphasized that Christ had submitted to the death which every man dies – even in this respect Christ completely identified Himself with the actual state of all men. Yet He who died the common death is the Head of humanity, and so every man, without any exception, has the right to see his own death encompassed by Christ's death.

As Christ's death was a sacrifice in which He surrendered Himself to God and trusted Him to sustain Him, so every man must understand his own death as a sacrifice in which he delivers everything back to God and throws himself upon Him and His love.[12] The Cross revealed that the death of self-surrender is the true law of human life. Being created in the likeness of Christ, man must continually sacrifice himself and die from self to live for God.[13] As was the case with Christ, so for every man the death of the body means the consummation of a life of self-denying sacrifice.[14] By sacrificing himself totally to God in death, man abandons unbelief and selfishness. Sin is abolished, when man fully trusts God to give him life according to His will. Death is a great blessing because it removes the barriers which man's sin has raised up in his relationship to God, thus bringing about true fellowship between God and man. Christ's death has, therefore, revealed the meaning and purpose of the death of every individual man.[15]

It is precisely this truth that St. Paul wished to bring home when he proclaimed that in baptism man had been planted with Christ in the likeness of His death (cf. Rom. 6,5).[16] As Christ's death implied His perfect fellowship with His Father, so in his death every man is united to God. What befell Christ in His death and resur-

---

12 Cf. *Theological Essays*, 43: "from it [the death of Christ] I am able to learn what other deaths are, – what the death of man is. Christ gave up all that was His own, – He gave *Himself* to His Father. He disclaimed any life which did not belong to Him in virtue of His union with the Eternal God. It is our privilege to disclaim any life which does not belong to us in virtue of our union with Him. This would be an obvious truth, if we were indeed created and constituted in Him, – if He was the root of our humanity. We should not then have occasion to ask how much perishes or survives in the hour of death. We should assume that all must perish, to the end that all may survive."

13 Cf. *Sacrifice*, 81: "the living sacrifice is that which God seeks for, – – it is this which interprets the mystery of death, – – it is this which purifies, – – it is this which unites."

14 Cf. p. 48: "we shall learn that we must be ready to present our souls and bodies, and all that is dear to us, every day as sacrifices to God. And then we may leave it to Him how and when it shall please Him to take these souls and bodies for other services than those to which He has appointed them here. – – At sunset or at cock-crowing, on the sick-bed, or in the midst of work, the voice may reach any of us. It is enough for us to know whose voice it is, and to what it is summoning us. – – It is calling us to make a real sacrifice, to present ourselves to God."

15 Cf. *Sermons* II, 189: "Henceforth look not for it [the death] in its particular forms and cases; in other men or in yourself. Look at it here. The Cross is the only interpreter of it. This only shows you its individual, its human, its divine significance."

16 Cf. p. 185: "He [St. Paul] does not only speak of our Lord being made like to us, but of our being made in His likeness. – – He speaks of our death being cast in the mould of His Death; of His being the only standard by which we can measure, the only type by which we can understand our own: "We have been planted together in the likeness of His Death"."

rection manifests the truth about the life of every man because He is the Head of humanity.[17]

Death, then, is not an anomaly in God's created Order. On the contrary, it is, in accordance with God's will, a blessing for mankind, since it means the fulfilment of the law under which man exists: to die from self in order to live with God. Furthermore, death is a benefit because it delivers man from his animal, fleshly nature, his mortal mould, which hinders the spirit in its flight to the eternal world.

We have previously noticed the ambiguity which marks Maurice's understanding of the term "the flesh". He used the word both as being synonymous with selfishness and as identical with the animal, fleshly nature with its gravitation downwards. The same ambiguity is displayed in his understanding of death. Maurice could interpret the fact of death to mean that man dies from his selfishness, renouncing every desire and attempt to live for himself. He could also understand it to mean the deliverance of the spirit from the fleshly nature, which is always drawing man away from the eternal world in order to bind him to transient, earthly things. In the latter case death could be considered to have ended the conflict between the spirit and the flesh, because the flesh is given up to the destruction of death.[18] Maurice interpreted the Scriptural phrase accordingly: "As in Adam all die, so in Christ shall all be made alive" to mean that the Adam-nature as man's fleshly nature is destroyed by bodily death while the spirit, by fellowship with Christ, shall live on; first then it can truly unfold itself when it has thrown off its "mortal mould".[19]

17 Cf. p. 191: "This Death, – this common Death, – the Death of Him Who died for all, is that in the likeness of which we are planted; here is the bond of perfect human fellowship, here is the assurance that Death cannot break the bonds which hold us to each other, because the Love which established them had, in death, proved itself to be stronger than Death," and *Life* I, 106: "the death of Christ – – is actually and literally the death of you and me, and the whole human race; the absolute death and extinction of all our selfishness and individuality. – – Let us believe, then, what is the truth and no lie – that we *are* dead, actually, absolutely dead; and let us believe further that we *are* risen; and that we have each a life, our only life – a life not of you nor me, but a universal life – in Him."

18 Cf. *Christmas Day*, 253: "Now the law may thunder at each of us, and say, 'Thou hast sinned; thy mind has been separated from God's mind'. But thou canst answer bravely, 'No; I am united to Christ; in my spirit I serve him; in my spirit I cleave to him; nought but my flesh serves the law of death, and that flesh death may have, I willingly give it up to him'."

19 It is obvious that, when speaking about the conflict of the spirit and the flesh in man, Maurice was reproducing a Platonic dualism. However, he was anxious to assert that the spirit is only immortal through fellowship with Christ. In *Christmas Day*, 332, he pointed out that the unfettered flight of the spirit to the heavenlies is due both to its emancipation from the mortal mould and to its dependence upon Christ: "When man has been conscious that there is a spirit within him, he has always cried for something higher than himself to help him; when he thinks only of himself, his wings soon drop, he falls back into the very charnel-house which he had found so degrading and so loathsome. Whenever he has been conscious that he had spiritual powers, he has lifted up his voice to a higher spirit to raise him to himself; he has felt that all his misery came from the separation between him and some being whom he ought to trust in and obey." It must be emphasized, however, that the idea of the animal, fleshly nature as something which resists the life of the spirit is only of secondary importance in Maurice's thought. Although it is a contributing factor in leading man astray, and debasing him through his serfdom to sensual things (cf. p. 331: "It is true that the mind which muses upon many things is held down by the low and earthly

Since Christ's death signifies that He sacrificed Himself in order to live in fellow-ship with God, His resurrection means that God accepted Christ's sacrificial surrender of self and sustained Him through death and the grave.[20] The Resurrection is a witness to the fact that the fellowship of the Son with the Father cannot be destroyed but remains unbroken, triumphant over all the powers of destruction.[21]

It was, therefore, quite consistent of Maurice to refuse to deal with the problem of historical evidence for the facticity of Christ's resurrection. That Christ had been resuscitated or, rather, had lived on by virtue of His fellowship with the Father does not need any specific proof. It is simply the necessary consequence of a life in which He had always sacrificed Himself to fulfil the will of His Father: "His Death is the consummation of His Incarnation, the fulfilment of the Sacrifice which He was offering up each day. His Resurrection and Ascension are not strange, perplexing additions to the narrative, but the orderly carrying out of its meaning; events without which all that goes before would be incomprehensible."[22] Conversely, Christ's life is always a life of resurrection since He continually surrenders Himself to the Father in order to be sustained by His life-giving power. According to Maurice this interpre-tation is the overriding theme of the Evangelists and the Apostles in their description of the resurrection of Christ. Indeed the attempt to provide evidence for the fact of the Resurrection only betrays a lack of understanding of its true significance.[23]

Maurice frequently expressed himself in such a way as to give the impression

appetites of the flesh. It is true that every exercise of the intellectual powers is a witness that such slavery was not intended for us. There must be an emancipation from it, and he who does not seek it, is content to part with the privileges of a man"), in the last analysis, the selfishness and unbelief of the spirit are the true causes of man's misery: "the soul has power to be its own tormentor, yea, is its tormentor" (p. 332).

20 Cf. *Sermons* II, 191–2: "If Death import a surrender to God, as of a child to a Father; Resurrection must import that the surrender has been accepted. – – It is proved that His union with the Father was not broken in that hour in which He poured out His soul to death. By that union His human soul is quickened, His human body is quickened; by it He becomes the source of a divine life to all creation."

21 Cf. *Sermons* VI, 5: "the Apostle always thought of the fact of the Resurrection as a mani-festation of the Divine relation in which Christ stood to the Eternal Father; of the Divine Life which dwelt in Him because He was the Son of God; of the Divine energy which was every hour sustaining that life, and which in weakness, agony, on the cross, in the sepulchre, sustained it still."

22 *The Prayer-Book*, 117–8.

23 Cf. *The Unity of the New Testament*, 164–5: "the Evangelists looked upon the Resurrection as the natural and inevitable sequel of their history. No pains are taken to shew how an event so strange and unparalleled could take place; no pains to bring any weight of testimony in support of it. – – The assumption is that another issue, if you take the premises of the story, would be incredible; that this was the exact fulfilment of the Divine order, the victory over irregularity and disorder. It was not *possible* that He could be holden of death – not possible if He was the Son of God and the King of Men, not possible if His baptism, His temptation, His miracles, His parables, His whole life, were what the three Evangelists declare them to have been," and *The Church a Family*, 122–3: "The Apostles did not look upon the resurrection as a strange episode in His history, as something altogether peculiar and unsuspected. To believe that He was the Son of God, the mediator between God and man, in whom all things consisted, and to suppose that He did not rise, would have been in their minds an utter incredible contradiction."

that the resurrection of Christ has constitutive significance for the relation between God and man. Thus, he described the Resurrection as the foundation of the Christian faith, since it meant the victory of life over death.[24] Christ rose from the dead in order to bestow a new life on man,[25] – indeed all mankind rose with Christ.[26] However, once again a closer analysis reveals the now familiar pattern of an incongruity between the literal meaning of what Maurice said and what he purported to say. In describing the significance of the Resurrection he made use of Biblical and traditional theological language, but the context and his whole chain of reasoning make it abundantly clear that he interpreted the Resurrection as a manifestation and revelation of the unchangeable constitution of the Divine Order. The Resurrection did not inaugurate a new reality for man, though it does impart the true knowledge of God and of human existence.[27]

This concern prompted Maurice to say: "We have dwarfed the New Testament doctrine respecting our Lord's resurrection, through our eagerness to disparage the condition and the expectations of those who lived before it."[28] This criticism was directed against the prevalent orthodox view, which maintained that the resurrection of Christ was the event that made it possible for man to enter upon a new life of salvation. Such a concept, however, narrowed the significance of Christ's resurrection, since it implies that those who lived after this event existed under conditions different from those that had prevailed before this event. Maurice maintained, in contrast, that the resurrection of Christ has a direct bearing on the life of every man irrespective of when he lived.[29] This sounds obscure until it is realised that for Maurice the Resurrection is an event which reveals the law and order of the universe and all human life. Because it imparts true knowledge of that which unchangeably constitutes

24 Cf. *The Commandments*, 69–70: "Have the priests or doctors of any part of Christendom really taught the nation that the law of life is stronger than the law of death; that mankind has been brought by its Head under that law of life? Is not our preaching altogether about the power of death, the feebleness of life? Who could gather from our language, that the Resurrection of Christ is the foundation of our faith; that to bear witness of Christ's triumph to the world is our main function? Have we not led men to think that the Resurrection is to be accepted as the great anomaly of all, not as the fact which clears away anomalies, which restores order to the universe?"

25 Cf. *The Conflict*, 126: "The whole teaching of the Apostles intimated that Christ had come to make the tree good; to establish them on a new root, to give them a new life. They could not separate the Resurrection from this new life: Christ has risen from the dead, that He might bestow it upon those who confessed themselves to be dead in trespasses and sins."

26 Cf. *Sermons* VI, 9: "in raising Him, He [God] raised up us also, whom He had created in Him to be His children."

27 Cf. *The Unity of the New Testament*, 486: "they [the Apostles] preach Christ's Cross and Resurrection and say that men are to learn from these God's will and their own condition."

28 *Sermons* III, 260.

29 Cf. *The Unity of the New Testament*, 462: "The law of death for the race is said to be manifested in Adam, the law of life for the race in the Christ. The Resurrection has proved the law of life to be stronger than the law of death. The Resurrection has not been to confirm the hopes of a few believers; not to assure those who came in after days how much better their condition is than that of their fathers. He is the first-fruits of those that have *slept*. All the men of the past world are concerned in his victory. It is a victory over their tyrant. It breaks their chains."

God's creation, the Resurrection proclaims the truth of the life of every man, no matter in what age he lives: "The Apostles unquestionably speak of our Lord's resurrection as an unprecedented fact in the world's history. But they say that its importance to human beings lay in this, that it declared Jesus to be the Son of God with power. It was an act retrospective and prospective. It revealed the Head of the human race. It revealed the relation of that human race, in the person of its Head, to the Father of all. That which was manifested to be true, when He Who had taken on Him our nature, and had died as we die, rose out of death because He could not possibly be holden of it, had been true always. Those who believed in Christ could not doubt that man was to learn his condition from Christ, that he could learn it only from Christ."[30]

Men have failed to see the true significance of the Resurrection because they have clung to the mere fact of the resurrection of Christ. What is essential, however, is not the outward event, but the principle or law which it manifests. Only when this is grasped will it be understood that the purpose of the Resurrection is to reveal Christ as the One who always displays and yields "the power of Resurrection".

During his entire earthly life Christ had been manifested as the Creator and Lord of the universe and of all mankind, always imparting life to His creation and upholding it against the destructive machinations of the powers of evil. This manifestation is ratified by the Resurrection because it demonstrated that the lifegiving power of Christ, received through His union with the Father, is victorious and triumphs over sin and death. From the Resurrection man learns that the creative life which Christ has imparted to the universe and mankind is the ultimate reality, which nothing can thwart or destroy.[31] Thus the Resurrection vindicates the order and harmony of God's creation.[32]

When Maurice stated that all mankind is risen with Christ and that, through

---

30 *Sermons* III, 260.
31 Cf. *Sermons* VI, 5–6: "You will find [in 1. Cor. 15] the doctrine of a divine power exercised first according to an eternal law in Christ as the Head of the race, then in all its members – coming forth in every sentence, I might say in every word. Take away this assertion of a power, – inward, mysterious, discernible to us only in its effects, but most orderly, uniform, incapable of being suspended without the subversion of the whole economy of the Universe, without the destruction of all its principles, – substitute for this assertion the announcement of the Resurrection merely as a great exception to the course of nature, – and that chapter loses not only all its sublimity, but all that has cheered the heart of any mourner, all that has given him strength to endure life and death," and p. 11: "We can explain the facts in no other way. The power of His resurrection has been there. It is that very power which first moved upon the face of the waters; that very power which has been striving with men in all ages, reclaiming, civilizing, renewing. It is the power of that Word who was in the beginning, without whom nothing was made that was made, whose life was always the Light of men. But it is that power concentrated and manifested in the Word made flesh; that power proved to be stronger than death, the grave, or Hell; that power asserting its right in and over the will of man and over the creation of which man is the lord."
32 Cf. *The Conflict*, 101–2: "The Resurrection for him [St. Paul] was not an interruption of its order, but an assertion of its order. Death was the disturber. The living Word took the flesh and blood of men that He might vindicate the order of creation." This happens because the Resurrection imparts the knowledge that Christ as the foundation of the universe possesses a victorious life.

Christ's resurrection, the entire human race has been brought from death to life and thereby been redeemed and restored to its true state,[33] his choice of language served to establish the fact that the human race is encompassed by the life of the risen Christ. Yet this union was not achieved by the Resurrection itself, which merely demonstrated that not even death could dissolve the bond between Christ, the Head of humanity, and man. As the Resurrection manifested the life-giving power of victorious Christ, so it vindicated man's true state: "In His Resurrection God declared that death had no power over Him, because He was united by an eternal bond to Himself. In His Resurrection He declared that death had no power over us, because we are united to Him in the Well-beloved."[34]

That the human race is risen with Christ signifies that every man is bound to understand his own life as a participation in Christ's risen life, and this means that he may know for certain that Christ upholds him by imparting His own victorious life to him. Although sin and death might appear to prove to man that he is doomed to destruction, he can now reject this view as a lie.[35] To live in fellowship with the risen Christ during earthly life is for man nothing but to believe that Christ is His victorious Head, who always upholds his life.[36]

33 Cf. *The Prayer-Book*, 271–2: "The Father has raised up the Son, and in raising Him up has raised us up, whose nature He took. He has declared to us that the Life which is in Him is capable of quickening, and shall quicken, our souls and our bodies; that we are restored in Him to our rightful state of union with God, of dependence upon God," and p. 272–3: "This is the fruit of the Resurrection – of that restoration of the Universe which He fulfilled when He broke from the tomb, and declared that Man was under a law of life, and not of death; the child of a living and loving Father, not the bondsman of Nature."

34 *The Prayer-Book*, 272. Cf. also *Theological Essays*, 75: "The Resurrection from the dead is a resurrection for us as well as for Him; it has vindicated man's true condition, not subverted it," and *Sermons* VI, 8: "they [the Apostles] looked upon the Resurrection-day as the New Birth-day of the world; as that which declared what man is, according to the true law of his being; what each man is bound to think of himself. – – He is to claim the condition of a redeemed creature; of one who has been reclaimed from the domination of death; of one who has been declared to be under the law of the Resurrection, to be under the power of Resurrection." As the resurrection of Christ revealed the true and unchangeable state of mankind, Maurice had no difficulty in giving it a central place in God's history of salvation. This does not mean, as J. H. Rigg contended, that Maurice asserted "the inauguration of a new era and the spring of new influences for the human race", and hence that "in Christ, as God incarnate, humanity is not only justified, but regenerate" (op. cit., 188). Consequently Rigg was wrong to maintain that Maurice's concept of the resurrection is "strangely incongruous with the whole tenor of [his] theology" *(ibid.)*.

35 Cf. *The Prayer-Book*, 276: "And though there are powers of death ever at work upon your souls and bodies both, threatening the destruction of both, there is a mightier power which is sustaining, preserving, quickening both; a power to which we cannot commit ourselves and you in too childlike dependence and trust," and p. 274–5: "Yet it requires nothing less than the faith that God is the restorer and regenerator of Humanity, and that He has commenced the restoration and regeneration of it from its root, to justify the witness of our reasons and consciences, and to persuade ourselves that the charnel-house does not interpret the law of the Universe."

36 The message of the Resurrection Maurice could describe in the following way: "The dream of man, that there is something near to him which is mightier than he knows, or can grasp, is not a dream, but a reality. The vague fear of man, that what is near him may be not a

The significance of the resurrection of Christ is, however, not restricted to explaining the truth about the actual life of every man. It reveals at the same time that man is meant to live beyond the grave. As Christ could not be bound by death but continued to live by virtue of His fellowship with the Father, so every man will continue to live, because Christ and His power of resurrection will always be sustaining him.[37] The resurrection of Christ demonstrates man to be an immortal being.

That Maurice's belief in the Resurrection is ultimately a belief in the immortality of man is evident from his attitude to those thinkers who had maintained this belief, for example Plato. There were, admittedly, deficiencies in Plato's argument, but he deserved all honour because he had sought an answer to a question which has persistently haunted men.[38] Although there appear to be good reasons for the belief that death and the grave mark the extinction of human life,[39] it is, nonetheless, a fact that man cannot surrender the idea of immortality. There has always been "in every man and in every race *some* faith in a victory over the grave."[40] Men cannot help believing that "life is stronger than death, and that there is another law for him than the law which binds natural things."[41] Men feel that there is something in them which cannot be the prey of death, but is immortal and belongs to the eternal world.[42]

The resurrection of Christ in no way invalidates this belief in the immortality of

thing but a Person, is a verity. The vague hope of man, that this Person may be gracious and not malignant, the source of all the good which he beholds, or believes, or imagines, and not of any of the evil, is established. The sense in every human heart that it must have one to lean upon who is higher than itself, and to whom it may give up itself, from whom it may be every moment a receiver, is shown not to be a delusion" *(The Prayer-Book*, 271).

37 Cf. *The Unity of the New Testament*, 593: "If they believed that Christ had died and risen again, they believed in a union of both worlds, a breaking down of the barrier that separated the state before death from the state after death, – the visible and the invisible world. Such a belief, if they truly entertained it, would assure them that those whom they called dead had fallen asleep, but that Christ was as much with them as He was with the daughter of Jairus or with Lazarus; that they could as much hear His voice as those departed spirits had done; that as they were members of Christ's body, and drew their life from Him, God would bring them with Him."

38 See *Sermons* III, 261–2.

39 Cf. p. 262: "It is not true that those who brought forward these arguments for immortality were opposing themselves to the belief of the rest of the world. They were trying to justify a belief which had expressed itself in every mythology, in every legend, against the unbelief which the falsehoods of those mythologies and legends, co-operating with natural appearances, – yes! and with very strong, if not the strongest, motives to the heart of man, – were producing in those about them and in themselves. The death of every flower, of every beast, of every man, was a broad, palpable argument addressed to the senses, which one might have supposed that no efforts of imagination or speculation could in the least have resisted."

40 p. 264.

41 *ibid.*

42 Cf. p. 267: "They [philosophers] asked whether there were not evidences in the constitution of the world, and in the constitution of man, that man was more than an animal, and that whatever there was in him which was above the animal, was not doomed to the death of the animal. They maintained that that thing in him which thinks, believes, hopes, must belong to life. They were therefore asserting, not a natural immortality for themselves, but an immortality which belonged to them by rising above nature."

man.[43] On the contrary, it substantiates it as true by revealing that Christ as the Head of mankind always imparts a life to man which triumphs over death and the grave. There is such a close relation between the resurrection of Christ and man's belief in immortality that the latter can even be said to furnish the evidence for the truth of the Resurrection. Throughout the history of mankind and in his own life man has been brought to understand himself as an immortal being, and since the resurrection of Christ ratifies this conviction, man intuitively perceives its truth.[44] Therefore it is labour lost to provide evidence for the fact of Resurrection. It is sufficient simply to proclaim this event; it will immediately prove itself to be true because it satisfies man's inmost longings and yearnings by revealing that man is immortal by virtue of his union with Christ.[45]

By showing the true foundation of the idea of immortality, the resurrection of Christ at the same time cleanses it from all the false theories and speculations which have mingled with and distorted this genuine conviction of mankind.[46] Thus, the Resurrection demonstrates that man is not immortal in his own right. In fact, such a belief issues in a virtual denial of the immortality of man, since it throws him back upon himself and makes him a slave of his own fickleness and the transient world of sense.[47] Against this falsehood the Resurrection proclaims that man is immortal because of the life which Christ imparts.[48] Furthermore, it refutes the idea entertained by philosophers and religious men that immortality will be the possession only of a select few. Christ identified Himself with the meanest members of the human race; when He rose, every man, irrespective of his intellectual and moral qualities, received the right to believe that the power of the risen Christ is at work in him too.[49] The re-

43 Cf. p. 261: "To think then that we are honouring the Resurrection by dishonouring the expectations of immortality which men in the foregone ages have derived from one source or another, is surely monstrous."

44 Cf. p. 260–1: "The evidence for the Resurrection, then, lay in all the history, in all the experiences and life of men, up to that hour."

45 Cf. *Theological Essays*, 42: "The testimony will be mighty, because the thing testified of is that which all men, everywhere, are wanting, – which some who do not crave for what is peculiar and distinguishing, who must have that which is human, are taught by many hard processes that they want."

46 Maurice always distinguished between convictions and theories or dogmas which threaten to falsify the convictions. Convictions are inspired by God whilst theories or dogmas originate in man's intellect. Thanks to this distinction Maurice was capable of finding "precious truths" hidden under the hard incrustation of the thought forms of the understanding. However, it cannot be denied that "the convictions" which Maurice worked out more often than not present a striking similarity to his own ideas, whilst a critical examination frequently reveals that what he designated as theories or dogmas is in fact central to the complex of ideas in question.

47 Cf. *The Prayer-Book*, 269: "Experience might prove – – that the soul, when it began to worship itself, lost its capacity of acquiring further light, and could only revolve in the narrow circle of its present acquisitions. – – He [St. Paul] held man, merely considered in himself, to be a miserable creature; – – he became the most dependent of all creatures – the slave of the things which he might have ruled."

48 Cf. *Sermons* III, 260: "the victory over the grave is God's gift in Christ, not an inherent right of our nature."

49 Cf. *The Prayer-Book*, 273: "Has Christ died and risen again to give a few proud Philosophers or ascetical Pharisees some high notion about the powers of the soul, and the meanness

230

surrection of Christ is universal, encompassing all mankind: "We have a right to say that the dreariest winter contains the pledge of a spring. We have a right to say that we cannot look into the heart of Death without discovering the certainty of a nobler birth. We have a right to say that nothing in this wide world lies out of the law of Christ's Cross and Passion, and that therefore there can be nothing which it not overshadowed by His Resurrection, and which has not the capacity of a glorious life."[50]

When Maurice spoke of the resurrection of man, he was primarily thinking of the spirit in man. Many statements of his even give the impression that he rejected the idea of the resurrection of the body. Indeed, this appears to be the logical conclusion from his assertion that the mortal mould of man remains in the grave, since it has no connection with what is truly human in man.[51] Although Maurice certainly laid himself open to the charge that he denied the resurrection of the body,[52] he, nevertheless, wanted to stand up for the idea that the whole of man, spirit and body, is encompassed by the resurrection of Christ.[53]

When Christ sacrificed Himself to God on the Cross, this self-surrender included both His spirit and body. Both were, however, sustained by God and kept alive because of the unbroken fellowship between the Father and the Son.[54] So even the body

of the body? Has He not entered into the state of the lowest beggar, of the poorest, stupidest, wickedest wretch whom that Philosopher or that Pharisee can trample upon? Has He not come to redeem the humanity which Philosophers, Pharisees, beggars, harlots share together? Has He not come to tell each man, 'There is no life for thee in thyself; there is perfect life for thee in God, and it is a restorative life, which can work in thee, at the very root of thy being, and make thee a new and holy creature'?"

50 *Sermons* II, 193.
51 Cf. *Theological Essays*, 44: "Nor does the thought then disturb them [the common people] that there is a want of identity between him that has been and him that is. Though the decaying, agonised frame is lying calm and at rest, they do not then doubt that he who spoke to them a few minutes before did not derive his powers of speech, any more than the celestial smile which still remains on the clay, from that clay. Faith and reason, however crushed and confounded, are too strong in that hour of reality for a notion so cold and so inhuman," and p. 43: "We shall be ready to believe stories of miracles wrought by them [the remains of the body]; we shall be half inclined to worship them. Or if we reject this temptation, – because Romanists have fallen into it, and we think that it must therefore be shunned, – we shall take our own Protestant way of asserting the sanctity of relics, by maintaining that at a certain day they will all be gathered together, and that the very body to which they once belonged will be reconstructed out of them. -- This demand is made upon our faith by divines who read to every mourner as he goes with them to the grave of a friend, that corruption cannot inherit incorruption; that flesh and blood cannot inherit the kingdom of God."
52 So R. S. Candlish's comment on Maurice's treatment of the resurrection of the body in *Theological Essays* was not without foundation: "The author would count it foul scorn to be charged with holding any of the heresies of the Gnostical teachers. And yet it would puzzle the most learned adept in these old controversies to draw the line between what they thought of the bodies which they burned and buried, and what this whole passage must be understood to mean, if it has any definite meaning at all" (op. cit., 249).
53 As a direct answer to Candlish's charge Maurice wrote: "But I contended as earnestly, that this emancipation of men's *spirits* was not the only or final effort of Christ's Resurrection. The redemption of the *body* was quite as much a part of His work for man; its redemption from death, the grave, and hell" (*Sacrifice*, XXXIV).
54 Cf. *Sermons* II, 192: "It is proved [by Christ's resurrection] that His union with the Father

231

of Christ was manifested as victorious over death and the grave. Because the life of Christ exhibits the law for the life of each individual man, man now knows that even his body will remain untouched by death: "Christ was buried in order that the body might be claimed as an heir of life, as redeemed from corruption."[55] Since Christ truly "brought back from the grave that body which was supposed to be the soul's cage and prison-house",[56] Maurice could polemicize against those who denied the resurrection of the body and were willing to accept only the immortality of the soul. In doing so they not only poured contempt upon the body, but scorned the experiences and expectations of mankind.[57]

It cannot be denied that Maurice's treatment of the resurrection of the body is ambiguous and betrays great tensions. And yet this is not surprising since it is an inevitable consequence of his equally ambiguous understanding of the relation between the spirit and the body in man. However, his two approaches to the problem of the resurrection of the body are not as disconnected as might first appear. Maurice did attempt to combine them by distinguishing between the substance of the body and the shameful accidents of the body.

was not broken in that hour in which He poured out His soul to death. By that union His human soul is quickened, His human body is quickened," and *Theological Essays*, 105–6: "The idea of a bodily *Resurrection* – – had been accepted by men, not as a fact to be attested by a great amount of evidence, but as the inevitable issue of the previous revelation."

55 *Theological Essays*, 46. Cf. *Sermons* VI, 261–2: "He [St. Paul] is affirming with the utmost vehemence the permanence of the human substance, even of the human body, through all vicissitudes. – – His argument is, that in the death and resurrection of our Lord we read the law under which all human creatures are placed. If we are not to rise, he argues boldly, Christ is not risen. – – It was a necessity of his faith to acknowledge the identity of Christ in all possible changes, from the cradle in Bethlehem till His body had entered into the glory which He had with His Father before the worlds were. How then could he doubt the identity, through all circumstances of birth, growth, decay, renovation, of any one who had been made a living soul like the first Adam, and who had received the quickening spirit of the second Adam?", and *Sermons* II, 193: "These souls cannot perish if His has not perished; these bodies cannot perish if He has brought His back from the grave. As He had no life apart from His Father, we have no life apart from His."

56 *The Prayer-Book*, 268.

57 Cf. p. 273–4: "If we claim some high glory and inherent immortality for the soul, we come inevitably – men always have come – to think that this wonderful frame of the body, this glorious sense of sight, with all that it has apprehended and may apprehend, this mystery of sound, this power of touch, and taste, and smell, the capacity of motion, even the organs of speech, are all to be cast aside, and become the prey of death. Some fine article, some pure essence of this which I call myself, is to survive; all that has been most intimately and dearly associated with me, that has been the instrument of my communion with the bright world around me, and with brethren of my own race, all this living machine, the mystery of which it has required six thousand years very imperfectly to penetrate, must be extinguished utterly for each man after threescore years and ten, during which it has been maintained through sorrow and strife, endured rather than enjoyed." This is a "strange and cruel faith" which makes it impossible to "admire men who devote themselves with honest zeal to the investigation of the truths of science, and of those laws of art, which concern the relation of our senses with the external world. Those truths, those laws bear witness, as the mythology of every civilised and savage people does, the dream of every Elysium and Walhalla, that men do look, must look, for a redemption of their bodies" (p. 274).

Maurice's concern emerges clearly in the following passage: "What I believed that orthodox Christians – – had done, was to exhaust the belief of the resurrection of the body of all its force, its meaning, its consolation, by substituting for the resurrection of the living powers and principles of which our bodies consist, the renovation of those elements which were the signs of its decay, its curse, its death."[58] According to Maurice, then, the body of man is made up of living principles and powers, which constitute its substance, and of corrupt degrading elements or accidents, which have their origin in sin and, as sinful, will be delivered up to death and corruption.[59] Maurice never precisely defined what he understood by these sinful accidents. Only so much is clear that they hinder the free exercise of the substance of the body and even lead it into rebellion against the spirit of man.[60] At any rate, he contended that through death man will be delivered from these sinful elements so that the substance of the body can be free to act according to the law of its creation. This is for Maurice the significance of the resurrection of the body. It should be noticed that, as in the case of the spirit, it is a question not of resurrection in the ordinary sense of the word but of the continued existence of the body.

This distinction between the substance of the body and its sinful, corrupt accidents enabled Maurice, on one hand, to maintain the identity between the body which man carries with him during his earthly life and that which he will possess after death and, on the other hand, to maintain the contrast between them: "I am – – zealous – – to assert the absolute identity of the body of humiliation with the body of glory. That truth cannot be asserted in stronger language than it is asserted by St. Paul in the 15th chapter of the 1st Corinthians, and by our own Burial Service. God forbid that any one should make it weaker! What I affirm is, that we do not gain the least strength

58 *Sacrifice*, XXXIV.

59 Cf. *Theological Essays*, 43: "If we did attach any meaning to that expression upon which St. Peter at Jerusalem, St. Paul at Antioch, dwelt so earnestly, that Christ's body saw no corruption, – if we did believe that He who was without sin showed forth to us in Himself what is the true normal condition of humanity, and showed forth in that body of His what the human body is, – we should not dare, I think, any longer to make the corrupt, degrading, shameful accidents which necessarily belong to that body in each one of us, because we have sinned, the rule by which we judge of it here: how much less should we suppose these to be the elements out of which its high and restored and spiritual estate can ever be fashioned?"

60 Cf. p. 47: "I may be sure that death, as Butler maintains from analogy, does not change the substance of the human creature, or any of its powers or moral conditions, but only removes that which had crushed its substance, checked the exercise of its power, kept its true moral condition out of sight," and *Sermons* VI, 189–90: "The Redemption of the body – – must, I apprehend, include the removal of whatever hinders the senses from receiving clear and satisfactory impressions of the world with which they are intended to converse – all which has made them feeble or rebellious ministers of the spirit." Maurice did not make it clear what hinders the senses in their true functions and what makes them the disobedient servants of the spirit. The reason is undoubtedly that these questions are unanswerable on Maurice's own premises. He was, in fact, never able to settle accounts with the problem of corporality. When he dealt with it he at times argued from a Platonic conception of the flesh and at times from the Biblical idea of the flesh. Now the first aspect prevails, now the second; hence the oscillations and uncertainties in his treatment of the body and the animal, fleshly nature.

for this conviction by setting aside St. Paul's assertion, that corruption shall not inherit incorruption; and that the Burial Service nowhere gives the slightest hint that what is committed as earth to earth, ashes to ashes, dust to dust, shall be reunited to constitute that body which we have a sure and certain hope will be raised, and will be made like unto Christ's glorious body."[61] Although Maurice knew that the "attempt to identify the corruption of the body, the effects of death with the substance which death is unable to destroy, -- has the sanction of great and venerable names,"[62] this conception remains, nevertheless, "an earthly and sensual explanation of a glorious reality, directly interfering with the scriptural account of it, and with many of the most practical and consolatory truths which flow from it."[63] For Maurice the substance of the body, with its living powers and principles, cannot be contained by death and will constitute man's heavenly body. In other words, man already possesses the body of resurrection during his earthly life, but it is hidden and even checked in the exercise of its functions by the sinful accidents. Only at the moment of death will the substance of the body be delivered from the sinful, degrading elements and attain its free and full development.[64]

2. The Ascension

We have seen that for Maurice Christ always has fellowship with every man. This fellowship is with his spirit. Christ is the Light which enlightens the reason and conscience of man, which are created to receive His revelation. Christ speaks directly and immediately to the inner man, and man can only receive and grasp the revealed truth when he rises above his fleshly nature and the visible world of time and space.[65]

This fact has in no way been changed by the Incarnation. Even during His earthly life Christ did not speak to or appeal to man's sense perceptions. His revelations were, as ever, directed to that organ in man which alone can attain to true knowledge because it has been created to grasp *that which is*.[66] So the spirit remains that in man

61 *The Gospel of St. John*, 484–5.
62 p. 485. This rendering is Maurice's version of the belief that through the resurrection man's dead body is made alive.
63 *ibid.*
64 Cf. *Christmas Day*, 249: "Consider then that if God gives a growth to that seed, and makes it turn to an ear, he will make the seed of life, which he has put into thy body, produce a body such as he pleases. It may be very unlike that which thou wearest here in this world of death, as different as the seed is from the fruit or the flower: but it will be *thy* body still. -- One -- is an Adam body, the other is a Christ body."
65 Cf. *Sacrifice*, 170: "the Kingdom of Heaven is -- the spiritual world, in contrast to the natural world. The spirit of man contemplated as the subject of God's teaching and government, must be one of the heavenly things."
66 Cf. *Sermons* IV, 181: "Divines are wont to make distinctions between Christ the Teacher of the world at large, and Christ the Teacher of the heart and conscience of each man. They talk of an outward Christ and an inward Christ. The Evangelists indulge in no such refinements. The Christ Who was born of the Virgin, Who suffered under Pontius Pilate, reveals Himself, not to the eyes of those who actually see and handle Him, but to a spirit within them. He calls forth faith, which is the proper organ and exercise of that spirit. He speaks to a man that was hidden within the man. And there is *always* an answer of some kind to His voice."

234

with which Christ has fellowship, educating it to perceive God in His eternal world.

As a corollary to this concept Maurice contrasts "faith" and "sight" as expressing the true and the false relation to God respectively. This does not mean that during his earthly life man is bound to rest content with faith instead of the direct vision of the eternal God.[67] For Maurice "sight" represents the sensual knowledge which refers only to the outward shape of visible things, whilst "faith" stands for that knowledge which, as specific for the spirit or the reason in man, consists in the immediate sight of true reality. Christ, therefore, appeals to "faith" and not to "sight".[68] By using the term "faith", Maurice also wanted to emphasize that it is only by self-denying trust in Christ that the spirit can receive His revelation and know *that which is.*[69] "Faith" is the only attitude by which the spirit is capable of penetrating Christ's outward shape, His "earthly mould", and know Him as the eternal Son of God and Son of Man.[70]

67 Cf. *Sermons* I, 193: "It is said to be the consequence of our exile from Heaven that we walk by Faith, not by sight. A time, we are promised, will come when Faith shall be lost in sight." Maurice bluntly rejected this view as false.

68 Cf. *The Gospel of St. John*, 183–4: "But if He was the Word who had in all times been the Light of men; if those who judged by the sight of their eyes had resisted this Light and become idolaters; if those who received it, received it into their hearts, and so rose to the stature of Sons of God; – then it was certain that He would speak to another organ than the eye, or than any of the senses; as much when He stood before them in an actual body, and spoke with fleshly lips, as when He was only their invisible Teacher and Reprover. It must be their faith, not their sight, which must now, as ever, see Him and answer to Him. They might touch Him, and yet not come to Him."

69 If Christ spoke to the senses, and man did not have any knowledge of Him other than that which he receives through sense perceptions, then for Maurice those who were His contemporaries and saw Him in the flesh would have had an advantage and privilege over the rest of mankind. As man's relationship to Christ, however, is not conditional on man's having known Him in the flesh, Maurice could say: "The apparent advantage of being on earth at the time of His appearing – of being in the streets in which He walked, of sitting with Him, of conversing with Him – would be nothing. All these privileges might belong to those who would reject Him, hate Him, betray Him" *(The Gospel of St. John, 184).*

70 For the two senses in which Maurice used "faith" the following quotations are most illuminating: "This trust or Faith then conversed with invisible things; with things which *were;* which it could not create more than the eye created the things which made themselves evident to it. In both cases there is a revelation. The outward world reveals itself to the eye. God reveals Himself to Faith. The eye being blind, there is no revelation to it, though all the Universe is revealing itself. Faith being absent in a man, there is no revelation of God to him; though God is ever revealing Himself. Faith is the evidence in one case, as Sight is in the other" *(Sermons* I, 195), and "Let us remember that when the Son of Man actually presented Himself in a body that might be seen and handled, to those whom He was not ashamed to call His brethren, it was to their Faith that He addressed Himself; it was their Faith that, by His words and His acts of healing, He sought to call forth. – – It was to Faith only that He revealed Himself, when the senses appeared most capable of giving a report concerning Him. And let us be sure that it must always be so. Faith must pierce though the robes of His visible Majesty, as Faith did pierce though the robes of His Humiliation. We must know what He is in Himself, His own pure, essential Nature, otherwise there can be no delight in His presence" (p. 196–7). As the spirit in man is not related to the world of the senses, it has no need of evidence of the truth: "faith itself is a higher evidence. Things not seen present themselves to it with a force and a demonstration as great as that with which the

The whole purpose of Christ's teaching and education of His disciples was to call forth "faith" in them:[71] "He chose out some of them to be the heralds of this Kingdom to the world. He led them by various methods to feel their own intimate relation to Himself, to feel that it was not a relation which was produced by His bodily presence with them, or which would be interrupted when He was visibly withdrawn; that it had a deep and eternal ground."[72] At the same time Christ's education implied that He wished to draw His disciples from the world of the senses and direct them to *that which is* as the proper object of the spirit.[73] Thus, Christ's work was in strict conformity with God's revelations to Israel. Here, too, the aim was to educate men as spirits to know God and His eternal Order by making them rise above their fleshly nature, which chained them to the visible things of the world.

But does not the Incarnation run counter to such an understanding of the purpose of God's revelation? Once God has revealed Himself completely in the incarnate Christ, must the consequence not be that man becomes chained to the world of time and space? When the incarnate Christ becomes the object of reverence and worship, does "not He who was leading them [the disciples] out of all visible idolatry Himself become the object of it?"[74] The acceptance of the Incarnation appears

things seen present themselves to the eye. The invisible Person who is the Light of men, makes Himself known to that organ which is created to receive His light. His life, His peace, are as near to us as they were to those to whom He showed Himself alive after His Passion. Our knowledge that He is risen may be as certain as theirs, and essentially of the same kind" (p. 194). Since "faith" stands for a self-denying trust in God as well as for a direct knowledge and vision of the eternal world, it is the true expression of that which unchangeably characterizes the relation between God and man. "Faith" remains the law for this earthly life as well as for the life beyond the grave: "Is God to be changed into an object of sense? Have we been fighting with idolatry all through our stay upon earth; fighting with it as the great earthly sin; as that which degraded God to the level and nature of earth; and are we to become idolaters as soon as our eyes close upon the earth? Is that to be the great celestial reward? Or is Faith, as identical with Trust, to cease? Is the glorified Saint no longer to depend upon God for all that he has and for all that he is? Will some new and higher security be conferred upon him than that which is derived from unceasing trust?" (p. 195–6). Of course Maurice was not in doubt that these questions must be answered in the negative.

71 Cf. *What Is Revelation?*, 54: "Revelation is always with him [St. Paul] the unveiling of a Person – and that Person the ground and Archetype of men, the source of all life and goodness in men – not to the eye, but to the very man himself, to the Conscience, Heart, Will, Reason, which God has created to know Him, and be like Him."

72 *The Prayer-Book*, 128–9.

73 Cf. *The Gospel of St. John*, 202: "The spirit in man is as impatient of those fetters that bind it to the earth, as the carnal understanding is of all that is not of the earth, earthy. The message which Christ brings from the living Father to that spirit is, – 'I can raise you above the earth; I can enable you to share those treasures of wisdom, and righteousness, and love which are the treasures of the kingdom of heaven. I can make you partakers of that Divine Humanity which I have redeemed and exalted to the Father's right hand," and *Theological Essays*, 66: "As He interpreted to them the nature of this kingdom, they more and more felt that He was drawing them from a world which they looked upon with their eyes, into an unseen world which another eye that He was opening must take in; yet a world which was intimately united to the one they were walking in, which gave the forms of that world a distinctness they had never had before."

74 *Theological Essays*, 66–7.

simply to lead men into idolatry, since to worship the incarnate Christ is nothing but to picture God in the categories of sense-perceptions and to worship the visible instead of the invisible God.

Maurice faced this problem clearly. He readily admitted that the belief in the Incarnation has often had such damaging consequences: "When I read some of those hymns "ancient and modern", which are intended to glorify the Incarnation, when I hear them sung with fervour by young men and women who cultivate High Church doctrines, – – I do believe that they are introducing among us a habit of feeling which must issue in the notion that the Godhead *was* controverted into flesh, and so in every possible development of sensuous and idolatrous worship."[75] Maurice had to protest against this interpretation of the Incarnation since it makes Christ's bodily appearance in the history of time and space and not the eternal God the object of man's awe and worship. This is a confounding of time and eternity with idolatry as the inevitable result.

Maurice certainly wanted to present the Incarnation as the great demonstration of the fact that God in His love stoops down to man to save Him. However, he was bound to emphasize that men fail to see the true purpose of the Incarnation if they stop short at Christ's earthly life and do not see His ascension as an integral part of God's history of revelation. Only the Ascension safeguards a right understanding because it unambiguously demonstrates that "the Incarnation is – – not the reasonable excuse for creature-worship, but especially the consummation of the Divine teaching for raising men out of it."[76]

The Gospel narratives bear witness to how Christ gradually revealed to His disciples that He had always had fellowship with them as spirits because they had been created in Him. It is true that the disciples continually yielded to the temptation

75 *The Contemporary Review* XV ("The Athanasian Creed"), 489.
76 *The Epistle to the Hebrews,* CVI. Cf. also *The Prayer-Book,* 290–1: "The impulse of ordinary polytheists was to bring God down to earth; to make Him like themselves. Against this impulse the philosopher protested, representing the Divine Nature as wholly inactive, self-concentrated, removed from mundane interests. The Gospel justifies the truth which was implied in the error of the first; Christ, taking flesh, and dwelling among men, declares that Heaven has stooped to earth. But here a great many would stop; they would bring back Paganism through Christianity. The Son of God, they say, has become incarnate; now fleshly things are again divine; earth is overshadowed by Heaven; it is no longer sin to worship that which He has glorified. In the manger of Bethlehem they sink the Resurrection and Ascension: they will only look at one part of the great Redemption, not at the whole of it; at the condescension to our vileness, not at the deliverance from that vileness, which the Son accomplished when he sat down at the right hand of the Father," and *The Gospel of St. John,* 206–7: "But starting from that which is the strong and vital truth of Mahometanism – proclaiming mightily an unseen God and a living God – we may go on to declare that which is the specially Christian truth, – that this God is united to His creatures in a Son; that this Son has taken man's flesh, and has given His flesh for the life of the world. The deepest mystery of our faith is the most universal; when we are most Christian, we are most human. Only we must not stop short at the Incarnation; we must go on to the Ascension; – so we do justice to the Mahometan demand that we should not exalt manhood above Godhead; so we escape the danger which Mahometans too justly imputed to Christians, that they turned the flesh of Christ into an object of idolatry; – when Christ Himself said, *'It is the spirit which quickeneth'.*"

to believe that their fellowship with Christ was conditioned by the fact that they knew Him in the flesh and with their senses had heard His words and seen His deeds. However, what Christ strove to make His disciples realize was unmistakably demonstrated to be true by His ascension. Now they knew for certain that Christ's fellowship with them was not dependent upon His appearance in the flesh.[77] Similarly the Ascension demonstrated that Christ had established a real, but invisible, relation with every man as a spirit and that He had always revealed the truth to man.[78]

As the Ascension only makes that stand out clearly which was implied in the relation of the incarnate Christ to His disciples, its historical truth does not need to be proved by external evidence. That Christ ascended to the right hand of the Father and was thereby manifested as the invisible Lord of all men was simply the necessary outcome of all that had preceded that event. Any other result would have meant a monstrous contradiction and would have broken the inner harmony and consistency of the account Christ had given of Himself as the Son of God and the Son of Man in His words and deeds.[79]

The fact that the Ascension is the consummation of the Incarnation means that it is not the incarnate Christ, but the ascended Christ that must be held forth to men as the object of their reverence and awe. The Ascension is the great bulwark against

---

77 Cf. *Theological Essays*, 75: "The Ascension, if we admit it to be a fact, not a mere idea, proves – – not that we are divided from Him, but that place cannot divide us," and p. 76: "The disciples who accompanied Him when He journeyed from Galilee to Jerusalem, and sometimes were amazed at the mystery of His being, and at His knowledge of their thoughts, understood first when He was parted from them how entirely independent that being and that knowledge were of the accidents which then surrounded Him, – how much these accidents had interfered with their recognition of Him. As long as they had any notion that they stood to Him only in the peculiar relation of disciples to a Master, as long as *that* relation seemed to them an external fleshly relation, they wanted the real awe and check, as well as the real help and support, of His presence."

78 Cf. p. 76: "they understood that this relation was common to them with a multitude of persons nowise bound to them by kindred, occupation, race; – – they learnt that the real bond between a disciple and a Lord is not a visible, but an invisible one."

79 Cf. p. 67: "If there was such a Son of God and Son of Man, as He had led them to believe there was, then it seemed to them strange and monstrous that He should die, but natural and reasonable that He should rise. And soon they seem to have felt it scarcely less natural and necessary that He should ascend to Him from whom they believed that He had come. They relate, in a few simple words, how they arrived at that conviction, how He educated them into it," and *The Unity of the New Testament*, 302: "If there has been a Resurrection, we feel there must be an Ascension. Men have believed it. Why? Because there was a great array of external proofs and evidences to confirm it? Where are they? Who has ever found them, or believed any stupendous fact of this kind, upon the strength of them? Men have for eighteen hundred years accepted the fact of the Ascension upon the testimony of this one Evangelist, confirmed by the few words of St. Mark, because it was not an incredible thing to those once believing in a Son of God, and King of men, that it should be so; but incredible that it should not be so; incredible that He should be bound by any chains of space and time, that He should not have led captivity to them captive, that He should not be as actual and personal, as when He was loaded with those fetters which hinder us from realizing our personality, from being what we are meant to be; that He should not be actually at the right hand of God, actually the bond of union and fellowship among men."

the misconception that the union of Christ with man is constituted by that which takes place in the world of time and space. Apart from the fact that this falsehood leads to idolatry in the form of worship of visible things, it restricts the significance of the life and work of Christ to those who by chance had seen Him in the flesh or had heard about His incarnation. Mankind is then divided up into those who have had this privilege and those to whom it has fortuitously been denied. Thus, the particular and exclusive dominate the understanding of the Incarnation. When, on the other hand, the Ascension is understood as revealing that the life and work of Christ are not subject to the bounds of time and space, then Christ is seen to be truly the Head of humanity, having an invisible, but nonetheless real and personal fellowship with every man. The Ascension demonstrates that Christ did not choose His disciples in order to give them privileges denied to other men. On the contrary, He chose them and educated them so that they could testify as to Christ's relation to every single member of the human race.[80] The fellowship of the incarnate Christ with His disciples is simply a visible demonstration of the true nature of His relationship to every man.[81]

Thus, the Ascension manifests Christ as the invisible Lord, whose relation to mankind is not restricted by the limitations of time and space. However, the Ascension revealed Christ not only as the Son of God, but also as the Son of Man, constituting the life of every man. In order to bring this knowledge home to man, Christ became man and identified Himself with human life even in its most wretched and most degrading shape. The fact that He nevertheless ascended consequently gives every man the right to see his own life included in the ascension of Christ and to understand that he is not chained to the visible world of time and space but is a spiritual being, intended to live in the spiritual Kingdom of God. This is what Maurice meant by

80 Cf. *Life* II, 614–5: "If we do not set forth the ascended Christ as the object of trust and hope to mankind, as Him who by ascending has led captivity captive and received gifts for men, as the centre to whom all may turn, and in whom all are one, the desire to bring Him down from Heaven – to see Him in the elements on the table – will be, as it has been, irresistible. Priests will be believed to possess the power, because the power must be conceived to reside somewhere; the denial of the Ascension will be called faith in the Incarnation. – – there must be a priest-king in Rome if the Priest-King at the right hand of the Majesty of Heaven is not reverenced there, but is sought to be brought back to His mortal conditions or to an image of His mortal conditions here. If these men are right we must give up saying the Lord's Prayer. Our Father is *not* in Heaven; there is no Heaven; all is of the earth, earthly. I have felt this feebly for a long time; now it comes to me with a tremendous demonstration."

81 Cf. *Country Churches*, 126: "It was not because the disciples saw Christ with their eyes, that they were able to receive His instruction. He spoke to something within them which could not see it. He spoke to their hearts; they understood Him better after they had ceased to see Him than when they could look into His face, and when His lips moved to answer their questions. And therefore do not doubt me when I say He is teaching you and me, even as He taught them. He is walking with us as He walked with them. Every one of us may believe that. As you sow, or reap, or go leasing, you may be sure there is an eye upon you, and that eye is the eye of the Son of Man; you may be sure that a teacher is with you, and that teacher is the Son of Man," and *Sermons* VI, 83–4: "He has gone up on high. He is there where our eyes cannot follow Him, with the God who is and was and is to come, His Father and our Father. He is there, not separated by space from the creatures whose nature He bears; not separated from them in any sympathy; in all things what He was, when He bore their infirmities, was made sin for them, died their death."

asserting that the ascension of Christ implied the ascension and glorification of all men to the right hand of God. The ascension signifies "a victory actually accomplished for the human race over all powers that held it in subjection, – – an actual glorification of Man in the person of Him who is declared to be the Head of every man."[82] In spite of all experience to the contrary man, because of the Ascension, knows for certain that he is a spiritual being who, through Christ, lives in the eternal world. The Ascension is "the practical vindication of our spiritual position and spiritual capacities."[83]

God had educated the Jews to know Him as the transcendent Lord and Creator, who must not be identified or fused with visible things. However, the idea of man as a spiritual being, meant to live in the spiritual world, beyond the world of space and time, was entirely alien to them. The Greeks, on the other hand, had asserted that there is that in man which ardently desires to leave the transient, changeable world of the senses and live in the eternal world as its true home. Maurice was in no doubt that it was due to God's inspiration that the Greeks had reached this view of man as a spiritual being – it was simply their vocation to stand up for this belief. Yet, what for the Greeks was only an idea and, often even, only a dim, groping feeling and desire, expressed in many myths and legends, was vindicated as the truth about man through the Ascension.[84]

Just as Christ's ascension proclaimed the truth about the spiritual capacities of man to His disciples, who, being Jews, had been educated in reverence and awe of the transcendent majesty of God,[85] so it revealed to the Greeks the true foundation of

82 *Sermons* II, 91. Cf. also *The Gospel of St. John*, 222: "we regard the Ascension as the redemption and glorification of Humanity at the right hand of God," and *The Epistle to the Hebrews*, 52: "Man was brought into the presence of God by the ascension of Christ, and – – he was treated as a spiritual being, to be ruled and guided by God's Spirit." Even with respect to the Ascension Maurice's presentation seems to indicate that this event had established a new relation between God and mankind. This was not, however, his intention. For him the Ascension reveals to man a true knowledge of his own life and its foundation in Christ. Once again we notice a disparity between what Maurice actually said and what he intended to say.

83 *Theological Essays*, 93. Cf. also p. 106: "the Ascension of Christ in their nature proclaimed that they did not belong to earth; that they were spiritual beings, capable of holding converse with Him who is a Spirit; able to do so, because that Son who had taken their flesh, and had offered it up to God, and had glorified it, had said that His body and blood should be their food and nourishment. This belief of the Ascension [is] the great triumph for man," and *The Epistle to the Hebrews*, 88: "He had gone into the unseen world; this might shew that men were not to dwell among visible things."

84 Cf. *Theological Essays*, 72: "the message which is contained in the old story of Christ's ascension to the right hand of God – – [is] not – – a legend but – – the fulfilment of all legends, not – – an idea but – – the substantiation of an idea in a fact."

85 Cf. *The Gospel of St. John*, 235: "The idea of an *ascent*, of a return of a spirit to its proper home, was utterly strange to them [the disciples]. This was a proof that they needed one to come from above, that they might be delivered from their downward, earthbound nature. This was a proof that they needed one who was not of this world to come, who might lift them above it; that they, too, might find their way to their Father's house," and *Theological Essays*, 67: " "We may ascend to God! Why, that is the ideal language. You are now translating Hebrew into Greek." If I am, I am doing what the Apostles did. Their minds – the minds of these dull Galileans – *were* idealised, spiritualised. It is what I wish you to ob-

their belief in man as a spiritual being, thereby cleansing it of the false elements with which it had been contaminated. Thus, the Greek philosophers had maintained that only a select few possessed spiritual capacities, whereas the great majority of men were brutes. The Ascension invalidated this great division of mankind because it demonstrated that every man is a spirit, meant to rise above his animal nature and the world of appearances in order to live in the spiritual world in direct knowledge of God.[86] Furthermore, the Ascension proved that man is unable to live as a spirit and ascend to the eternal world by virtue of his own abilities. This ascent can only be achieved by dependence upon Christ, who alone can ensure that man's destiny is fulfilled.

From this account of Maurice's interpretation of the ascension of Christ the conclusion suggests itself that he was only thinking of man's spirit in contrast to his fleshly, animal nature – the one binding him to the eternal heavenly world, the other drawing him to the transient world of time and space. This line of thought is certainly dominant, and, as it presupposes the Platonic dualism of the spirit and the flesh in man, it is not surprising that Maurice basically approved of the Greek idea of man. But the ambiguity which we have repeatedly noticed in Maurice's understanding of the flesh and the world of the senses also makes itself felt in his treatment of Christ's ascension. Besides contending that the flesh belongs to the transient changeable world, he also claimed that even the body of man is encompassed by the ascension of Christ.

Thus, Maurice maintained that "the Gospels and Epistles assert not merely that man has a spiritual nature, but that he is a spiritual being."[87] This means that man consists both of spirit and body, and that even the latter belongs to the spiritual

serve." Christ had also educated St. Paul "to know that the spirit is the substantial part of man; that he *is*, because he is made in the image of God, who is a Spirit; that he is in a fallen, anomalous condition, when the senses which connect him with the earth are his rulers, and he judges what he is from them; that he is in a restored, risen, regenerate condition, when he is able to assert his glory as a spiritual being by asserting his relation to God" (p. 69–70).

86 Cf. *Theological Essays*, 70: "If the Greeks, with their high spirituality, had anything to produce which was more spiritual than this, – if, with their Humanity, they had anything which was more human, – it is a pity they did not bring it forth in those three centuries when they were struggling, with every possible advantage, against the Christian Church. But I think the more we look into the history of that Church in those centuries, and in all that have succeeded them, the more we shall perceive that it has become earthly, debased, superstitious, inhuman, just in proportion as it has lost hold of this truth of Christ's actual ascension; just in proportion as it has substituted a mere symbolical or ideal ascension for that; just in proportion as the Greek notion of men rising and ascending by dint of high gift of soul into gods, has superseded the notion of the fishermen and the tentmaker, that they and the humblest men are risen with Christ, and may therefore seek those things that are above." – That the message of the Ascension has been universally accepted was, according to Maurice, due to the fact that through the hardships of their daily life ordinary people had been trained to seek *that which is*, the invisible, eternal world (cf. p. 95: "we – – owe them [the best men in the old world] gratitude unspeakable, for having testified that man's business in life is to seek for that which is, to believe that he may find it, and to strip himself of all phantoms and shadows which interfere with the apprehension of it. God be thanked for having raised up such witnesses to Himself. What I say is, that the witness has been found to be real and substantial by tens of thousands who have known nothing of dialectics, whose only training has been that of poverty, sickness, the prison, the rack").

87 p. 93.

world since it, as created by God, is meant to be subject to the spirit as its obedient servant. This truth was vindicated when Christ's body, as well as His spirit, ascended to the right hand of the Father. Because the Ascension proved the body to be a spiritual body,[88] it rules out the idea that the body is a recalcitrant element which hinders the spirit in its heavenly ascent.[89] It demonstrates that the body is meant to subordinate itself to the spirit and that man only realizes himself as a person when his spirit lives in dependence upon God and makes his body its obedient servant.[90]

This interpretation enabled Maurice to maintain that neither the body of man nor, even, the outward world of the senses constitute a hindrance to the invisible fellowship of the spirit with God. Even during his earthly life man is related to the eternal world. Consequently there can be no question of leaving the earth in order to live with God. Indeed, because the Ascension established that man as a spirit is meant to be the master of his own body and the world of nature, making them subservient to the will of God, the belief in the ascension of Christ provides the most powerful motive for man faithfully to carry out the tasks of ordinary human life.[91]

As the purpose of the Ascension was to illuminate and explain existing reality, it cannot be considered an event which breaks the laws which constitute the harmonious order of the universe. On the contrary, they are ratified by Christ's ascension. The Resurrection and the Ascension are "acts, attesting the power of spirit over body, the capacity of men to overcome the powers of nature, the possibility of rising into communion with the Infinite"; both events are "instances of an actual connexion between the spiritual and the external world, and of the dominion of the first over the second."[92] As the same testimony is supplied by science and art,[93] there can be

88 Cf. p. 68: "It was the great witness and demonstration to them that they were spirits having bodies, that they were not bodies into which a certain ethereal particle, called spirits, was infused. That which conversed with God was not something accidental to them, but their substance."

89 Cf. *ibid.*: "For this is the pledge of their union to Him; His victory in the body, over the body, for the body, is theirs also. They could claim the dignity of spirits, because they were one with Him who had redeemed the body and made it spiritual."

90 Cf. p. 93: "Christ has shown that the body which He took did not constitute His personality, but that, because He was a Person, because He was the Son of God, He could raise, redeem, and glorify His body; – – He has shown a man not to be a person because he has a body, but that he only claims and realises his personality then when he maintains his relation to God, and holds his body as a subject."

91 Cf. p. 70: "the most quiet, reasonable life you can lead is that of creatures who are raised into union and fellowship with a higher creature; who are continually looking up to Him, in weakness and dependence leaning upon Him, confident that He can lift you, and is lifting you, above all the things which He has put in subjection to you, and is giving you the power to use them as your ministers, and to consecrate them to Him." *Sermons* VI, 75–91 gives an excellent illustration of how the belief in the ascension of Christ furnishes the strongest motivation for fulfilling the duties of daily life.

92 p. 71.

93 Cf. *ibid.*: "Science itself is becoming dynamical rather than mechanical; powers and agencies are discovered in nature itself, not less mysterious than those which miracle workers spoke of. Man is able, through science, to exercise such powers as seem to attest the dominion of spirit over nature more completely than any signs they wrought. The victories of the old artist over the marble, the mysterious energy by which he compelled it to express the thoughts and emotions of living beings, are leading many whom these facts do not impress,

242

no conflict between the belief in the ascension of Christ and the acceptance of science and art. Indeed, the conviction of the truth of the Ascension will only prompt scientists and artists to a faithful carrying out of their work, since it substantiates their research and artistic aspirations respectively. Conversely, those who believe in the Ascension will hail each new discovery and conquest of man over nature as a further confirmation of its truth: "With what delight might we then trace the unfolding mysteries of science, believing that each new fact is revealing some step in the ascending scale of creatures, the lowest of which is an object of creating and redeeming love, the highest of which is in communion with the Son of God! How the triumphs of art would then be felt as witnesses for the subjection of all things to man, a subjection accomplished in Him who has gone through death and has ascended to His Father!"[94]

Summing up the results of our examination of Maurice's interpretation of the ascension of Christ, we find it in complete accord with his idea of revelation. The Ascension "exhibits eternal laws" and "vindicates the true order and constitution of human existence" by manifesting Christ as the Lord of all mankind, who always stands in an invisible fellowship with each single man, just as it demonstrates that man as a spirit lives in the eternal world. Ambiguity was to be found in Maurice's treatment of the flesh and the visible world of the senses. Although he frequently contrasted the spirit and the flesh, he nevertheless contended that the Ascension reveals that the spirit of man is meant to rule over the body and the world of the senses and make them subservient to the will of God. Being encompassed by the ascension of Christ, the body must be defined as a spiritual body.

With this conception of the Ascension Maurice was also convinced that he had solved the difficulty which belief in the Incarnation apparently presented to his basic convictions. This belief threatened to bind men to the world of the senses and make them think that specifice events in the history of time and space were the means by which man's fellowship with Christ was established. The Ascension proved this view to be false. It safeguarded the true understanding of the Incarnation by showing that its purpose was to reveal that all mankind, by virtue of its invisible union with Christ as its Head, is in actual fact related to the eternal world, redeemed from the fetters of time and space.

in the same direction," and p. 76: "History shows how confident men have been in all times that they were meant to ascend above their earthly conditions, and to have fellowship with an unseen world; their noblest dreams have had this origin, – their wildest and most degrading superstitions have arisen from their incapacity to claim what they felt was their right. Physical science shows how many violations of true and divine laws men commit when they become slaves of their bodies, and into what ignorance they fall when they accept the testimony of their senses as determining those laws; in either case they are evidently not obeying reason, but setting it at nought."

94 p. 72. Cf. *ibid.*: "What joyful testimony would every mythological story then bring in, not to the wishes and aspirations of men only, but to God's satisfaction of them! Why may not the countrymen of Bacon, and Shakespeare, and Milton, aspire thus to declare to all mankind, the significancy of science and art, the essential and practical connection of earth with heaven, of the human and the divine?"

Chapter X

THE CHURCH

The idea of the Church played a prominent part in Maurice's thought. In his numerous writings he repeatedly described the Church as a divine society, existing by virtue of God's presence acting through the divinely instituted ordinances: baptism, the eucharist and the ministry. The life of the Church is expressed in the common faith and love of its members and in the common praise and worship of the Triune God.

This view of the Church did not fail to capture the attention of Maurice's contemporaries. As early as in 1838, after the publication of *The Kingdom of Christ*, he was immediately placed as a man who stood for "Church principles". In this great work he had strongly maintained that the Established Church was the authentic representative of the one Catholic Church, in whose divine ordinances the whole revelation of God had received a full and perfect embodiment. He elaborated this idea in contrast to the religious and theological views of Nonconformist Churches and to various philosophical systems. Maurice did not deny that these theological and philosophical bodies of thought all stood for important aspects of the truth, but their convictions were one-sided and could be fully developed only in the life and doctrine of the Church of England.

It is understandable that with such views Maurice was lumped together with the Tractarians, who maintained that the Church was a divine institution through which God, by means of the sacraments and the ministry, whose validity was guaranteed by the apostolic succession, drew men out of the world in order to assemble and build up His holy people, the Body of Christ. It is true that his readers were well aware that Maurice presented and argued his case in his own way, but there was no doubt that in the final analysis he lined up with the Tractarians in defence of the Catholic Church and in sharp opposition to the Latitudinarians, the Evangelicals and the Nonconformists.[1] This was the general view of Maurice throughout the 1840's.

Although misgivings increased as to the soundness of Maurice's churchmanship, it was, however, not until the publication of *Theological Essays* in 1853 that it became clear to everybody that he had little in common with those who stood for Church principles. The Tractarians now definitely stigmatized him as a foe of the desposit of faith which had been delivered to the Catholic Church. The Evangelicals could join forces with them in so far as they considered him to have forfeited his calling as a

---

1 Thus a Unitarian reviewer characterized *The Kingdom of Christ* in the following way: "We cannot better describe the present work than by saying that it is an elaborate attempt prompted by the resuscitated spirit of popery in the Church of England to philosophize Puseyism into a transcendental theology" *(The Eclectic Review* VII (February 1840), 151).

minister of the Church of England – his teaching obviously conflicted with the doctrinal standards of his Church.

By then Maurice had become isolated in his own Church. Nevertheless what he had maintained in 1838 he persisted in saying right up to his death. Stubbornly and indefatigably he maintained that in his preaching and theological thinking he was only expounding the principles of the Catholic Church. His unsparing and incessant chastisement of the clergy and the laity of the Church and his harsh accusations against them of religious egoism and self-sufficiency were, as he saw it, the necessary consequences of his desire to keep watch over the Catholic Church and to show it its high calling. He was bound to wage war against the religious world because it had hindered the Church from fulfilling its true vocation and proclaiming that which God had put into its mouth.

But what did Maurice, in actual fact, understand by the Church? How did he view its calling? What concern prompted his sharp polemics against what he styled the religious world of his day? An examination of the fundamentals of Maurice's idea of the Church is needed to answer these questions.

1. The Idea of the Church

Maurice's thinking is dominated by an ardent desire for unity and fellowship, for that which is universal and common to all and which can unite all men irrespective of rank and worth. Maurice was the sworn enemy of individualism. Where he saw it loom large in the Church and in society, where he saw its fruits in the shape of barriers and dividing-lines between men, where he perceived particularism and exclusiveness, it aroused his passionate anger and called forth his sternest criticism.

For Maurice the history of mankind and the life of every single man are ultimately one great longing and search for a centre of unity, capable of binding all men together in a universal fellowship.[2] Now the Incarnation means the fulfilment of man's longing and search for unity. This is so because it revealed that men are not isolated beings, sentenced to a self-seeking preoccupation with their own destinies, but that they all exist as members of the human race with Christ as its life-giving centre.[3] Christ did

---

2 Cf. *Sermons* VI, 127: "Unity is, consciously or unconsciously, the end for which we are all striving"; *Sacrifice*, 230: "Whence comes it [the strife]? what is it that we have lost? what is it that we want? And the answer will come in due time; it comes from a want of a *Centre* of Unity. That Centre men will seek for, high and low; in one sect and school, then in another; in one dogma and another, in one man and another, in one city and another," and *The Prophets*, 272: "And then ask yourself whether you can meditate on such a world as this, whether you can explain how society has been possible in it, how families, nations, churches can have existed in it, how there has been order and fellowship amidst so much hatred and anarchy, – unless there were a centre of unity, a divine source of life and regeneration – –. I know that there is a conscience and reason within us which say, 'Such a One there *must* be'."

3 Cf. *Sermons* IV, 25: "No schemes, doctrines, systems of men can unite nations together. God has united them in His Son. God does bind them together by His Spirit. Schemes and systems do build up new barriers between men, because they set up new and contradictory conceptions of God," and *The Conflict*, 172: "Men are not united in opinions; they are not bound together under sophists. Christ is the Head of a living body: all are members of Him – members therefore of each other."

not come, as the religious world mistakenly imagined, to withdraw a small flock of believers from the multitude of men and bestow His benefits upon them alone. On the contrary, Christ became incarnate in order to demonstrate that He is the Creator and Saviour of all men and has that life in which all may participate provided they do not exalt themselves above their fellow-men and are satisfied to receive Christ's gifts in fellowship with the meanest and most despised members of the human race.

This truth is apparent from the fact that the Kingdom of God is at the core of Christ's words and deeds. At times Maurice expressed himself as if Christ had become incarnate in order to establish the Kingdom of God.[4] Once again, however, this is an instance of how his mode of expression fails to convey his meaning accurately. The Kingdom of God has always existed.[5] What happened in the Incarnation is that Christ revealed its existence to men who, because of their unbelief and sin, had been ignorant of it, imagining that they were living under the dominion of sin and the Devil. The Kingdom of God is simply the Divine Order, God's created universe.[6] Owing to the revelation of Christ incarnate man now knows for certain that all mankind is always encompassed by the Kingdom of God and lives, moves and has its being in God.[7]

Against this background Maurice's idea of the Church appears to present a problem. He could describe the Church as a new, universal human fellowship, founded upon the incarnation of Christ,[8] and assert that it was called into existence through the sending of the Holy Spirit after Christ's ascension.[9] Maurice could even

---

4 Cf. *The Kingdom of Christ* I, 248: "this person [Christ] came into the world to establish a Kingdom. Every act and word which is recorded of Him has reference to this kingdom."

5 Cf. *The Kingdom of Christ* I, 223: "the spiritual and universal society must be involved in the very idea of our human constitution, say rather, must be that constitution, by virtue of which we realise that there is a humanity, that we form a kind. – – the character of this constitution has been revealed to us in an inspired Book," and *Sermons* IV, 93: "He will have found that what he needed, what he was to seek, was an Eternal Kingdom, – a Kingdom of God, – the manifestation of which might be different in one age or another; which might come more mightily into prominence at one particular time; but which *is* the same yesterday, to-day, and for ever; which is really about all."

6 Cf. *The Unity of the New Testament*, 52–3: "the actual King of men [came] to make manifest the nature of his government to them, to shew what rule he had been exercising over them, and for what ends, how it was thwarted, why they were unaware of its presence; – – The King of Men [was] also the King of nature, the Creator and Lord of the world in which man is dwelling," and *Christmas Day*, 193–4, in which Maurice had Christ say: "It is not only true that the God of righteousness will be King hereafter when I shall have established my Church upon the earth. It is true now. It has been true always. This book, this record which is preserved in durable letters that it may testify of indurable, unchangeable things, this book bears witness to His dominion; I am come to claim it as His, I am come to set aside all Satan's pretensions to be the master of this earth, and of those who inhabit it. So far as this I am come to change the condition of the world. But it will not have a new king. Only He whose right it is will drive all usurpers out of it."

7 Cf. *Social Morality*, 372: "That a Fatherly Will is at the root of Humanity and upholds the Universe was the announcement which shook the dominion of capricious dæmons and the throne of an inexorable fate in the Roman Empire."

8 Cf. *The Kingdom of Christ* (1838) I, 243: "the incarnation, – the foundation of the church's being."

9 Cf. *The Acts of the Apostles*, 27: "Out of that dying Jewish commonwealth must spring up

246

view the establishment of the Church as the culminating event in God's history of revelation: "what we sometimes speak of very lightly, as if it were only an accident of the New Testament, – the calling in of the Gentiles – the unfolding of a universal society out of the Jewish national society, – is treated by our Lord Himself, and by His Apostles, as that wonderful event to which all God's purposes, from the beginning of the world, had been tending."[10] The Church represents the people of the new covenant, meant to embrace all the nations of the earth.[11] The Church is the manifestation of the Kingdom of God upon earth.

Such statements certainly provide support for the contention that Maurice reproduced the New Testament idea of the Church – and this in contrast to the theological thinking of his time.[12] If this is so, then it must be added that there is a contradiction in Maurice's thought beween his concept of the Kingdom of God as identical with the created universe and encompassing all men and his concept of the Church as having been established with the sending of the Holy Spirit after the resurrection and ascension of Christ as the realization of the Kingdom of God upon earth. Although several students of Maurice have noticed this contradiction, there has been no attempt to deal with it adequately despite the fact that it raises the issue of the coherence and consistency of Maurice's theological thinking.[13]

We have already seen that Maurice could speak of God's revelation as progressive.

---

a new and human commonwealth, quickened with a divine life. Man could not effect such a renovation and new birth. He who raised His Son out of the bonds of death and the grave will effect it"; *Sermons* VI, 109: "the Church stands upon the gift of a divine Spirit – this is the very ground of its stability and universality," and *Theological Essays,* 92: "The Christian kingdom cannot be described as a dispensation of the Spirit if these anticipations were not fulfilled. The Apostles must have deceived their hearers, if the condition of those who lived after Christ's glorification was not better in this respect than that of those who waited for His coming. The story of the descent of the Spirit on the day of Pentecost, and of the signs which accompanied it, and of the preaching which followed it, must be thrown aside altogether, if no great blessing was then vouchsafed to *mankind*."

10 *The Gospel of St. John*, 332.
11 Cf. *Sermons* II, 83–4: "The Scripture has been teaching us how God chose out a family to testify of Him and of His relation to men; how He chose out a nation to testify of Him and of His relation to men; how, finally, He sent forth members of that family and that nation, to bid men of all lands enter into covenant and fellowship with Him, because He had sent forth His Son – –. On that warrant men were invited to come to be baptized."
12 Thus A. M. Ramsey remarks: "It was not at the time common to expound the Church as the Israel of God, and to seek its meaning within Scripture as a whole; and no other exponent of the doctrine of the Church in Maurice's day – Newman, Palmer, Arnold, Gladstone – succeeded in treating the Church in a manner so thoroughly scriptural. Maurice sees in Scripture the principles of the Church which now is, because there still exists the holy nation, the people of God" (op. cit., 29–30).
13 A. R. Vidler hints at the problem when he writes: "some might infer that, since according to Maurice Christ is the Head of the whole human race (and not only of a portion of it), since all men are created in Christ and have been redeemed by Him, and since Christ is the Head of every man, no place is left for what the New Testament calls the Ecclesia or Church as a distinct society. Does not the Church on this view become coterminous with humanity? Are the Church and the world then simply alternative names for humanity? But this is of

He made it perfectly clear, however, that this must not be understood as the gradual realization of a divine economy of salvation. As reality, being founded upon the immutable will of God, always remains the same, a progressive revelation only implies a progressive manifestation and demonstration of *that which is*.[14] Throughout history God had educated man to ever deeper insights until full and perfect knowledge was given through the Incarnation.[15] Maurice accordingly maintained that God's progressive revelation took place as a gradual unveiling of Himself and the Divine Order through the family, the nation and, finally, the Church. They represent three distinct phases in God's history of revelation. The fact that the latter does not abrogate the former clearly indicates that they do not refer to different grades of reality, but to a gradual growth in the knowledge of reality.

When God constituted the family of the Patriarchs, this act was accompanied by

course very far from being the case." (op. cit., 64–5). Dr. Vidler does not attempt to prove the correctness of his interpretation. A. M. Ramsey has faced the difficulties presented by Maurice's statements about the Church and offers the following solution: "Maurice was, like the Tractarians, contending for the dogma of the Holy Catholic Church; but his methods and his emphasis were different from theirs. – – He viewed the Church not only as the home of the redeemed, but as the sign that God had redeemed the whole human race and that the whole human race was potentially in Christ" (op. cit., 34). Although Dr. Ramsey does not elaborate, it is possible to adduce statements which appear to prove his case (see for instance *The Kingdom of Christ* (1838) III, 316: "the Church is a fraternity not united in the profession of a certain opinion, but actually united together by a common relation to a divine Person; – – this relationship existed implicitly for all men, but actually and effectually for those who renounce their selfish position, and enter this society"). As the further exposition of Maurice's idea of the Church should prove, his standpoint is that the Church manifests the truth that all mankind stands in Christ and is united with Him. So the contrast between the Church and the rest of mankind consists in the former having, and the latter not having, knowledge of this fact.

14 Cf. *Life* I, 333: "There must be a perpetual growth, but a growth which does not falsify any previous stage, because it is a growth into the knowledge of Him who is the same yesterday, to-day and for ever; a growth which, instead of being the same thing with change, is out of change to fixedness and certainty"; *The Gospel of St. John*, 31: "the greatest progress consists in the assertion and elucidation of first principles," and *Theological Essays*, 91: "If all Progress consists in the advancing farther into light and the scattering of mists which had obstructed it, the Bible contains the promise of such *Progress*." In *The Kingdom of Christ* II, 235 Maurice deliberately rejected "a notion of progress, which is inconsistent with the permanency of God's order and truth", on the grounds that "there was no alteration in the counsels of the Divine mind". So Maurice was not a forerunner of the theological exploitation of the idea of evolution as we find it in the *Lux Mundi*-school and its prominent representative, Charles Gore. This view was maintained by J. Scott Lidgett: "The Prophetic vision and teaching of Maurice anticipated the coming conflict between the static view and the dynamic, brought about by the doctrine of Evolution, and supplied religious faith with the means of so transforming theological thought as, not only to escape the danger, but actually to illuminate the situation. Maurice saw that the concepts of the Absolute and Infinite are empty abstractions, and that the Fatherhood of God, rightly construed, brings together for Religion transcendence and immanence, perfection and process, eternity and time" (op. cit., 30). Maurice spoke of "progress", not of "evolution", and the term refers only to knowledge, not to reality itself.

15 Cf. *The Epistle to the Hebrews*, 28–9: "We often say that Revelation is progressive. – – But by *progress*, some seem to understand a continual journeying away from the inmost centre;

a revelation of God's being and was sealed with a visible sign to safeguard the knowledge which had been imparted. This happened again when God called Israel into existence and made a covenant with it. Its political, social and religious institutions were given by God as signs to keep the Israelites in the new revelation that God was their Lord to whom they owed their life and well-being as a nation. The last and final step in God's history of revelation occurred through the Incarnation. As the Old Testament covenants and their signs were related to that partial and imperfect revelation, which had been given to the Patriarchs and Israel, they were inadequate for the full and perfect revelation which Christ brought. A new fellowship with new signs was needed which could adequately express this complete knowledge of God and His Divine Order.[16]

Although the Church was constituted after the resurrection and ascension of Christ, it only exists to bear witness to unchangeable reality. Therefore the Church does not supersede the fellowships of the family and the nation or render them superfluous. Indeed, by proclaiming that they are created and sustained by God, the Church stands up for their continued existence and their God-given tasks.[17] "The Church," Maurice asserted, "– – is a part, the highest part, of that spiritual constitution of which the nation and the family are lower and subordinate parts; implied in the acts we do and the words we speak, established before all worlds, manifested as the true and everlasting kingdom when the Son of God died, rose, and ascended on high, testified

a movement towards the circumference. Here we seem to be taught that each step of it is bringing us nearer to the ground of things – nearer to the throne of God. The revelation of God in this sense is truly the unveiling of Himself. First, He speaks in that which is most distant from Him, the mere things which He has formed; then in men whom He created to rule over these things; lastly, in Him who by the eternal law is the inheritor of all things, in whom and for whom they were created."

16 Cf. *The Kingdom of Christ* (1838) II, 127: "But when the Son of God came in human flesh, to proclaim himself the source of all the order of the universe, it was inevitable that the outward organization, which had been foretelling his advent, should be converted into one which assumed it for its ground," and *The Kingdom of Christ* I, 287: "Thanks be to God, that He has not left eternal truths, which concern all men, to the custody of the wise and prudent of the earth; that He has embodied them in forms which from generation to generation have been witnesses of his love to the humble and the meek, and which all the contradictions of pride and self-will only help to illustrate and interpret."

17 Cf. *The Kingdom of Christ* I, 268–9: "I have maintained, upon the authority of Scripture, that the Catholic Church is emphatically a kingdom for *mankind,* a kingdom grounded upon the union which has been established in Christ between God and man. I have maintained that it grew out of a family and a nation, of which social states it proved itself to be the proper and only foundation," and *The Kingdom of Christ* (1838) I, 283–4: "Admitting a holy order and constitution in Christ, the national life, the family life, being – – holy and divine ordinances, were of course esteemed parts, though subordinate parts of it. The church-life was in one sense the flower and consummation of all the rest. In one sense it included them all, – it might be spoken of as root, and stem, and flower; for the church was the great kingdom which God had set up on earth; grounded upon a fellowship established with himself in the person of his Son, and this kingdom ruled over all." Against this background Maurice could maintain that each individual undergoes the same education as that experienced by mankind throughout its whole history. As a member of a family and a nation, each man is led to an ever growing knowledge of reality, reaching its culmination in the perfect knowledge which the Church imparts to him.

as the common property and inheritance of men by certain forms and ordinances which convert it from an idea for the mind into an actual reality for all who will enter into it and enjoy it, and which prove God to be true though all men be liars."[18]

There is, therefore, no contradiction between Maurice's description of the Kingdom of God as embracing the entire creation and his contention that the Church had been called forth after the resurrection and ascension of Christ as the manifestation of the Kingdom of God. For him it is an established fact that the creation is coterminous with the Kingdom of God, since its existence is always dependent upon the self-sacrificing love of the Triune God. However, it is only in the Church that this knowledge of the Divine Order has found an adequate visible expression. Therefore the Church eminently represents and manifests the Kingdom of God. On these premises Maurice could contend that the Church as "a *family* of men, claiming to be the sons of God, feeling that they were so, and therefore that they were brethren to each other, shewing forth their filial relation and their brotherly relation in act, proving that selfishness was not the law of the universe, but was the contradiction of its law, – – was a novelty in the history of mankind."[19]

Maurice once declared that "there is a very distinct obligation laid upon us all to explain what we understand by the language of Scripture respecting the gift of the Spirit and the foundation of the Church."[20] He does not appear to have fulfilled this obligation himself! We have previously seen how Maurice maintained that the Spirit is at work in every man and that all good in man and society is due to its inspiration. At the same time he asserted that the sending of the Holy Spirit marked the foundation of the Church and that, owing to "the dispensation of the Spirit", new life and blessings had been bestowed upon mankind. Even here, however, it turns out in the end that the contradiction is only apparent although, it must be conceded, this is obscured by the fact that in his description of the Church he made use of the language of the Bible and traditional theology, of terms which are notoriously associated with the idea of the sending of the Spirit as an event inaugurating the Church as a new unique stage in the divine history of salvation.

Maurice regarded it as a historical fact that the Holy Spirit descended upon the disciples at Pentecost and that this event issued in the foundation of the Church. He even described this outcome as "the end of all God's dispensations".[21] Yet the aim was not to introduce a new principle of life into the world. The sending of the Spirit meant the revelation of the Spirit as a person who eternally proceeds from the Father and the Son and together with them constitutes the Divine Unity.[22] The descent of

18 *Life* I, 306–7.
19 *The Church a Family*, 44.
20 *Theological Essays*, 98.
21 *Sermons* VI, 109.
22 Cf. *The Kingdom of Christ* (1838) II, 137: "The deep mystery of it [the Pentecost] – – consisted in the formal declaration of the Holy Spirit as a Person, the assertion of the Divine Unity of the Father and the Son in Him, and in the establishment of a universal Church," and p. 126–7: "The priests and sacrifices in the Jewish commonwealth testified of a divine constitution established in the Word. The order of prophets testified of a divine Spirit actuating and energising in man; but as the person of the Word was not yet manifested, so neither was the person of the Spirit. This mystery was hid for ages and generations. Each new step in the divine plan is a preparation for the discovery of it."

250

the Holy Spirit is a visible manifestation of the fact that the Holy Spirit is a living, acting person, always at work in the universe and in man. While it is true that the Church has received the gift of the Spirit, this fact must not be taken to mean that the activity of the Spirit is exclusively restricted to its sphere.[23] The granting of the gift of the Spirit signifies that the Church has received perfect knowledge of the Holy Spirit and its work in order to explain and unveil the truth about human life to all men.[24]

Man had always felt himself possessed by inspirations which prompted him to perform acts of truth and goodness and fight that which would lead him into sin. In his blindness and ignorance he had, however, been unaware of the origin of these inspirations – most often he had imagined that they originated in his own nature. The event of Pentecost unveiled the true facts of the case. It substantiated the experiences of mankind by revealing that man can only be true man when he lives by inspired guidance, and that this inspiration proceeds from the Holy Spirit as a living person.[25] In other words, Pentecost proclaims that "the indwelling of a Spirit in man – – is implied in his original constitution."[26] It is the law of man's being always to live under the guidance of the Holy Spirit, which leads him to true humanity, the essential characteristics of which are truth and goodness. Moreover, the very fact that the

23 Cf. *Sermons* II, 101–2: "The truth that He [the Holy Spirit] is *the* gift which the Son, when He had ascended on high and led captivity captive, received for men, is the truth of which the Holy Catholic Church exists to bear witness. Churches have dared to invert the order of God's revelation, to transpose the articles of the Creed. They have placed the faith in the Church first, in the Holy Ghost second. They have made the Spirit dependent upon the body which He quickens; not the body upon the Spirit. So the divine gifts have been shrivelled into enchantment and tricks of legerdemain. So men have been taught to shut God out of His own universe, and to suppose that He was exercising no real government over their acts, confining Him to certain sudden and casual and trivial interferences with the course of Nature and with human affairs. So science has been divorced from Faith, and the empire of Chance set up to subvert the Kingdom of Heaven." In this passage Maurice attacked the idea that the Holy Spirit is to be found in the Church exclusively and acts only in and through the Church. If this is so, membership of the Church is necessary in order to receive the Spirit and His gifts. Such a particularist and exclusive view of the Holy Spirit and His activity implies that the universe with the greater part of mankind must be regarded as godless, being outside the orbit of the Spirit.

24 Cf. *Religions*, 191: "One therefore who believes this [St. Peter's] statement cannot look upon this descent of the Spirit, with all that was implied in the circumstances of it, as violating the laws of the human constitution, as an exception in the plan of the Creator. He must look upon it as expounding that constitution, as carrying out that plan."

25 Cf. *Theological Essays*, 106: "But though the minds of men had always felt that they must look upwards to some Ruler above them, they had equally confessed the presence of an Inspirer within them. The Christian revelation – – explained to us whence all *Inspirations* had proceeded, who was the Author of them, how they are to be received, how they may be abused," and *The Kingdom of Christ* (1838) II, 155: "We say that the inward call was made intelligible by the descent of the Holy Spirit, who thus declared Himself to be the source of all the impulses and movements in the heart of man."

26 *Religions*, 201. Cf. *Sermons* VI, 95: "The Apostle, believing as he did that the day of Pentecost spoke of a real, not of an imaginary gift – of a living Person, not of a floating influence – of that which was implied in the creation and constitution of Man, but which could not be actually conferred, in its fulness and universality, till Christ had glorified the nature of Man at the right hand of his Father."

sending of the Spirit united the disciples in a fellowship demonstrated that it is owing to its work that human fellowships have continued to exist in spite of man's persistent attempts to tear them asunder by living for himself apart from his fellow-men.[27]

The significance of Pentecost is that it reveals the truth about human existence; for Maurice this is evident from St. Paul's preaching to the Greeks. St. Paul came to a people "whose traditions told them of an Inspiration which poets, prophets, priestesses, received from some divine source. These traditions had facts for their basis. Men were actually seen to be carried far above the level of their ordinary thoughts; they spoke as they did not speak when they were buying and selling; their words entered into other men's minds, and worked mightily there."[28] The Greeks felt that this inspiration demanded their obedience because it was of divine origin but they were incapable of answering the question: *"What* God, what is His *name?"*[29] However, St. Paul provided the answer by proclaiming that it was God who through the Holy Spirit had sent these inspirations. At the same time his message taught the Greeks to distinguish between that part of their concept of inspiration which originated from God and the part which stemmed from sinful man.[30] St. Paul's message also disposed of the idea that the gift of the Spirit was the possession of a few exceptional persons and reserved even for the most exceptional moments of their lives by making it perfectly clear that the Holy Spirit was at work in every man and was necessary for the discharge of the duties of ordinary human life.[31]

Thus, Maurice's interpretation of the event of Pentecost accorded completely with his idea of revelation. The sending of the Holy Spirit to the disciples was a visible manifestation of unchangeable reality. It removed the blindness and ignorance of man by declaring the Holy Spirit to be a divine living person, ever working in the universe and in man. Consequently the Church, founded as the result of the descent of the Holy Spirit, had received perfect knowledge of reality. Its calling was to proclaim to

---

27 Cf. *Theological Essays*, 102, where Maurice spoke of "the law which was proclaimed on the day of Pentecost; – – the assertion that it is the law of human Society, – the one by which Society *is* governed, – however much men may be denying it or rebelling against it," and *What Is Revelation?*, 463–4: "Shall we never ask whether the Day of Pentecost is not the explanation of the Constitution of human society, the interpretation of the difference between that Universality, which is grounded upon a Spirit of Truth, who binds together and quickens the spirits of men, – and the Universality of Despotism, Imperial, Ecclesiastical, Democratical?"

28 *Theological Essays*, 84.

29 *ibid.*

30 Cf. p. 85: "The opposition between the divine and either the animal or the devilish, which had been confounded with it in the old mythology, was manifested just in proportion as those very powers and gifts, which man had felt before he could not ascribe to himself, were ascribed to the Spirit of God, the Spirit of Order and Truth."

31 Cf. *ibid.*: "But it is equally evident that there was another great and broad distinction between the old and new belief. The first had been partial, narrow, peculiar. It had tried to explain how extraordinary men, or men in some extraordinary crisis of their lives, were able to do strange acts, to speak unusual words. St. Paul's Gospel was human and universal. It explained, indeed, the influence of seers and prophets; it asserted the existence of special endowments; it put all honour upon distinct callings. But first, it asserted that the Spirit was necessary for all human beings, and was intended for all."

all men that the whole creation lives, moves and has its being in the Triune God, the Father, the Son and the Holy Spirit.

The correctness of this interpretation receives further corroboration from Maurice's analysis of the relationship between the Church and the world. This subject occupied a central place in contemporary preaching and theological debate, and it was incumbent upon Maurice to make his position clear.[32]

Maurice accepted that there is a contrast between the Church and the world. The world, being temporal, changeable and transitory, must be opposed to the Church as the visible manifestation of the Kingdom of God, which stands for the eternal, unchangeable and permanent, in other words, for *that which is*.[33] However, the world must not be identified with the visible creation; although the latter is part of the mutable world of time and space, its life is rooted in the eternal world, since it is called forth and sustained by the loving will of God. Therefore all human beings and all human fellowships can be described as consisting of "a Church element", the substantial, eternal principle, which constitutes their being, and "a world element", which chains them to the sensible, changeable world.[34] There is bound to be a continual struggle between the Church and the world, between the permanent and the transitory, because the sensual shape of things always attempts to drag man away from eternity.[35] The task of the Church in this situation is to proclaim the truth about the Divine Order so that man can know the law of his existence and live and act accordingly.[36]

32 The Evangelicals had strongly emphasized the contrast between "believers" and the godless, unbelieving world, whilst the Tractarians had underlined that the Church, as the divinely instituted ark of salvation, must be opposed to the world, which lives under the law of sin and death.

33 Cf. *What Is Revelation?*, 91: "We oppose the Kingdom of Heaven to the Kingdom of Earth. We call the one eternal, the other temporal or transitory. That is ordinary language; none, whatever their theory may be, object to it," and *Sermons* II, 110: "it is the very nature and law of the world to be continually changing, to have no permanent principle. That is the reason why it is so ignominious a thing for a man to be conformed to it: he must abandon all his prerogative of looking before and after; he must become merely a creature of to-day; he must be fluctuating, capricious, insincere, – a leaf carried about by every gale, floating down every current. How is it possible that such a one can know anything of the Will of God, which is fixed, eternal, capable of no accidents?"

34 Cf. *Sermons* I, 256: "The world is seen in each age. It is embodied in the various customs, habits, fashions of the age; it is a series of shifting dissolving views. It always *implies* something permanent, but that permanence is not in it. And it is always trying to separate itself from that which is permanent, trying to make itself self-sufficient, trying to make us live in the transitory, the momentary."

35 Cf. *Christmas Day*, 351: "from this love [of God] the images and pictures of this world, the created, temporal things, are seeking to withdraw us. We cannot enjoy them without it; from it they borrow their lustre. Yet they would tempt us to forsake it for them; to dwell in them and not in it. The invisible guide of our hearts is drawing them by a thousand gracious acts and influences, and invitations, from the perishable to the eternal; from that which is the likeness of the thing they long for, to the thing itself; from that which loses its beauty when we can no longer give it beauty, to that first source of beauty from which we and they alike draw our life."

36 He who does not dwell on the visible and outward, but pierces through it to the eternal and unchangeable, will be able to see the entire visible creation as good: "The world in itself is

Maurice was only stating this fact in other words when he expressed the contrast between the Church and the world as the contrast between those who have attained to a true knowledge of reality and those who are living without this knowledge, believing man to be fettered to the world of time and space and capable of living for himself without God.[37] The Church cannot, however, allow the world to rest content with its false knowledge. It must fight it by declaring the truth about the universe and mankind.[38] "The Church," Maurice maintained, "exists in the world as a witness to mankind that there is a continual, divine, gracious government over it − −. The Church is to declare, that the spiritual and eternal kingdom which God has prepared for them that love Him, is about men now, and that they may enter into it − −. To bring these truths practically home to the minds and hearts of human beings, is, it seems to me, the great function of a Church."[39]

It can now be seen that Maurice's idea of the Church represents a consistent development of his idea of revelation. He fully accepted that the resurrection and ascension of Christ issued in the sending of the Spirit and the establishment of the Church. However, he emphatically rejected the view that the Church stands for a unique spiritual reality. The Church differs in no way from that which constitutes the life of all mankind. Its sole distinction is that God has entrusted it with His perfect revelation and given it visible signs which embody the truth about the Divine Order. This view entirely invalidates any claim to exclusiveness. The Church is simply mankind when it has surrendered its lies and falsehoods and attained a true knowledge of reality.

not our enemy: it is loved by God; it has been redeemed by Christ. The world of nature is precious in God's sight, and should be precious in our sight. The world of human beings is more precious to Him, and should be more precious to us. But the pomps and vanity of the world, those mere outside phantoms which dazzle our eyes and hinder us from looking into the heart of nature, from knowing her substantial worth and secret loveliness; the fashions among human beings which shut them up in a little circle of time and place, and cut them off from all that is essentially human, from all that unites them to each other and to God; these are the signs of a *wicked* world, of a world which chooses to exclude the sun, and to dwell in its own darkness" (*Sermons* I, 280).

37 Cf. *The Gospel of St. John*, 392–3: "The one difference − − between the world and those whom He chooses out of it, is that they confess a Centre, and that the world confesses none; that they desire to move, each in his own orbit, about this Centre, and that the world acknowledges only a revolution of each man about himself. The world, indeed, cannot realize its own principles. It must have companies, parties, sects, − bodies acknowledging some principle of cohesion, aspiring after a kind of unity. Still, as a world, this is the description of it; and therefore, as a world, it must hate all who say, 'We are a society bound together, not by any law of our own, not by an election of our own, but by God's law and election. And His law is a law of sacrifice'."

38 Cf. *Sermons* I, 251: "The Universal Church, constituted in its Universal Head, exists to protest against a world which supposes itself to be a collection of incoherent fragments without a centre, which, where it reduces its practice to a maxim, treats every man as his own centre. The Church exists to tell the world of its true Centre, of the law of mutual sacrifice by which its parts are bound together," and *The Gospel of St. John*, 212: "The world must hate those who tell it that the Creator of all good and truth is close to it, − that it has no good apart from that Creator, − that its works will always be evil while it is not owning Him."

39 *The Patriarchs*, XX–XXII.

Maurice repeatedly emphasized that it is the calling of the Church to be "a witness to all mankind of what Christ has done for them, and what they really are, created in Christ, and redeemed by Christ."[40] The Church must be "the witness of the true constitution of man in Christ"[41] and proclaim "a permanent divine order, belonging not to the individuals – – but to their race."[42]

"To make Churchmen feel," Maurice once declared,[43] "that they are not members of a corporation bound together by certain professions of opinion, but that they exist to testify of a body to which men as men belong, has been the aim which I have tried to keep before me and which I have, with shameful feebleness, pursued." To achieve this purpose, however, it was necessary to oppose the false ideas of the Church which were rampant in the preaching and theological thinking of his day.

Maurice could have nothing to do with Tractarians and others who held High Church doctrines, since they deified the Church by placing it before God Himself[44] and thus paved the way for sacerdotalism with its despotic rule over men and human life.[45] These accusations, which Maurice never tired of launching, might easily lead one to the conclusion that he stood out as a man who wanted to make the Church realise that it is nothing in and by itself but is solely dependent upon God and His revealing and redeeming acts.[46]

---

40 *Christmas Day*, 196.

41 *The Gospel of St. John*, 499.

42 p. 146.

43 *Life* II, 325.

44 Cf. *The Contemporary Review* XIV ("Grammar of Assent"), 165: "I have said that I believe in God the Father, and in Jesus Christ his Son, and in the Holy Ghost; *after that* in the Holy Catholic Church. That I have understood to stand in His name, to have no existence apart from it. If I am to believe in the Church first and then in God, I do not know what the Church is; I do not know how it came into existence, or what function it can have. Just so far as it ceases to be a witness for God, and supposes that it has a theology or a religion of its own, just so far I think it proclaims itself apostate."

45 Cf. *Sermons* I, 52–3: "men who thought their function was only to preach the word, might substitute for that hard dogmas and hard practices, which misrepresent the character of God, and make themselves objects of faith instead of Him. – – All things are no longer referred to God. The Gospel is not a message from Him, that He has reconciled the world to Himself. Men are by certain acts of faith to bring themselves into reconciliation with Him; divines must ascertain the quality and degree of those acts of faith. They must define the ways in which men may approach God, and ascertain that they are at peace with Him. Whatever ministers may call themselves, when they undertake this office they must cultivate all the arts of priestcraft"; *The Prayer-Book*, 390–1: "we do not affirm Theocracy in the sense which some persons give to that word, and which may well have made it hateful. We do not say 'Thine is the kingdom', meaning that it belongs not really to an invisible Father, but really to certain visible priests, who claim the homage due to Him for themselves, and bring men into bondage by the perversion of that truth which is alone able to set them free," and *Sermons* I, 51–2: "God is living and reigning and – – He has not delegated His powers to any body of ministers, or shut up His grace in any ceremonies."

46 The following passage is one example of many which at first sight seem to justify such an interpretation: "We feel that the Holy Catholic Church must be worthy of all the honour which we can pay to it. But we can pay it no honour while we set it before God and His revelation of Himself. When we do that, we make it no longer God's Church, but man's

Simply to see Maurice as a staunch opponent of any idea of priestly rule and of the deification of the Church is, however, to miss the fundamental point in Maurice's polemics. His true aim was to eradicate the idea that the Church mediates God's salvation to mankind. If membership of the Church is made the *conditio sine qua non* of fellowship with God, then the Church is set above God.[47] This idea necessarily leads to sacerdotalism, since priests have to decide what profession of faith men are to make, and what ceremonies they must undergo in order to be considered the children of God.[48] "We are not to pretend," Maurice emphatically declared,[49] "that they must come to Church in order that they may be brought under the the discipline of the Son of Man, in order that the Word of God may work in their hearts. They come here to learn that they cannot escape from the Son of Man; that He is with them when they lie down, and when they rise up; that He is spying out all their ways. They come here to be told what that flame is, which ever and anon breaks out within them; what those smouldering ashes, which they always fear may burst into a flame after it seems to have been extinguished. We are to tell them that the Word of God kindles that fire; that it is seeking to burn up what is evil and false within them; that it will not cease to scorch and torment *them* till they have yielded to this process, and desired that it should be an effectual one. We are to preach this to you; we are to preach it to ourselves, knowing well that God is preaching it to us all – not here, but out of the whirlwind. The sermon is a poor godless *substitute* for the lessons of life. It may be a godly *interpreter* of those lessons. It may remove some of the confusions which hinder us from doing our work manfully; this confusion most of all, that we do not know whether the Creator of the Universe, the Lord of ourselves, is working with us or against us." Christ is always united to every man. But man does not recognize this fact, being mislead and led astray by his self-will and his subjection to the world of the senses. Therefore he needs the witness of the Church to tell him that there is "a foundation for all men, an everlasting Name in which all are living and moving and having their being."[50]

The true idea of the Church and its divinely appointed task was also contradicted, and even opposed, by what Maurice termed the religious world. What this favourite term of his covers the following passage makes evident: "A religious world is a so-

Church. We can pay it no honour when we do not regard it as set up among sinful men and as claiming sinful men for its members. When we do that, it becomes a mere artificial body, not a real body" *(The Faith of the Liturgy, 28–9).*

47 Cf. *What Is Revelation?*, 392: "[that] "High Church doctrines" – – put the Church before God, and suppose the Church to be our teacher respecting God, not God respecting the Church, is the real, earnest English objection to them," and *Tracts for Priests and People No. VI* ("Morality and Divinity"), 29: "If I think the Church is above God, or that I derive any knowledge of God from the Church and not from Him, I shall be obliged to change its method and its substance."

48 Cf. *Sermons* I, 100: "We are always ready to fancy that we are not redeemed, not claimed as God's children, not grafted upon a true and holy root. We are always supposing that by some painful acts, devised by ourselves or borrowed from the practice of other days, we are to bring ourselves into a condition which we ought to attain, but which God has not yet bestowed upon us."

49 p. 186–7.

50 *Life* II, 443.

ciety by itself, witnessing for itself, for its own privileges, for its difference from the rest of mankind. It acknowledges no vocation from God; it has no living connection with the past; it is subject to all the accidents and mutations of public opinion. Yet it has no hold upon human life in any of its forms. It treats politics, science, literature, as secular; but it dabbles with them, pretends to reform them by mixing a few cant phrases with them, is really affected by all the worst habits which the most vulgar and frivolous pursuit of them engenders. It trembles at every social movement, at every thought which is awakened in human hearts, at every discovery which is made in the world without. But it does not tremble at its own corruptions."[51]

Thus, the religious world believes that, in contrast to the rest of mankind, it stands in a unique relationship to God. It maintains that it alone, by virtue of its faith and works, has procured God's benevolence. In fact, however, it is prompted by selfishness, cares only for its own salvation and leaves the world to its own fate.[52] It jealously guards its privileged status.[53] It prides itself upon its own excellence.[54] It demands that people must accept its opinions and patterns of behaviour in order to be recognized as the children of God. It considers itself entitled to decide who is encompassed by God's salvation and who is condemned to everlasting perdition. The religious world regards human life as godless and pretends that it can deal with it only when it is made to conform to its maxims. Under the pretext that it has been entrusted with responsibility for God and His Kingdom, it has set up a tyrannous rule and considers any attack on itself as a rebellion against God and a violation of His glory and honour – and this contrasts sharply with the indulgence which it displays towards its own sins.

However, the pretensions of the religious world are null and void. They are simply the product of religious selfishness, manifestations of the sect-principle or party-spirit with exclusiveness as its distinguishing mark.[55] The religious world has put itself in God's place and deals with God and its fellow-men at will. Consequently

---

51 *The Patriarchs*, XXIII.
52 Cf. *The Epistles of St. John*, 110: "We are very apt to think thus, 'We belong to a guilty race; God looks upon us all as sinners. But perchance *I* may get Him to treat me differently; *I* may procure a separate pardon'. No! that will not do. There is selfishness, there is separation from *thy* brother, there is the very essence of sin in that thought."
53 Cf. *Sermons* I, 175: "Wherever men have tried to construct a Church which should be ascertained by tests of theirs to consist only of chosen men it has ended by the members of that Church being angry that others should receive the same wages with them, and by their denying that the King has really made a Marriage for His Son with their race."
54 Cf. *The Prophets*, 409: "How comfortable when we can thus sever ourselves from the sins of the world around, and make them a foil to shew off our own excellence!"
55 Cf. *Sermons* IV, 8: "the sect-profession is: *"We* have bound ourselves together for the purpose of promoting certain great objects; *we* have adopted certain distinct badges of *our* faith; *we* are pledged to oppose that which interferes with it." Christ chooses the *Church* to be a witness of His love to mankind. The *sect* chooses Christ because it is convinced that His doctrine is better than that of the founders of other religions," and *The Patriarchs*, XXIV: "Its faith is essentially exclusive, and so is its charity; for though it devises a multitude of contrivances for relieving the wants of human beings, nearly all these seem to proceed upon the principle, that they are creatures of another race, on behalf of whom religious people are to exercise their graces; not creatures who have that nature which Christ took, as much sharers in all the benefits of His incarnation and sacrifice, as their benefactors are."

there is bound to be enmity between God and the religious world: "So the prophets of old found; so the apostles found; so the reformers found; so it was in the days when our Lord walked on earth. All had to contend with the religious world of their day – He most of all."[56]

Although Maurice reckoned the Tractarians as part of the religious world, he primarily had the Evangelicals in mind when describing its distinctive character. It is easy to point out that the well-established Evangelical party, with its powerful institutions, displayed many of the traits which Maurice found typical of the religious world. But both Maurice's contemporaries as well as a later age have astonishingly failed to see the essential point behind his fierce attacks on the religious world. It is true that many passages can be quoted which make Maurice out to be a prophet, chastising the representatives of the religious world for their exclusiveness and arrogance towards their fellow-men, and scorching them for their complacency about their doctrinal systems and their religious practices and calling upon them to rely upon the living God alone and to love and bear the burdens of their neighbours.[57] It is easy to present Maurice as a man who combated the religious parties and cliques of his time for monopolizing the Word of God and fought for a Church which proclaims God's salvation as a free and unconditional gift to be received by everybody.[58] Without being false such interpretations do not, however, strike at the root of Maurice's criticism of the religious world.

The basic reason for Maurice's antagonism to the religious world is that all its preaching and activity imply that mankind has fallen from God and can be saved only through the life and death of the incarnate Christ, a salvation made accessible to the individual through the preaching of the Gospel and the administration of the sacraments as the divinely instituted means of grace. It is this idea of Christianity which for Maurice ultimately constitutes the denial and apostasy of the religious world. Because it has not recognized that Christ is the living Head of humanity and always has fellowship with every man, it is a sect which has reduced Christ to the status of the founder of a religion and the Saviour only for those who belong to the sect.[59] When Maurice charged the religious world with having exalted its own

56 *Sacrifice*, XLI.

57 Cf., for example, *The Gospel of St. John*, 348: "I would have you observe how carefully we are told that these disciples were chosen by Him; that His love to them did not depend upon their faith, but their faith upon His love. I would have you observe how this love was manifested to them all as a body – to one and another of them individually; how they were taught that it was only this love which was sustaining them then, or could sustain them afterwards. Unless we do that, we shall never understand how they were witnesses against that religious world out of which they were called, – that world of sects and parties, – that world where all were choosing for themselves, and none were acknowledging a loving Will which was ruling them; where all were striving for their own views and opinions, and none were confessing their relations to each other; where each was fighting for ascendency, and none was content to be a servant."

58 Cf., as one instance among many, *The Kingdom of Christ* (1838) II, 207: "We open the Church to all; we declare that none are excluded from the benefits of Christ's redemption and the gift of the Spirit; we invite all to claim them. But the sects, each in their own way, declare that this privilege is not theirs."

59 Cf. *Sermons* IV, 11: "There is a plant in your heart and mine which our Heavenly Father has not planted, and which must be rooted out. It is that same plant of self-seeking, of

258

beliefs and made acceptance of them the necessary condition of fellowship with God, his ultimate aim was to eradicate the idea that man's salvation is accomplished through God's acts in a particular history and is mediated through the proclamation of Christ's incarnation, death and resurrection.[60]

3. The Signs of the Church

The religious world was constantly threatening to usurp the Church and lead it into apostasy.[61] It tempted the Church to deny its vocation to bear witness to Christ as the Head of all mankind.[62] The Church of England was not exempted from this danger, and Maurice considered its actual state most deplorable. Party-spirit dominated and tended to eclipse the good tidings which it was its charge to proclaim to the nation. It was on the verge of becoming a sect itself – consequently it had no right to exalt itself and boast of its superiority to other Churches.[63]

Nevertheless Maurice did not withdraw his allegiance from the Church of England, but even supported it steadfastly. His reason was that by its mere existence as an Established Church and through its liturgy and doctrinal standards it bore the strongest witness against the sect-spirit of its parties. Despite their practical atheism the Church was enabled by these mean continually to proclaim the truth about the life

opinionativeness, of party-spirit, which has shed its poison over the Church and over the world. It springs in us from that same root of unbelief in One Who is the Head of us all, Whose Life is the common Life of all, out of which all sects and parties have proceeded, – from that root of pride which has led to the amazing delusion, that God has not called us to be His servants and children, but that we are taking Him to be our Lord and Father."

60 Cf. *The Gospel of St. John*, 346–7: "The Jewish sects had refused to believe in a Father. They had refused to believe in a Son of Man. They had refused to believe in a Lord of their own hearts. For a Father they had substituted a lawgiver, who hated all Gentiles, and to whom Jews could only look up with terror, not with confidence. For a Son of Man they had substituted their sect and its leaders. For a Lord over their hearts they had substituted the notion of an outward Christ, who was to be identified by certain particulars of place and time, which must be ascertained by studying the letters of a book." Maurice considered the Jewish parties in Jesus' own time as displaying all the characteristics of the religious world.

61 Cf. *Life* II, 272: "the sin of the Church – the horrible apostasy of the Church – has consisted in denying its own function, which is to proclaim to men their spiritual condition, the eternal foundation on which it rests, the manifestation which has been made of it by the birth, death, resurrection and ascension of the Son of God, and the gift of the Spirit."

62 Cf. *The Conflict*, 186: "How ready *every* church is to make itself heretical by separating itself from the rest, how ready it is to fraternise in some opinions, and so to deny the Head of the whole body," and *Sermons* II, 84: "If this society called Christian had not courage to say, "We are called out to be members of a body of which Jesus Christ, the Son of Man and the Son of God, is the glorified Head, we are actually one with Him where He is, He is actually dwelling with us where we are," they disclaimed their history; they renounced the charter on which their calling and their privileges rested; they made themselves something which God had not made them; and, of necessity, just so far as they were guilty of this apostasy, they made themselves a curse to the world which they were appointed to bless."

63 Cf. *Life* II, 324: "With respect to the English Church I have felt and do feel bitterly how it is always on the point of drifting into mere sectarianism; and I know that it may make itself the most proud and self-exalting of sects."

of man.[64] It was precisely as a loyal and faithful member of the Church of England that Maurice felt bound to wage war against the religious world. His task was to make the Established Church see the significance of its own existence, its Creeds, its ministry and worship. No new foundation had to be laid for the Church of England. What was needed was to sweep away the falsehoods which the religious parties were attempting to substitute for its true ground.[65]

Since the vocation of the Church is to bear witness to the fact that Christ is the living Head of the human race and constitutes its life, the Church embraces all mankind.[66] Every man must be considered a member of the Church.[67] Likewise every nation in its totality is an integral part of the Church. The reason for the Church's existence as a distinct, visible body is that only in this way can it perform its task of being a witness to the whole nation and to all men. Since it is part of the proper ordering of human life that the various functions and offices are assigned to different men, there must be a ministry set apart to teach the nation the truth about its foundation and to educate its members to understand the Divine Order and their place in it.[68]

64 Cf. *Life* II, 524: "I prize the Church of England very greatly, because it bears continual witness to the truths which we, its members, are most habitually denying; because it testifies for that unity in Christ with the whole family in heaven and earth which we by our acts and words are seeking to destroy," and *The Kingdom of Christ* II, 291: "The idea of a unity which lies beneath all other unity, of a love which is the ground of all other love, of Humanity as connected with that love, regarded by it, comprehended in it; – – this idea is the basis of our Liturgy, our Articles, our Church."

65 Cf. *Life* II, 299–300: "I think the Church of England is the witness in our land against the sect principle of "forming churches" which is destroying us – –. As long as we think we can form churches we cannot be witnesses for a Humanity and for a Son of Man. We cannot believe that we do not choose Him, but that He chooses us and sends us to bear witness of His Father and of Him. Everything seems to me involved in this difference. I admit that the English Church is in a very corrupt, very evil condition. I am not afraid to own that, because I believe it is a Church and not a sect. The sect feeling, the sect habit is undermining it. The business of us who belong to it is to repent of our sectarianism and to call our brothers to repent, to show that we have a ground on which all may stand with us."

66 Cf. *The Prayer-Book,* 10: "If they will not have a Common Prayer with us, we can make our prayers large enough to include them. Nay, to take in Jews, Turks, Infidels and Heretics, all whose nature Christ has borne. For He is theirs as well as ours. He has died for them as for us, He lives for them as for us. Our privilege and glory is to proclaim Him in this character; we forfeit our own right in Him when we fail to assert a right in Him for all mankind. The baptized Church is not set apart as a witness *for* exclusion, but against it. The denial of Christ as the root of all life and all society – this is the exclusive sectarian principle."

67 Cf. *Sermons* V, 241: *"This* signifcation [of the Church as a body] which connects it with the natural body, *this* signification which identifies it with that universal body politic of which Christ is the Head, because He is the Head of every man, shall remain. Of your relation to this Church you cannot rid yourselves, any more than you can change the law under which your natural bodies and the members of them exist. It is one which you must confess along with us, because you are human beings as well as we are."

68 Cf. *The Church a Family,* 158–9: "This distinction between the internal ground or constitution of a society, and its external economy or management, is to be traced in every orderly community which the world has ever seen. It has been felt strongly just in proportion as the body has been firm and coherent, or loose and inorganic. And it has always exhibited

260

The Church of England testifies to this true understanding of the relation between Church and nation by the mere fact that it is a Church established by Law. Consequently Maurice strongly repudiated the Tractarian view of the Establishment as a *mésalliance*, which had been brought about by mere historical chance and which had only had the effect of obliterating the true character of the Church as the Body of Christ. The responsibility of the Church towards the nation can only be fulfilled when it exists as an Established Church. The Establishment is a visible demonstration of the fact that the Church and the nation are coterminous. It safeguards the Church from yielding to the religious world and becoming a sect which considers itself saved in contrast to the rest of the nation. At the same time the Establishment is a continual protest against the false notion that the nation is a society accidentally brought into existence through man's own endeavours. The mere existence of the Establishment is a declaration to the effect that the nation is created and sustained by God and is called to live according to His will. The idea of disestablishment must be rejected as a denial of the Divine Order.[69]

Because the Church is "a body instituted by God Himself, to which men, as men, are invited to belong, and to which no one can refuse to belong without abandoning his own privileges, and denying the privileges of his fellow-men,"[70] any attempt at distinguishing between believers and non-believers is ruled out. All men belong to the Kingdom of God irrespective of their personal attitude.[71] Maurice, therefore,

itself in the assignment of different functions or offices to different persons. That there should be some persons who express to a nation the idea that its existence has a divine ground, who shall keep up the feeling of a communion between the visible and the invisible world; that this class should be distinct from those who regulate its outward workings, and keep in order the different parts of its machinery; this has been the most serious conviction of all people, the clearest apprehension of all thoughtful statesmen, however differently they may have embodied it." – It follows from this understanding of the necessary union of Church and nation that the Church alone is capable of educating the nation. All true education aims at illuminating human existence and developing true humanity. Since the Church has received the knowledge of what man truly is, it alone is fitted for the task of being the educator of the nation: "our formularies enable us to embrace the people; – – sects and Secularists alike ignore their necessities, even their insatiable cravings; – – the State can only bring them to the water without the least power of giving them drink" *(Life* II, 613).

69 Cf. *The Kingdom of Christ* (1838) III, 76: "If we once settle in our minds, that the State is as much God's creation as the Church, even as the body is just as much his creation as the spirit, we shall be saved from a world of difficulties; we shall no more talk of a spiritual body forming a low and dishonourable alliance with an earthly body – –. That connection as much exists in the nature of things, – is as much based on an eternal law, as that which binds father to child, or brother to sister," and p. 106: "God hath ordained an eternal connection between the law, which is embodied in the State, and the religious, life-giving principle which is embodied in the Church, so that one shall always sigh and cry till it has found the other to be its mate."

70 *The Kingdom of Christ* (1838) II, 1.

71 Cf. *Sermons* II, 41: "I can assert that Humanity in the very terms of the Creed, against those who would separate believers from the rest of human beings, – who would exalt the *sect* of Christians against the race which the Church of Christ, which Christ Himself represents." Although Maurice strongly repudiated any attempt to draw a line between believers and non-believers (cf. *Social Morality*, 103: "We *have* no means of determining in any man's case how much he has in him of gold or of alloy; it is assuming the throne of the supreme

strongly opposed the contention of the Evangelicals that man only becomes a child of God through his conversion and personal belief in the forgiveness of his sins by virtue of Christ's expiatory death upon the Cross. This view simply founded man's salvation upon his own efforts – whether it was a question of doing good works or producing a living faith in order to enter into fellowship with God did not in Maurice's eyes make any difference. Instead he referred to baptism as indicating how man's salvation was dependent upon God's will alone.

Maurice placed great emphasis upon baptism. When describing its significance he appears to follow closely the Anglican formularies, which defined baptism as "a sign of Regeneration or new Birth, whereby, as by an instrument, they that receive Baptism rightly are grafted into the Church; the promises of forgiveness of sin, and of our adoption to be the sons of God by the Holy Ghost, are visibly signed and sealed" (Article XXVII). Thus, Maurice maintained that "by our baptism we are born into the new covenant",[72] or admitted into the Kingdom of God[73] with the right to call God the Father and to draw near to Him as His children through Christ.[74] In baptism man is grafted onto Christ and receives His life.[75] By the act of baptism he is made a member of the Church and receives the Holy Spirit as his guide and guardian.[76] Because, through baptism, God has accepted man and made him His child without any effort or merit on his part, there can be no question of forfeiting the privileges of baptism and losing the fellowship with God. What remains is to exhort men to adhere to their baptism as the foundation of their Christian life and become what their baptism has made them to be.[77]

judge to attempt *that* discrimination") he did acknowledge that, within each man, a dividing-line exists between that which receives Christ and that which opposes Him, in other words, between the spirit in man and his animal, fleshly nature: "there is no need of artificial rules and distinctions, such as doctors invent for their own confusion. The Light makes the distinction. It is not the distinction of Pharisee or Publican, or religious men or irreligious. It goes deeper than that. It is the distinction between that in every man which welcomes the light and claims kindred with it, and that in every man which eschews the light and would fain extinguish it for ever" *(Sermons* IV, 181–2).

72 *The Prophets*, 441.

73 Cf. *Sermons* I, 124: "To be baptized into the name of the Father, the Son, and the Holy Ghost is, it seems to me, to be admitted into that kingdom, which Christ said was at hand."

74 Cf. *Christmas Day*, 28: "By your baptism you have been admitted into the family of God; the right of calling God your Father has been conferred upon you; the right of believing that he has redeemed you and reconciled you to himself; the right of approaching him at all times and in all places through his well-beloved Son."

75 Cf. p. 17: "By your baptism God hath given you a portion in him who was made flesh," and *The Kingdom of Christ* I, 289: "He does not by Baptism, faith, or by any other process, become a new creature, if by these words you mean anything else than that he is created anew in Christ Jesus, that he is grafted into Him, that he becomes the inheritor of His life and not of his own."

76 Cf. *The Kingdom of Christ* (1838) I, 119: "And now this child, admitted into the Church of Christ, receives that Spirit which is given to the church and to us, so far as we are members of it," and *The Kingdom of Christ* II, 92: "It follows from that doctrine of Baptism, which lies at the threshold of our Churchmanship, that we suppose every Christian infant to be taken under the guardianship and education of God's Holy Spirit."

77 Cf. *The Patriarchs*, 344: "Why is any teacher raised up in the Christian age except to tell baptized men that God's Spirit is with them, and that the greatest and the least of them

Such statements certainly convey an understanding of baptism which runs counter to the idea of Christ as the Head of every man. The inconsistency is not to be denied but here, as elsewhere, it is due to the fact that Maurice simply reproduced the language of the Bible and the Anglican formularies. A closer scrutiny makes it evident that he also interpreted baptism in accordance with his basic idea of revelation.

Maurice definitely rejected the idea of baptism as a means through which God takes man into fellowship with Himself and incorporates him into the fellowship of the Church. Neither the baptismal act nor man's faith in the significance of baptism bring about any change in the relation between God and man or create anything new in man.[78] Admittedly, baptism is "the ordinance of God for men",[79] but its function is to be a witness of the fact that man unchangeably lives in Christ. Baptism is a sign in which God declares "that which is true concerning men, of the actual relation in which men stand to Him".[80] Baptism consequently "interprets our existence to us; – – it interprets the condition of mankind".[81] Thus baptism imparts to every single man the true knowledge of reality which dispels the lies and falsehoods under which he has been living.[82] It was on these premises that Maurice was able to point to baptism as a decisive act on God's part towards man and describe its significance in the terms of the Anglican formularies.

The extent of Maurice's consistency in his understanding of baptism is revealed in a letter to Charles Kingsley on the meaning of the words of the Catechism: "[in baptism] I was made a member of Christ, the child of God, and an inheritor of the

must give account for a trust so awful; for the presence of a Guide whom they may trifle with and grieve, but whom they cannot banish, and who is speaking to them continually, whether they heed His voice or despise it?", and *The Kingdom of Christ* II, 281: "the sacrament is not believed to have conferred on men a temporary blessing, but to have admitted them into a permanent state, which is at all times theirs, which they are bound at all times to claim, and by which they will be judged."

78 Cf. *The Contemporary Review* XV ("The Athanasian Creed"), 481: "A few earnest people refuse the ceremony [of baptism] only because they are afraid to connect with something visible and external a truth which they say must be at the very root of our lives. Heartily do I agree with these – – objectors, that no ceremony can be a bond between nations or men. Even more incredible is the notion that some opinion about the ceremony or the amount of meaning which attaches to the ceremony, can be a bond between them."

79 *Theological Essays* (1853), 201.

80 *ibid.*

81 *Sermons* V, 77. Cf. also *The Kingdom of Christ* I, 280: "the idea of Baptism – – assumes Christ to be the Lord of men; it assumes that men are created in Him, that this is the constitution of our race," and II, 2: "Philosophers say that man can only be that or do that which is according to his constitution; he cannot be made by some miraculous process something else than he is; or, if he can, that power must be an injurious one. Baptism declares man's true and right constitution to be that of union with God."

82 Cf. *The Church a Family*, 42: "the command, 'Be baptized', [means] yield to an ordinance which implies that God is the source and spring of all that is good in you; of the pricking in your hearts, of your repentance, of your faith, of every movement towards heaven now going on in you, or that has gone in you at any time, of all moral and spiritual acts whatsoever, of any kindly affection you have ever manifested towards a child or a parent, of every wish and hope that has not been selfish and shameful. That is the meaning of the act to which He bids you submit – –. I affirm baptism to be the assertion of an absolute, undoubted, unconditional truth concerning the condition of that person who comes to it."

kingdom of heaven."[83] Kingsley, his faithful and straightforward disciple, had completely adopted Maurice's idea of baptism but felt that it contradicted the teaching of the Catechism on baptism – and asked for help in solving this difficulty. Maurice complied, underlining the necessity of only using words which convey an unambiguously clear meaning.[84] "You know," he wrote,[85] "– – how much it has been the effort of my life to assert a ground for men's sonship to God, which is deeper than any external rite and which is grounded on the eternal relation of God to man in the Living Word." Maurice readily admitted that this basic idea apparently conflicted with the words of the Catechism – the Tractarians seemed therefore justified in appealing to them to prove their concept of baptismal regeneration.[86] However, though the use of the word "made" is beset with difficulty because it appears to deny man's "original sonship in Christ",[87] it would be wrong to drop it. The word "made" safeguarded a truth which would otherwise easily be lost sight of: "You lose the witness of men being above nature, above their law of the ordinary birth; you lose a witness of their being the spiritual creatures you want to affirm that they are. The *made* sounds formal, sounds legal, just as legitimate does. But I do not know if we exchanged it for any other that we should not slide back into the very notion against which our whole lives are a fight, that we are in our flesh, merely as animals, sons of God."[88] In other words, if the word "made" is left out in any explanation of the significance of baptism, the conclusion will be drawn that man is by nature, that is, as a creature with a fleshly, animal nature, a child of God. This is false, since it is only the spirit in man which has fellowship with God.[89] Thus the retention of "made" serves the function of stressing the distinction between spirit and flesh in man and emphasizing that it is man's spirit only which God has adopted and deals with as His child.[90]

83 *Life* II, 271–5.
84 Cf. p. 271: "most heartily do I rejoice to find you again working at that old puzzle about "made" which you rightly think we have not got to the bottom of yet. It deserves all sifting that we may be sure we are not cheating ourselves and cheating mankind of that which is most precious, and that we are not making words mean what they do not mean."
85 p. 271–2.
86 Cf. p. 273: "We are *made* sons of God in baptism. "There", says the Puseyite, "is not that conclusive? How dare you go farther? You have spoken the words. Now talk about an original sonship – a sonship in Christ before all worlds if you please"."
87 Cf. p. 274: "You are not satisfied with the word *made* children of God in baptism. You ought not to be."
88 *ibid*.
89 Cf. *ibid*.: "I think it is the hardest of all struggles for you with your right and eager assertion of the worth of man's animal nature, not to confound it with the spirit and so to unsay all you mean to say. I have felt the difficulty too, but more in a logical way – –. Meantime, I am quite certain that you will be taught to preach a Gospel to men that they are spirits and that they are born of God, and that it is their duty to believe so. If baptism were in the way of such a proclamation, I should throw it off as St. Paul did circumcision."
90 In *Family Worship*, 59–60, Maurice again discussed the significance of the word "made": "May it not be exceedingly difficult to guard by *any* form of speech against two opposite dangers: the first, of losing sight of this distinction and merging the spiritual in the natural birth; the second, of diminishing the universality of the blessing and confining it to certain persons? There have been times when I have felt the last danger much more than the first; when I have feared so much to narrow the Redemption of Mankind, that I have used language which might easily convey the impression that men as natural creatures were sons

264

Maurice clearly realised that baptism has often been made a pretext for raising a barrier between men, dividing the baptised from the unbaptised, the saved from the lost. But this stems only from the misunderstanding that baptism confers a specific righteousness and holiness which make men new creatures in Christ.[91] Maurice, on the other hand, emphatically asserted that baptism "can confer no separate or independent grace upon any creature. It can only say: 'Thou belongest to the Head of thy race; thou art a member of His body; thou dost not merely carry about with thee that divided nature which thou hast inherited from the first Adam – a nature doomed to death, with death stamped upon it – thou hast the nature of the Divine Son, thou art united to Him in Whom is life, and from Whom the life of thee and of all creatures comes'."[92]

Just as God, through baptism, declares that Christ is the Head of every man, so the act of being baptised signifies that man acknowledges this to be the truth of his own life.[93] Since baptism reveals that this applies to every individual, the baptised

of God. Then I have tried to find a more comprehensive phrase than the one of the Catechism, and have secretly or openly murmured against that. But the greatness of my own mistake has been brought home to me by some strong inward experience. I have felt that I was not really more universal, but was cheating men of a conviction, which is of the most radical and universal kind, cheating them also of the message of God which has met that conviction. Then I have come back to this word *made,* and while fully admitting how open it is to misapprehension, have been led to doubt whether I could invent any other." In a sermon on Eph. 2,3–5: *Nature and Grace. The Service for Infant Baptism* Maurice interpreted "by nature a child of wrath" as "a child of passion, of mere impulse, governed by the things about me, and the impressions they make on my senses, apt to look to them, as if I sprang from them, as if they had some title of paternity over me" *(The Church a Family,* 22–3). Baptism, on the other hand, is "the witness to us that we are in a state of grace, and are redeemed out of nature" (p. 39); through it we are vindicated as "spirits", "susceptible of spiritual blessings" and having "the capacity for the knowledge of God, the chief of all treasures" *(ibid.).* That man is living under grace and not under law and wrath is tantamount to saying that, as spirit, he can rise above his animal, fleshly nature with its carnal appetites whereas the latter always remains under the domain of law and wrath.

91 Here Maurice had the baptismal doctrine of the Tractarians especially in mind. To assert that baptism imparts to man a *gratia infusa,* a righteousness and holiness which he must keep inviolate as his personal property, is a blunt denial of its purpose and significance. Baptism simply proclaims that man lives in Christ and receives everything from him in self-denying trust and obedience: "this state – – precludes the notion that goodness, purity, holiness belongs to any creature considered in itself. To be something in himself is man's ambition, man's sin. Baptism is emphatically the renunciation of that pretence. A man does not, therefore, by Baptism, by faith, or by any other process, acquire a new nature, if by nature you mean, as most men do, certain inherent qualities and properties" *(The Kingdom of Christ* I, 288–9).

92 *Sermons* I, 81.

93 Cf. *The Kingdom of Christ* II, 5: "by that act we are acknowledged as spiritual creatures, united to a spiritual Being, by this act we claim our spiritual position, we assert our union with that Being," and *Theological Essays,* 52: "If it [baptism] marked him [St. Paul] out as a Christian, that was because it denoted that he would no more be the member of any sect, of any partial society whatever, – that he was claiming his relation to the Son of God, the Head of the whole human race. It must import his belief that this Son of God, and not Adam, was the true root of Humanity; that from Him, and not from any ancestor, each man derived his life. It must import his acknowledgement that in himself, in his flesh, dwelt no

know that their fellow-men are likewise members of the human race which is created and upheld by Christ.[94] So, far from separating men from each other, baptism binds them together, making them realise that all men belong to the Church, the universal human fellowship of which Christ is the lifegiving centre. As "the simplest and fullest witness of a redemption which covers those who are not baptised," baptism is a sign which is "inclusive and not exclusive."[95]

Like baptism, the eucharist must be understood as an inclusive sign. Its significance is in no way limited to those who participate in the Holy Communion.[96] As a divine ordinance it declares the truth about human existence, since the bread and the wine "remind us of the daily, hourly temptation to be seeking a life of our own, to be forgetting that we are bound by the eternal law of God, by the unchangeable conditions of our own being, to our fellows, and to their Father and ours, in the Well-beloved Son."[97]

Thus, the ordinances of the Church, baptism, the eucharist and the ministry,[98] are visible signs which reveal eternal truth. Therefore Maurice rejected any idea of them

good thing; but that he was not obliged or intended to live as a creature of flesh, as a separate self-seeking being; that it was utterly contrary to God's order that he should."

94 Cf. *The Conflict*, 179: "We tell all men, those who are most incredulous of our message, most hostile to it, that this Name is about them, that they are living, moving, having their being in it. They do not acquire this privilege by baptism; we baptize them because they have it," and *The Church a Family*, 30–1: "If – – all these [words of the Baptismal Service] are merely enigmatical phrases with which we may play fast and loose as we please, which may signify something for some of those to whom they are spoken, and nothing at all to the great majority, – – the Gospel has no hold upon human life; it concerns a few individuals, excepted out of the mass of perishing creatures; but it does not concern us as men; it gives us no place in a human fellowship."

95 *Macmillan's Magazine* XI ("On the Revision of the Prayer Book and the Act of Uniformity". April 1860), 425. Cf. also *The Unity of the New Testament*, 278: "At the same time it [baptism] contains the most earnest encouragement to spread far and wide the Gospel (that is to say, the good news to men of their sonship), and a warning of the great guilt of turning Baptism into a plea for exclusiveness, into a denial of that human privilege which it asserts and upon which its glory rests," and *The Epistles of St. John*, 66: "Our race, our manhood is glorified in Him. Whether we live in London, or Paris, or Constantinople, we are no longer separated. There is a common Lord of us all. There is a common life for us all. Confessing that common Lord, renouncing by the strength of this common life our selfish divided life, we become men indeed; we obtain the rights, the stature, the freedom, the dignity of men."

96 Cf. *Sermons* IV, 100: "Do you think that any ordinance of Christ can have reference merely to the advantage or enjoyment of those who submit to it? – – If this feast does not show forth or declare something to the world, – if we only seek in it for some benefit to ourselves, – it cannot be a communion in the body or in the mind of Jesus Christ."

97 *Sermons* IV, 123. Cf. also *Sermons* I, 11–2: "Surely we must be reminded of His [Christ's] presence with us. The natural notion that what is invisible is unreal; that He does not govern us because our eyes do not see Him; that He does not govern the world because the world fancies that it governs itself, this must be set at naught. We must have an assurance – a continual assurance – that the senses are as little judges of what is true in morals, as they are in physics; that self, which appears to be the centre round which everything here revolves, is no more really the centre than our earth is the centre round which the heavenly bodies revolve."

98 Maurice's understanding of the ordination as "an inclusive sign" appeared from our examination of his concept of every vocation as "a divine office", see pp. 92–5.

as instruments through which God saves man, since such a concept only binds men to the visible things of time and space and makes God's dealings with man subservient to particularism and exclusiveness. However, once it has been made clear that the divine ordinances do no more than reveal how God, in and through Christ, always acts towards mankind, then their importance cannot be overstressed.[99] They can even be called necessary in the sense that they make it unambiguously clear that every man stands in Christ and through Him is encompassed by God's love.

If man did not have these visible signs which witness to the unchangeable truth of human existence, he would easily fall prey to a false knowledge of reality deduced from the changeable world of time and space. He would make his own experiences of sin and evil the basis for his concept of God and His dealings with man. He would believe that there is no other knowledge of God than that which the intellect imparts or imagine that fellowship with God is dependent upon the strength of his personal feelings and the quality of his own endeavours.[100] Even the clergy yielded repeatedly to the temptation of interpreting God's revelation by means of these false measuring-rods: the consciousness of sin and evil and the intellect which, because of its categories of thought, only deals with the visible world of time and space. But this falsification of the Gospel of Christ has never been allowed to remain unchallenged. Through His ordinances God has raised up signs which continually bear witness to the truth: "He has taken care of His own name and His own kingdom in this earth of ours, – – His Church has stood firm in His Son; – – in every land He has testified of its existence by His ordinances, which no corruptions of men could set aside."[101]

Our analysis has in no way exhausted what Maurice said about the Church and its vocation.[102] Its sole purpose has been to work out the basic principles determining his view of the Church and its task in the world.[103] Our examination should have

---

99 Cf. *Christmas Day*, 287: "Do not suppose that I am limiting the operations of God on the hearts and minds of men to these ordinances; I am urging you to take the privileges which they offer you, because I am sure, they interpret to us all His other operations, because they enable us to feel His presence, to hear His voice in all the common events and accidents of life," and *The Acts of the Apostles*, 244: "The worship of ordinances and institutions destroyed the faith which ordinances and institutions embodied. Those who could not look above them had really no sense of their worth. Those who received them as messages from God saw in them a perpetual pledge of His presence, an assurance that His will could not be confined by the limitations which it had fixed for them."

100 Cf. *The Kingdom of Christ* I, 267, where Maurice maintained that the Quakers' rejection of baptism means that "they cannot keep the faith that we are related to the Divine Word; they can only substitute for it certain individual feelings and impressions."

101 *Sermons* IV, 11.

102 Cf. *Life* II, 495: "For if sacraments express the purpose, and the relation of God to man, dogmas *cannot* express it. To dogmatise about sacraments is to destroy their nature. To dogmatise about God is to assume that man does not receive the knowledge of God from Him, but imputes the forms of his own intellect to Him. Sacraments are, as I think, the necessary form of a revelation, precisely because they discover the Divine nature in its union with the human, and do not make the human the standard and measure of the Divine."

103 A. R. Vidler has provided excellent material on which to base an elucidation of Maurice's ideas on the Church (see op. cit., 35–154), although he has not subjected it to that penetrating analysis which is necessary for an understanding of Maurice's intentions.

proved that Maurice's interpretation of the Church entirely accords with his idea of revelation. His solution of the problem of the relation of the Church and the world and the way he deals with the apparently most recalcitrant material afford further proof of the inner coherence and consistency of his theological thought.

Chapter XI

ETERNAL LIFE AND THE LAST THINGS

The great Revivalist movement, which had so greatly affected the Church of England and the Nonconformist Churches since the beginning of the nineteenth century, was of diverse origins. Although John Wesley and his followers played a prominent part in the great outburst of revivalism, it was supported by many others who had independently, but via the same experiences arrived at the same conclusions as to the essentials of Christianity. Despite their variety of doctrinal and ecclesiastical outlook the Revivalists nevertheless constituted a common front in the religious life of England. They were united in their opposition to the Latitudinarian interpretation of Christianity and in their belief that the Bible and the orthodox view of the depravity of man and of his salvation through Christ's life, death and resurrection were the mainstay of Christian faith.

This was also true of the Evangelicals and the Tractarians. Although they were sharply opposed on the question of the Church, baptism, conversion and justification by faith, what united them was far stronger and deeper than that which separated them. Thus, they were determined to fight the Latitudinarian concept of Christianity and take their stand upon the Bible and the doctrinal standards of their Church. The domination of the Church of England by the Evangelicals and the Tractarians in the second third of the nineteenth century meant the victory of orthodox theology. The leaders of both parties felt a responsibility for safeguarding what they regarded as the orthodox faith of their fathers. Anybody reproducing Unitarian ideas or showing even the slightest affinity with German idealistic philosophy and Biblical criticism was pretty sure to be opposed as a rationalist and infidel.

This common religious and theological outlook was also evident in the doctrine on the Last Things. It was the firm conviction of all who considered themselves orthodox, whether Anglicans or Nonconformists, that Christ would come again at the end of the world to judge the living and the dead. The future destiny of an individual would be decided by his personal attitude in this life as "the accepted time of salvation". On the day of judgment the believers would receive everlasting life in fellowship with God, whereas the impenitent and infidels would be condemned to everlasting perdition. Heaven and hell were places where man lived in everlasting bliss and suffered everlasting punishment respectively. The idea of the terrible day of judgment and the possibility of being condemned to everlasting hell-fire figured strongly in Victorian preaching.

Maurice had fought orthodox eschatology directly and indirectly ever since the publication of The Kingdom of Christ in 1838. The culminating point occurred, however, with the appearance of Theological Essays in 1853. Even though Maurice's orthodox contemporaries had difficulty in grasping his eschatological teaching, they were in no doubt that he in effect denied the idea of everlasting perdition and asserted that all would be saved. The Council of King's College was simply reflecting orthodox opinion when its majority resolved that in Maurice's *Theological Essays* and subsequent statements "the opinions set forth and the doubts expressed – – as to certain points of belief regarding the future punishment of the wicked and the final issues of the day of judgment, are of dangerous tendency, and calculated to unsettle the minds of the theological students of King's College."[1] Admittedly, many of the orthodox felt that both the Principal of King's College, Dr. Jelf, and its governing body had, from a strictly legal point of view, treated Maurice unfairly.[2] Yet, Evangelicals, Tractarians and Nonconformists all agreed that King's College had discharged its responsibility for the maintenance of sound doctrine in dismissing him as a heretic.[3]

However, our task here is not to relate the actual history of the controversy between Maurice and King's College,[4] but to work out the motives, prompting his rejection of orthodox eschatology, and to lay bare his own teaching on the Last Things.

1. Time and Eternity

Maurice's *Theological Essays* together with his dismissal from King's College made a tremendous stir in Great Britain and gave rise to a great discussion in the religious and theological press. Although the reviewers of *Theological Essays* all complained that they found it hard to grasp Maurice's constructive thought, they generally made a sincere attempt to see what he had at heart. To an amazing degree, however, they failed to understand the core of Maurice's protest against orthodox eschatology. Since they believed that the essential thing for him was to maintain Universalism, they were puzzled by his emphatic repudiation of the doctrine of apocatastasis. They were even more puzzled when he elaborated and substantiated his ideas by a long exposition of the original meaning of the word "eternal".[5] They were at a loss to see the bearing of such a linguistic analysis on the points at issue. Some even imagined that Maurice was only trying to escape a straightforward discussion and ward off criticism by

1 *Life* II, 191.
2 Thus the accusation of heresy was based exclusively on the last seventeen pages, of four hundred and forty-nine, in the first edition of *Theological Essays*. Here in an Appendix Maurice had treated, with great brevity, the problem of the eternal life. Dr. Jelf, who appeared not to have read the rest of the book, even admitted that the Appendix did not contain any clear statements on the points at issue: "the impression it gives seems to throw an atmosphere of doubt on the simple word *eternal* and to convey a general notion of ultimate salvation" (R. V. Jelf and F. D. Maurice: *Grounds for Laying before the Council of King's College, London, Certain Statements Contained in a Recent Publication, Entitled "Theological Essays" by the Rev. F. D. Maurice, M. A.* (3rd edit. 1853. Cit. *Grounds*), 1).
3 On the other hand, Maurice's position evoked great sympathy from many people. *The Record*, the powerful Evangelical weekly, found that the whole "infidel world" had given Maurice their support, whereas the true defenders of the faith were in the minority.
4 This has been done in *Life* II, 188–203. See also *King's College and Mr. Maurice No. 1. The Facts by a Barrister of Lincoln's Inn* [J. A. Ludlow], London 1854.
5 Maurice further developed his views on this point in the second edition of *Theological Essays*, which appeared in the autumn of 1853, as well as in his correspondence with Dr. Jelf, published in *Grounds*.

throwing a smokescreen over the questions under discussion.[6] This was completely beside the mark and only betrayed the extent to which even competent critics were unable to grasp the basic ideas of Maurice's theological thinking in general and of his eschatological views in particular.

Maurice's anxiety to define the precise meaning of the word "eternal" clearly indicated that he saw his disagreement with contemporary orthodoxy as ultimately stemming from a different concept of eternity and its relation to time.[7] This issue was decisive for an understanding of the fundamentals of the Christian faith, and Maurice saw in it the essence of his controversy with Dr. Jelf and King's College. He therefore welcomed the confrontation in the confident expectation that it would force the Church to an awareness of the true content of the Gospel.[8]

6 Thus, the otherwise so discerning R. S. Candlish remarked: "As to the word "eternal", of which the author makes so much in his correspondence with Dr. Jelf – as well as in the concluding Essay in the second edition of his book, manifestly arising out of that correspondence – I confess myself to have been not a little puzzled at first to make out what the exact bearing of his somewhat subtle criticism was meant to be. I am inclined to think, however, that it is, after all, a mare's nest he has found. He will not hear of "eternal" signifying endless duration" (op. cit., 38). F. J. A. Hort testified that many others thought as Candlish did: "I have been astonished at the small number of even thoughtful men at Cambridge who were able to recognise the distinction between time and eternity. The prevalent idea seemed to be that, right or wrong, Maurice had invented it to meet a particular case. No one seemed to enter into the impossibility of a theology, or of the existence of a spiritual world, without it. Thompson [Professor of Greek at Cambridge] was the only one I met who knew that it was to be found in Plato" (Life and Letters I, 266).

7 Cf. What Message have the Clergy for the People of England? A Letter to the Right Hon. and Right Rev. the Bishop of London in Reference to the Controversy on the Future State of Sinners (Cambridge 1864. Cit. What Message), 9: "I know no one who feels so strongly on this object [eternal life] as I do, or whose thoughts on every other divine and human topic are so much determined by their thoughts upon it."

8 Maurice considered his discussion with Dr. Jelf on the meaning of eternal life to be the climax of the battle between God and the Devil, the critical moment in which God directly put before the Church of England the question as to whether it preached a Gospel or not. While Maurice was writing Theological Essays, he was convinced that the result would be his dismissal from King's College. He felt compelled to finish the work, however, because God Himself would be using it as an instrument to chastise and cleanse His Church. "I knew when I wrote the sentences about eternal death," Maurice told Charles Kingsley months before his dismissal was an established fact, "that I was writing my own sentence at King's College. And so it will be. – – Hard fighting is in store for us, dearest friend; but those that are with us are stronger than those who are against us, though we ourselves my be often among the latter. Let us hope mightily for the future. There will be a gathering of Christ's host, as well as the Devil's, out of the ranks of Pharisees and Sadducees, of publicans and harlots. We shall not have to choose our own ground, it will be fixed for us; all we shall have to do is to keep it" (Life II, 168–9 (19/7 1853). Cf. also p. 170–1: "I feel the tremendous responsibility of maintaining this position; it must appear to be the condemnation of other men. But I cannot help it. God must see to His own cause. He knows well enough that I cannot defend it, but if He chooses that I should just at this moment maintain the truth that He is the deliverer of men and not their destroyer, I suppose He knows best. The question becomes more serious and awful to me the more I think of it. I feel more astonished at the crisis to which we have come. I can only ask that the Church may be brought through it, and that I may not do mischief by doing anything out of my own head. – – The religious people, High Church and Evangelical, will be as much blessed ultimately if they get their

271

By insisting on the elucidation of the meaning of the word "eternal" as the basic problem, Maurice gave his opponents a direct clue to an understanding of his fundamental principles and pointed out to them what was at the core of his criticism of traditional orthodox theology, including its eschatology.[9] His critics failed to grasp the help which Maurice offered them and so missed the opportunity to confront him on their fundamental divergences.[10] Their spokesmen did not attack the leading ideas of *Theological Essays* but picked out only certain of his expositions which they found called for criticism. What Maurice considered essential was brushed aside as irrelevant subtleties – and what he maintained to be issues of minor significance became their chief concern. In other words, Maurice's critics forfeited the chance to debate the basic question at issue, that of the compatability of the Platonic and the Biblical idea of reality. This was, in effect, what Maurice had asked for by challenging his orthodox opponents to clarify their views on the relation between time and eternity.

For Maurice "eternity" with its cognates is a key-word in the New Testament, because it indicates the very purpose of the divine economy.[11] The orthodox religious world, however, had cut itself off completely from grasping its significance by confounding time and eternity. This was apparent from their having taken "eternity" to

minds cleared on this subject [of time and eternity] (very many after a long process will) as the infidels"). Even allowing for Maurice's strong, emotional temperament, his evaluation of the situation appears both astonishing and out of all proportion until it is recognised that the problem of the relation between time and eternity was for him the basic issue of theology.

9 Thus Maurice wrote to Dr. Jelf: "It is not, then, mainly for its bearing on the question of punishment, that I reject the popular (if that can be called popular which has certainly no hold whatever on the mind of people) notion [of eternity]. If you will do me the honour to look at the other Essays in my book, you will see that I am far more disturbed by the effects which that notion produces on our theology and on our preaching generally" (*Grounds*, 14). Cf. also *The Word "Eternal"*, XIX: "Those questions do not concern only, or chiefly, the duration of punishment or the future state of mankind – they concern the whole meaning of the Christian Revelation, the Gospel we have to preach to the world, the foundations of sound morality," and *Life* II, 520: "Everything in the work of our ministry as well as in our interpretation of the New Testament, depends upon the force which we give to those continually recurring words "eternal life"." – Both at the time of its publication and later, *Theological Essays* was found to be extremely misty and obscure. For instance A. M. Ramsey considered it "one of the weakest of Maurice's books. It is the work of a man on edge; and throughout it the proportions of theological exposition are distorted by a preoccupation with those points where Maurice was irritated by contemporary theologians" (op. cit., 48). This is definitely wrong. The book is basically clear if understood on Maurice's own premises (cf. *Grounds*, 2: "the final Essay in my book is connected with the principle which I have maintained through the whole of it. If I may not assert a distinction between time and eternity, the whole mystery of Godliness, as I have endeavoured to set it forth, in opposition to the Locke Materialism of one class of Unitarians, and the Emersonian Spiritualism of another, vanishes into air; I cannot say that things earthly are fleeting and things heavenly substantial; I do not know what earth or heaven, shadow or substance, would mean"). Maurice was certainly right in considering *Theological Essays* as that of his works which gave the clearest exposition of his thought (see *Life* II, 544).

10 This is true even of Dr. Candlish's work. The only notable exceptions were J. H. Rigg and James Martineau.

11 Cf. *Theological Essays* (1853), 436: "The word 'eternal' – – is a key-word of the New Testament. To draw our minds from the temporal, to fix them on the eternal, is the very aim of the divine economy."

mean endless, or everlasting, time. But this was to make God and His revelation subject to the intellect which can only conceive of things in categories of time and space and must therefore understand eternity as absolute duration of time.[12] The consequence is that eternity is swallowed up by time – God and His eternal world are submerged in, and judged by, the changeable, transient world of time and space.[13] Maurice's position was that the New Testament, far from endorsing such a blasphemy, liberates man from it.[14]

The Bible teaches that God, and not man, must be the starting-point of theology. This is also true of the question of the meaning of "eternity" and "eternal": "Whenever the word *Eternal* is used, then, in the New Testament, it ought first, by all rules of reason, to be considered in reference to God. Its use when it is applied to Him must determine all its other uses."[15] If this method is followed it becomes clear that "eternity" has no relation to time in the sense of endless time, but stands for a definition of quality with respect to God's being.[16] It is most important, Maurice argued, that "there should be a word expressing a permanent fixed state, not a succession of moments. The word αἰών, or *Ætas*, served this purpose. Like our own word "period" it does not convey so much the impression of a line as of a circle. It does not suggest perpetual progress, but fixedness and completeness. The word αἰώνιος or *æternus*, derived from these, seemed to have been divinely contrived to raise us out of our Time notions, – to suggest the thought of One who is the same yesterday, to-day, and for ever; to express those spiritual or heavenly things which are subject to no change or succession."[17] God's eternity denotes, therefore, His perfect, unchangeable being, just as eternal life is that life of perfect love, righteousness and holiness which is to be found only in God.[18] But since eternity stands for the unchangeable, permanent and

12 Cf. *The Word "Eternal"*, 8: "mere negative words, such as "endless", "never ending", start from a ground of Time; when I predicate them of God, I make Him a mere negation of Time; I conceive of Him just as the Magicians did as "Time without bounds"."

13 Cf. p. 9–10: "I say, then, that it is not safe to conceive the nature of God according to our conditions, to bring down His eternity to our notions. I say, that if we do that, the blessedness of heaven vanishes; the things that eye hath not seen nor ear heard become imaginary things, and we do not restore their reality or their worth by calling them "endless"."

14 Cf. *Life* II, 470: "That we make eternity a very, very long time is what I have always affirmed to be the great contradiction of the religious world, the contradiction from which the New Testament (or rather the Spirit who spoke in the writers of the New Testament, and would open to us the meaning of the New Testament) would deliver us if we did no prefer our own notions, derived from earthly things, to the Divine illumination." Maurice admitted that the Authorised Version paved the way for an un-Biblical understanding of the meaning of αἰώνιος by rendering the word both as "eternal" and as "everlasting". The first rendering is correct, the second is misleading since it induces men to believe that αἰώνιος means "endless time".

15 *Theological Essays*, 114.

16 Cf. *The Word "Eternal"*, 12: "The eternal life which Christ manifested, the eternal life which He has given, are surely spoken of without the least reference to duration; simply with a reference to the nature of the being in whom it dwells and on whom it is bestowed." It is "an eternity which is not subject to Time, or merely a negation of Time" (p. 7).

17 p. 6.

18 Cf. *Theological Essays*, 115: "His Righteousness, His Truth, His Love, the Jew came more and more to perceive, were the substantial and eternal things, by seeking which he was delivered from the worship of Gods of Time and Sense, as well as from the more miserable

perfect, it follows that it is generically different from time which signifies the changeable, transient and perishable. Eternity is before all time and always exists independent of time,[19] being "the same yesterday, to-day, and for ever".[20]

Although eternity and time must never be confounded and merged, there nevertheless exists the most intimate relation between them. They represent the invisible, spiritual world and the visible world of time and space respectively and stand in the relationship of archetype to image. To maintain the distinction between eternity and time, then, in no way implies a contempt for the visible world. This would be the case if eternity were taken to stand for endless time following upon the short duration of man's earthly life. In that case there would be no connection between man's human existence and the Kingdom of God, this being thought of as belonging to the future in the sense of the endless extension of time. When it is realised that eternity is God's immutable and perfect being, which has nothing to do with the succession of time, it becomes clear that man's life in the visible world of time and space is encompassed by God's eternity: "the eternal is always standing side by side with the changeable and temporary."[21] God's eternal world is the foundation of the temporal world since it imparts life and being to it. Maurice maintained, therefore, that only by distinguishing between eternity and time is it possible to arrive at a true understanding of the universe and human existence. If, however, eternity is confounded with time and understood as the endless duration of time, then it inevitably follows that the world and the life of men must be considered as "fleeting shadows", as a transient meaningless chaos.[22]

Maurice was certainly not exaggerating when he pointed out how our interpretation of God's dealings with man is bound up with our understanding of the relation between eternity and time. Because time has no substance and permanence, it can never have any constitutive significance for the relationship between God and man. As

philosophical abstraction of a God who is merely a negative of time; *without* beginning and *without* end," and *The Epistles of St. John,* 27: "It was the eternal life. Not a life of years, and months, and days, and instants; but a fixed permanent life – the life of a Being in whom is no variableness, nor the shadow of a turning."

19 Cf. *Theological Essays,* 119: "Eternity is not a mere negation of time, – – it denotes something real, substantial, before all time."

20 Maurice acknowledged that the Bible used notions of time to describe the eternity of God but this was only to show that eternity encompasses all time: "The "measures of duration" which you try to escape, by speaking of an absolute duration, may be used – are used in Scripture – to raise us above notions of Time. "I am Alpha and Omega, the beginning and the end, the first and the last"; "the same yesterday, to-day, and for ever"; "which is, and was, and is to come", are forms of speech which do not chain us to a beginning or to an end, to yesterday or to-day, to the past, to the present, or to the future; but teach us of One who is living in these "measures of duration", and is not confined by them" *(The Word "Eternal",* 8).

21 *Sermons* VI, 274.

22 Cf. *Life* II, 473: "if eternal things are not future things more than they are present, more than they are past, if they are distinct in kind from temporal things – each may have its own honour, they may be inseparably linked together in the nature of man. – – Whilst you *distinguish* the Eternal and the Temporal, you see their relation to each other; you can feel what a blessing appertains to each. When eternity is merely a vast interminable future, it swallows up everything. Yet there is no joy in contemplating it."

time is only able to reflect eternity as "a fixed permanent state", God's revelation in the history of time and space can only be conceived of as a visible manifestation of *that which is,* that is, God's eternal world which embraces the visible world and gives it its ordered and harmonious existence. Maurice was certainly well aware of the fundamental divergences between his own theological thinking and the orthodox theology and preaching of his day and was right in maintaining that in the last analysis they originated in different conceptions of the relation between time and eternity.

2. Eternal Life and Eternal Death

Eternity, then, denotes God's unchangeable perfect being, which is generically distinct from the changeable, transient, temporal world. For Maurice, this idea of eternity must also determine our understanding of eternal life and eternal death.[23] Accordingly, they do not signify an everlasting or endless life or death after the cessation of man's earthly life; they denote fellowship with God and separation from God respectively.[24] Since eternity is not the endless extension of time, eternal life or eternal death can never be thought of as future states. Consequently, during his earthly life man has the possibility of living either in the state of eternal life or in the state of eternal death. In other words, eternal life means that man, being a spirit, has fellowship with God in the eternal world and is redeemed from the chains of the world of time and space, just as eternal death denotes man's rebellion against, and opposition to God, and his subjection to the world of the senses.[25] Hence it follows that eternal life is not a privilege, imparted to a select few; it is an expression of the true state of every man. By the will of God man is created to have eternal life, since as a spirit he is created to know God and live in fellowship with Him in the eternal world.[26]

Maurice was accused of being abstract and incomprehensible in his exposition of eternity and of eternal life and eternal death. Thus, Dr. Jelf wrote to him: "Your positions, if established at all, must rest upon very abstract assumptions, or at the best upon very abstract reasonings, such as (to judge from those to whom I have shown your Essays) even highly gifted, and cultivated, and theologically educated minds find the utmost difficulty in grappling with. What effect are they likely to have, I will not

23 Cf. *Theological Essays,* 115: "If it is right, if it is a duty to say that Eternity in relation to God has nothing to do with time and duration, are we not bound to say that also in reference to life or to punishment it has nothing to do with time or duration?"
24 Cf. *The Word "Eternal",* 18: "I have considered *eternal* punishment or *eternal* death as expressly the loss of God's presence, – the word "eternal" having that force – – that it always has in Scripture."
25 Cf. *Life* II, 219–20: "The eternal state, I apprehend, is the state of a spiritual being, out of time, living in spiritual relations, enjoying or suffering a spiritual inheritance."
26 Cf. *The Unity of the New Testament,* 643: " 'Lay hold of eternal life,' the life of a spirit, the life of a man, the life which is opposed to that of an animal, to that of time or sense," and *Sermons* IV, 217: "Such an Eternity is not cast in the mould of time; not an interminable series of years; but a solid possession for each moment; a treasure which we are to claim now, that we may hold it, into whatever new circumstances life or death may bring us. St. Paul speaks of looking at, or looking into, the things which are unseen and eternal. That he regards as the highest privilege, as the proper occupation of a man."

say only on our half-trained students, but on ignorant country congregations?"[27] Now Maurice in no way wished to contest that his interpretation of eternity ran contrary to that advocated by the leading philosophers and theologians of his day. This fact, however, did not impress him. They were bound to reject his understanding of eternity as an absurdity, because they accepted only the intellect and its thought forms, which related exclusively to the world of time and space.[28] But this was not the case with the common people. Through the toils and sufferings of their daily life they had been taught to reject the intellect and its notions and concepts as void of reality and to yearn for true unchangeable reality. Intuitively they understood that they were not limited by time and space and longed to live in that eternal world which alone could give their lives substance and meaning.[29] Nor were they interested in an ever-lasting life in the future. They demanded communion with the eternal world here and now. Consequently, Maurice asserted, the ordinary people would immediately under-stand that eternal life means the life and fellowship of the spirit with God in the in-visible world. That is why he rejected Dr. Jelf's accusation that he was abstract and incomprehensible as totally unfounded: "I have felt – I do feel more every day – that in proclaiming this [eternal] life to men, in warning them of this [eternal] death, I am speaking to something which can answer me, and which, if it never hears *my* voice, will one day hear the voice of the Son of Man and live. – – You wish that I would adapt my lessons to simple people. If there is anything in them which men in smock-frocks, which pure-minded women cannot take in, I would fain get rid of that. But I do not think they will understand me better if I talk of an eternity *a parte post*, and an eternity *a parte ante*, if I exchange the language of St. John for that of the schools."[30]

27 *Grounds*, 10–1.
28 Cf. p. 14: "I find that, in order to adopt it [the idea of eternity as endless time], I must set aside the grand distinction of St. Paul (which must affect the whole meaning of Christianity and of our spiritual life) between the things that are seen and temporal, and the things that are not seen and eternal. I find that the loss of this distinction is connected with a philo-sophy, which rejects all belief in a spiritual substance, in any mystery not measurable by the understanding, ultimately by the senses."
29 Cf. *Sermons* IV, 216: "There is a perpetual witness within him that phantoms and supersti-tions belong to Time and Sense; that Eternity is the great Reality, which alone gives reality to that which he sees," and *Theological Essays*, 110: "We feel that we are under a law of change and succession; that we live in days, and months, and years. We feel also that we have to do with that which is not changeable, which cannot be represented by any divisions of time. – – We experience the utter vanity and emptiness of chronology as a measure of suffering, of thought, of hope, of love. All these belong to another state of things. We perceive that Scripture is speaking to us of that state of things; that it is educating us into the apprehension of it. The more we attend to the New Testament, the more we find it to confirm the witness of our reason that eternity is not a lengthening out or continuation of time; that they are generically different – –. The spiritual world, – we are obliged to confess it in a thousand ways, – is not subject to temporal conditions."
30 *Life* II, 474. Cf. also *Theological Essays*, 120: "Nearly all people, therefore, in this country, who speak of such matters [time and eternity], are agreed that the words of the Gospel, if they were taken strictly and fairly, must have the hardest (I do not say the most awful, for I believe the sense I contend for is much more awful) meaning which has ever been given them. Only the tens and hundreds of thousands who cannot speak dissent from that decis-

Being created as spirit man must always be haunted by the problem of eternal life. He feels that he is meant to live with God in the eternal world, while at the same time, because of his selfishness and his subjection to the world of the senses, he strongly feels that he is in the state of eternal death, without union with God. To know how to be redeemed from the temporal world and be related to the eternal world is therefore the essential question for all human beings.[31] God's revelation, culminating in the Incarnation, provides the answer to this fundamental problem.[32]

Eternity belongs exclusively to God – to know God is therefore to have eternal life. As Christ has revealed God's true being and has thus given mankind true knowledge of Him, He has imparted eternal life to man: "This is the eternal life, that which Christ has brought with Him, that which we have in Him, the knowledge of God; the entering into His mind and character, the knowing Him as we can only know any person, by sympathy, fellowship, love. And so the meaning and order of the Divine revelation become evident to us; God has been declaring Himself to us that we might know Him, because He would have us partakers of this eternal life."[33]

On this subject, too, Maurice sometimes expressed himself in such a way that he

ion." Their dissent is due to the fact that they have not been educated in a philosophy which only accepts a knowledge, based upon sense perceptions. Being unspoiled by a false philosophy they are able, by virtue of the reason, to recognise the truth of Maurice's exposition of the eternity of God immediately. Maurice did not want to betray the common man in order to please those who represent a philosophical school which is unable to arrive at a true knowledge of reality: "When any one ventures to say to an English audience that Eternity is not a mere negation of time, that it denotes something real, substantial, before all time, he is told at once that he is departing from the simple intelligible meaning of words; that he is introducing novelties; that he is talking abstractions. This language is perfectly honest in the mouths of those who use it. But they do not know where they learnt it. They did not get it from peasants or women or children. They did not get it from the Bible. They got it from Locke. And if I find that I cannot interpret the language and thoughts of peasants and women and children, and that I cannot interpret the plainest passages of the Bible or the whole context of it, while I look through the Locke spectacles, – I must cast them aside" (p. 119).

31 Cf. *Sermons* IV, 220: "Men tremble at eternity, whether they think of it as present or to come; they must tremble at it, unless there comes forth from it a Gospel of forgiveness and reconciliation. It is no sham terror, begotten by the arts of priests, which I feel when the thought flashes on me, 'I am an eternal being. I cannot shake eternity from me. It belongs to me; it goes with me where I go; it stays with me where I stay'." In fact, Maurice saw the same fundamental question posed in all genuine philosophy: "I find every Heathen Philosopher embarrassed and bewildered in the search of Him in whom he was living and moving and having his being, by these Time-negations; I find him now flying to the popular mythology at the peril of conceiving God under a multitude of visible forms and images, now flying from the mythology and resting in a vague abstraction of unity. The heart and reason of these philosophers confessed that there was a Substance which they could not measure by their notions, which was the great reality which was before all Time, not the unreality which they made it by merely contradicting what they beheld in Time. They longed to be told what this Substance is, that it should reveal itself to them. I have been taught that the revelation of God in Christ is the answer to that longing" (*The Word "Eternal"*, 8).

32 Cf. *Sermons* IV, 212: "Who will uphold *him*? Who will show him that other world to which he belongs, of which he thinks he is an inheritor, but which seems full of indistinct phantoms? This, St. Paul teaches us, is the very end of God's Revelations."

33 *Theological Essays*, 111.

appeared to be saying that, through His incarnation, Christ brought man from eternal death to eternal life. Such an interpretation, however, falls short of Maurice's true concern. Being the perfect image of God, Christ always has eternal life, and being the Head of the human race, He has always imparted eternal life to every man.[34] This means, in other words, that man, by the very fact that he is created as a spirit, lives with God in His eternal world because of his union with Christ.[35] This is the true situation of man, a situation which Christ has revealed. It is not a question of acquiring eternal life, since, living in Christ, man always participates in His eternal life, His life with God.[36]

Those who have eternal life live in heaven, whereas those who have chosen the state of eternal death live in hell. Just as eternity and its derivatives must not be understood on the basis of the time notions of the intellect, so heaven and hell must not be interpreted on the basis of its space notions. Heaven and hell do not stand for places but signify states where man either lives in the fellowship of love with God or in unbelief and selfishness respectively. Consequently, life in heaven or life in hell is the alternative which always confronts every man at every moment of his life. Man is created to live in heaven already in his earthly life, but he may deny this law of human existence and decide to live in hell.[37]

The attempt to interpret eternal life and eternal death as an endless life and an endless death leads, in Maurice's view, to the most disastrous consequences. Since they only become a reality upon the cessation of earthly life, they are reduced to

34 Cf. *The Epistles of St. John,* 28: "He who came into the world, and showed forth that life in it whereof St. John speaks, said, 'I come from a Father. My life is the image of His life. Therefore it is an eternal life. It did not begin at a certain time; it will not end at a certain time. And as you are partakers of my nature, you are intended to partake of this eternal life; you are the children of Him who has declared me to be His only-begotten Son'," and *Life* II, 18: "there is a great and awful idea of eternity which our Lord would teach us, which belongs to our inmost selves."

35 Cf. *Sermons* IV, 216–7: "To think of Him [Christ] as the eternal ground of all things, from Whom they come, by Whom they consist, in Whom they shall be gathered up; Who is the same yesterday, to-day and for ever – – this is an eternity which we can contemplate. For in it is included the endurance and permanence of every person and thing that the Word has created and redeemed," and *Life* II, 17: "Our Lord has been training us by His beautiful, blessed teaching to see eternity as something altogether out of time, to connect it with Him who is, and was, and is to come. He has been teaching me that I have a spirit which cannot rest in time, which must strive after the living, the permanent, the eternal, after God Himself. He has been telling me that He has come to bring me into this state, that He is the way to it."

36 Cf. *The Gospel of St. John,* 420: "It is enough to know – – what love is above all and beneath all, how that love has been manifested and accomplished on this earth of ours. To dwell in it must be eternal life; to be separated from it must be eternal death."

37 Cf. *Theological Essays,* 117: "Hell as the state of unrighteousness, Heaven as the state of righteousness, Earth as the battlefield between the two," and *The Contemporary Review* XV ("The Athanasian Creed"), 482: "The kingdom of heaven would then be the eternal kingdom of righteousness, peace and joy in the Holy Ghost. The kingdom of hell would then be the kingdom of evil, hatred, despair. Both would be about every man; both would be kingdoms into which they could only enter by the spirit. Communion with either would be most real and actual, would determine the course of man's thoughts and acts."

abstract notions without any bearing upon man's actual life.[38] Furthermore, when, as a necessary corollary, orthodox preaching thinks it right to induce men to abstain from evil by threats of endless punishment in hell and to exhort them to live a holy and righteous life by holding out everlasting bliss as a reward, man's selfishness is made the driving force in his relation to God.[39] Man does not obey the will of God for His own sake but only to secure his own future safety and felicity – God has been made subservient to man's selfishness.[40] This is just to turn heaven into the hell of selfishness. The only reward which is held out to man is to do God's will and to become the servant of His love towards his fellow-men. This alone is heaven, when man, filled by the love of self-sacrifice, is set free from selfishness.[41]

A further consequence of orthodox eschatological preaching is that it makes man fear punishment more than sin. A consuming anxiety to avoid future punishment in hell replaces man's anxiety to be set free from sin, which, for Maurice, is to turn things upside down. It is sin, and not punishment, which man has to fear. Far from being a curse, punishment is a blessing since it proves that God, being perfect love, has not left man to himself and his sin. Through punishment God educates man to know his own misery so that he may willingly turn to God to be released from his sin.[42] There is "a vision – – far more fearful than the vision of punishment; that of being *left alone;* of being permitted to be out of discipline – to have our own way."[43] This is the experience of the common man – he feels the self and its sins as the true

38 Cf. *The Apocalypse*, 85–6: "we picture to ourselves a heavenly world which is not interested in the doings of the earth, which stands altogether aloof from it; – – the heavenly world which was revealed to St. John enters into all the concerns of men, the highest and the lowest; is not indifferent to the needs of the most insignificant creature who feeds or starves below; is not indifferent about our sordid ways."

39 Cf. *The Kingdom of Christ* II, 269: "The wretched notion of a private selfish Heaven, where compensation shall be made for troubles incurred, and prizes given for duties performed in this lower sphere – – had infused itself into our popular teachings and our theological books."

40 Cf. *Life* II, 470: "That a certain prize called Happiness is to pay us for being righteous and for a good life, and that righteousness and the Divine life are not themselves the ends which Christ sets before us, the highest blessings we can seek – this seems to me the terrible confusion which has come to us from mixing partly the philosophy of Aristotle, partly the philosophy of the money market, with the message of the Son of God," and *Life* II, 18: "For the idea of enjoying God or being without God, we unawares substitute that Mahometan felicity or Mahometan torment which you speak of, and the whole of Christianity becomes depraved in consequence."

41 Cf. *The Word "Eternal"*, 16: "Had you ever read a single book of mine, I believe you would have discovered that it is from first to last an assertion of the doctrine that man can only be blessed when he becomes the free servant of God, choosing His will; – – I not only hold goodness to be the necessary means to happiness, but that happiness apart from it is a dream and an impossibility," and *Social Morality*, 390: "[God's] reward is that likeness to Him, the unselfish Being, which such self-seeking makes impossible."

42 Cf. *Life* II, 369–70: "I do – – desire to assert the inseparable union of sin with misery, and the impossibility of any blessing to man till he is delivered from sin. I desire also to assert that the pure and holy will of God is always in conflict with that which is evil and rebellious in the will of the creature," and p. 470: "Punishment, the Bible teaches me, is always God's protest against sin, His instrument for persuading men to turn from sin to righteousness."

43 *Theological Essays* (1853), 439.

burden of his life. Therefore orthodox eschatological teaching cheats men by virtually maintaining that God can be persuaded to dispense with His holy love and its opposition towards sin if they can only produce a certain faith and certain prescribed works. Indeed, such a position is plain blasphemy and a falsification of the Gospel.[44]

Maurice did not dispute that the sinner is condemned to eternal death and hell. However, this condemnation is not due to God but to man himself. Man's rebellion against God brings its own condemnation with it, since he, by choosing to live without God, condemns himself to death and hell.[45] That this condemnation is called eternal denotes that the separation from God is its distinguishing mark. It has, on the other hand, nothing to do with endless duration, and consequently the state of eternal condemnation will cease when man decides to give up his rebellion against God.

Far from leaving man to his self-chosen condemnation God in His love works to redeem him from death and hell.[46] In spite of man's resistance God continues to persuade him to surrender his resistance and receive eternal life, fellowship with God in faith and love in the invisible world.[47] This is good tidings for toiling and suffering men – and Maurice was in no doubt that they would eagerly embrace it. He wrote to Dr. Jelf: "If I thought the great end of God's revelation was to tell men of future bliss or future woe, it might be a legitimate question whether your denunciations of fire and worms, or mine of being left without God, would be the most or least ineffectual; I believe they would be nearly on a level. But as I speak of a present evil which may grow harder and deeper every day, and of a present deliverance from that which God's grace offers to the will and conscience of a voluntary and conscious being, I think the dark vision of being left without such a friend, – of being left to himself, – is something more real, more dreadful to a man, than any which you can conjure up; even as the hope of living under His government and enjoying His friendship would be far more blessed and full of immortality than one of some unknown reward of services never performed."[48]

44 Cf. *The Word "Eternal"*, XXII: "To me the ordinary doctrine seems full of the most miserable mitigations and indulgences of evil. I plead for the Love of God, which resists sin, and triumphs over it, not for a mercy which relaxes the penalties of it."

45 Cf. *Life* II, 17: "The condemnation is declared to be choosing darkness rather than light, "hating Christ and the Father". A rebel state of will, at war with God, is the highest, completest misery."

46 Cf. *The Word "Eternal"*, 16: "it is the will of God, acting through the Mediator who has died for man, upon a man's will, which can alone raise him from sin to holiness, from death to life, whenever he is, in whatever circumstances he is."

47 Cf. *Theological Essays*, 121: "This [eternal] life is that for which God has created man, for which He has redeemed man in His Son, which He is sending His Spirit to work out in man. – – This eternal death is that from which God sent His Son to deliver men, from which He has delivered them. If they fall into it, it is because they choose it, because they embrace it, because they resist a power which is always at work to save them from it."

48 *The Word "Eternal"*, 27. Cf. also *Theological Essays*, 122: "Every man who knows what it is to have been in a state of sin, knows what it is to have been in a state of death. He cannot connect that death with time; he must say that Christ has brought him out of the bonds of *eternal* death. Throw that idea into the future, and you deprive it of all its reality, of all its power. – – It becomes a mere vague dream and shadow to me, when you project it into a distant world. And if you take from me the belief that God is always righteous, always maintaining a fight with evil, always seeking to bring His creatures out of it, you take every-

3. Christ as the Living Judge

Maurice also sharply opposed orthodox eschatological thought when it maintained that Christ would come again at the end of time to judge the living and the dead by condemning unbelievers to everlasting perdition in hell and by rewarding believers with everlasting bliss in heaven.[49] Such a view of the day of judgment implied that Christ is only considered the saviour during man's earthly life while He afterwards appears as a vengeful and condemning judge.[50] Against this background it was for Maurice small wonder that man feared and trembled at the thought of the coming day of judgment.

The attempt to establish a contrast between Christ as saviour and Christ as judge is, however, rooted in a failure to grasp the Biblical concept of judgment. We have previously seen that, for Maurice, judgment denoted "distinction", "discrimination" or "separation" between the true and the false so that the contrast between them could be made manifest. That Christ is called judge implies, consequently, that He distinguishes and separates between the true and real and the false and unreal.[51] Christ judges by imparting the perfect knowledge of reality so that man can discern things as they truly are.[52] Judgment throws light upon human existence by revealing what originates in God's will and love and what is due to man's sin.[53] Because Christ's acts of

thing from me, all hope now, all hope in the world to come. Atonement, Redemption, Satisfaction, Regeneration, become mere words to which there is no counterpart in reality."

49 Cf. *Sermons* I, 155: "There is a disposition – it must not be denied – among religious men, to look for *something else* than the manifestation of Christ. They think that He has come in the flesh and died for them, that they may escape Hell and that they may obtain Heaven. But when they are asked what Hell is, and what Heaven is, their answers are vague. One is something infinitely evil, which Christ has delivered them from; one is something infinitely good, which Christ has won for them. But they seem to regard the infinite evil as consisting in certain inflictions which God has appointed *for* evil; the infinite good as consisting in certain blessings which God has promised *to* good. Christ is, according to them, a means to an end, but not the end; the sight of Him is not itself what they covet; the loss of Him is not itself what they dread."

50 Cf. *The Conflict*, 116: "We shall think, "All has been done for our race that could be done, and all has been done in vain. Christ was once a Saviour, so far as He could be; now His mind and purpose have changed. He will be manifested to take vengeance on those who have not accepted the offer which He has made them." I need not tell you that such is the language of our pulpits, of those in which no extravagant doctrine is preached, which best represent the ordinary religious opinions of the day."

51 Cf. *Sacrifice*, 309: "This Faithful and True Knight, the Apostle says, is the Righteous Judge; the discerner of the thoughts and intents of the heart; the perfectly clear and equitable and effectual divider between that which is, and that which is not, – between the real thing, and the counterfeit which waits upon it."

52 Cf. *What Is Revelation?*, 437: "Such a Judgment, – that which is called, in the New Testament, the unveiling of the Son of Man, [is] the discovery of the real Head and Source of all Life, Order, Peace, in God's Universe, the overthrow and destruction of all Death, Disorder, War."

53 Cf. *Theological Essays*, 80: "Do we not require a redemption of all that is human from its changeable accidents – a judgment and separation, which shall come from the revelation of Him who has redeemed and glorified our whole humanity, between that in us which is His, and that which we have contracted by turning away from Him? Do we not ask for a day in which all the scattered limbs of Christ's body in heaven and earth shall be gathered together in Him, for a day in which light and darkness, life and death, shall never be mingled or confounded again?"

281

judgment unveil true reality they separate and deliver truth from falsehood, goodness from evil. Seeing that it is an integral part of Christ's saving work to perform the function of judging, there can be no distinction between Christ the saviour and Christ the judge.[54]

Since they held this view all the Apostles and Evangelists awaited Christ's coming as a judge with confidence and joy. Thus St. Paul exhorted men "to look boldly up to God, in His Son, to judge them, and justify them from that evil. And our failure to do this, – – our want of belief that God has sent His Son to justify us, and to deliver every one of us from his iniquities – our failure to believe that we do stand in Christ, pure and holy, and without blame, before Him, is the reason why we do not feel as the Apostle did about His judgments upon the world, but cherish just the opposite feeling, a desire that they should not come, or that they should not reach us."[55]

Maurice also criticized the idea that Christ would only come and perform the office of a judge by means of a visible manifestation at the end of time. The concept of judgment day as a future event must necessarily induce men to believe that Christ has absented Himself from His creation until then and has left men to live their own lives without any interference from Him.[56] Such a misconception arose because men, by accepting only the knowledge of their sense perceptions, were unable to conceive of Christ as a living person, unless He made His appearance in visible shape. Consequently they could only imagine Him performing the office of a judge through a new outward manifestation at the end of time.[57]

54 Cf. *Sermons* III, 63: "the coming of Christ as a Deliverer *necessarily* involved His coming as a Judge," and *The Conflict*, 118–9: "You will not distract their minds with thoughts of two Christs, one that has come to save, another that will come with quite another mind to judge. You will represent the judgment as the completion of the divine work of salvation. You will teach them what are the enemies from whom He came to save them, what are the enemies between whom and them He is judging now and will judge hereafter."

55 *The Apocalypse*, 290–1. Cf. also *The Word Revelation*, 27–8: "The Day stands here and everywhere in opposition to night. The belief in Christ, the Light of Men, the Light of the World – visionary or mystical, if you like to call it so – was the belief of the Apostles and Evangelists. The Day therefore is the coming forth of this Light; the discovery of the source whence all light has flowed into the hearts and understandings of men. Being such, it must be the test or judgment of all acts, thoughts, purposes of men."

56 Cf. *Sermons* III, 11: "And then, though we say that we believe that He shall come to be our Judge, it is merely as we might say, we believe any one else shall come to be our judge. The Judgment we expect is not of a Person Who is near to us, Who has to do with our lives at every moment, to Whom our thoughts are open and naked at every moment; but of one who is standing aloof from us, who, till that day, is leaving us very much to take our own course, to settle for ourselves, without persuasion or remonstrance on his part, what we shall do and what we shall be," and *Theological Essays*, 76: "they suppose that they are, at some distant, unknown period, to be brought into the presence of One who is far from them now, and who is not now fulfilling the office of a Judge, whatever other may be committed to Him."

57 Cf. *The Unity of the New Testament*, 125, in which Maurice had Christ say the following concerning His coming to judgment: "the greatest temptation possible to human beings [is] to seek Me in the outward world, and not to seek Me as the Lord of the hearts and reins, to change Me into a Cæsar, and not regard Me as a real, divine King, to think of Me as a judge sitting upon some exalted seat like that on which the lords of the earth sit, and not to think of Me as the Judge who looks down into the depth of every spring and principle

Such a view is, however, expressly repudiated in the Creeds. The fact that they mention Christ's coming for judgment immediately after His ascension means that Christ is the invisible Lord who always stands as the judge before man.[58] Christ continually judges man by laying bare his inmost thoughts and purposes and by distinguishing between the true and the false in him. Every moment is therefore "critical" and, in fact, represents "a day of judgment".[59] Far from having left mankind, Christ is always present with every man in order to unveil true reality so that he can become aware of falsehood and sin and renounce it: "To believe that there is such a Judge at the heart of society, close to the heart of each man, is an infinite security that the crude and random apprehensions, and the selfish schemes of individuals, or of ages, shall not have power to make good evil, or evil good, however they may labour to do so."[60]

Maurice was well aware that because of his understanding of the day of judgment he would be charged with having diluted its true significance and turned it into a mere fiction without any hold upon men's minds; faced with this criticism, he simply retorted that precisely the opposite was true.[61] To imagine that in a dim future Christ will appear to judge men is simply to empty the idea of judgment of all meaning and force. What ordinary men need is that someone will continually guide and judge them – and this practical demand is fulfilled through the proclamation of Christ as the ever-present judge, who is near every man.[62]

of action, into the very inmost heart of society; before whose presence every thing must stand revealed in its inward nakedness; before whom every falsehood must fly away." Maurice added: "Mighty and divine words to shatter in pieces all sensual dreams which substitute an apparent for a real Christ!" *(ibid.)*.

58 Cf. *Theological Essays*, 77: "If I read the words, *From thence He shall come*, following immediately upon the account of an ascension into heaven, which is described as a great triumph for Him and for mankind, I do not think my first notion would be that they implied that He would descend from that state – that He would assume again the conditions and limitations of the one which He had left."

59 Cf. *Sermons* VI, 274: "We shall feel that every moment is a critical moment, that God's judgments are always proceeding," and *Sacrifice*, XXXVI: "A judgment of the hearts and reins, a judgment of the man, a judgment of the principles from which acts flow – this is what Scripture teaches me to believe in here, to expect hereafter. Under the sense of this judgment – in the confidence that the Judge is always at the door – it desires that I should live every day and every hour."

60 *Sacrifice*, 309–10.

61 Cf. *Theological Essays*, 79: "I am quite prepared to hear the charges that I have now been defending an ideal, and not an actual, judgment day, and that I confound the spiritual kingdom of Christ with His reign over the earth. I can only answer – – that I have found the current notions of a judgment, not exactly ideal, but exceedingly fantastic, figurative, inoperative, and that I have tried to ascertain whether Scripture does not give us the hint of something more practical and more substantial."

62 Cf. p. 80: "If, again, the popular notion on this subject is wanted as an influence to act habitually on the lives of ordinary worldly men, – and it is alleged that I have substituted for it the notion of a mysterious judgment, of which it is impossible that such men can make any account, – then I reply, that it is precisely this kind of mysterious judgment which these men do recognise – –. Such men demand for *themselves* an habitual government, inspection, judgment, reaching to the roots of their heart and will; such men demand for the earth some complete deliverance from all that defiles it and sets it in rebellion against a true and righteous King."

Maurice felt it his vocation to proclaim the eternal Kingdom of God, which always embraces the life of mankind and to which all men belong. That every man always stands in Christ and through Him receives everything was the overwhelming truth which he considered it his appointed task to lay before the world. Because this truth had been neglected and had even been denied by contemporary orthodox theology and preaching, he had been so anxious, he once explained, to emphasize its significance for actual human life that he had dealt less with "the future state and its occupations" than was perhaps justified.[63] Maurice had, however, no doubt that the idea of Christ as the Head of humanity not only did not exclude but directly demanded the expectation of a full manifestation of God's will and love: "If we think that *nothing* is given yet; that we are merely to look for something to come, we are most miserable, for the something to come is as shadowy as that which is about us. If we think that *all* has been given, – that we have nothing to long for, – we are most miserable, for that which is good here becomes a lie if it is not the germ of what is to be perfectly good."[64]

The Incarnation had revealed that God was perfect love and that Christ was the Head of the universe and of mankind. The actual life of the world and men appear, however, as a glaring contradiction of this truth. Selfishness and subjection to the sensible forms of the world characterize the life of men; human distress and suffering are rampant and apparently demonstrate the powerlessness of God's love. That is why it is necessary to hope for a day when the Divine Order will finally be vindicated with a display of the absolute impotence of sin and the Devil.[65] It is true that Christ

63 Cf. *Life* II, 242: "I am much more desirous to learn than to teach upon the future state and its occupations. I feel that I have been driven by the necessities of my own being to seek so much more for a present deliverance from cruel and pressing enemies, than for any future bliss, that the vision of the latter has often been almost entirely obscure to me. I am sure that this has been a grievous loss to myself, and has put me at a distance from many with whom I should wish to be in sympathy. – – The necessity of confessing a kingdom of Heaven within – a kingdom of Heaven ever present with us now; different in kind from the visible world, but affecting it, and swaying its movements continually – has been with me an overwhelming one." That Maurice so strongly stressed the relevance of the Kingdom of God to human life must be understood as a highly needed protest against much current preaching in which "the future state, as we are wont to hear it described, is so vague, so selfish, so much a denial of that truth concerning the redeemed state of man, which I have been sent to bear witness of" (p. 243). As another reason for the unobtrusive place which the idea of a future state had occupied in his thinking, Maurice pointed to his personal temperament, "the dreariness and coldness of my own heart and imagination", and "the hollow of my head where the organ of hope should be" *(ibid.)*.

64 *Sermons* V, 38.

65 Cf. *Sermons* III, 228: "No man who feels the oppressions of the world, and tries to bear up against them, can help utterly fainting, if he does not verily believe that this earth shall not always be a den of robbers, but that its true Saviour and Helper shall Himself purge it and restore it. But the men of old were able verily to believe this truth; because they verily believed, in their own day, that the universe was not the Devil's but God's – –. Our faith in its future establishment rests wholly on our belief in its present truth," and *Theological Essays*, 96: "There is a sense of Judgment, of some great decision, that is to settle for ever which of these is the stronger, the Evil, or the Good with which the Evil has been so intricately combined."

is invisibly present in His created universe and always judges and separates between truth and falsehood so that man may know the Divine Order and his place in it,[66] indeed, the history of each man and of all mankind is, in fact, an incessant day of judgment with the imparting of an ever increasing knowledge of true reality.[67] Nevertheless, all history, as guided and governed by God, moves towards and culminates in a final day of judgment which is to inaugurate the complete fulfilment of God's will and purpose.[68]

The hope of a future state is legitimate but its implications can only be seen on the basis of the idea of Christ as the Son of God and the Son of Man. Since Christ is already the actual Lord of the creation, the final day of judgment cannot involve the destruction of the universe and the establishment of a new heaven and a new earth. On the contrary, there is an inner connection between the present state and the future state which is to follow upon the final manifestation of Christ.[69] Therefore, man's hope for the future state must be a hope that he will receive perfect knowledge of that which has always been true of the universe and mankind: "The appearance of a light which shall show things as they are, and before which the darkness shall flee away, the day of judgment and distinction, the gathering of all together in one, the restoration of all things, this is the language in which we are taught to express our thoughts and anticipations respecting the future. – – And what do such words imply, but the full evidence and demonstration of that which *is now;* the dispersion of all the shadows and appearances which have counterfeited it or have hidden it from view? What do they imply, but the existence of a kingdom, or order, or constitution, which men have been trying to set at nought and deny, but under which they have been living notwithstanding, and which, in the clear sunlight of that day, is shown to be the only one under which they can live?"[70]

---

66 Cf. *The Unity of the New Testament,* 350: "that day of the Lord which cannot be measured by the rules and conditions of time, which lies out of them and beyond them, and yet which is at certain crises presented in its full brightness and glory to eyes that are waiting for it, and prepared to welcome it."

67 Cf. *The Prayer-Book,* 17: "each day of the Lord carries in it the foretaste of a final day, when no spirit in the universe shall be able to evade the sense and certainty of its being naked and open before God," and *Theological Essays,* 80: "Is there any one who seriously believes that it [the day of judgment] is a day of twenty-four hours in duration which we are thus expecting? Is it not one which has dawned on the world already? which our consciences tell us we may dwell in now? which therefore Scripture and reason both affirm must wax clearer and fuller, till He who is the Sun of righteousness is felt to be shining everywhere, and till there is no corner of the universe into which His beams have not entered?" See furthermore *Sequel,* 277–8.

68 Cf. *Sermons* II, 112: "they could contemplate the great drama of history, not as a succession of shifting scenes, but as a series of events tending to a divine catastrophe; to the fulfilment of that Will which is seeking good and good only."

69 Cf. *Life* II, 243: "the words of the Apostle, "Looking for the revelation of our Lord Jesus Christ", have seemed to me the only words that gave me any glimpse into the state, or into the use which we are to make of it, in urging ourselves and others to fight," and *Sacrifice,* XLVI: "the future state [is] – – not as the commencement of a new state of things, – but as the carrying out and consummation of all God's plans and government, – as the state in which the victory of good over evil is no longer a question of doubt or uncertainty."

70 *The Kingdom of Christ* II, 270. Cf. also *Sermons* V, 19: "This salvation from all which

The final day of judgment is to be awaited as a joyful event for the entire creation. None of God's involuntary and voluntary creatures will be delivered up to destruction, but when sin and falsehood are separated and banished, all things will be rectified and consummated according to the will of God. The order and harmony of the creation will stand forth in its true splendour[71] so that all men will confess Christ as the Head of the universe and mankind.[72] The final day of judgment is the day of salvation for all creation.

Just as the history of the universe moves towards the final day of judgment, so the life of each man is directed towards a day in which he will see everything clearly in the light of God. This event occurs, however, at his death when he puts off his animal, fleshly nature, "the vesture of mortality", which had drawn him towards the visible world and, together with his selfishness, impeded his fellowship with God in the eternal world.[73] The death of each individual is a final day of judgment because he now unambiguously sees that Christ has always been the foundation of his life and clearly realises what has prevented him from living according to the law of his creation[74] – and this insight means that he is separated and redeemed from his sin.

clogged their progress and hindered them from seeing things as they were, – this salvation from lies, from hatred, from indifference, – was all contained in the promise that He in whom is light and no darkness at all, should be fully manifested. Every day and hour was hastening on this manifestation, and therefore this salvation."

71 Cf. *Introductory Lectures Delivered at Queen's College* ("On Theology"), 262: "The day we look forward to is that in which every insect and flower, every order of Creation, from the lowest upwards, shall be seen in its perfect distinctness, in its fulness of life, in its perfect relation to every other, because He will be fully revealed who called them into existence, who renews their life day by day, in whom they find their purpose and their harmony."

72 Cf. *Sermons* IV, 68: "The day of Christ, as the Apostles set it forth to us, is not a day in which a few are to look for their triumph, and for the defeat of their enemies. It is the day when the Son of Man will be revealed as the King of the Universe, when His victory for mankind shall be proved to be a real, not an imaginary one. The day of Christ is not the proclamation of One Who has been for ages a stranger to the world which he visited for a few years; it is the assertion that He Who sacrificed Himself is, and always has been, the prince of all the kings of the earth, from Whom all their power has been derived, Who alone has prevented it from being destructive of themselves and of those they have governed, to Whom they must give account of it. The day of Christ is not the ascent of a new sun into the firmament, it is the meridian splendour of that light which has been lightening every man that has come into the world," and *Sermons* I, 214–5: "assuredly we have a right to expect a day when laws shall be asserted and anomalies swept away, when we shall see ourselves and all the creatures of God as they are in His sight, not as they have appeared to us through the mists of our lower world."

73 Cf. *Theological Essays*, 45: "Since he [St. Paul] held that in Adam all die, and that in Christ all are made alive, he of necessity believed also that a day was at hand for every man – a day of revelation and discovery – a day which should show him what life was and what death was – what his own true condition, what his false condition, was. And everything which warned a man that such a day was at hand, which roused him to seek for light and to fly from darkness, was a note of the Archangel's trumpet – a voice bidding him awake, that Christ, the Lord of his spirit, might give him light. And in a moment, in the twinkling of an eye, by a fit of apoplexy, by the dagger of an assassin, the vesture of mortality which hides that light from it might drop off from him, and he might be changed."

74 Cf. *Life* II, 245: "I conceive we may confidently look forward to death as a step in the revelation of Christ, as the rending asunder of a veil which has obstructed our vision of

Therefore, in the moment of his death, man is changed so that he is now able truly to live as a spiritual being in the eternal world.[75]

Yet life after death is not generically different from life on earth. It is simply the consummation of all that has distinguished man as man during his earthly life: "we shall feel that this earth is but the first stage for the exercise of these powers [of the spirit]. It will not be a difficult thing to us to believe that they are intended for a higher expansion and for nobler services; it will be hard, almost impossible, to think otherwise; for, believing that we are united to One who has himself shared our weakness and has himself entered into a state of perfection and glory, we must believe that everything in us which is in an imperfect seminal condition, is destined somewhere or other to attain its complete growth, to put forth its perfect fruits."[76] Whether in this life or in the life to come there is only one law for man: he must always depend on God in trust and obedience and sacrifice himself for his fellow-men. Death only means that men, redeemed from sin and the fetters of the visible world of time and space, can now truly live and act as the servants of God in His spiritual kingdom, which spans the whole universe: "No idleness, no luxurious indulgence was offered them; they would enter into the glory of their Lord; they would have the delight of knowing more and more of His purposes, of working more and more in conformity with them.

> Him who died and rose again, as a removal of shadows and falsehoods; as a means of bringing us out of the confusions which have made God's ways unintelligible to us; as the accomplishment of a long series of discipline and processes which we have understood very little, and repined at very much," and *The Epistles of St. John*, 172: "They believed Him to be the King of the World; they could not doubt that what we describe as crises or revolutions in the condition of society were, in very deed, discoveries of His purpose, the destruction of something which had interfered with them. Such a doctrine was involved in the belief which they had in Him as the Son of Man. But that same belief obliged them to suppose that a very thin veil is interposed between us and Him, and that when we shut our eyes upon this world that veil is removed. Then the outsides of the world which present themselves to our senses will vanish; the substantial principles and realities which the eye cannot see, but which the spirit confesses and believes in, will stand forth. Christ the Lord of our own selves will appear, when those things that have only been surrounding us disappear."

75 Cf. *Christmas Day*, 336–7: "In the brightness of that judgment, every person will then understand his own responsibility for that which has been lent to him, and which must then be restored. Each one will feel and understand how every relation in which he stood upon earth was pointing the way to him, who is the common Lord and brother of man; how each duty was a call to ask for his strength, and an assurance that it would be granted. And, therefore, in that day, all self-seeking must be confounded, and shewn to be a vain thing, under whatever names or disguises it may have been concealed; and all who, under whatever clouds and confusions, have struggled after Him who is the one good and life of the world, must obtain what they seek, and find that infinite reward which eye hath not seen nor ear heard, nor hath it entered into the heart of man to conceive; which only love can give and only love can take in."

76 p. 333. Cf. also *Sermons* I, 198: "Let us believe then, with St. Paul, that Faith must abide always with us, if we are to be blessed creatures. No distinction which belongs to God's divine order can be abolished. Faith and Sight may both be pefected; the invisible things may become more real and certain to us than the things of sense. We may be sure that they are the substances apart from which the others would be mere shadows. Hereafter, this world, which has been so full of unfathomed secrets, may disclose them and their deepest signification to the purified searcher. Every sense may put forth its fullest energy. The glorified body may be fit to understand the glorified earth."

They should be set free from the miserable vanity and selfishness which clogged and disappointed their efforts here; they should understand their own spheres of labour, and co-operate with all to whom other spheres were assigned; they should live as He lives, they should work as He works, for the good of His subjects; they should judge, as He judges, between the right and the wrong, between the pure and the impure."[77]

5. The Restitution of All Things in God

Our previous account has demonstrated how, according to Maurice, God, being perfect love, had in Christ created the Divine Order. As the Head of the universe and mankind Christ had continually imparted life to the creation and upheld and sustained its order and harmony. Admittedly, sin and the Devil were always attempting to frustrate God's purposes and lead His creation into destruction. In spite of the fierceness of their attacks, however, they never succeeded. Their powerlessness would be clearly revealed on the final day of judgment, when all that had defied God and His love would be exposed, separated and annihilated – then the unchangeable order and harmony of God's created universe would become evident to everybody.

Although Christ has always had fellowship with man as a spirit, he in his unbelief and selfishness and through his attachment to the sensible world again and again denies this union with his Head and attempts to live for and by himself. That this attempt is abortive and futile is made manifest when man in the moment of his death experiences the final day of judgment. Having surrendered his mortal mould, his animal, fleshly nature, he continues to live in the direct vision of God in the eternal world; by this light he sees things as they truly are. Having been separated from sin, man is restored to his true position as a spiritual being, created to live in fellowship with the eternal God.

Yet man is the crown of the creation. This implies that the involuntary creatures are subordinated to him and stand and fall with him. Therefore when all men have been restored to perfect fellowship with God, the whole involuntary creation will immediately be restored and find its true place in the Divine Order. The apocatastasis, the restitution of all things in God, appears to be the necessary outcome of Maurice's eschatological teaching.

Maurice's exposition presupposes that sin is basically due to ignorance and a false knowledge of God and the Divine Order. Therefore the essential question is to attain to a true knowledge of reality. This is clearly to be seen in Maurice's interpretation of God's history of revelation and in his idea of judgment and of the final day of judgment. His insistence upon the necessity of true knowledge implies that when man knows truth he will live and act accordingly. Indeed, this cannot be otherwise since man is created to know God and live with Him in the eternal world. Man is therefore always restless until he finds God. When God, the goal of all man's longings and

---

77 *The Apocalypse*, 309. Cf. also *The Gospel of St. John*, 355: "If we are members of one body, if He is the Head, why should not there be a continual circulation of life from each member of the body to every other? How can the departure of men out of this world hinder that circulation, or cause us who are here to feel it less? May not their power have become greater as the mortal fetters have been taken from them? May not we feel it more?"

the ultimate object of all his quests, has revealed Himself and imparted a perfect knowledge of reality, man cannot but embrace this revelation and enter into fellowship with God. On these premises the question of apocatastasis can pose no problem.

We have, however, previously seen that Maurice strongly contended that sin originates in man's rebellious will. Although this view in no way influenced Maurice's idea of revelation, it nevertheless expressed a genuine conviction and contributed to his understanding of the relation between God and man. That this fact introduces an inner tension in his thought is especially apparent in his treatment of the question of the salvation of all men. The doctrine of apocatastasis did after all present a problem to Maurice.

Maurice had asserted that man had rebelled against God of his own free will and decided to live by and for himself. Since God has created man to live in free and willing trust in and obedience to Him, He cannot compel man to give up his defiance and selfishness, however much misery they draw upon him. Nor can God crush and destroy sinful man, since He in His love desires his salvation. Nevertheless man can be saved and attain to his true destination only when he has surrendered his rebellious will and joyfully and willingly submitted to God. Now the means which God employs to persuade men to live in fellowship with Him are manifold. Through Christ's invisible presence in every man, through Christ's incarnation, death and resurrection and through the Church and its signs God impresses upon all men that He is unchangeable love so that they may choose life instead of death. Similarly, God punishes man to make him aware of the misery and sufferings of being separated from Him in order to urge him to return to God.

Yet God's work for the saving of rebellious man is not limited to this earthly life. Far from bringing it to an end death itself is a means of achieving His purpose. Thus, besides the idea that at the moment of death man is released from his animal, fleshly nature and receives the perfect knowledge of God which separates and banishes sin from him, Maurice maintained that at the moment of death it will be manifest whether man lives in fellowship with God or apart from Him, and that he will be recompensed according to his will and desire.[78] He who has desired to have fellowship with God, trusting Him in all things, shall live in the vision of God and have the privilege of being the obedient servant of His love, while he who has desired to rebel and defy God will be punished with eternal death and hell – and for Maurice this means that he will be allowed to continue the life of selfishness which he has chosen. But as rebellious man at the moment of his death also receives a perfect knowledge of God and His love as the sole power in the universe, he can no longer base his resistance towards God upon a false knowledge of reality. Thus his death, by revealing his true state, involves an urgent new appeal to turn towards God.

However, even if defiant man should harden himself and decide to continue in his

---

78 Cf. *The Unity of the New Testament*, 607–8: "The recompense of the wicked corresponds exactly to that of the righteous. The true judgment of God ascertains the condition of both. Each obtains what he is seeking after. As the state of knowing God and being like Him is the reward of the one, the state of not knowing Him and being without Him is the punishment of the other. This is called æonian or eternal destruction, the most awful state to which a spiritual being can be reduced." See also *The Church a Family*, 196–7.

rebellion against God he is not able to escape His love. Even beyond the grave God urges man to give up his selfishness and receive the true life in God. To this end God also inflicts punishments upon recalcitrant man in the next world.[79] They may be called eternal since they make man experience the misery of living in separation from God but they are not everlasting because they will cease when man, overwhelmed by the divine love, decides to live in God or, in other words, to pass from eternal death into eternal life.

By maintaining the possibility of a conversion after death Maurice clashed with orthodox theology and preaching, which categorically asserted that he who did not accept God's salvation during his earthly life was irretrievably lost and condemned to everlasting punishment in hell. For Maurice this denial of the possibility of conversion beyond the grave only meant, however, that the religious world had usurped the right "to dogmatise about the limits of God's love and willingness to save".[80] The orthodox view was an outrage, even a blasphemy against God and His justice since all men did not have the same opportunities, and some even had none at all, of receiving God's offer of salvation during the short span of their earthly life.[81] It directly ran counter to the message with which the Church was entrusted: "How dare we define God? How dare we say that Christ is not the Lord of both worlds? How can we check the Spirit of Love who bids us pray "for all men", or tell them that the prayer must be limited by barriers of space and time, which Christ has broken down?"[82] Christ's death on the Cross had clearly demonstrated that the love of God is unchangeable and limitless and embraces the whole universe and every man.[83] Therefore, wherever there are rebellious wills opposing God, in this world or in the next, He is working to save them from the death and hell of selfishness and persuade them to receive eternal life in fellowship with God.[84]

79 Cf. *What Message*, 32: "Who is so resolute [as Butler] in maintaining the uniformity of the divine government? Who is so eager to prove that we may estimate the nature and objects of punishment hereafter, by the nature and objects of punishment here? Is not the notion that it is the will of God to save men before the event which we call death and to destroy them after; that punishment is inflicted for men's good here and with no reference to their good after, nay – I tremble while I say it, but I must say it – expressly to keep them in evil hereafter?"

80 *The Word "Eternal"*, 25. Cf. also *Theological Essays*, 119: "there has been a tendency throughout the history of the Church to determine the limits of God's love to men, and to speak of all but a few as hopelessly lost."

81 Cf. *What Is Revelation?*, 433: "it is a cruel fiction to speak of the knowledge of that power by which God acts upon men's Wills to raise them, as being offered to us all during this state of trial. To say that the prostitutes in our streets, that the Hindoos, that the Australian Bushmen, have had the same means of learning what power there is to reform and regenerate the Will, as Mr. Mansel and I have had, is to outrage all sense. To insist that the Scripture obliges us to utter so monstrous a contradiction of fact, is to blaspheme it as no German Rationalist ever did."

82 *Theological Essays* (1853), 441.

83 Cf. *Theological Essays*, 123: "Christ's sacrifice compasses the whole universe; we cannot limit the extent of its operations by measures of space and time."

84 Cf. *What Is Revelation?*, 432–3: "What is the whole Gospel but a message to the Will? What is Redemption but a redemption of the Will? – – What we say is, that the revelation of that deliverance which God has wrought out, of that power by which He acts upon the

The question as to whether those who remained unbelievers and impenitent in this life could be saved afterwards loomed very large in Maurice's controversy with King's College and its Principal. Maurice's insistence upon the possibility of a conversion after death was taken to mean that he was advocating the doctrine of Universalism.[85] However, Maurice strongly repudiated such an interpretation. Although he had been educated to accept Universalism, he explained to Dr. Jelf, he had come to realise that the arguments for this doctrine were just as untenable as those which were brought forward in defence of the opposite view.[86] To maintain that even unbelieving and disobedient men would be saved was simply to confound the love of God with a tolerant good-will which connived at sin. In fact, the doctrine of Universalism involved the greatest cruelty towards man, since it represented God as conniving at man's sins by not punishing them – in other words, as allowing man to live in his selfishness for ever.[87] As sin is the true misery and curse of man, God, because of His love towards man, must necessarily hate sin and work for its destruction. Punishment, being the means which God uses to persuade a rebellious will to return to Him, must therefore continue as long as man remains a sinner.[88] Because salvation implies that man willingly denies himself and lives in trust and obedience to God, it is out of the question that unbelievers and the impenitent can be saved. It is therefore unwarranted, Maurice pointed out, to draw the conclusion from his teaching that men may confidently continue in their sins since after all everybody will be saved. On the contrary, his teaching contained the strongest appeal to men to cast off sin by making it perfectly clear that there can be no peace between God and sinful man.[89]

Will of men, has nothing in its nature which fixes death as the limit of it, but everything which defies and breaks through that limit."

85 Cf. *Grounds*, 29, where Dr. Jelf wrote to Maurice: "The Essay and your letters together, I do not hesitate to affirm, unquestionably hold out the hope that the punishment of wicked, unbelieving, and impenitent sinners may, after all, not be everlasting. This hope is set forth with more or less distinctness in more than one part of these writings. I should say also, that you appear to look upon it as a special part of your mission to inculcate it wherever circumstances may seem to require it."

86 Cf. *The Word "Eternal"*, 14: "I have said distinctly that I am not a Universalist, that I have deliberately rejected the theory of Universalism, knowing what it is; and that I should as much refuse an Article which dogmatised in favour of that theory as one that dogmatised in favour of the opposite." See also *Life* II, 15.

87 Cf. *Life* II, 19: "I cannot speak of God punishing for a number of years, and then ceasing to punish, or of the wicked expiating their crimes by a certain amount of penalties. The idea of a rebel will is, to those who know in themselves what it is, far too awful for such arrangements as these. A man who feels what sin means, who feels it as the contradiction to God's nature, the perfectly holy, and blessed, and loving nature, cannot find any comfort in the thought of God leaving men alone, or hold out such a prospect as a comfort to his fellows."

88 Cf. *The Word "Eternal"*, 20: "I have thought and spoken of that love as only removing punishment by removing sin; I have desired, and hope always to desire, for myself and for all men, that we may never cease to be punished by God till we cease to punish ourselves by rebelling against Him."

89 Cf. *What Message*, 21–2: "I do not at all doubt that the vague notion, "Our present probation may be final", will have this effect [of encouraging careless sinners to continue in sin], so long as punishment is dreaded more than sin – so long as sin is not felt to be the curse out of which God, by His punishments, is showing us that we need to be saved. If I teach a careless sinner that God will some day or other give over punishing him for sin, and will

God's unceasing battle with sin aims at nothing but the salvation of all men. As man is not able to grasp the unfathomable depth of the divine love which never tires of sacrificing itself for sinners, no limit can be set to its endurance and converting power.[90] This does not, on the other hand, entitle anybody to pronounce that all men will be saved. It is for Maurice a fact that the will of man is able to defy and resist God, and nobody is capable of measuring its power of hardening itself in the rejection of God and His saving love.[91] Consequently it is impossible to pass any verdict affirming or denying the doctrine of Universalism. The problem must simply be left open, as Maurice wrote to Dr. Jelf: "What I dare not pronounce upon is the *fact* that every will in the universe must be brought into consent with the Divine will. – – I should indeed tremble to affirm the contrary, and I think any man would. Dare you make it a positive article of faith that God's will, being what the Scripture says it is, shall *not* finally triumph? Nevertheless there is such a darkness over the whole question of the possible resistance of the human will, that I must be silent, and tremble and adore."[92]

Even so Maurice could not relinquish the idea of the restitution of all things in God. However rebellious and recalcitrant the human will may be, it was for him inconceivable that God should not triumph in the end: "I know that no man can be blessed, except his will is in accordance with God's will. I know it must be by an action on the will that love triumphs. Though I have no faith in man's theory of Universal Restitution, I am taught to expect "a restitution of all things, which God who cannot lie has promised since the world began". I am obliged to believe that we are living in a restored order; I am sure that that restored order will be carried out by the full triumph of God's loving will. How that should take place while any rebellious will remains in His universe I cannot tell, though it is not for me to say that it is impossible; I do not want to say it, I wish to trust God absolutely, and not to trust in any conclusion of my own understanding at all."[93]

leave him alone in it, I believe I tell him the most horrible news that I can tell him. I tell him that God does not will that he should be saved, and should come to the knowledge of the truth. I tell him that his Father does not care that he should be a partaker of His holiness."

90 Cf. *Grounds*, 13: "But, when I am asked to dogmatize on the other side, to say that there is some place, or time, or mode in which the resistance of man to God shall be effectual, and when the resources of His converting grace shall be exhausted, I dare not."

91 Cf. *ibid.*: "I know also that the will of man has an awful power of resisting the will of God. How far that power may go, I dare not ask myself. It is an abyss into which I cannot look."

92 p. 17.

93 *Life* II, 19–20. Cf. also p. 19: "And can it [a rebel will] not fix itself in misery? Has it not a power of defying that which seeks to subdue it? I know in myself that it has. I know that we may struggle with the Light, that we may choose death. But I know also that Love does overcome this rebellion," and *Theological Essays*, 122: "I ask no one to pronounce, for I dare not pronounce myself, what are the possibilities of resistance in a human will to the loving will of God. There are times when they seem to me – thinking of myself more than of others – almost infinite. But I know that there is something which must be infinite. I am obliged to believe in an abyss of love which is deeper than the abyss of death: I dare not lose faith in that love. I sink into death, eternal death, if I do. I must feel that this love is compassing the universe. More about it I cannot know. But God knows. I leave myself and all to Him."

Despite all his reservations, then, Maurice felt certain that God would prove the stronger and that the entire creation, headed by man, would confess Him as the foundation of all things and find its true destination by receiving all life from Him. It was this faith in God's inexhaustible and unfailing love which inspired Maurice to expect the apocatastasis and even turned this hope into a certainty. It was, however, just as much a consequence of his idea of the Divine Order. As God had from eternity decided to create the universe and mankind in Christ, so all that attempted to thwart His will and purpose must necessarily be annihilated. God, as the only true being and omnipotent love, must ultimately triumph and be acknowledged and worshipped as He in whom all creation lives, moves and has its being.

CONCLUSION

In the Introduction it was pointed out that none of the previous studies on Maurice had provided an exhaustive and detailed analysis of his theological thinking. They had, in effect, all limited themselves to examining and discussing certain aspects of his thought and had arrived at the most divergent estimates of its basic character. This state of affairs, together with the apparent obscurity of Maurice's exposition of his ideas, raised the question whether it was not hopeless to expect coherence and consistency in his thinking. We observed, however, that, although it was tempting to dismiss Maurice as an uncritical, eclectic and confused thinker, there was much to indicate that his thought displayed an inner unity. Therefore it seemed to be worth while to subject his teaching to a fresh examination.

Our detailed analysis of Maurice's theological thought should have demonstrated its basic clarity and coherence. It is dominated by the leading idea of the Divine Order. Maurice's teaching is nothing but a magnificent exposition of how God, being perfect love, had eternally decreed the creation of the universe and mankind and how His will was carried out in and through Christ, the Son of God and the Son of Man. To proclaim this Divine Order as an existing reality and to show its implications for the actual life of man was the task which Maurice felt convinced that God had laid before him.

The idea of the Divine Order determined all that Maurice said and wrote and gave his thought its inner unity. It provided him with the measuring-rod by which he evaluated the problems of the day in Church and nation and judged the various religious, theological and philosophical movements and schools of thought. Confronted with other views and doctrines Maurice immediately realised what to appropriate and what to reject. He welcomed all that might help to demonstrate the truth of his teaching and waged, on the other hand, an unflinching war against everything that seemed either to contradict or deny his basic convictions. Both in his constructive thought and in his polemics with others he always knew what he was about.

Maurice developed his thinking under the impact of widely different influences. He had learnt from the Unitarianism of his childhood, from Coleridge's Romantic-Idealistic thinking, from the teaching of Thomas Erskine and Edward Irving and, not least, from the Dialogues of Plato and the Bible. They all supplied him with material for the construction of his thought. Yet Maurice's extraordinary systematic powers enabled him to weld these various influences into a coherent whole. His thought was the outcome of the struggle of an independent mind to arrive at the knowledge of truth and solve the riddles of human existence, his own and those of all men. That is why it possessed a truly existential character and displayed the freshness of originality.

We have seen how, during Maurice's lifetime, J. H. Rigg had launched a vehement attack against him for teaching undiluted Platonism under the cover of Christianity.

James Martineau, although far more generous and sympathetic to Maurice's concern, argued fundamentally the very same thing: that Platonic realism constituted the basis of Maurice's thought. It is true that neither Rigg nor, even less, Martineau substantiated this verdict by any extensive documentation. Rigg, moreover, had weakened his case by a one-sided and frequently distorted exposition of many fundamental points in Maurice's thinking. Subsequent Maurice students were also to acknowledge that traces of Platonism were to be found in Maurice, but the general trend has clearly been the insistence that the Bible was the decisive influence in shaping his teaching.[1] They have, on the other hand, been equally unconcerned to substantiate their interpretation, and there the case rests – assertion, so to speak, stands against assertion.

Our analysis of Maurice's thought should, however, have provided enough evidence to make it possible to arrive at a solution of the problem of Maurice's Platonism. But first a word regarding its historical aspect! We have repeatedly observed that Maurice's sole desire was to expound God's revelation as contained in the Scriptures. Indeed, he maintained that he was only proclaiming what he had found in the Bible. On the other hand, Maurice once directly stated in a letter to J. F. A. Hort that next to the Bible he had learnt most from Plato.[2] Unfortunately he never directly indicated what Plato had actually taught him – the explanation for this is undoubtedly that he was convinced that the essentials of Plato's thought were to be found in the Bible. Furthermore, we know that the great Christian Platonist, Clement of Alexandria, found great favour with him.[3] Apart from this, with the exception of Coleridge, we cannot demonstrate with any certainty what Pagan and Christian thinkers of the Platonic tradition had attracted and influenced him. Just as it is impossible to give an account of the various shades of Platonism with which Maurice may have been

1 Cf. Pieter Blaauw: *F. D. Maurice. Zijn Leven en Werken* (Amsterdam 1908), 268: "Nu is ontegenzeggelijk Plato's denktrant op Maurice van invloed gewest, of in elk geval Maurices denkwijze Platonisch getint. Maar veel liever spreek ik bij Maurice van een *Bijbelsch-realisme*. Want ten slotte is het toch de wereld van den Bijbel, die de wereld van Maurices realia vormt," and A. R. Vidler, op. cit., 32: "It was in sifting his own words and thoughts that he received help from Plato and Socrates. Beyond that, Maurice was no more, though surely no less, of a Platonist than the Fathers or than St. Paul and St. John." Far more discerningly A. M. Ramsey recognizes that it is "a moot question how far Platonism affected Maurice's basic assumptions – –. Inevitably his Platonism coloured his Biblical exegesis; and it led him to a tendency to expound the whole Bible through the spectacles of his own interpretation of the Johannine prologue" (op. cit., 23). However, "he stood as a theologian *within* the Bible – –; and, while he went as far as it is possible to go in recognizing the light that lighteth every man, his soul rested in the unique *act* of the Incarnation" (p. 20).

2 Cf. *Life* II, 37: "But I have never taken up any dialogue of Plato without getting more from it than any book not in the Bible." It was Julius Hare's lectures on Plato which aroused Maurice's fascinated interest in him during his Cambridge years. The important point to make in this connection is that Hare was strongly influenced by Schleiermacher's interpretation of Plato and therefore presented a view of Plato and his significance which clearly contrasted him with Plotinus.

3 Cf. *Lectures on the Ecclesiastical History of the First and Second Centuries* (Cambridge 1854), 239: "On the whole, I do not know where we shall look for a purer or a truer man than this Clemens of Alexandria. – – We must be content to make his acquaintance through the words which he has spoken. Judging from them, he seems to me that one of the old Fathers whom we should all have reverenced most as a teacher, and loved best as a friend."

acquainted, so we are unable to make out in detail what he had appropriated from them and to map out the way in which they had been influential in shaping his thinking. We can only ascertain that the impact of Platonism was of the greatest importance for his thought. The actual extent of Plato's influence can, however, only be gathered from an examination of Maurice's teaching itself.

Now, our analysis should have made it abundantly clear that Maurice completely accepted the Platonic idea of reality. Only that can be designated as true being which unchangeably is the same. This implies that *that which is* is only to be found in the unchangeable, eternal world, which is generically different from the changeable, transient world of time and space. The two worlds are, on the other hand, correlated to each other as archetype to image. Supersensual reality imparts to the visible world that being which constitutes its life, its order and harmony.

In Maurice's thought, however, this Platonic ontology was fused with the Biblical idea of creation. God is a personal will, just as His nature is perfect love. Because God, as the totality of being, is unchangeable, so His will must be unchanging. The fact that God, prompted by His love, has willed the creation of a universe and a mankind by an eternal decree means, therefore, that this decision will be accomplished. Inasmuch as the creation is completely dependent upon the almighty divine will, Maurice was able to maintain the absolute distinction between God and man. Since God's eternal purpose will necessarily be achieved, it follows that the relation between God and His creatures can never be broken nor brought to an end. If the creation were able to separate itself from God and live independently, this would imply that God had ceased to be the Creator, being subject to mutability and made subservient to His creation.

The merging in Maurice's thought of the Platonic idea of reality and of the Christian belief in God as the almighty Creator displays many affinities with that which earlier Christian Platonists had propounded. Maurice may have been influenced by some of them – St. Augustine, for example – but even so Maurice's idea of the creation has a character of its own. This is primarily due to his understanding of the divine love as self-sacrificing love. This concept of love is central to his interpretation of the Trinity. Since the essence of the divine nature is love, God must eternally exist as the Father and the Son, united in the Holy Spirit as the bond of love. The divine creative activity is nothing but a carrying out of the purposes of self-sacrificing love. The existence of the entire creation is founded upon self-sacrificing love. When describing man's position in the creation, Maurice did indeed reproduce the Reformers' idea of man as a creature, entirely dependent upon God, but profiled it in an original way. Self-sacrifice is the law of man's being since he is created to sacrifice himself in a trusting dependence upon God and in the service of love towards his fellow-men. Thus, the Platonic ontology has, so to speak, been permeated by the New Testament concept of self-sacrificing love. The unchangeableness and permanence of the Divine Order is ultimately rooted in God's love, which always sacrifices itself for the sake of His creation.

Maurice not only accepted the Platonic ontology, but – quite consistently – approved of the Platonic epistemology. It was axiomatic for him that the sole object of true knowledge is unchangeable being, *that which is*. Similarly, he was convinced that man can arrive at knowledge because his true self participates in the eternal world. Yet, Maurice did not appropriate these ideas without modifications, interpreting them in the light of his idea of man as created to depend upon Christ as his only source of life. Man is not a self-existing being who can arrive at true knowledge by virtue of his inherent powers. It is true that man has been created with the reason as the organ through which he can directly perceive *that which is,* but true knowledge of reality is only imparted to him by Christ. Even epistemologically man is dependent upon his Creator.

Maurice's exposition of the contrast between the spirit or the reason and the flesh in man also betrays a Platonic structure. However, as man can achieve nothing by himself but always lives because of his union with Christ, Maurice was able to maintain that all men, being spirits, will arrive at their true destination: fellowship with God in the eternal world. The idea that God has accepted man as His child, irrespective of personal qualities and virtues, has been blended with the Platonic concept of man.

Maurice's view of God as the personal will of love, acting in and through Christ, is so dominant in his exposition of the Divine Order that the Platonic ontology is often difficult to detect. Nevertheless it forms the basic structure of his thinking. This is most evident in his concept of reality and his theory of knowledge but is also to be discerned in his interpretation of God's history of revelation as contained in the Scriptures.

Maurice's continual insistence that man must take his starting-point in the eternal God in order to arrive at true knowledge presupposes the Platonic idea of reality. Accordingly, God's acts of revelation in the history of space and time can have no constitutive significance for the relationship between God and man. The sole purpose of the divine history of revelation is to unveil eternal, universal truth. Maurice's idea of revelation represents a fusion of the Platonic idea of reality and the Biblical history of salvation. Although it is not difficult to point out affinities with what earlier Christian Platonists had maintained regarding the significance of revelation in the Scriptures, Maurice's independence and originality are once again striking. This is particularly evident in the unrelenting consistency with which he brought his idea of revelation to bear upon the interpretation of the history of Israel, Christ's incarnation, death, resurrection and ascension and the Church.

Maurice was a great original thinker. With extraordinary systematic talent he had, so to speak, set out to unite Plato and the Bible, and by appropriating leading ideas from both of them he constructed a new, fundamentally coherent and consistent view of totality. The success of his achievement is indicated not least by the fact that it is a most difficult task to point out precisely where Plato gives way to the Bible and *vice versa.* Both Plato and the Bible had equally attracted and overwhelmed a great mind, passionately intent on discovering the truth about human existence. Out of this encounter, and through the interaction of these powerful influences, emerged a Christian Platonism of a truly remarkable spiritual and intellectual quality.

It is true that Maurice expounded his teaching in a way which appears extremely fragmentary and obscure. Nevertheless he had provided his readers with sufficient clues to grasp the core of his thought and see its inner unity. This is not, however, to say that the repeated criticisms of Maurice for obscurity and indistinctness are without any foundation. Thus, we have frequently noticed an incongruity between what Maurice actually said and what he intended to say. This observation certainly points to a weakness in the way in which Maurice presented his message. Apart from the fact that it made him appear a confused thinker, it has helped to blur his true concern and even led students on the wrong track in their interpretation of his basic convictions.

This deficiency is undoubtedly due to the fact that Maurice was not a discursive and analytical thinker, carefully sifting and testing the precise meaning of the words he used. He presupposed that what immediately appealed to him as truth would vindicate itself in the same way to other men. This explains why he could use terms and ideas taken from widely different doctrines and systems of thought, on the grounds that they expressed vital truths, without considering whether they adequately conveyed his own convictions. At best he would suggest, through a polemical and supplementary aside, how they were to be understood. This is why Maurice employed the phraseology of the Bible and of the doctrinal standards of his Church although it often conveyed ideas which, seen in their context, were entirely different from his own basic assumptions. This explains why Maurice thought himself to be clear and lucid in the exposition of his teaching!

A critical analysis of Maurice's phraseology reveals many of the obscurities and inconsistencies as being only apparent. Yet not all of them can be resolved in this way. Thus, in Maurice we find lines of thought which do not fit into a consistent pattern, and this is ultimately due to the fact that not even a man of his intellectual calibre could engraft the Biblical history of salvation onto a Platonic ontology in such a way that the result became a consistent whole in every respect – they are different entities which, by virtue of their very structure, defy such a fusion. Despite Maurice's truly remarkable synthetic endeavours it is therefore not surprising that there remain ambiguities and inconsistencies in his thinking. This is the case with his concept of the flesh and the world of the senses. Another example is the way in which he attempted to tackle the problem of sin and evil, proposing various mutually incompatible explanations as to their origin and character which do not display any coherent pattern.

It is obvious that Maurice wished to maintain the idea of sin as a terrible destructive power which has invaded God's creation, and, at the same time, he was anxious to define it so that it became clear that it had not achieved its purpose of destroying the Divine Order. The ambiguity which characterizes Maurice's description of sin and its effects – and this is the crucial point in any encounter between Plato and the Bible – was bound to effect his whole thinking. We have noticed it in his exposition of the significance of God's history of revelation for the salvation of man and, not least, in his attitude to the problem of apocatastasis. These incongruities, which are only rendered more conspicuous by Maurice's frequently inadequate phraseology and his often fragmentary way of expounding his convictions, are undoubtedly responsible for the ambiguity and obscurity of his teaching.

We have seen that Maurice emphatically maintained that his teaching was based upon the Bible and the liturgy and doctrinal standards of his Church. Yet Victorian orthodoxy, whatever its shade, contended that Maurice had evaded and subverted the message of the Bible. Posterity has virtually reversed this verdict, acknowledging that Maurice's teaching was ultimately what he claimed it to be. His contemporaries had because of their narrow and rigid orthodoxy failed to realise his theological greatness in having fathomed the foundations of the Christian faith afresh and worked out its implications for human life.

It cannot be denied that there is some justification for this reaction. Though from a special angle, Maurice had disclosed deficiencies in the teaching of Victorian orthodoxy and had brought aspects of the message of the Bible to light which it had been apt to forget. He had fought any tendency to base man's fellowship with God on his own endeavours and achievements. He had protested against religious exclusiveness and self-assurance and emphasized how God's saving love always transcended the boundaries which men were liable to set up. In many respects Maurice had pursued the same ends as the Reformers – it is therefore not surprising that many Lutheran theologians have seen a *Lutherus Anglicanus* in him. However intent his contemporaries had been on giving him a fair hearing, they failed to see that much of what he said could be substantiated from the Scriptures and the teaching of the Reformers. Neither his criticism nor his constructive thought was heeded to such an extent that it challenged them to search the Bible anew and discover those aspects of Biblical truth to which Maurice had directed their attention.

Despite this concession it must, nonetheless, be maintained that the verdict of Victorian orthodoxy was justified. If the Bible and the doctrines of the Church of England were to be the touchstone of sound teaching – and on this Maurice insisted – then its spokesmen were entitled to repudiate his teaching as deficient and unsound. Maurice was decidedly wrong when he maintained that he had only expounded and proclaimed the message of the Scriptures. While it is true that the arguments for the rejection of Maurice's theology had their defects, those who pronounced their *Non placet* had grasped more of its true characteristics and argued their case better and more intelligently than posterity has been inclined to believe. Nor was it only the orthodox who rejected Maurice. Even the representatives of the Broad Church movement and the most eminent thinkers of the age, in spite of their admiration and appreciation of Maurice's noble endeavours, found his teaching inadequate and unconvincing.

Against this background it truly appears strange that, after his death, Maurice acquired the reputation of being one of the greatest thinkers of the Church of England, a man who had expounded the Christian faith in such an original and profound way that his findings have not yet been exhausted. Whether strange or not, posterity arrived at a new estimate of Maurice and the significance of his teaching. Those who became acquainted with Maurice's *Life and Letters* and his writings received an overwhelming impression of the man and his work. That he had strongly opposed Victorian orthodoxy and the contemporary religious world was no longer detrimental to his reputation. On the contrary, Maurice students were already aware of the religious and theological shortcomings of Mid-Victorian Christianity and found his attacks justified. Even more important was their feeling that Maurice had opened up new horizons and given new insights leading to a truer understanding of Christianity and its relevance for the modern age and its issues. A changed spiritual climate had made men see in Maurice a religious depth, a breadth of humanity and an abundance of original seminal ideas. Without doubt J. Scott Lidgett spoke for many when he wrote: "I regard Frederick Denison Maurice as having been by far the most important and significant personality – the most potent and pervasive influence – in the religious life and thought of England during the past century. A very great man, he owes his pre-eminent importance and influence to his marvellous – I am inclined to say unique – combination of prophetic witness, systematic thought, and creative endeavour, unified and inspired by the ceaseless aspiration and pursuit of a wholly consecrated and truly saintly life. His influence has been far-reaching and is still abundantly fruitful in every realm of Christian concern."[4]

In 1964 W. Merlin Davies stated: "The importance of Maurice as in some sense "the father of modern English theology" has been sufficiently demonstrated."[5] Considered as a summing up of what so many have said about Maurice's importance and influence, this statement might seem to be justified. Yet it ought to be added that nobody has demonstrated the impact Maurice has actually had on the development of English theology. The naked truth is, however, that apart from his having contributed to the downfall of Victorian orthodoxy through his criticism, the influence which Maurice wielded on the theological thinking of his own day was negligible. This was also the case after his death. Maurice found no new followers in what he had considered the essentials of his teaching, nor did it become a formative influence in the religious and theological debate of a later age. It is true that students have been anxious to point out the significance of Maurice's teaching for contemporary religious, theological and social issues. When, however, they attempt to exploit it, they, in effect, only make use of that in Maurice's theological thinking which appears to corroborate their own preconceived positions. What we have pointed out to be deficiencies and obstacles to an understanding of Maurice's basic convictions and the perception of the coherence and consistency of his thinking proved advantageous in a later age in the sense that it opened the way for an eclectic use of his theology. Yet, from the fact that Maurice has fascinated and impressed posterity it is quite unwarranted to conclude that he has exercised any great influence on the emergence and shaping of modern English theology.

The task of proving this in detail falls, however, outside the scope of this work. Its sole purpose has been to subject Maurice's teaching to an exhaustive analysis, an analysis which has demonstrated him to be a great and original thinker, the spiritual and intellectual qualities of whose theology place him amongst the foremost representatives of the Christian Platonist tradition.

4 op. cit., 13.
5 *An Introduction to F. D. Maurice's Theology* (London 1964), IX–X.

Acta Theologica Danica

EDENDA CURAVERUNT
TORBEN CHRISTENSEN . EDUARD NIELSEN
REGIN PRENTER . HEJNE SIMONSEN